fourth edition

English File

Pre-intermediate

Teacher's Guide

WITH TEACHER'S RESOURCE CENTRE

Christina Latham-Koenig
Clive Oxenden
Jerry Lambert

Paul Seligson
with Anna Lowy
Krysia Mabbott

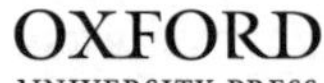
OXFORD
UNIVERSITY PRESS

Great Clarendon Street, Oxford, OX2 6DP, United Kingdom

Oxford University Press is a department of the University of Oxford.
It furthers the University's objective of excellence in research, scholarship,
and education by publishing worldwide. Oxford is a registered trade
mark of Oxford University Press in the UK and in certain other countries

ISBN: 978 0 19 403762 4   Teacher's Guide

Printed in China

This book is printed on paper from certified and well-managed sources

ACKNOWLEDGEMENTS

Back cover photograph: Oxford University Press building/David Fisher

*The authors would like to thank all the teachers and students round the world whose
feedback has helped us to shape* English File.

The authors would also like to thank: all those at Oxford University Press (both
in Oxford and around the world) and the design team who have contributed
their skills and ideas to producing this course.

*Finally very special thanks from Clive to Maria Angeles, Lucia, and Eric, and from
Christina to Cristina, for all their support and encouragement. Christina would also like
to thank her children Joaquin, Marco, and Krysia for their constant inspiration.*

*The publisher would like to thank the following for their permission to reproduce
photographs*: Getty pp.242 Scarlett Johansson/Paul Zimmerman/WireImage,
Rihanna/Jerritt Clark, Justin Timberlake/Peter Andrews/Corbis via Getty
Images, 243 (Bob Dylan/Kevin Mazur/WireImage, Jakob Dylan/Steve Granitz/
WireImage); Oxford University Press p.265 (Gareth Boden); Shutterstock
pp.173, 185, 188, 195, 220, 223, 228, 230, 237, 242 (Orlando Bloom, Oprah
Winfrey, Robert de Niro), 253, 254, 257, 258, 261, 262, 264, 267.

Illustrations by: Bill Brown pp.182, 184, 196, 199, 259, 266; Emma Brownjohn
pp.181, 193, 200, 201; Mark Duffin pp.192, 197, 244; Joy Gosney p.240; Ben
Hasler p.204, 206; Joanna Kerr/New Division pp.176, 180, 225, 235, 263, 271;
Roger Penwill pp.175, 177, 178, 186, 194, 199, 205, 268; Kath Walker pp.174,
183, 202, 203, 206, 247, 251, 263, 269.

Grammar photocopiable activities written by: Amanda Begg

Contents

p.4 Syllabus checklist

p.8 Course overview

- **Introduction**
- **What do Pre-intermediate students need?**
- **For students**

  Student's Book

  Online Practice

  Workbook

- **For teachers**

  Teacher's Guide

  Teacher's Resource Centre

  Classroom Presentation Tool

  Class audio

  Video

p.12 Lesson plans

p.12	File 1 A–C	Practical English Episode 1
p.28	File 2 A–C	1&2 Revise and Check
p.41	File 3 A–C	Practical English Episode 2
p.55	File 4 A–C	3&4 Revise and Check
p.66	File 5 A–C	Practical English Episode 3
p.80	File 6 A–C	5&6 Revise and Check
p.92	File 7 A–C	Practical English Episode 4
p.106	File 8 A–C	7&8 Revise and Check
p.119	File 9 A–C	Practical English Episode 5
p.132	File 10 A–C	9&10 Revise and Check
p.143	File 11 A–C	Practical English Episode 6
p.157	File 12 A–C	11&12 Revise and Check

p.167 Photocopiable activities

p.167	Introduction
p.168	Grammar activity answers
p.172	Grammar activity masters
p.208	Communicative activity instructions
p.217	Communicative activity masters
p.253	Vocabulary activity instructions
p.257	Vocabulary activity masters

Syllabus checklist

		GRAMMAR	VOCABULARY	PRONUNCIATION
1				
6	**A** Are you? Can you? Do you? Did you?	word order in questions	common verb phrases	the alphabet
8	**B** The perfect date?	present simple	describing people: appearance and personality	final *-s* and *-es*
10	**C** The Remake Project	present continuous	clothes, prepositions of place	/ə/ and /ɜː/
12	**Practical English** Episode 1	calling reception		
2				
14	**A** OMG! Where's my passport?	past simple: regular and irregular verbs	holidays	regular verbs: *-ed* endings
16	**B** That's me in the picture!	past continuous	prepositions of time and place: *at*, *in*, *on*	weak forms: *was*, *were*
18	**C** One dark October evening	time sequencers and connectors	verb phrases	word stress
20	**Revise and Check 1&2**			
3				
22	**A** TripAside	*be going to* (plans and predictions)	airports	the letter *g*
24	**B** Put it in your calendar!	present continuous (future arrangements)	verbs + prepositions, e.g. *arrive in*	linking
26	**C** Word games	defining relative clauses	paraphrasing	silent *e*
28	**Practical English** Episode 2	at the restaurant	**V** restaurants	
4				
30	**A** Who does what?	present perfect + *yet*, *just*, *already*	housework, *make* or *do*?	the letters *y* and *j*
32	**B** In your basket	present perfect or past simple? (1)	shopping	*c* and *ch*
34	**C** #greatweekend	*something, anything, nothing*, etc.	adjectives ending *-ed* and *-ing*	/e/, /əʊ/, and /ʌ/
36	**Revise and Check 3&4**			
5				
38	**A** I want it NOW!	comparatives adjectives and adverbs, *as…as*	types of numbers	/ə/
40	**B** Twelve lost wallets	superlatives (+ *ever* + present perfect)	describing a town or city	sentence stress
42	**C** How much is enough?	quantifiers, *too*, *(not) enough*	health and the body	/ʌ/
44	**Practical English** Episode 3	taking something back to a shop	**V** shopping	
6				
46	**A** Think positive – or negative?	*will / won't* (predictions)	opposite verbs	*'ll, won't*
48	**B** I'll always love you	*will / won't / shall* (other uses)	verb + *back*	word stress: two-syllable verbs
50	**C** The meaning of dreaming	review of verb forms: present, past, and future	modifiers	the letters *ea*
52	**Revise and Check 5&6**			

SPEAKING	LISTENING	READING
exchanging information	understanding personal information	
describing a person	identifying the person being described	understanding a description
describing a picture, talking about preferences	checking hypotheses	
talking about your last holiday	understanding the key events in a story	understanding the key events in a story
talking about preferences	listening for gist and detailed information	checking hypotheses (using visual evidence)
retelling a story	listening for specific information	
planning a tour	listening for specific information	understanding text cohesion – connectors
making arrangements	understanding times, dates and appointments	understanding a questionnaire
describing and paraphrasing	guessing words from definitions	understanding rules of a game
talking about housework	checking hypotheses using background knowledge	understanding opinions
talking about shopping experiences	understanding a theory	
describing your weekend	understanding historical information	checking and correcting information
comparing habits: present and past	identifying key points	scanning for data (facts and numbers)
talking about memorable experiences	understanding ranking	
talking about your lifestyle	understanding advice	identifying pros and cons
making predictions	using existing knowledge to predict content	summarizing the main point of a text
giving examples and reasons	understanding specific details	understanding the order of events
talking about the past, present, and future	checking hypotheses, understanding specific information	

		GRAMMAR	VOCABULARY	PRONUNCIATION
7				
54	**A** First day nerves	uses of the infinitive with *to*	verbs + infinitive: *try to, forget to*, etc.	weak form of *to*, linking
56	**B** Happiness is …	uses of the gerund (verb + *-ing*)	verbs + gerund	*-ing*, the letter *o*
58	**C** Could you pass the test?	*have to, don't have to, must, mustn't*	adjectives + prepositions: *afraid of*, etc.	stress on prepositions
60	**Practical English** Episode 4	going to a pharmacy	**V** feeling ill	
8				
62	**A** Should I stay or should I go?	*should*	*get*	/ʊ/ and /uː/
64	**B** Murphy's Law	*if* + present, + *will* + infinitive (first conditional)	confusing verbs	homophones
66	**C** Who is Vivienne?	possessive pronouns	adverbs of manner	reading aloud
68	**Revise and Check 7&8**			
9				
70	**A** Beware of the dog	*if* + past, *would* + infinitive (second conditional)	animals and insects	word stress
72	**B** Fearof.net	present perfect + *for* and *since*	words related to fear, phrases with *for* and *since*	sentence stress
74	**C** Scream queens	present perfect or past simple? (2)	biographies	word stress, /ɔː/
76	**Practical English** Episode 5	asking how to get there	**V** directions	
10				
78	**A** Into the net	expressing movement	sports, expressing movement	word stress
80	**B** Early birds	word order of phrasal verbs	phrasal verbs	linking
82	**C** International inventions	the passive	people from different countries	/ʃ/, /tʃ/ and /dʒ/
84	**Revise and Check 9&10**			
11				
86	**A** Ask the teacher	*used to*	school subjects	*used to / didn't used to*
88	**B** Help! I can't decide!	*might*	word building: noun formation	diphthongs
90	**C** Twinstrangers.net	*so, neither* + auxiliaries	similarities and differences	/ð/ and /θ/
92	**Practical English** Episode 6	on the phone		
12				
94	**A** Unbelievable!	past perfect	time expressions	the letter *i*
96	**B** Think before you speak	reported speech	*say* or *tell*?	double consonants
98	**C** The *English File* quiz	questions without auxiliaries	revision of question words	question words
100	**Revise and Check 11&12**			

102 **Communication**   113 **Writing**   120 **Listening**   126 **Grammar Bank**

SPEAKING	LISTENING	READING
retelling an article	understanding a problem	text coherence / understanding content words
describing feelings	understanding how something works	
talking about language learning	understanding the events in a story	using topic sentences
discussing habits and preferences	understanding opinions	understanding opinions
using the right word in conversation	understanding an anecdote	scanning for specific information
reacting to a story	using information to interpret a story	understanding a short story
Would you know what to do?	understanding facts	understanding specific information
How long…?	taking notes	recognizing topic links
talking about life events	understanding biographical information	using textual clues to match information with a person
responding to opinions		understanding opinions
retelling a person's day	understanding reasons	extracting main points from a text
passives quiz	understanding historical information	
talking about school days	understanding attitude	finding key information in a text
choices and decisions	identifying the main points in a talk	
finding similarities and differences	understanding similarities and differences	understanding similarities and differences
retelling a news story		understanding the order of events
gossip	understanding a conversation	recognizing text type
general knowledge quiz	understanding quiz questions	

150 **Vocabulary Bank**   164 **Irregular verbs**   165 **Appendix**   166 **Sound Bank**

Course overview

Introduction

Our aim with *English File fourth edition* has been to make every lesson better and to make the package more student- and teacher-friendly. As well as the main A, B, C Student's Book lessons, there is a range of material that you can use according to your students' needs, and the time and resources you have available. Don't forget:

- videos that can be used in class in every File: Practical English, Video Listening, and Can you understand these people?
- Quick Tests and File tests for every File, as well as Progress Tests, an End-of-course Test, and an Entry Test, which you can use at the beginning of the course
- photocopiable Grammar and Communicative activities for every A, B, C lesson, and a Vocabulary activity for every Vocabulary Bank

Online Practice and the **Workbook** provide review, support, and practice for students outside the class.

The **Teacher's Guide** suggests different ways of exploiting the Student's Book depending on the level of your class. We very much hope you enjoy using *English File fourth edition*.

What do Pre-intermediate students need?

Pre-intermediate students are at a crucial stage in their learning. Students at this level need material that maintains their enthusiasm and confidence. They need to know how much they are learning and what they can now achieve. At the same time they need the encouragement to push themselves to use the new language that they are learning.

Grammar, Vocabulary, and Pronunciation

If we want students to speak English with confidence, we need to give them the tools they need – Grammar, Vocabulary, and Pronunciation (G, V, P). We believe that 'G + V + P = confident speaking', and in *English File Pre-intermediate* all three elements are given equal importance.

Each lesson has clear G, V, P aims to keep lessons focused and give students concrete learning objectives and a sense of progress.

Grammar

- Clear and memorable presentations of new structures
- Regular and varied practice in useful and natural contexts
- Student-friendly reference material

We have tried to provide contexts for new language that will engage students, using real-life stories and situations, humour, and suspense. The **Grammar Banks** give students a single, easy-to-access grammar reference section, with example sentences with audio, clear rules, and common errors. There are at least two practice exercises for each grammar point. Students can look again at the grammar presented in the lesson on **Online Practice**. The **Workbook** provides a variety of practice exercises and the opportunity for students to use the new grammar to express their own ideas.

Vocabulary

- Revision and reactivation of previously learnt vocabulary
- Increased knowledge of high-frequency words and phrases
- Tasks which encourage students to use new vocabulary
- Accessible reference material

Every lesson focuses on high-frequency vocabulary and common lexical areas, but keeps the load realistic. All new vocabulary is given with the phonemic script alongside, to help students with the pronunciation of new words.

Many lessons are linked to the **Vocabulary Banks** which help present and practise the vocabulary in class, give an audio model of each word, and provide a clear reference so students can revise and test themselves in their own time. Students can review the meaning and the pronunciation of new vocabulary on **Online Practice**, and find further practice in the **Workbook**.

Pronunciation

- A solid foundation in the sounds of English
- Targeted pronunciation development
- Awareness of rules and patterns

There is a pronunciation focus in every lesson, which integrates clear pronunciation into grammar and vocabulary practice. There is an emphasis on the sounds most useful for communication, on word stress, and on sentence rhythm. **Online Practice** contains the Sound Bank videos which show students the mouth positions to make English vowels and consonants. They can also review the pronunciation from the lesson at their own speed. There is more practice of pronunciation in the **Workbook**, with audio, which can be found on **Online Practice**.

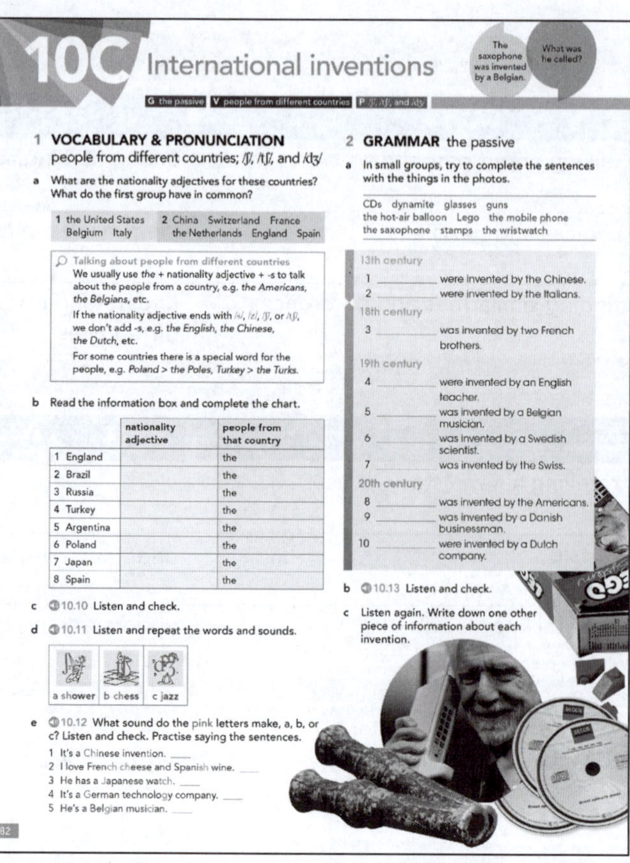

Speaking

- Topics that will inspire students' interest
- Tasks that push students to incorporate new language
- A sense of progress in their ability to speak

The ultimate aim of most students is to be able to communicate orally in English. Every lesson has a speaking activity which activates grammar, vocabulary, and pronunciation. The tasks are designed to help students to feel a sense of progress and to show that the number of situations in which they can communicate effectively is growing. Every two Files, students can use **Online Practice** to record themselves doing a short task.

Listening

- A reason to listen
- Confidence-building tasks
- Help with connected speech

At Pre-intermediate level students need confidence-building tasks which are progressively more challenging in terms of speed, length, and language difficulty, but are always achievable. They also need a variety of listening tasks which practise listening for gist and for specific details. We have chosen material we hope students will want to listen to. On **Online Practice**, for each File students can find further listening practice related to the topic. They can also access the listening activities from every lesson, to practise in their own time, and to read the script to check anything that they have found difficult.

Reading

- Engaging topics and stimulating texts
- Manageable tasks that help students to read

Many students need to read in English for their work or studies, and reading is also important in helping to build vocabulary and to consolidate grammar. The key to encouraging students to read is to give them motivating but accessible material and tasks they can do. In *English File Pre-intermediate,* reading texts have been adapted from a variety of real sources (the British press, magazines, news websites, online forums, etc.) and have been chosen for their intrinsic interest and ability to generate discussion. The opinions expressed in these texts do not necessarily reflect the views of the *English File* authors or of Oxford University Press.

Writing

- Clear models
- An awareness of register, structure, and fixed phrases.

English File Pre-intermediate provides guided writing tasks covering a range of writing types from a biography to a social media post. Students can use **Online Practice** to develop their writing skills further. The Discussion board also provides opportunities for informal written interaction.

Practical English

- Understanding high-frequency phrases
- Knowing what to say in typical situations
- Learning how to overcome typical travel problems

The Practical English lessons give students practice in key language for situations such as explaining that there are problems in a hotel or in a restaurant, or taking something back to a shop. To make these everyday situations come alive, there is a storyline involving two main characters, Jenny (from New York) and Rob (from London). There is a clear distinction between what students will hear and need to understand and what they need to say. The lessons also highlight other key 'Social English' phrases. On **Online Practice**, students can use the interactive video to record themselves and hear their own voice in the complete conversation. They can also listen and record the Social English phrases. The **Workbook** provides practice of all the language from the Practical English lessons.

Revision

- Regular review
- Motivating reference and practice material
- A sense of progress

Students will usually only assimilate and remember new language if they have the chance to see it and use it several times. Grammar, Vocabulary, and Pronunciation are recycled throughout the course. After every two Files there is a two-page Revise & Check section. The left-hand page revises the grammar, vocabulary, and pronunciation of each File. The right-hand page provides a series of skills-based challenges, including street interviews, and helps students to measure their progress in terms of competence. These pages are designed to be used flexibly according to the needs of your students. On **Online Practice**, for each File, there are three **Check your progress** activities. The first is a multiple choice activity for students to test themselves on the Grammar and Vocabulary from the File. The second is a dictation related to the topic and the language of the File for students to practise the new language in context. Finally, there is a **Challenge** activity, which involves a mini-research project based on a topic from the File. Every two Files, the **Workbook** contains a *Can you remember...?* page, which provides a cumulative review of language students have covered in the **Student's Book**.

Course overview

For students

Student's Book

The Student's Book has 12 Files. Each File is organized like this:

A, B, and C lessons

Each File contains three two-page lessons which present and practise **Grammar**, **Vocabulary**, and **Pronunciation** with a balance of reading and listening activities, and lots of opportunities for speaking. Every two Files (starting from File 2), the C lesson ends with a **Video Listening** section. All lessons have clear references to the **Grammar Bank**, **Vocabulary Bank**, and where relevant, to the **Sound Bank** at the back of the book.

Practical English

Every two Files (starting from File 1), there is a two-page lesson with integral video which teaches language for typical situations (for example buying medicine or complaining in a restaurant) and also 'Social English' (useful phrases like *By the way, You must be tired.*). The video is in the form of a drama, featuring the two main characters, Rob and Jenny. The lessons have a storyline which runs through the level.

Revise & Check

Every two Files (starting from File 2) there is a two-page section revising the **Grammar**, **Vocabulary**, and **Pronunciation** of each File and providing **Reading**, **Listening**, and **Speaking**. The *'Can you…?'* section challenges students with engaging reading texts and street interview videos, which give students exposure to real-life English.

The back of the Student's Book

The lessons contain references to these sections: Communication, Writing, Listening, Grammar Bank, Vocabulary Bank, and Sound Bank.

The Student's Book is also available as an eBook.

Online Practice

For students to practise and develop their language and skills or catch up on a class they have missed.

- **Look again:** students can review the language from every lesson.
- **Practice:** students can develop their skills with extra Reading, Writing, Listening, and Speaking practice.
- **Check your progress:** students can test themselves on the main language from the lesson and get instant feedback, and try an extra challenge.
- **Interactive video** to practise the language from the Practical English lessons.
- **Sound Bank videos** to learn and practise pronunciation of English sounds.
- **Resources:** All Student's Book audio, video, scripts, wordlists, dyslexia-friendly texts, and CEFR Language Portfolio.

Workbook

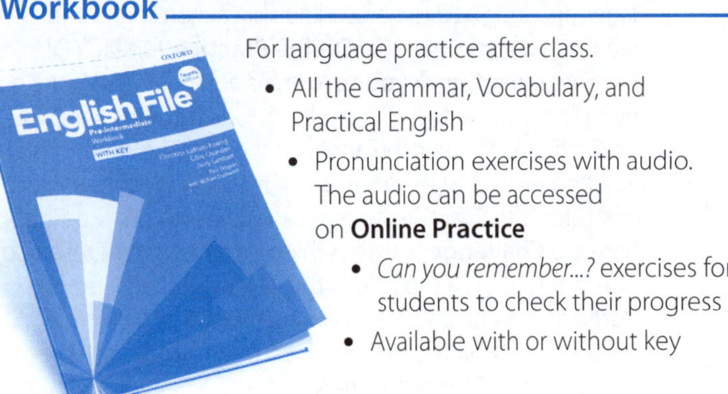

For language practice after class.

- All the Grammar, Vocabulary, and Practical English
- Pronunciation exercises with audio. The audio can be accessed on **Online Practice**
  - *Can you remember...?* exercises for students to check their progress
  - Available with or without key

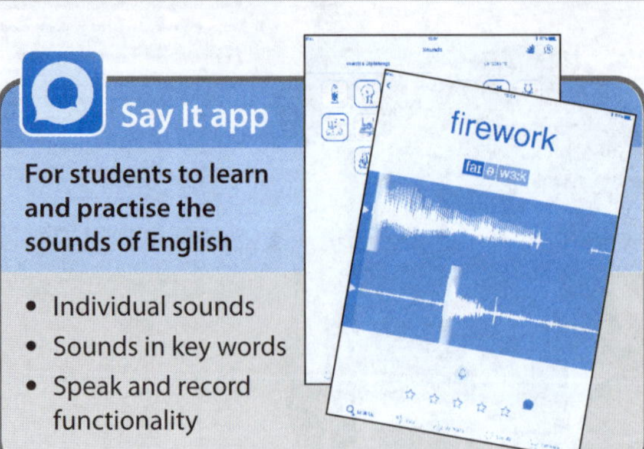

For teachers

Teacher's Guide

Step-by-step procedural notes for all the lessons including:

- an optional 'books-closed' lead-in for every lesson.
- **Extra challenge** suggestions for ways of exploiting the Student's Book material in a more challenging way if you have a stronger class.
- **Extra support** suggestions for ways of adapting activities or exercises to make them work with weaker students.
- **Extra ideas** for optional activities.

All lesson plans include answer keys and audio scripts.

Over 80 pages of photocopiable activities.

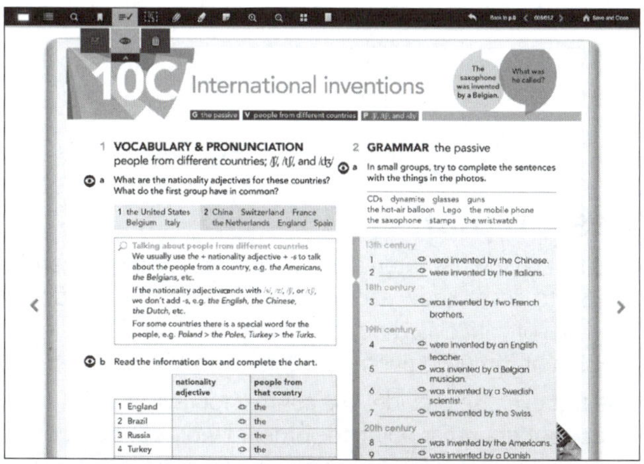

Grammar

see pp. 168–207

- An activity for every Grammar Bank, which can be used in class or for self-study extra practice

Communicative

see pp.208–252

- Extra speaking practice for every A, B, C lesson

Vocabulary

see pp.253–271

- An activity for every Vocabulary Bank, which can be used in class or for self-study extra practice

There is more information on page 167 of this Teacher's Guide about the photocopiable worksheets and tips on how best to use them.

Teacher's Resource Centre

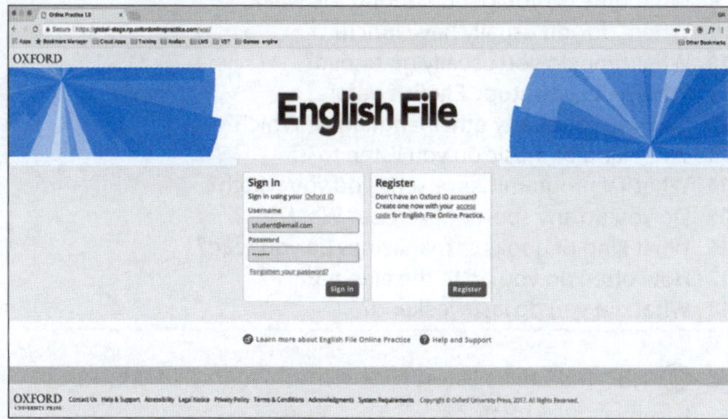

- All the Student's Book audio/video files and scripts
- Detailed lesson plans from the Teacher's Guide
- Answer keys
- All the photocopiable activities from the Teacher's Guide, including customisable versions
- All the Workbook audio files and scripts
- Tests and assessment material, including: an Entry Test; Progress Tests; an End-of-course Test; a Quick Test for every File; and complete test for every File. There are A and B versions of all the main tests and audio files for all the Listening tests
- CEFR documents

Classroom Presentation Tool

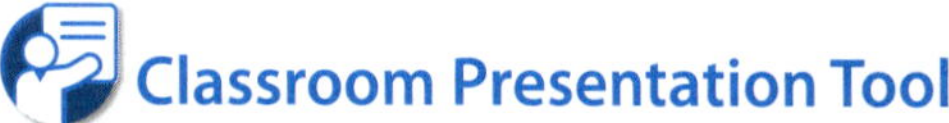

- The complete Student's Book
- Photocopiable activities from the Teacher's Guide
- All class audio and video, with interactive scripts
- Answer keys for exercises in the Student's Book and photocopiable activities
- Dyslexia-friendly texts

Class audio

All the listening materials for the Student's Book can be found on the **Teacher's Resource Centre**, **Classroom Presentation Tool**, **Online Practice**, **Student's eBook**, and the **Class Audio CDs**.

Video

Video listening

- Short documentary, drama, or animation for students at the end of even-numbered C lessons (2C, 4C, 6C, etc.)

Practical English

- A unique series of videos that goes with the Practical English lessons in the Student's Book

Revise & Check video

- Street interviews filmed in London, New York, and Oxford to accompany the Revise & Check section

All the video materials for the Student's Book can be found on the **Teacher's Resource Centre**, **Classroom Presentation Tool**, **Online Practice**, **Student's eBook**, and the **Class DVD**.

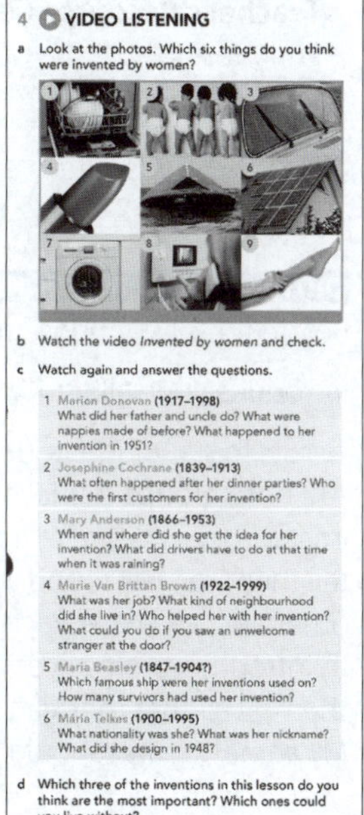

G word order in questions
V common verb phrases
P the alphabet

Lesson plan

This first lesson has three main objectives: to help you and the Sts to get to know each other, to give you a clear idea of the level of your class, and to provide some quick, efficient revision of some Elementary language points.

The first exercise provides the context for revising an important grammar point: the order of words in questions. The vocabulary focus is on common verb phrases. Sts use these to complete the questions, which they then ask each other. They then focus on the word order and practise it in the Grammar Bank. The pronunciation of the alphabet is revised, and the listening activity gives Sts the chance to revise spelling. Sts then bring all the language together by interviewing each other and completing a form.

There is an Entry Test on the *Teacher's Resource Centre*, which you can give Sts before starting the course.

More materials
For teachers
Photocopiables
Grammar word order in questions *p.172*
Communicative Student profile *p.217*
(instructions *p.208*)
Teacher's Resource Centre
Entry test
For students
Workbook 1A
Online Practice 1A

OPTIONAL LEAD-IN (BOOKS CLOSED)

Before the class, choose some party music.

Introduce yourself to the class. Say *Hello, I'm…* .

Tell Sts to stand up. Divide the class into two groups, **A** and **B**. Ask both groups to make a circle, **A** inside **B**. Tell them to imagine that they're at a party. When you play the music, tell them to walk round in their circle, one clockwise and the other anticlockwise. Each time you stop the music, tell them to introduce themselves to the person standing opposite them. Elicit that they can say *Hello* or *Hi, I'm…*, or *My name's…*, and should respond *Nice to meet you.*

1 VOCABULARY & SPEAKING
common verb phrases

Vocabulary notes

Sts at this level should be familiar with all these verb phrases. You may want to highlight the two meanings of *have*, as in *have brothers and sisters* and *have lunch*.

a If you didn't do the **Optional lead-in**, and your Sts don't know each other, set a time limit of, for example, two minutes, and tell Sts to stand up and move round the room, introducing themselves to other Sts. Tell them to say *Hello / Hi, I'm…* and *Nice to meet you*, and to try to remember other Sts' names.

Books open. Focus on the photos and the questions in *Getting to know you*. Point out to Sts that the first two (*are*, *were*) have been done for them.

Tell Sts to complete the other questions, individually or in pairs, with the correct verbs.

b ◉ **1.2** Play the audio for Sts to listen and check.

Check answers, making sure that Sts understand the whole question, not just the missing verb.

3 live	**4** live	**5** have	**6** have	**7** do	**8** get	**9** have
10 go	**11** study / learn	**12** speak	**13** listen	**14** watch / like	**15** do	**16** read	**17** go	**18** do

◉ **1.2**
1 Where are you from?
2 Where were you born?
3 Where do you live?
4 Do you live in a house or a flat?
5 Do you have any brothers and sisters?
6 Do you have any pets?
7 What do you do?
8 What time do you get up during the week?
9 Where do you usually have lunch?
10 What time do you usually go to bed?
11 Where did you study English before?
12 Can you speak any other languages? Which?
13 What kind of music do you listen to?
14 What TV programmes or series do you watch?
15 Do you do any sport or exercise? What?
16 What kind of books or magazines do you read?
17 How often do you go to the cinema?
18 What did you do last weekend?

c ◉ **1.3** Tell Sts to listen to the rhythm and intonation in the first six questions.

Play the audio once for Sts just to listen.

◉ **1.3**
See questions 1–6 in script 1.2

Now play it again, stopping after each question for Sts to repeat. Remind Sts that we usually stress the important words in a question, e.g. question words, verbs, and nouns, and say the other words less strongly, e.g. **Where** were you **born**? Do you **have** any **brothers** or **sisters**?

Then repeat the activity, eliciting responses from individual Sts.

d Focus on the **'Returning' a question** box and go through it with the class.

Now focus on the instructions and the example.

Demonstrate the activity by getting Sts to ask you questions first. Give full answers, with extra information.

EXTRA CHALLENGE Encourage Sts to ask follow-up questions, e.g.:

A *Do you have any brothers and sisters?*
B *I have one brother.*
A *How old is he? / What's his name? / What does he do?*

! You may have Sts who are neither at school / university nor working, e.g. they are unemployed or at home with children. If so, point out that question 7 (*What do you do?*) can be answered with, for example, *I'm unemployed / looking for a job / looking after my children*, etc.

Put Sts in pairs. Give them time to ask and answer all the questions. Monitor their conversations to give you an idea of their oral level.

Get feedback from several pairs to see what they have in common. At this point, you could teach them the word *both* and its position (before all verbs except *be* and modal verbs like *can*), e.g. *We both live in the city centre. We're both doctors. We can both speak German.*

2 GRAMMAR word order in questions

a Focus on the instructions and point out that the first one has been done for them.

Give Sts time to read questions 2–6 and tick or correct them.

Get Sts to compare with a partner, and then check answers.

2 ✗ Where does your father work?
3 ✓
4 ✓
5 ✗ Do you have cereal for breakfast?
6 ✗ Where did you go for your last holiday?

EXTRA IDEA Put Sts in pairs and get them to ask and answer the six questions.

b Tell Sts to go to **Grammar Bank 1A** on *p.126*. Explain that all the grammar rules and exercises are in this part of the book.

Grammar notes

In questions with the auxiliaries *do*, *does*, and *did*, Sts might leave out the auxiliary or get the word order wrong. Typical mistakes are: ~~*You live with your parents? Why she didn't like the film?*~~

The memory aids **ASI** (**A**uxiliary, **S**ubject, **I**nfinitive) and **QuASI** (**Qu**estion word, **A**uxiliary, **S**ubject, **I**nfinitive) may help Sts here.

In questions with *be* and *can*, Sts sometimes forget to invert the subject and verb. Typical mistakes are: ~~*Ana is a student? Where I can sit?*~~

If a verb is followed by a preposition (e.g. *talk about*, *listen to*), the preposition goes at the end of the question: *What did you talk about?*

Focus on the example sentences and play both audio 1.4 and 1.5 for Sts to listen and repeat. Encourage them to copy the rhythm. Then go through the rules with the class.

Now focus on the exercises for **1A** on *p.127*. Sts do the exercises individually or in pairs.

Check answers, getting Sts to read the full questions.

a
1 Where **can** we park?
2 How **old** are you?
3 Does **the class** finish at 8.00?
4 Where do your friends **live**?
5 Why **didn't** you answer my email?
6 Do you often **go** to the cinema?
7 What **does** this word mean?
8 What time did **your friends** arrive?
9 Who are you talking **to**?
10 Where were **you** last night?

b
1 Do you have a car?
2 Where was your brother born?
3 How often does he phone you?
4 What time does their flight arrive?
5 Is your girlfriend from Brazil?
6 How many languages can you speak?
7 How was the party?
8 Where did you go last summer?
9 Is there a doctor here?
10 Did you come to school by bus?

Tell Sts to go back to the main lesson **1A**.

EXTRA SUPPORT If you think Sts need more practice, you may want to give them the **Grammar** photocopiable activity at this point.

c Focus on the instructions, the questions, and the example. Demonstrate the activity by asking the first question (*Do you drink a lot of tea or coffee?*) until someone answers *Yes, I do*. Then ask the follow-up question (*How many cups do you drink a day?*).

Give Sts a few minutes to work out how to form the questions.

EXTRA SUPPORT Put Sts in pairs and get them to write the questions.

Check answers.

PRESENT
What gym **do you go** to?
How many hours **do you sleep**?
What games **do you play**?
What sports **do you like watching**?

PAST
What time **did you go** to bed?
What **did you cook**?
Where **did you go**?
What film **did you see**?
What **did you buy**?

d Focus on the instructions and make sure Sts understand what they have to do.

Ask Sts to stand up and move around the class, asking each other the questions. If it's difficult to move around the class, do this in pairs or small groups.

Get some feedback from the class.

3 PRONUNCIATION the alphabet

Pronunciation notes

Emphasize the importance of being able to spell in English, particularly your name or email address. Point out that it is very useful to be able to recognize and write down letters correctly when people spell words to you.

If your Sts didn't use *English File* Elementary, this will be the first time that they have seen the sound pictures (*train*, *tree*, etc.). Explain that the pictures will give Sts a clear example of the target sound and that they will help Sts remember the pronunciation of the phonetic symbol. This is very important if Sts want to check the pronunciation of a word in the dictionary. Even if they have a dictionary app, the phonetic symbol will help to clarify which sound it is.

Tell Sts that the two dots in /iː/, /uː/, and /ɑː/ mean that they are long sounds.

a 🔊 **1.6** Put Sts in pairs and get them to say the groups of letters to each other.

Now play the audio for Sts to listen and check.

🔊 **1.6**
See the alphabet in Student's Book on *p.7*

EXTRA CHALLENGE Elicit the alphabet from the class before playing the audio.

Now play the audio again, pausing after each group of letters for Sts to listen and repeat.

b 🔊 **1.7** Focus on the box **The alphabet** and go through it with the class.

Now focus on the sound pictures and instructions. Point out that the first one (*train*) has been done for them.

Play the audio for Sts to listen and write the words. Check answers.

2 tree **3** egg **4** bike **5** phone **6** boot **7** car

🔊 **1.7**
1   train /eɪ/
2   tree /iː/
3   egg /e/
4   bike /aɪ/
5   phone /əʊ/
6   boot /uː/
7   car /ɑː/

Now play it again, pausing after each one for Sts to repeat.

EXTRA SUPPORT If these sounds are difficult for your Sts, it will help to show them the mouth position. You could model this yourself or use the Sound Bank videos on the *Teacher's Resource Centre*.

EXTRA IDEA Tell Sts to go to the **Sound Bank** on *pp.166–167*. If your Sts didn't use *English File* Elementary, explain that this is a reference section of the book, where they can check the symbols and see common sound–spelling patterns. Look at the spelling rules for the seven sounds. Model and drill the example words for the vowels and elicit / explain their meaning.

Tell Sts to go back to the main lesson **1A**.

c Now focus on the letters in the list, but <u>don't</u> elicit their pronunciation yet. Tell Sts, in pairs, to write the letters in the correct column according to their sound. Tell Sts that this exercise is easier to do if they say the letters aloud. Point out that the first one (*J*) has been done for them.

d 🔊 **1.8** Play the audio for Sts to listen and check. Check answers.

🔊 **1.8**

1	train	A H **J K**
2	tree	B C D **E G** P T V
3	egg	F L **M N** S **X** Z
4	bike	I **Y**
5	phone	O
6	boot	Q U W
7	car	R

Now play it again for Sts to listen and repeat.

Ask Sts which letters are difficult for them. Highlight the difference between pairs and groups of letters which are often confused, e.g. *a / e / i, g / j, k / q*, etc. You could tell Sts that *zed* is pronounced *zee* in American English and is the only letter of the alphabet that is different from British English.

In pairs, Sts practise saying the letters in each column.

e Put Sts in pairs, **A** and **B**, and tell them to go to **Communication Alphabet quiz**, A on *p.102*, B on *p.108*.

Tell Sts to take turns asking and answering their questions. Point out that the answers are in italics after each question.

When they have finished, find out if any Sts got all the answers correct.

Tell Sts to go back to the main lesson **1A**.

4 LISTENING & SPEAKING understanding personal information

a ◁)) **1.9** Focus on the instructions. Make sure Sts understand that they aren't going to listen to six complete conversations. They must listen to six people giving some information and write down the letters and numbers.

Go through the words in 1–6, making sure Sts know what they mean, e.g. *first name*, *postcode*, etc. Point out that the first one (*Wayne*) has been done.

Play the audio for Sts to listen and write the letters and numbers. Play again if necessary.

Get Sts to compare with a partner, and then check answers by eliciting the information onto the board.

EXTRA SUPPORT Before playing the audio, you might want to check that Sts know how to say an email address, e.g. that @ = *at* and . = *dot*. You might also want to check that Sts understand the term *double*, e.g. *My name's Anna – A-double N-A.*

> **2** SE21 8GP **3** 07700 987782 **4** jvine64@kings.co.uk
> **5** Rathbone **6** 16 Russell Street

◁)) **1.9**
1 A How do you spell your first name?
  B W-A-Y-N-E.
2 A What's the postcode?
  B It's S-E-twenty-one-eight-G-P.
3 B Oh-seven-seven-double oh-nine eight-seven-seven-eight-two.
4 A It's J-V-I-N-E-six-four at kings dot co dot U-K.
  B Can you repeat that, please?
  A Yes, J-V-I-N-E-six-four at kings dot co dot U-K.
5 B Ann Rathbone. R-A-T-H-B-O-N-E.
6 A It's sixteen Russell Street. That's R-U-double S-E-double L. Let me show you on the map.

---

b ◁)) **1.10** Focus on the instructions and make sure Sts understand what they have to do. Go through situations a–f and point out that the first one (*1b*) has been done for them.

Play the audio, pausing after each conversation to give Sts time to number a–f. Play again if necessary.

Now play the audio again, pausing after each conversation, and check the answer.

> **2** a **3** c **4** e **5** f **6** d

◁)) **1.10**
(script in Student's Book on *p.120*)
1 A Good afternoon. How can I help you?
  B I have a reservation for five nights.
  A What's your name?
  B Wayne Roberts.
  A How do you spell your first name?
  B W-A-Y-N-E.
  A Just a moment.
2 A So, the sofa is eight hundred and ninety-nine pounds and ninety-nine p in total. What's the address for delivery? Is it a London address?
  B Yes, it's in south London.
  A What's the postcode?
  B It's S-E-twenty-one-eight-G-P.
  A And the address is…?
  B Fourteen Dangerford Road, flat two. That's in Forest Hill, London.

3 A Welcome to our mobile phone helpline. Please say the number of the mobile phone you have a problem with.
  B Oh-seven-seven-double oh-nine-eight-seven-seven-eight-two.
4 A Now, every Friday I'm going to give you some writing to do for homework at the weekend. You can either give it to me in class on the Monday, or you can send it to me by email. I'm going to give you my email address and I'd like you to write it down. OK? It's J-V-I-N-E-six-four at kings dot co dot U-K.
  B Can you repeat that, please?
  A Yes, J-V-I-N-E-six-four at kings dot co dot U-K. OK, now I'm going to write it on the board for you. Did you get it right?… Well done. Remember, this symbol is called *at* in English, and this one is *dot*.
5 A Good evening.
  B Hi. We have a table booked for seven thirty.
  A Yes, madam. What name, please?
  B Ann Rathbone. R-A-T-H-B-O-N-E.
  A Ah, yes, here we are. Can you come this way, please?
6 A OK, Susannah, that's great. Here's your student card. Your classes start on Monday at nine a.m. Now, the classes are not here in the main school, but in a different building.
  B Oh?
  A But it's very near – just five minutes' walk from here, in Russell Street.
  B Sorry, what's the address?
  A It's sixteen Russell Street. That's R-U-double S-E-double L. Let me show you on the map.
  B Thank you.

EXTRA SUPPORT If there's time, you could get Sts to listen again with the script on *p.120*, so they can see exactly what they understood / didn't understand. Translate / Explain any new words or phrases.

c Focus on the instructions and the form.

Put Sts in pairs and get them to interview each other. If Sts don't want to give their real address and phone number, tell them to invent one. Remind Sts that when we say phone numbers in English, we say the individual digits, and that *0* can be *oh* or *zero*. Elicit how to say an email address, e.g. that @ = *at* and . = *dot*.

When they have finished, get Sts to show each other their forms to check the information.

Get some feedback.

G present simple
V describing people: appearance and personality
P final *-s* and *-es*

Lesson plan

In this lesson, the present simple (all forms) is revised in detail through a British newspaper article. A daughter tries to find a suitable partner for her father, who is divorced. The lesson begins with Vocabulary and Reading. Basic language for physical description is revised, and in the Vocabulary Bank, new language is presented and adjectives of personality are introduced. Sts then read the article about Charlotte's dad, Clint, and focus on the grammar of the present simple. This is followed by a pronunciation focus on the final *-s* and *-es* endings in verbs and nouns. Sts then read about two possible dates for Clint and discuss who they think is the better date. In Listening, Sts listen to Elspeth, an Irish journalist, talking about a dating experiment in which her mother chooses dates for her from a dating app. The lesson ends with Sts describing a single person – a member of their family, or a friend – in detail, and writing a short description.

More materials	
For teachers	
Photocopiables	
Grammar present simple *p.173*	
Vocabulary Describing people *p.257* (instructions *p.253*)	
Communicative Ask me some questions… *p.218* (instructions *p.208*)	
For students	
Workbook 1B	
Online Practice 1B	

1 VOCABULARY & READING describing people

a ◗) **1.11** Books open. Focus on the instructions and the two photos.

Play the audio for Sts to listen and decide which speaker is the woman in the photos (describing her father).

Check the answer, eliciting the words and phrases which helped Sts to identify Charlotte's father, e.g. *quite good-looking, he's not very tall – a bit taller than me.*

Charlotte is speaker 2.

◗) **1.11**
1 My dad's very tall and thin, with a big nose. He looks a bit like a tall, thin bird! He has blond hair and blue eyes, which is typical of Sweden – his grandmother was from Sweden. Um, he looks a bit serious, but he isn't, really. He's very funny – he has a great sense of humour.
2 I think my dad's quite good-looking. He's not very tall – a bit taller than me – and he still has his hair: it was dark, but it's grey now. He's not thin, but he isn't overweight – he's careful about what he eats. And he's got a lovely smile.
3 My dad's short and thin, and he wears glasses. He isn't exactly good-looking, but he's not unattractive, either. He's very friendly, and very talkative – in fact, he never stops talking.

b ◗) **1.12** Focus on the instructions and make sure Sts understand *height, hair, weight,* and *smile*.

Play the audio.

Get Sts to compare with a partner, and then check answers. Get Sts to try to spell *overweight*, and write it on the board. Elicit its meaning, as it is probably the first time Sts have seen the word.

height not very tall
hair was dark, now grey
weight not thin, but isn't overweight
smile lovely

◗) **1.12**
I think my dad's quite good-looking. He's not very tall – a bit taller than me – and he still has his hair, but less than before – it was dark, but it's grey now. He's not thin, but he isn't overweight – he's careful about what he eats. And he's got a lovely smile.

Vocabulary notes

Sts are often confused by the difference between the questions *What does he look like?* and *What's he like?*. *What does he look like?* only refers to appearance, but *What's he like?* can refer to both appearance and personality.

You may want to explain that *blonde* is used to describe women's / girls' hair and *blond* is used for men's / boys' hair.

c Tell Sts to go to **Vocabulary Bank** Describing people on *p.150*. Focus on **1 Appearance**. Focus on the question *What does he / she look like?* and elicit that it refers to a person's physical appearance. Get Sts to do **a** individually or in pairs. Point out that the first one has been done for them.

◄))) 1.13 Now do **b**. Play the audio for Sts to listen and check.

Check answers. Make sure Sts understand the individual words in the descriptions.

◄))) 1.13

1 Appearance What does he look like? What does she look like?
2 She has curly red hair.
3 She has long, straight hair.
1 She has big, blue eyes.
6 She has short, blonde hair.
5 He has a beard and a moustache.
4 He's bald.
7 He's very tall and thin.
9 He's medium height and very slim.
8 He's quite short and a bit overweight.

Now either use the audio to drill the pronunciation of the sentences, or model and drill them yourself. Give further practice of any words your Sts find difficult to pronounce, e.g. *curly, straight, beard*, etc. Highlight the different pronunciations of *height* /haɪt/ and *weight* /weɪt/.

Now go through the information box with the class. After going through the **Using two adjectives together** section, you might also want to elicit from Sts typical colours for hair, i.e. *fair / blond(e), red, grey, light / dark brown, black, white*. In the **Handsome or beautiful?** section, highlight the silent *d* in *handsome*.

Finally, focus on **c**. Get Sts to cover the sentences and use the photos to test themselves or their partner. If they are testing a partner, encourage them to use the question *What does he / she look like?*.

Focus on **2 Personality** and get Sts to do **a** individually or in pairs. Point out that the first one (*friendly*) has been done for them.

Check the answers to **a** before moving on to **b**.

2 talkative **3** generous **4** kind **5** lazy **6** funny **7** clever
8 shy

Now Sts do **b** by putting the adjectives from the list into the **Opposite** column in **a**.

◄))) 1.14 Now do **c**. Play the audio for Sts to listen and check.

Check answers and make sure Sts understand the individual words in the descriptions.

◄))) 1.14

Personality
1 friendly, unfriendly
2 talkative, quiet
3 generous, mean
4 kind, unkind
5 lazy, hard-working
6 funny, serious
7 clever, stupid
8 shy, extrovert

Now either use the audio to drill the pronunciation of the adjectives, or model and drill them yourself. Give further practice of any words your Sts find difficult to pronounce. You could tell Sts that *mean* in American English has a different meaning (= *unkind*) and it is sometimes used with this meaning in British English.

Focus on the **What does she look like? What is she like?** box and go through it with the class to remind them of the difference between the two questions.

Focus on **d**. Get Sts to cover the adjectives and look at the definitions to test themselves or their partner.

Finally, for **Activation**, put Sts in pairs and get them to ask and answer questions about a member of their family or a good friend. Get some feedback from a few individual Sts.

Tell Sts to go back to the main lesson **1B**.

 If you think Sts need more practice, you may want to give them the **Vocabulary** photocopiable activity at this point.

d Focus on the instructions and make sure Sts understand all the lexis, e.g. *job, marital status*, etc.

Focus on the title of the article and elicit the meaning of the verb *date* (= go out with someone in a romantic relationship) and the noun *date* (= a romantic meeting) at the beginning of the article. Give Sts time to read the article and complete the task.

Get Sts to compare with a partner, and then check answers.

 Before Sts read the article the first time, check whether you need to pre-teach any vocabulary.

his age 52
his job businessman
his marital status divorced
his personality warm, generous, a gentleman, romantic, fun
his perfect partner a woman who works, independent, funny, clever

e Focus on questions 1–4 and go through them with the class.

Give Sts time to read the article again and answer the questions.

Get Sts to compare with a partner, and then check answers.

1 Because she doesn't want him to end up alone.
2 They go out together and are planning a trip together.
3 You met people face to face, and, for example, invited them for a drink.
4 He finds dates online / on the internet. Charlotte has helped by writing his profile.

f Focus on the instructions and do this as a whole-class activity.

1 funny **2** fun

Finally, deal with any other new vocabulary. Model and drill the pronunciation of any tricky words.

g Do this as a whole-class activity and elicit Sts' opinions.

2 GRAMMAR present simple

a Focus on the instructions. Give Sts a few minutes to complete the gaps.

Check answers.

> ⊞ needs ⊟ doesn't ? do, does

b Tell Sts to read the four sentences and tick the ones that are correct. Highlight that the correct answer depends on the position of the adverbs of frequency *often* and *always*.

Check answers.

> 1 A 2 B

EXTRA CHALLENGE Ask Sts why the other sentences are wrong and elicit the rules for word order.

> Adverbs of frequency go before main verbs, but after the verb *be*.

c Tell Sts to go to **Grammar Bank 1B** on *p.126*.

Grammar notes
Present simple
Remind Sts:
- of the difference in pronunciation between *do* /duː/, *don't* /dəʊnt/, and *does* /dʌz/
- of the pronunciation of *goes* /gəʊz/ and *has* /hæz/
- that the contracted forms *don't* and *doesn't* are always used in conversation

Adverbs and expressions of frequency
You may want to point out that *usually / normally* and *sometimes* can also be used at the beginning of a present simple sentence, e.g. *Sometimes I get up late on Saturday*.

Other common expressions of frequency using *every* are *every week*, *every month*, and *every year*.

In expressions like *once a month*, *twice a day*, etc., remind Sts that *once* and *twice* are irregular (NOT ~~one time~~, ~~two times~~); *times* is used with all other numbers, e.g. *ten times*, *thirty times* (*a year*).

Focus on the example sentences and play both audio 🔊 **1.15** and 🔊 **1.16** for Sts to listen and repeat. Encourage them to copy the rhythm. Then go through the rules with the class.

Now focus on the exercises for **1B** on *p.127*. Sts do the exercises individually or in pairs.

Check answers, getting Sts to read the full sentences.

> **a** 1 Does Anna like music?
> 2 My sister has a lot of hobbies.
> 3 I don't get on very well with my parents.
> 4 My brother studies English at university.
> 5 My neighbours don't have any children.
> 6 What time does the film start?
> 7 He goes out twice a week.
> 8 We don't often talk about politics.
> 9 How often do you see your brother?
> 10 Sally doesn't go on Facebook very much.

> **b** 1 I always go to bed before 11.00.
> 2 Kate hardly ever sees her family.
> 3 We never go shopping on Saturdays.
> 4 I go to the dentist's twice a year.
> 5 They sometimes have breakfast in bed. / Sometimes they have breakfast in bed.
> 6 I usually listen to the radio in the car.
> 7 Alan runs in the park every day.
> 8 Sam is often late for work.
> 9 John doesn't often go to the theatre.
> 10 I visit my mum once a month.

Tell Sts to go back to the main lesson **1B**.

EXTRA SUPPORT If you think Sts need more practice, you may want to give them the **Grammar** photocopiable activity at this point.

3 PRONUNCIATION & SPEAKING
final *-s* and *-es*

Pronunciation notes
The pronunciation rules for adding an *-s* (or *-es*) to verbs (e.g. *smokes*) and nouns (e.g. *books*) are the same.

The difference between the /s/ and /z/ sounds is very small and only occasionally causes communication problems. The most important thing is for Sts to learn when to pronounce *-es* as /ɪz/.

You may want to give Sts these rules:
- The *s* is pronounced /s/ after these unvoiced* sounds: /k/, /p/, /f/, and /t/, e.g. *walks*, *stops*, *laughs*, *eats*.
- In all other cases, the final *s* is voiced and pronounced /z/, e.g. *plays*, *parties*, etc.

*Voiced and unvoiced consonants
Voiced consonant sounds are made by vibrating the vocal chords, e.g. /b/, /l/, /m/, /v/, etc. Unvoiced consonant sounds are made without vibration in the vocal chords, e.g. /k/, /p/, /t/, /s/, etc.

You can demonstrate this to Sts by getting them to hold their hands against their throats. For voiced sounds, they should feel a vibration in their throat, but not for unvoiced sounds.

a 🔊 **1.17** Explain that the final *-s* and *-es* in the third person of the present simple and in plurals can be pronounced in three different ways.

Focus on the sound pictures. Elicit and drill the words and sounds: *snake* /s/, *zebra* /z/, and /ɪz/.

❗ Sts may have problems distinguishing between the /s/ and /z/ sounds. Tell them that the /s/ is like the sound made by a snake and the /z/ is a bee or fly.

Play the audio once for Sts just to listen.

🔊 **1.17**
See sentences in Student's Book on *p.9*

Then play it again, pausing for Sts to listen and repeat.

Now focus on the **Pronunciation of final *-s* and *-es*** box and go through it with the class.

b 🔊 **1.18** Write the three phonetic symbols, /s/, /z/, and /ɪz/ on the board. Elicit the third person pronunciation of the first verb in the list (*chooses*) and ask Sts which group it belongs to (group 3). Write it on the board under the correct heading. Get Sts to continue with the other verbs. Then tell them to do the same thing with the plural form of the nouns.

Play the audio once the whole way through for Sts to listen and check.

Check answers.

	/s/	/z/	/ɪz/
verbs	cooks	goes	chooses
	stops	lives	teaches

	/s/	/z/	/ɪz/
nouns	books	boys	classes
	shops	friends	languages

🔊 **1.18**
chooses, cooks, goes, lives, stops, teaches
books, boys, classes, friends, languages, shops

> Highlight that the most important thing to get correct is that *lives* and *dates* are pronounced /lɪvz/ and /deɪts/, NOT /lɪvɪz/ and /deɪtɪz/, but that in *chooses*, *teaches*, *classes*, and *languages* the -es is pronounced /ɪz/.
>
> Now play the audio, pausing after each group of words for Sts to repeat.
>
> Then repeat the activity, eliciting responses from individual Sts.

EXTRA SUPPORT If these sounds are difficult for your Sts, it will help to show them the mouth position. You could model this yourself or use the Sound Bank videos on the *Teacher's Resource Centre*.

c Put Sts in pairs, **A** and **B**, and tell them to go to **Communication A date for Clint**, **A** on *p.102*, **B** on *p.108*. Go through the instructions with them carefully.

Sit **A** and **B** face-to-face if possible. When they have finished reading their profiles, **B** starts by asking **A** questions 1–7 about Maggie.

When **B** has finished, they swap roles.

When they have finished, tell them to compare photos and decide who they think is a better date for Clint.

Tell Sts to go back to the main lesson **1B**.

d With a show of hands, find out if the class think Maggie or Tessa is the better date and why.

4 LISTENING identifying the person being described

a 🔊 **1.19** Focus on the photo of Elspeth Gordon and the instructions. Now focus on the four questions and point out the **Glossary**. Demonstrate the meaning of *swipe* to make sure Sts have understood the definition.

Play the audio once the whole way through.

Get Sts to compare their answers with a partner, and play the audio again if necessary.

Check answers. When checking the answer to question 2, elicit what you do if you don't like someone (*swipe left if you don't like someone*).

EXTRA SUPPORT Read through the scripts and decide if you need to pre-teach any new lexis before Sts listen.

> **1** She uses a dating app.
> **2** You swipe right if you like them.
> **3** Elspeth's mother is going to choose the men she likes for her daughter.
> **4** Elspeth is going to go on a date with the men her mother chooses.

🔊 **1.19**
(script in Student's Book on *p.120*)
My name's Elspeth. I'm twenty-five, I'm a journalist, I live in Dublin, and I'm single. It's not easy to meet people here. So who can help me? My mother…and a dating app. My favourite dating app, called Tinder, shows you photos of possible partners, with a bit of information about them. You look at the photos and swipe, swipe, swipe. Swipe right if you like them, and swipe left…well…swipe left if you don't. If a guy likes you and you like him, you have a match. Then you can start messaging the person, and from this, romance follows…or so they say. I've tried it, but with no success. So I decide to give my mother my phone. She can swipe all the men she likes, and then look at my matches and choose the people that she likes the best. I've promised to go on a date with the men she chooses.

b 🔊 **1.20** Focus on the instructions and the question. Play the audio for Sts to listen and answer the question. Get Sts to compare with a partner, and then check the answer.

EXTRA SUPPORT Pause after the date with John and elicit the answer, then repeat for Sebastian.

> She likes her mum's choices and has fun, but she isn't sure the men are right for her.

🔊 **1.20**
(script in Student's Book on *p.120*)
Date 1
My first date is with a nice guy called John. I sit at a table in a bar and wait for him to arrive. An old man walks towards the table, and for two awful seconds I think it's all a terrible mistake, but he walks past, and then my date arrives. He's very tall: one metre ninety. Well done, Mum! I'm tall myself, so I always look for tall men, as my mum knows well. We start chatting, and it's all very easy. Mum has good taste. He's a teacher. We get on well and it's a fun date, but sadly, there isn't a spark. So I try again.
Date 2
I arrive a bit early again, and I sit there waiting for Sebastian to arrive. Suddenly, I realize that I can't remember anything at all about him, not even where he's from. Then he comes through the door: tall, dark, and handsome. *Mum, you're amazing*, I say to myself. He's from Germany, but he lives in Dublin. He's a real gentleman. At the end of the evening, he asks for a second date. Mum is very pleased. I agree to the date, but I don't really think it's going to work.

c Give Sts time to read 1–6 and see if they can remember which man each phrase refers to. Elicit that *a spark* means a feeling of excitement.

Play the audio again.

Get Sts to compare with a partner, and then check answers.

> **1** S **2** J **3** J **4** S **5** J **6** S

Ask Sts which man they think Elspeth prefers and why.

d ◀》 **1.21** Tell Sts they are now going to listen to Elspeth talking about a third date and they must answer the two questions. Before playing the audio, pre-teach *enthusiastic*. Model and drill pronunciation /ɪnˌθjuːziˈæstɪk/.

Now play the audio the whole way through.

Get Sts to compare with a partner.

Check the answer to the first question and elicit ideas for the second.

 Ask Sts more questions about the date, e.g. *What's his name? What problem is there at the beginning? What does George do?*, etc.

Yes, it is. The date is going well.

◀》 **1.21**
(script in Student's Book on *p.120*)
Date 3
Date number three is George. He suggests a bar on South William Street. I arrive early – I'm definitely the most punctual person in the world. I stand outside, very confused: the bar is closed. For a moment, I think Mum has finally got it wrong. But a few minutes later, he arrives – he just didn't know the bar was closed. We go somewhere else and start chatting. He tells me he works in IT and is from just outside Dublin. This guy is great fun. He's very relaxed and interesting – he's travelled a lot. He tells a lot of funny stories. It's all going well, and I'm getting very enthusiastic, when my phone pings.

e ◀》 **1.22** Tell Sts they are now going to listen to the end of the date. They must check their ideas from **d** and answer the two questions.

Play the audio the whole way through.

Check the answers to the first two questions and elicit opinions on whether Elspeth and George have a second date.

The message was from her mother.
She feels very embarrassed and wants to die.

◀》 **1.22**
It's all going well, and I'm getting very enthusiastic, when my phone pings. It's on the table between us and it's a text. From my mother. *Well, is he lovely? Love Mum.*
George looks at my screen and reads the text. I want to die.

 If there's time, you could get Sts to listen again to all parts of the audio with the scripts on *p.120*, so they can see exactly what they understood / didn't understand. Translate / Explain any new words or phrases.

f Do this as a whole-class activity and elicit Sts' opinions. Tell them what you think, too.

5 SPEAKING & WRITING describing yourself

a Give Sts five minutes to make a few notes about a person they know well who is single and looking for a partner. Monitor and help with vocabulary.

 Tell Sts to make notes about their person in the form.

b Put Sts in pairs, **A** and **B**. **A** describes his / her person and **B** listens and asks for more information.

Sts swap roles and **B** describes his / her person to **A**. Do they know someone who would be a good partner for this person? Get feedback from various pairs.

c This is the first time Sts are sent to the **Writing** section at the back of the Student's Book. In this section, Sts will find model texts, with exercises and language notes, and then a writing task. We suggest that you go through the model and do the exercise(s) in class, but set the actual writing (the last activity) for homework.

Tell Sts to go to **Writing Describing yourself** on *p.113*.

Focus on **a** and get Sts to read Charlie's profile and answer questions 1–7.

Get Sts to compare with a partner, and then check answers.

1 Carlos
2 Guadalajara, Mexico
3 He's a (physics) student.
4 His parents and his dog
5 He has black hair, brown eyes, and a Roman nose.
6 He's positive and funny, but he can be serious, too.
7 He watches TV and plays computer games.

Now do **b** and tell Sts to read the profile again and correct the ten mistakes.

Get Sts to compare with a partner, and then check answers.

1 I'm 21 years old.   2 studying   3 photo   4 brown
5 friends   6 can be   7 don't   8 much   9 because
10 English

Now focus on the chart in **c**. Get Sts to first write the topics from the list in the first column of the chart (**Content**), and then write the highlighted phrases from the profile for each paragraph. Point out that Paragraph 1 has been done for them.

Check answers.

	Content	Phrases
Paragraph 2	work / study, family	I'm going to tell you about…; I live with…
Paragraph 3	physical appearance	As you can see from the…; My father always says…
Paragraph 4	personality	I think I'm a…; My…say…
Paragraph 5	hobbies and interests	…when I'm not in class…; …when I can, I like…

Focus on **d** and tell Sts they are now going to plan their own profile. They should add notes to the last column (**My information**) in the chart.

When Sts are ready, focus on **e** and tell them to write their own profiles on a piece of paper. As this writing task is quite short, you may like to get Sts to do it in class. Otherwise, set it for homework.

In **f**, Sts check their work for mistakes before giving it in.

G present continuous
V clothes: *boots*, *skirt*, etc., prepositions of place: *under*, *next to*, etc.
P /ə/ and /ɜː/

Lesson plan

The context for this lesson is a project called Remake, in which modern photographers recreate famous paintings. The images from one example, a painting by Vermeer called *The Milkmaid* and its corresponding photo, are used to present clothes vocabulary, and this is followed by a pronunciation focus on two common vowel sounds, /ə/ and /ɜː/. Sts then focus again on the images and answer questions, and this leads them to the Grammar section, which is on using the present continuous for things that are happening now, or around now, and for describing what is happening in a picture. The present continuous is also contrasted with the present simple for habitual actions or permanent situations. When Sts come back from the Grammar Bank, they have a listening activity where they hear an art expert talking about Vermeer and the painting. They then revise prepositions of place, and all the language of the lesson is pulled together in a final speaking activity, where Sts describe two more examples of paintings and their remakes to each other in order to find the similarities and differences.

More materials

For teachers

Photocopiables
Grammar present simple or present continuous? *p.174*
Vocabulary Things you wear *p.258*
(instructions *p.253*)
Communicative What are they doing? *p.219*
(instructions *p.208*)

For students

Workbook 1C

Online Practice 1C

1 VOCABULARY clothes

a Books open. Focus on the instructions and then give Sts time to look at the painting and photo and read about the Remake Project.

Elicit opinions from the class. You could also tell Sts what you think.

b Tell Sts to look at both the painting and the photo and look for the items of clothing. Elicit 1 from the class and explain the meaning of *apron*. Sts then continue to say who is wearing the other items.

Check answers.

1 W	2 M	3 W	4 W	5 M	6 W

c Tell Sts to go to **Vocabulary Bank Things you wear** on *p.151*. Focus on the four sections (*clothes*, *footwear*, *accessories*, and *jewellery*) and make sure Sts know what they mean and how to pronounce them (/kləʊðz/, /ˈfʊtweə/, /əkˈsesəriːz/, /ˈdʒuːəlri/).

Vocabulary notes

Some clothes words only exist in the plural, e.g. *jeans*, *leggings*, *pyjamas*, *shorts*, *trousers*, *tights*. These words cannot be used with *a*, e.g. NOT *a trousers*. If Sts want to use an indefinite article, they should use *some*, e.g. *I bought some trousers / some shoes*.

You could also teach *a pair of*, which is often used with plural clothes words, e.g. *a pair of trousers*. Other words for clothes, e.g. *footwear*, *socks*, and *gloves* are usually plural, but can be used in the singular.

· Now get Sts to do **a** individually or in pairs.
1.23 Now do **b**. Play the audio for Sts to listen and check.

Check answers.

1.23
Things you wear

Clothes		Footwear		Jewellery	
11	blouse	24	boots	33	bracelet
13	cardigan	25	flip-flops	32	earrings
3	coat	22	sandals	35	necklace
2	dress	23	shoes	34	ring
9	jacket	21	trainers		
5	jeans				
14	leggings	**Accessories**			
18	pyjamas	26	belt		
8	shirt	30	cap		
1	shorts	31	hat		
6	skirt	28	gloves		
20	socks	29	scarf		
7	suit	27	tie		
16	sweater				
19	tights				
4	top				
10	tracksuit				
12	trousers				
15	T-shirt				
17	underwear				

Now either use the audio to drill the pronunciation of the words, or model and drill them yourself. Give further practice of any words your Sts find difficult to pronounce.

Focus on **c**. Give Sts a minute to cover the words and look at the photos to test themselves or each other.

Focus on the information box for **wear, carry, or dress?** and **a pair**, and go through it with the class.

Finally, focus on **Activation** and put Sts in pairs, **A** and **B**. **A** starts by telling his / her partner what someone is wearing and **B** has to guess who it is. They then swap roles.

Tell Sts to go back to the main lesson **1C**.

 If you think Sts need more practice, you may want to give them the **Vocabulary** photocopiable activity at this point.

2 PRONUNCIATION /ə/ and /ɜː/

Pronunciation notes

The schwa /ə/ is the most common sound in English. It is a short sound, and always occurs in an unstressed syllable, e.g. _doctor_ /ˈdɒktə/, _address_ /əˈdres/.

You may want to point out to Sts that unstressed _-er_ or _-or_ at the end of a word are always pronounced /ə/, e.g. _teacher_, _better_, etc. and that _-tion_ is always pronounced /ʃən/.

/ɜː/ is a similar sound, but it is a long sound and is always a stressed syllable, e.g. _nurse_ /nɜːs/, _worker_ /ˈwɜːkə/.

a ◀ **1.24** Focus on the instructions and the question. Play the audio once for Sts just to listen.

◀ 1.24
See sounds and words in Student's Book on _p.10_

Then play it again, pausing after each word for Sts to repeat.

Ask Sts which sound is only in unstressed syllables.

The schwa sound /ə/ is only in unstressed syllables.

b Focus on the instructions and make sure Sts understand that they have to underline the stress in the words in the list and then decide if the highlighted sounds belong to 1 or 2 in **a**. Point out that the first one (_painter_) has been done for them.

Put Sts in pairs and give them time to complete the task.

c ◀ **1.25** Play the audio for Sts to listen and check. Check answers by writing the words on the board in the two groups and underlining the stressed syllable.

her 2   first 2   photograph 1   picture 1   prefer 2   curly 2
attractive 1   occasion 1   work 2   university 2

◀ 1.25
painter 1   her 2   first 2   photograph 1   picture 1   prefer 2
curly 2   attractive 1   occasion 1   work 2   university 2

Play the audio again, stopping after each word for Sts to repeat.

 If these sounds are difficult for your Sts, it will help to show them the mouth position. You could model this yourself or use the Sound Bank videos on the _Teacher's Resource Centre_.

d Put Sts in pairs and get them to ask and answer the questions. You could get Sts to ask you a couple of questions first.

Get some feedback from the class.

3 GRAMMAR present continuous

a Focus on the instructions and sentences 1–6. Make sure Sts know the meaning of _pour_ /pɔː/. Model and drill pronunciation.

Now tell Sts to look at both the Vermeer painting and the photo, and complete gaps 1–6.

Check answers.

1 They're   **2** She's   **3** He's   **4** She's   **5** They're   **6** They're

b Focus on the sentences and give Sts time to choose the correct form.

Check answers.

1 isn't wearing   **2** wear

 When Sts have chosen the correct form in each sentence, put them in pairs to discuss why the other is wrong.

1 isn't wearing (because we are describing a photo and saying what is happening at that moment)
2 wear (because it's something that happens habitually / frequently)

c Tell Sts to go to **Grammar Bank 1C** on _p.126_.

Grammar notes

Some languages do not have an equivalent to the present continuous and may always use the present simple. Typical mistakes are: ~~The man in the picture wears a hat. We live with friends at the moment because builders work on our house.~~

The present continuous is used to describe what is happening in a painting because it is as if we were looking at a scene through a window.

The future use of the present continuous (_I'm leaving tomorrow_) is presented in **3B**.

Focus on the example sentences and play both audio ◀ **1.26** and ◀ **1.27** for Sts to listen and repeat. Encourage them to copy the rhythm. Then go through the rules with the class.

Now focus on the exercises for **1C** on _p.127_. Sts do the exercises individually or in pairs.

Check answers, getting Sts to read the full sentences.

a
1 Oliver is wearing a suit today!
2 It's hot. Why are you wearing a coat?
3 Jane isn't sitting in her usual place today.
4 Hey! You're standing on my foot!
5 What book are you reading?
6 We're renting a small flat at the moment.
7 Is she wearing make-up?
8 I'm planning a trip to the USA.
9 Is your brother working in London this week?
10 They aren't getting on very well at the moment.

b
1 He **doesn't bite**
2 Why **are** you **wearing** sunglasses? It**'s raining**.
3 I**'m not listening** to it.
4 I **need** to find a cash machine.
5 The baby**'s putting** your pen in her mouth!
6 **Do** you usually **cook** at weekends?
   No, we normally **eat** out.
7 What **are** you **doing** here?
   I**'m waiting** for Emma.
8 I usually **drink** tea, but I **want** a coffee today.
9 She **works** from 9.00 to 5.00.
10 Marc **lives** in Paris, but he**'s working** in Nice at the moment.

Tell Sts to go back to the main lesson **1C**.

EXTRA SUPPORT If you think Sts need more practice, you may want to give them the **Grammar** photocopiable activity at this point.

4 LISTENING checking hypotheses (using visual evidence and background knowledge)

a Tell Sts that they are going to find out more about the painter Vermeer and *The Milkmaid*. Go through questions 1–6, making sure Sts understand all the lexis, e.g. *a pudding*.

Put Sts in pairs and get them to discuss the questions.

Elicit some answers from the class, but don't tell them if they are right or not.

b 🔊 **1.28** Now tell Sts to listen and check their answers to **a**.

Play the audio once the whole way through.

Get Sts to compare with a partner, and then check answers.

EXTRA SUPPORT Read through the script and decide if you need to pre-teach any new lexis before Sts listen.

1 b 2 a 3 a 4 c 5 b 6 b

🔊 **1.28**
(script in Student's Book on *p.120*)
Johannes Vermeer was a seventeenth-century painter from the city of Delft, in Holland. He mainly painted the people and things he saw around him: the rooms in his house, the people who lived or worked there – usually women – and the things they did every day. For example, in his work you will see women who are playing music, reading or writing letters, or working in the kitchen. Vermeer was especially good at painting light coming into a room through windows. Partly for this reason, people often describe his work as being like photography or film – his paintings can seem very 'real'. This painting, *The Milkmaid*, is one of these very 'photographic' images. The woman, a maid or a servant, is pouring milk into a bowl. Perhaps she's making a bread and milk pudding, because there are pieces of broken bread on the table. Nobody knows if the woman he painted was a real servant or a model. However, most people think Vermeer usually painted his wife, his daughter, and his servant, not models. A famous book and film called *Girl with a Pearl Earring*, inspired by one of his best-known paintings, is an imaginary story about Vermeer and his relationship with his young servant.
People admired Vermeer's paintings a lot in his lifetime, but he was never rich. There are two reasons for this. First, because he painted very slowly. Today, there are only thirty-four paintings which we can be sure are by him. Second, because he used very expensive paints. The blue paint he used for the milkmaid's apron was made of lapis lazuli, which was a very expensive stone.
People loved this painting from the very beginning, and although it is very small – only forty-six by forty-one centimetres – twenty years after Vermeer died, somebody bought the painting for one hundred and seventy-five Dutch guilders. That was an enormous amount of money for the time.

c Tell Sts to look at 1–6 and focus on the example for 1. Then ask Sts to tell you anything they can remember about 2–6.

Play the audio again for Sts to make notes.

EXTRA SUPPORT Pause the audio after each paragraph to give Sts time to take in the information.

Then play it again, pausing if necessary.

Get Sts to compare with a partner, and then check answers.

2 **light coming through windows** He was especially good at painting this.
3 **his wife, his daughter, and his servant** Most people think they are the women in his paintings.
4 ***Girl with a Pearl Earring*** It's a film and a book about his relationship with a young servant, inspired by one of his paintings.
5 **the milkmaid's apron** The blue paint he used for this was very expensive (made from lapis lazuli, a very expensive stone).
6 **175 Dutch guilders** What someone paid for the painting 20 years after his death. It was then a lot of money.

EXTRA SUPPORT If there's time, you could get Sts to listen again with the script on *p.120*, so they can see exactly what they understood / didn't understand. Translate / Explain any new words or phrases.

5 VOCABULARY prepositions of place

a Tell Sts that when you are describing a picture, it's important to use the correct prepositions to say where things are. Focus on the prepositions and phrases in the list.

Tell Sts to complete each gap with a word or phrase from the list. Point out that the first one (*in*) has been done for them.

Get Sts to compare with a partner.

EXTRA SUPPORT If Sts don't remember the prepositions very well, you could spend a bit more time recycling them, using things in the classroom, e.g. *Where's the TV? It's on a shelf behind the table*, etc.

b 🔊 **1.29** Play the audio for Sts to listen and check. Check answers.

> **2** in front of **3** On **4** in the middle of, between
> **5** under **6** Behind **7** on the left of **8** In the corner
> **9** on, above **10** next to

🔊 **1.29**

1 The young man is in the kitchen.
2 There's a table in front of him.
3 On the table there are some eggs, some bread, and some strawberries.
4 The bread is in the middle of the table. It's between the eggs and the strawberries.
5 There's a board under the bread.
6 Behind the man, there's an old washing machine.
7 There's a window on the left of the photo.
8 In the corner of the room there's a sink and some cleaning products.
9 There's a flower on the wall above the sink.
10 The sink is next to the window.

Now put Sts in pairs. Get them to cover the sentences in **a** and look at the photo, and ask each other where the things are.

Get some feedback from the class.

6 SPEAKING

a Focus on the **Describing a picture** box and go through it with the class. You might also want to teach Sts the words *foreground* (= the part of a picture that is nearest to you when you look at it) and *background* (= the part of a picture behind the main objects, people, etc.). Model and drill pronunciation.

Put Sts in pairs, **A** and **B**, and get them to sit face-to-face if possible. Then tell them to go to **Communication Remakes**, **A** on *p.102*, **B** on *p.108*.

Go through the instructions with them carefully and make sure Sts are clear what they have to do. Stress that they have to find the similarities and differences between the original painting and the modern photo.

Give Sts a few minutes to look at their pictures and think about how they are going to describe them. Remind them to use the present continuous to say what the people are doing.

Tell **A** Sts to start by describing their painting. When they have finished, they should swap roles.

When Sts have finished, they must look at the paintings and photos together.

Tell Sts to go back to the main lesson **1C**.

b Go through the questions and make sure Sts remember the meaning of *posters*, and the difference between *paint* and *draw*. Put Sts in small groups to discuss the questions.

Get some feedback from the class for each question. Tell them what you think for the first question, too.

Practical English Hotel problems

Function   calling reception

Lesson plan

This is the first in a series of six Practical English lessons (one every other File) which teach Sts functional language to help them 'survive' in English in travel and social situations.

There is a storyline based on two characters, Jenny Zielinski, an American journalist who works in the New York office of a magazine called *NewYork 24seven*, and Rob Walker, a British journalist who works in London for the same magazine, but who is now in New York for a month. If your Sts did *English File* Elementary, they will already be familiar with the characters. If your Sts didn't do *English File* Elementary, you might want to point out that in the **You Say** section of the lessons, they will be watching or listening and then repeating what the people say. If the speaker is Jenny, they will be listening to an American accent, but they do not need to copy the accent when they repeat her phrases. The main focus of this lesson is on describing problems and asking for help.

These lessons can be used with *Class DVD*, *Classroom Presentation Tool*, or *Class Audio* (audio only). Sts can find all the video content and activities on *Online Practice*.

More materials
For teachers
Teacher's Resource Centre
Video Practical English Episode 1
Quick Test 1
File 1 Test
For students
Workbook Practical English 1
Can you remember...? 1
Online Practice Practical English 1
Check your progress

OPTIONAL LEAD-IN (BOOKS CLOSED)

If your Sts did *English File* Elementary, elicit anything they can remember about Rob and Jenny, and write it on the board in columns under their names. Leave it on the board so when Sts do exercise **c**, they can see if Jenny mentions any of the points on the board.

If your Sts didn't do *English File* Elementary, introduce this lesson by giving the information in the Lesson plan.

Focus on the first two photos at the top of the page and tell Sts that the woman is Jenny and the man is Rob, and that they are the main characters in these lessons.

Get Sts to describe them, using language that they learned in **1B**, e.g. *Jenny is blonde. She has long, straight hair*, etc.

1 ▶ INTRODUCTION

a ◀)) 1.30 Books open. Focus on the instructions and the six photos. Make sure Sts understand the meaning of *mention*. Give Sts a few minutes to think about which order to put them in.

Now play the video / audio once the whole way through.

Then play it again and get Sts to number the photos 1–6 in the order Jenny mentions them.

Get Sts to compare with a partner, and then check answers.

1 B **2** D **3** C **4** F **5** A **6** E

◀)) 1.30

My name's Jenny Zielinski. I live and work in New York. I'm the assistant editor of a magazine called *NewYork 24seven*. A few months ago, I visited our office in London to learn more about the company. I met the manager, Daniel O'Connor. I had lots of meetings with him, of course. And a working dinner on my birthday… But I spent more time with Rob Walker. He's one of the writers on the London magazine. We had coffees together. We went sightseeing. I even helped Rob buy a shirt! He was fun to be with. I liked him a lot. I think he liked me too. Rob isn't the most punctual person in the world, but he is a great writer. We invited him to work for the New York magazine for a month…and he agreed! So now Rob's coming to New York. I know he's really excited about it. It's going to be great to see him again.

b Focus on questions 1–7 and give Sts time to read them.

Play the video / audio again for Sts to watch or listen a second time, and answer the questions.

Get Sts to compare with a partner, and then check answers. Make sure Sts understand the meaning of *punctual*. Model and drill pronunciation /ˈpʌŋktʃuəl/.

1 She works for a magazine. / She is the assistant editor of a magazine.
2 She went to London.
3 Rob is one of the writers for the magazine.
4 They had coffee and went sightseeing and shopping.
5 She likes him a lot. He was fun.
6 He isn't very punctual. / He's always late.
7 He is going to be in New York for a month.

EXTRA SUPPORT If there's time and you are using the video, you could get Sts to watch again with subtitles, so they can see exactly what they understood / didn't understand. Translate / Explain any new words or phrases.

2 ▶ CALLING RECEPTION

a 🔊 **1.31** Focus on the photo and ask Sts *Where is Rob?* (in his hotel room) and *What is he doing?* (making a phone call).

Now either tell Sts to close their books, and write the questions on the board, or get Sts to focus on the two questions and cover the conversation on page 13.

Play the video / audio once the whole way through and then check answers.

> Rob calls reception because he has some problems in his room.

🔊 **1.31** 🔊 **1.32**
Re = receptionist, R = Rob
Re Hello, reception.
R Hello. This is room six-one-three. (repeat)
Re How can I help you?
R There's a problem with the air conditioning. (repeat) It isn't working, and it's very hot in my room. (repeat)
Re I'm sorry, sir. I'll send somebody up to look at it right now.
R Thank you. (repeat)
***
Re Good evening, reception.
R Hello. I'm sorry to bother you again. This is room six-one-three. (repeat)
Re How can I help you?
R I have a problem with the wi-fi. (repeat) I can't get a signal. (repeat)
Re I'm sorry, sir. I'll put you through to IT.
R Thanks. (repeat)

b Now focus on the conversation in the chart. Ask Sts *Who says the* **You hear** *sentences?* and elicit that it is the receptionist. Ask *What nationality is he?* (American). Then ask *Who says the* **You say** *sentences?* and elicit that here it is Rob. These phrases will be useful for Sts if they have a problem in a hotel.

Give Sts a minute to read through the conversation and think what the missing words might be. Then play the video / audio again, and get Sts to complete the gaps. Play again if necessary.

Get Sts to compare with a partner, and then check answers.

> **1** help **2** send **3** evening **4** put

You might want to model and drill the pronunciation of *wi-fi* /ˈwaɪ faɪ/ and *signal* /ˈsɪɡnəl/. Elicit / Explain what *to put someone through* means and that *IT* stands for *Information Technology*, so here it means the people responsible for wi-fi at the hotel.

Go through the conversation line by line with Sts, helping them with any words or expressions they don't understand.

c 🔊 **1.32** Now focus on the **You say** phrases and tell Sts they're going to hear the conversation again. They should repeat the **You say** phrases when they hear the beep. Encourage them to copy the rhythm and intonation.

Play the video / audio, pausing if necessary for Sts to repeat the phrases.

🔊 **1.32**
Same as script 1.31 with repeat pauses

d Focus on the *I'll* information box and go through it with the class.

Put Sts in pairs, **A** and **B**. **A** is the receptionist. Get Sts to read the conversation aloud, and then swap roles.

e Put Sts in pairs, **A** and **B**. Tell them to read their instructions, and help them to understand exactly what they have to do.

A is the receptionist and has his / her book open. He / She reads the **You hear** part with the new information. Elicit that he / she may need to change *Sir* to *Madam* if **B** is a woman.

B has his / her book closed. He / She should quickly read the **You say** phrases again before starting.

Sts now role-play the conversation. **A** starts. Monitor and help.

> **EXTRA IDEA** Before Sts start the role-play, elicit some other things they could have in a hotel room, e.g. a TV, a towel, a chair, etc., and write them on the board. Then elicit some problems they might have with these things in the room, e.g. the TV doesn't work, there's no towel, the chair is broken, etc.

f When Sts have finished, they should swap roles.

You could get a few pairs to perform in front of the class.

3 ▶ JENNY AND ROB MEET AGAIN

a 🔊 **1.33** Focus on the photo and ask Sts where they are and how Rob looks.

Focus on the instructions and on sentences 1–7. Go through them with Sts and make sure they understand them.

Now play the video / audio once the whole way through, and get Sts to mark the sentences *T* (true) or *F* (false). Make it clear that they don't need to correct the false sentences yet.

Get Sts to compare with a partner, and then check answers.

> **1** F **2** F **3** T **4** F **5** F **6** T **7** F

1.33

J = Jenny, R = Rob

J   So, here you are in New York at last.
R   Yeah, it's great to be here. It's really exciting.
J   And how's your hotel?
R   It's fine. My room is really…nice.
J   Do you have a good view from your room?
R   I can see lots of other buildings.
J   Tomorrow, I'm going to show you around the office and introduce you to the team. Barbara's looking forward to meeting you…You remember Barbara, my boss?
R   Oh…yeah, sorry.
J   And then you can start thinking about your blog and the column. Have you got any ideas yet, Rob?…Rob?
R   What? Sorry, Jenny.
J   You must be really tired.
R   Yes, I am a bit. What time is it now?
J   It's nine o'clock.
R   Nine o'clock? That's two o'clock in the morning for me.
J   Let's finish our drinks. You need to go to bed.
R   I guess you're right.
J   So, I'll see you in the office at eleven in the morning.
R   At eleven?
J   Is that OK?
R   It's perfect. Thanks, Jenny.
J   There's just one thing.
R   What's that?
J   Don't be late.
R   By the way, it's great to see you again.
J   Yeah. It's great to see you, too.

b Play the video / audio again for Sts to watch or listen a second time and correct the false sentences.

Get Sts to compare with a partner, and then check answers.

> 1   Rob says the hotel is **fine**.
> 2   Jenny is going to show him round the **office** tomorrow.
> 4   Rob is **tired**.
> 5   It's **two** in the morning for Rob.
> 7   Jenny thinks that Rob is going to **be late**.

EXTRA SUPPORT   If there's time and you are using the video, you could get Sts to watch again with subtitles, so they can see exactly what they understood / didn't understand. Translate / Explain any new words or phrases.

c Focus on the **Social English** phrases. In pairs, get Sts to see if they can remember any of the missing words.

EXTRA CHALLENGE   In pairs, get Sts to complete the phrases before they listen.

d **1.34**   Play the video / audio for Sts to watch or listen and complete the phrases.

Check answers. If you know your Sts' L1, you could get them to translate the phrases.

> 1   great   2   good   3   must   4   right   5   way   6   too

1.34

1   It's great to be here.
2   Do you have a good view?
3   You must be really tired.
4   I guess you're right.
5   By the way…
6   It's great to see you, too.

Now play the video / audio again, pausing after each phrase for Sts to watch or listen and repeat.

e Focus on the instructions and make sure Sts understand what they have to do.

Get Sts to compare with a partner, and then check answers.

> **A** 3, 1   **B** 2   **C** 6   **D** 4   **E** 5

Now put Sts in pairs and get them to practise the conversations.

Finally, focus on the **CAN YOU…?** questions and ask Sts if they feel confident they can now do these things. If they feel that they need more practice, tell them to go to *Online Practice* to watch the episode again and practise the language.

G past simple: regular and irregular verbs
V holidays
P regular verbs: *-ed* endings

Lesson plan

The past simple (regular and irregular verbs) is revised in detail in this lesson, through the context of holidays, with three stories about trips where people lose something important. Sts begin by reading about Stuart, who went on holiday with a group of friends and misplaced his phone. Sts then listen to a similar story. Sts then thoroughly revise the past simple of both regular and irregular verbs. There is a pronunciation focus which revises *-ed* endings in regular verbs. After Sts learn new holiday vocabulary, they listen to four conversations which focus on showing interest and using 'interested' intonation. Finally, Sts interview each other about their last holiday using a short questionnaire.

More materials
For teachers
Photocopiables
Grammar past simple: regular and irregular *p.175*
Vocabulary Holidays *p.259* (instructions *p.253*)
Communicative Truth or lie? *p.220* (instructions *p.208*)
For students
Workbook 2A
Online Practice 2A

OPTIONAL LEAD-IN (BOOKS CLOSED)
Write MY LAST HOLIDAY on the board and tell Sts they have two minutes to find out from you as much as possible about your last holiday. Elicit questions in the past simple, e.g. *Where did you go?*, etc.

1 READING & LISTENING

understanding the key events in a story

a Books open. Focus on the title of the lesson and ask what Sts think the title means (*OMG* stands for *Oh my God* or *Oh my Goodness*). Tell Sts this abbreviation is very informal and is used in, e.g. tweets and WhatsApp messages.

Now focus on the instructions and make sure Sts know the meaning of *lose*. Model and drill pronunciation /luːz/. You could also elicit the opposite (*to find*).

Either put Sts in pairs or do it as a whole-class activity.

If Sts worked in pairs, get some feedback.

b Give Sts time to read the story and answer the questions. Get Sts to compare with a partner, and then check answers.

EXTRA SUPPORT Before Sts read the story the first time, check whether you need to pre-teach any vocabulary.

He lost his phone.
Yes.

c Focus on the instructions and make sure Sts know what they have to do. Point out that the first one has been done for them. Now tell Sts to read the story again.

When they have finished reading, they should cover it and look at 2–11.

Check answers.

2 One day, they **went for a long walk**.
3 It took **about two hours** to get to the top of the mountain.
4 They had **lunch** at the top of the mountain.
5 The view **was amazing**.
6 Stuart wanted to take another photo, but he couldn't find **his phone**.
7 He went back up the mountain with **all his friends**.
8 They spent **about half an hour** looking for the phone.
9 It started to get **colder**.
10 He found his phone in his **jacket pocket**.
11 His friends were **very nice** about it.

Deal with any other new vocabulary. Model and drill the pronunciation of any tricky words.

d 🔊 **2.1** Now tell Sts they are going to listen to another story about someone losing something, and they must answer the two questions. You could write the two questions on the board and get Sts to close their books.

Play the audio once the whole way through.

Get Sts to compare answers, and then play the audio again if necessary.

Check answers.

EXTRA SUPPORT Read through the script and decide if you need to pre-teach any new lexis before Sts listen.

Marta lost her ID card.
No.

🔊 **2.1**
(script in Student's Book on *p.120*)
Marta's story
This happened two years ago. I'm Spanish, but I was in Ireland at the time because I had a job in Dublin. Some friends of mine who lived in Lyon, in France, invited me to come and stay, so I decided to have a short holiday, a long weekend, from Friday to Tuesday. I looked for cheap flights, but I couldn't find any direct ones. The only thing I could find was Ryanair from Dublin to Brussels, and then Air France from Brussels to Lyon.
Anyway, the flight to Brussels was fine, and when I arrived, I went to the gate for my next flight to Lyon, but then when I needed to show my boarding pass and my ID, I couldn't find my ID card. I looked everywhere – in my bag, in my case – but it wasn't there. The people at the gate were very nice and they made some phone calls, but nobody could find it. So they told me to wait in a small room and I sat there for more than an hour, and my flight to Lyon left without me.
It was awful – I cried – I was so stressed and unhappy. In the end, a policeman came and he said that I couldn't go to France because I didn't have any ID – the only place I could go was to Spain to get a new ID card! I waited another five or six hours for the flight to Madrid, feeling very depressed.
So I never had my holiday! I spent the weekend in Madrid getting my new ID card!

e Tell Sts they are going to listen to Marta again. Give them time to read questions 1–7.

Play the audio again and get Sts to answer the questions.

Get Sts to compare with a partner, and then check answers.

1 Two years ago
2 Lyon. Her friends invited her to come and stay.
3 There were no cheap direct flights.
4 She couldn't find her ID card.
5 She felt stressed and unhappy.
6 He said that she couldn't go to France because she didn't have any ID.
7 Madrid. She got a new ID card. / She spent the weekend getting a new ID card.

EXTRA SUPPORT If there's time, you could get Sts to listen again with the script on *p.120*, so they can see exactly what they understood / didn't understand. Translate / Explain any new words or phrases.

f Put Sts in pairs or small groups and get them to answer the questions.

EXTRA SUPPORT To help Sts tell their story, write the following questions on the board:
1 WHERE WERE YOU AND WHO WERE YOU WITH?
2 WHAT HAPPENED?
3 WHAT DID YOU DO NEXT?
4 HOW DID IT END?

Get some Sts to tell their stories to the class. If you have ever lost anything important on holiday, tell Sts about it.

2 GRAMMAR past simple: regular and irregular verbs

a Focus on the verbs and tell Sts that some are regular and some are irregular. Make sure Sts know what they mean, but don't spend too much time on the pronunciation, as Sts will be focusing on this later. Elicit the past simple of the first one (*went*) and then get Sts to do the others in pairs. Encourage them to do as many as they can without looking back at the story and then check their answers in Stuart's story.

Check answers.

go – went
climb – climbed
be – was, were
take – took
have – had
can – could
sit – sat
get – got
want – wanted
think – thought
decide – decided
say – said
spend – spent
start – started
feel – felt

b Tell Sts to complete the gaps in 1–3 with negative past simple verbs.

They then check their answers in Stuart's story.

Check answers.

1 wasn't   2 couldn't   3 didn't

c Put Sts in pairs or do this as a whole-class activity. Give them a minute to remember how to make negatives and questions.

If Sts worked in pairs, check answers.

with *was / were*:
[–] = *wasn't* or *weren't*, e.g. *It wasn't cold.*
[?] = *Were (you, etc.)?, Was (he, etc.)?*, e.g. *Was it nice?*
with *could*:
[–] = *couldn't*, e.g. *We couldn't stay very long.*
[?] = *Could (I, you, etc.)?*, e.g. *Could you swim there?*
with other verbs:
[–] = *didn't* + infinitive, e.g. *I didn't show them, I didn't want it.*
[?] = *Did (you, etc.) + infinitive?*, e.g. *Did you go…?*

d Tell Sts to go to **Grammar Bank 2A** on *p.128*.

Grammar notes
You may also want to remind Sts:
• that irregular forms (*went, had*, etc.) are only used in positive sentences
• that the vast majority of verbs are regular. The irregular verbs need to be learned, but Sts already know the most common ones

Tell Sts to go to **Irregular verbs** on *p.164* and explain that this is their reference list. Get Sts to go through the list quickly in pairs, checking that they know what the verbs mean. Encourage them to highlight verbs they didn't know or had forgotten the past form of.

Let Sts test each other, or test round the class.

🔊 **2.2** Focus on the example sentences and play the audio for Sts to listen and repeat. Encourage them to copy the rhythm. Then go through the rules with the class.

Now focus on the exercises for **2A** on *p.129*. Sts do the exercises individually or in pairs.

Check answers, getting Sts to read the full sentences.

a
1 drove   2 broke   3 spent   4 got   5 went   6 couldn't
7 were   8 didn't know   9 found   10 stayed   11 saw
12 bought   13 wanted   14 didn't have   15 was   16 wasn't
17 started   18 left   19 stopped
b
1 **Did you have** a good time?
2 **Who did you go** with?
3 **Where did you stay**?
4 **How much did** the plane tickets **cost**?
5 **What was** the weather like?
6 **What did you do** in the evening?

Tell Sts to go back to the main lesson **2A**.

EXTRA IDEA Remind Sts that a very good way of learning irregular verbs is through reading stories. Show them a few Graded Readers if you can, and if you have a class library, encourage them to take out a book to read at home.

EXTRA SUPPORT If you think Sts need more practice, you may want to give them the **Grammar** photocopiable activity at this point.

3 PRONUNCIATION -ed endings

Pronunciation notes

The regular past simple ending -ed can be pronounced in three different ways:

1 -ed is pronounced /t/ after verbs ending in these unvoiced* sounds: /k/, /p/, /f/, /s/, /ʃ/, and /tʃ/, e.g. *looked, hoped, laughed, passed, washed, watched.*

2 After voiced endings, -ed is pronounced /d/, e.g. *arrived, changed, showed*. This group is the largest.

3 After verbs ending in /t/ or /d/, the pronunciation of -ed is /ɪd/, e.g. *hated, decided.*

The difference between 1 and 2 is very small and rarely causes communication problems. The most important thing is for Sts to be clear about rule 3.

* For information on **Voiced and unvoiced consonants**, see **Pronunciation & Speaking 1B** on *p.18.*

a ◉ **2.3** Focus on the task and play the audio for Sts to listen to the three sentences from Marta's story.

Check answers.

> **1** looked **2** happened **3** waited

◉ **2.3**
1 I looked everywhere – in my bag, in my case – but it wasn't there.
2 This happened two years ago.
3 I waited another five or six hours.

b ◉ **2.4** Focus on the three sound pictures. Elicit and drill the words and sounds: *tie* /t/, *dog* /d/, and /ɪd/.
Play the audio once for Sts just to listen to the sounds and sentences.

◉ **2.4**
See sounds and sentences in Student's Book on *p.15*

Then play it again for Sts to listen and repeat.
Now focus on the **Regular past simple verbs** box and go through it with the class.

c Give Sts a minute to practise saying the verbs in the list in the past and to decide which ones have /ɪd/ endings.

  Draw three columns on the board for the sounds. Get Sts to write the verbs in the correct column.

d ◉ **2.5** Play the audio for Sts to listen and check.
Check answers. Remind Sts that you only pronounce the *e* in -ed endings when verbs finish in a /t/ or /d/ sound, and then the -ed ending is pronounced /ɪd/.

> decided, rented, started, wanted

◉ **2.5**
asked, called, checked, decided, happened, lived, rented, started, stopped, thanked, wanted

  Play the audio again, pausing after each verb for Sts to listen and repeat.

  Elicit whether the other verbs are /t/ or /d/.

> asked /t/   called /d/   checked /t/   happened /d/   lived /d/   stopped /t/   thanked /t/

4 VOCABULARY holidays

a Focus on the instructions and the examples. Highlight that the verbs are in the -ing form because they are things you <u>like doing</u>.

Give Sts a minute to write five things, then get them to compare their list with a partner.

Elicit some of the verb phrases Sts have used and write them on the board, e.g. *swimming, going to restaurants, seeing new places*, etc.

  Tell Sts to decide which activity on the board is their favourite and take a vote with a show of hands.

b Tell Sts to go to **Vocabulary Bank Holidays** on *p.152.*

Vocabulary notes

Highlight:

- the difference between *go out* (*at night*) = leave your house / hotel, e.g. go to a restaurant, a club, etc., and *go away* (*for the weekend*) = leave your town, e.g. go to the country, to another town, etc.
- the difference between *swim* and *go swimming* (which applies to all the other expressions, e.g. *go walking, sailing, surfing,* etc.). We use *go + swimming*, etc. when we refer to it as an activity rather than an ability or way of moving. Compare *I go swimming every day* and *I can swim very well,* and *We went walking in the hills* and *We walked to the shops.*

Focus on **1 Phrases with go** and get Sts to do **a** individually or in pairs. Some of these phrases should already be familiar to them.

◉ **2.6** Now do **b**. Play the audio for Sts to listen and check.
Check answers.

◉ **2.6**
Holidays 1 Phrases with *go*
7 go abroad
10 go away for the weekend
4 go by bus
8 go camping
9 go for a walk
5 go on holiday
3 go out at night
1 go sightseeing
6 go skiing
2 go swimming

Now either use the audio to drill the pronunciation of the phrases, or model and drill them yourself. Give further practice of any words and phrases your Sts find difficult to pronounce.

Focus on **c** and get Sts to cover the phrases and look at the photos. They can test themselves or their partner.

Focus on **2 Other holiday phrases** and get Sts to do **a** individually or in pairs.

🔊 **2.7** Now do **b**. Play the audio for Sts to listen and check.

Check answers.

🔊 **2.7**
2 Other holiday phrases
stay in a hotel / **stay** at a campsite / **stay** with friends
take photos
buy souvenirs
sunbathe on the beach
have a good time
spend money
rent an apartment
hire a bicycle
book a flight online

Now either use the audio to drill the pronunciation of the phrases, or model and drill them yourself. Give further practice of any words and phrases your Sts find difficult to pronounce.

Focus on the **rent or hire?** box and go through it with the class. You could tell Sts that *flat* is British English and *apartment* is American English, although British people use both words.

Now focus on **c**. Get Sts to test themselves by covering the verbs and remembering the phrases.

Focus on **3 Adjectives**. Elicit the meaning of the *What was the…like?* questions. Then give Sts a minute to match the questions and answers.

🔊 **2.8** Now do **b**. Play the audio for Sts to listen and check.

Check answers.

🔊 **2.8**
3 Adjectives
1 What was the weather like?
   It was warm. It was sunny.
   It was very windy. It was foggy. It was cloudy.
2 What was the hotel like?
   It was comfortable. It was luxurious.
   It was basic. It was dirty. It was uncomfortable.
3 What was the town like?
   It was beautiful. It was lovely.
   It was noisy. It was crowded.
4 What were the people like?
   They were friendly. They were helpful.
   They were unfriendly. They were unhelpful.

Now either use the audio to drill the pronunciation of the sentences (*It was warm*, *It was sunny*, etc.), or model and drill the adjectives (*warm*, *sunny*, etc.) yourself. Give further practice of any words or phrases your Sts find difficult to pronounce.

Focus on the **General positive and negative adjectives** box and go through it with the class.

Finally, focus on **Activation**. Put Sts in pairs to discuss which alternatives they prefer.

Get some feedback.

Tell Sts to go back to the main lesson **2A**.

5 SPEAKING

a 🔊 **2.9** Focus on the task and make sure Sts understand what they have to do.

Play the audio once the whole way through.

Now play it again and get Sts to complete the gaps.

Check answers, making sure Sts understand the meaning of the phrases.

1 Wow   **2** no, pity   **3** Fantastic   **4** Really, awful

---

🔊 **2.9**
1 **A** I went to New York last week.
   B Wow! Did you like it?
2 **A** The weather was terrible – it rained every day.
   B Oh no! What a pity! What did you do?
3 **A** We went to a show in the West End.
   B Fantastic! What show was it?
4 **A** I lost my phone on the first day.
   B Really? How awful! How did you lose it?

---

b Now play the audio again, pausing after **B**'s responses for Sts to listen and repeat. Encourage them to copy **B**'s intonation.

c Focus on the questions and elicit what the missing words are (*did you* in most questions and *was / were* in others).

1 Where did you go?
2 When did you go?
3 Who did you go with?
4 Where did you stay? What was it like?
5 What was the weather like?
6 What did you do during the day?
7 What did you do in the evening?
8 Did you have a good time?
9 Did you have any problems?

Drill the complete questions quickly round the class.

d Give Sts time to think about their answers to the questions. Tell them that they can talk about another holiday they remember well, not necessarily their last holiday.

e Put Sts in pairs, **A** and **B**. **A** answers **B**'s questions. **B** must try to show interest and ask for more information. Monitor and correct.

Sts swap roles.

Get some feedback from the class.

G past continuous
V prepositions of time and place: *at*, *in*, *on*
P weak forms: *was*, *were*

Lesson plan

This lesson starts with a photo from a feature in the *Guardian* called *That's me in the picture*. The photo by Henri Cartier-Bresson, a well-known French photographer, is of a couple in a park in Paris. Sts read an article in which the woman in the photo tells the story behind it. They then focus on vocabulary and the correct use of the prepositions *at*, *in*, and *on*, both for time (revision) and place. The story behind the photo also provides the context for the presentation of a new structure, the past continuous. Sts then focus on the weak forms of *was* and *were* in the past continuous. This helps them when they go on to listen to a woman describing six photos on her Instagram page. The lesson ends with Sts talking about their own favourite photos, and then writing about one of them.

More materials
For teachers
Photocopiables
Grammar past continuous *p.176*
Vocabulary Prepositions *at*, *in*, *on* *p.260*
(instructions *p.253*)
Communicative Who did it? *p.221* (instructions *p.209*)
For students
Workbook 2B
Online Practice 2B

OPTIONAL LEAD-IN (BOOKS CLOSED)

Write PHOTO on the board. Ask Sts what it is short for (*photograph*) and elicit the verb we use with it (*take*). Elicit / Teach the words for a person who takes photos (*photographer*) and the subject (*photography*). Write them on the board and model the pronunciation. Ask Sts how the word stress changes and underline it on the board:

PHOTOGRAPH   PHOTOGRAPHER   PHOTOGRAPHY

1 READING checking hypotheses (using visual evidence)

a Books open. Focus on the instructions and the photo on *p.16*. Find out if any Sts have heard of Henri Cartier-Bresson. You could tell them that he is considered one of the major photographers of the 20th century. He was born in 1908 and died in 2004.

Now focus on questions 1–4 and make sure Sts know what *a decade* is. You might also want to check that Sts know the meaning of *time of year* (= season).

Put Sts in pairs and give them time to discuss the questions.

Elicit ideas, encouraging Sts to say why, but <u>don't</u> tell Sts if they are correct or not yet.

b Get Sts to read the article to check their answers to **a**. Check answers.

EXTRA SUPPORT   Before Sts read the article the first time, check whether you need to pre-teach any vocabulary.

1 the 1970s   **2** autumn   **3** an owl in a tree   **4** bread, to give the animals in the zoo

c Focus on questions 1–6 and go through them with Sts. Give Sts time to read the article again and answer the questions.

Get Sts to compare with a partner, and then check answers.

1 She was living in London, in her early twenties, working for an advertising agency.
2 She met him at a nightclub on a beach in the south of France. She found a job in Paris because she wanted to be with him.
3 They went for a walk.
4 They stopped because they heard a lot of noise coming from a tree. They saw an owl and some little birds attacking it.
5 She called Cartier-Bresson, and he sent her a copy.
6 Because it was a happy time for her.

Deal with any other new vocabulary. Model and drill the pronunciation of any tricky words.

d Do this as a whole-class activity. You could also tell the class if there is a photo with you in it that you really love.

2 VOCABULARY *at*, *in*, *on*

a Focus on the instructions and give Sts time to complete the gaps.
Check answers.

1 In, in   **2** at   **3** On   **4** in, in

b Tell Sts to go to **Vocabulary Bank** Prepositions on *p.153* and focus on **1** *at / in / on*.

Vocabulary notes
Place
Sts are often confused about the difference between *at* and *in* + places, as they often encounter both. At this level, it is probably better to simplify the rules, and to point out that with shops and buildings, e.g. the supermarket or the cinema, you can use *at* or *in* when you answer the question *Where were you?*. With *airport* and *station*, we normally use *at*.
Time
Remind Sts that years from 2000 to 2010 are usually *two thousand and one*, etc. From 2011 onwards, we normally say *twenty eleven*, *twenty twelve*, etc.
Point out to Sts that we say *in the morning / afternoon / evening*, but *at night*.

Focus on **a** and get Sts to complete the left-hand column of the chart.

2.10   Now do **b**. Play the audio for Sts to listen and check. Track **2.10** is quite long, so you might want to check answers without playing the audio.

2.10

Prepositions 1 *at / in / on*
1 *in*
countries and cities: in Spain, in Madrid
rooms: in the kitchen
buidlings: in a shop, in a museum
closed spaces: in a park, in a garden, in a car
months: in February, in June
seasons: in winter
years: in 2018
times of day: in the morning, in the afternoon, in the evening
2 *on*
transport: on a bike, on a bus, on a train, on a plane, on a ship
a surface: on the floor, on a table, on a shelf, on the balcony, on the roof, on the wall
dates: on the first of March
days: on Tuesday, on New Year's Day, on Valentine's Day
3 *at*
places: at school, at home, at work, at university, at the airport, at the station, at a bus stop
times: at six o'clock, at half past two, at quarter to eight, at night, at the weekend
festival periods: at Christmas, at Easter

Now either use the audio to drill the pronunciation of the phrases, or model and drill them yourself. Give further practice of any words your Sts find difficult to pronounce.

Focus on **Activation**. Put Sts in pairs, **A** and **B**. **A** (book open) tests **B** (book closed) for two minutes. Then they swap roles. Allow at least five minutes for Sts to test each other. Then get Sts to close their books, and test them round the class, saying a word, e.g. *home*, for Sts to say the preposition *at*.

Tell Sts to go back to the main lesson **2B**.

  If you think Sts need more practice, you may want to give them the **Vocabulary** photocopiable activity at this point.

c Put Sts in pairs, **A** and **B**, and tell them to go to **Communication** *at, in, on*, **A** on *p.103*, **B** on *p.109*.

Go through the instructions with them carefully.

Sit **A** and **B** face-to-face. **A** asks his / her questions to **B**, who replies using a preposition and then asks *What about you?*.

B then asks **A** his / her questions.

When they have finished, get some feedback from the class.

Tell Sts to go back to the main lesson **2B**.

3 GRAMMAR past continuous

a Focus on the highlighted verbs in the two sentences and do the questions as a whole-class activity.

1 were looking   **2** was living, was working

b Tell Sts to go to **Grammar Bank 2B** on *p.128*.

Grammar notes

If Sts have an equivalent of the past continuous in their L1, then it doesn't normally cause problems. If they don't, it's important to make the use very clear.

We often use the past continuous at the beginning of a story, to set the scene and to say what was happening, e.g. *On 1st April, I was staying with some friends in the country. It was a sunny day and we were having lunch in the garden.*

Very often these 'actions in progress' (past continuous) are 'interrupted' by a short, completed action (past simple), e.g. *We were having lunch in the garden when suddenly it started to rain.*

Highlight the similarity in form with the present continuous. It is identical except for using *was / were* instead of *am / is / are*.

You may also want to remind Sts of the spelling rules for the *-ing* form (see **Grammar Bank 1C**).

when or *while*?

We can connect two actions with *when* or *while*:
when + past simple, *while / when* + past continuous.

Focus on the example sentences and play both audio 2.11 and 2.12 for Sts to listen and repeat. Encourage them to copy the rhythm. Then go through the rules with the class.

Now focus on the exercises for **2B** on *p.129*. Sts do the exercises individually or in pairs.

Check answers, getting Sts to read the full sentences.

a
1 I took this photo when we **were travelling** in Greece.
2 He met his wife when he **was living** in Japan.
3 **Was** she **wearing** a coat when she went out?
4 The sun **was shining** when I went to work.
5 What **were** you **doing** at 7.30 last night?
6 I **wasn't listening** when you gave the instructions
7 They **weren't watching** TV when I arrived.
8 It started to rain when we **were running** in the park.
b
1 I **broke** my arm when I **was playing** football.
2 **Were** you **driving** fast when the police **stopped** you?
3 It **was snowing** when we **left** the pub.
4 I **didn't see** the match because I **was working**.
5 When you **called** me I **was talking** to my boss.
6 We **were studying** in Cambridge when we **met**.
7 **Were** they **living** in Rome when they **had** their first baby?

Tell Sts to go back to the main lesson **2B**.

  If you think Sts need more practice, you may want to give them the **Grammar** photocopiable activity at this point.

c 🔊 **2.13** Focus on the instructions and the example. Make sure Sts understand they are only going to hear sound effects and that they must write a sentence using the past continuous and the past simple. Put Sts in pairs.

Play the audio, pausing after each sound effect to give Sts time to discuss what they think was happening and to write a sentence.

Check answers and write the sentences on the board.

🔊 **2.13**
(Sound effects to illustrate the following)
1 *They were playing tennis when it started to rain.*
2 *She was driving when somebody phoned her.*
3 *They were having a party when the police came.*
4 *He was having a shower when somebody knocked at the door.*
5 *They were sleeping when the baby started to cry.*
6 *She was walking her dog when she met a friend.*

4 PRONUNCIATION & LISTENING weak forms:
was, were

Pronunciation notes

Native speakers use two different pronunciations of *was* and *were*, depending on whether the words are stressed or not, i.e. they can have a strong or weak pronunciation.

Was and *were* always have a strong pronunciation in short answers and negatives, and can have a strong pronunciation in *yes / no* questions, e.g. *Was he working when you phoned him?*. The pronunciation is /wɒz/ and /wɜː/.

Was and *were* tend to have a weak pronunciation in positive sentences and are pronounced /wəz/ and /wə/, e.g. *He was a teacher* /wəz/, *They were walking in the park* /wə/.

It is useful for Sts at this level to be aware of these differences, but unrealistic to expect them to be able to use them properly, and Sts will probably use mostly strong forms of *was* and *were*.

However, it's important for Sts to be able to recognize *was* and *were* when they hear them in speech, and **b** and **c** are designed to help them with this.

a Focus on the instructions and make sure Sts know what *Instagram* is (= a photo-sharing and social media site).

Do this as a whole-class activity and elicit Sts' ideas.

b 🔊 **2.14** Tell Sts they are going to hear six sentences and they must write the missing words.

Play the audio, pausing after each sentence to give Sts time to write.

Check answers.

1 It was   2 was staying   3 were doing   4 We were
5 were visiting   6 were…drinking, was doing

🔊 **2.14**
1 It was my first term at university.
2 I was staying with him in the Easter holidays.
3 We were doing a music course.
4 We were at school together.
5 She took this when we were visiting the Colosseum.
6 We were all drinking champagne, and Roz was doing the hard work!

c Now play the audio again for Sts to answer the question. Check the answer.

unstressed

d 🔊 **2.15** Tell Sts they are now going to listen to Anya talking about her Instagram photos. They must number them 1–6 in the order she describes them. Point out that the first one (*E*) has been done for them. Also point out the **Glossary**.

Play the audio once the whole way through for Sts to listen and complete the task.

Get Sts to compare with a partner, and then check answers.

EXTRA SUPPORT Read through the script and decide if you need to pre-teach any new lexis before Sts listen.

🔊 **2.15**
(script in Student's Book on *p.120*)
A = Anya, F = friend
1 **A** This is me and my mum in York. It was my first term at university, and she came to visit me, and I took her on a tour round the city.
   F Is that, er, the cathedral there?
   A Yes – well, it's called York Minster, but it's really a cathedral.
2 **A** And this one's on the beach in Cornwall with my boyfriend, Ollie. I was staying with him in the Easter holidays, and he took me to the beach and we went for a walk.
   F It looks windy!
   A Yes, it was really windy and cold. I think we were the only people on the beach!
3 **F** Nice photo! I like the moustache.
   A Yeah, that's me and my friend Maisie. We were doing a music course – I do it twice a year, and this was at the party at the end of the course.
   F Why the moustaches and the picture frame?
   A There was this corner that the teachers made where people could take funny photos with the big frame, and hats and moustaches and things.
4 **A** OK, this one is me and two of my best friends – we were at school together. One of them, Libby, the one on my right, has a house by the river, and we went there in September, before we all went to university.
5 **F** That's a nice photo. In Rome, I guess?
   A Yes, I was there for a holiday with my mum the summer before I went to university. She took this when we were visiting the Colosseum – as you can see.
6 **F** That's your mum again, isn't it?
   A Yes, that's her and her partner, and my sister Roz, on the river in Oxford. My mum's birthday is in July, and every year we go punting and then we go for dinner. We were all drinking champagne, and Roz was doing the hard work!

e Play the audio again, pausing after each photo has been to mentioned, to check answers and elicit any more information Sts can remember about each photo.

> 1 **E** The photo was taken in York, where Anya is / was at university. She took her mother on a tour of the city. In the background is the Minster (cathedral).
>
> 2 **C** The photo was taken in Cornwall. It was really windy and cold. Anya and her boyfriend were the only people on the beach.
>
> 3 **A** The photo was taken at a party on the last day of a music course, which Anya does twice a year. The teachers had put the big frame in a corner, as well as hats and moustaches, etc., for people to take funny photos.
>
> 4 **F** The photo was taken at a friend's house in September, before going to university. It shows Anya with her two best friends. She went to school with them.
>
> 5 **B** The photo was taken in Rome. She went there for a holiday with her mother the summer before she went to university. Her mother took the photo when they were visiting the Colosseum.
>
> 6 **D** The photo was taken on the river in Oxford, in July. It shows her sister, her mother, and her mother's partner. They are drinking champagne because it is her mother's birthday.

EXTRA SUPPORT If there's time, you could get Sts to listen again with the script on *p.120*, so they can see exactly what they understood / didn't understand. Translate / Explain any new words or phrases.

5 SPEAKING & WRITING describing a photo

a Most Sts will have photos on their phones which they can show each other during this activity. Focus on the four questions. Make sure Sts understand all the vocabulary. Demonstrate the activity by getting Sts to ask you the questions.

Get Sts to discuss the questions in pairs. Encourage them to give more information if they can.

Get feedback from a few pairs.

b Tell Sts to go to **Writing Describing a photo** on *p.114*.

Focus on the information at the top of the image and establish that this is for a photo competition on the internet.

Now focus on **a** and get Sts to complete the gaps in the description.

Get Sts to compare with a partner, and then check answers.

> 1 of   2 in   3 with   4 in   5 like   6 of   7 at   8 away
> 9 on

Now focus on **b** and get Sts to match the questions to paragraphs 1–3.

Check answers.

> 2 What was happening when you took the photo?
> 3 Where do you keep it?
> 3 Why do you like it?
> 1 Where were you when you took the photo, and who were you with?
> 1 What's your favourite photo?
> 1 Who took the photo? When?

Focus on **c** and give Sts time to plan their description. They should use the questions in **b** to help them.

Set the writing in **d** in class or for homework, and ask Sts to include the photo if they can. Tell Sts to answer the questions in **b** in the correct order and not as they appear on the page, so the first question they write about is *What's your favourite photo?*. They should also try to include the highlighted phrases if they can.

In **e** Sts check their writing for mistakes and attach the photo if they can.

G time sequencers and connectors: *suddenly, when, so,* etc.
V verb phrases
P word stress

Lesson plan

In this lesson Sts learn to use time sequencers, e.g. *after that, later,* etc. and the connectors *so, because, but,* and *although.* They also revise the past simple and continuous. The context is a short story with a twist. After Sts have read most of the story and worked on the grammar, they have a pronunciation focus on word stress in two-syllable words, and then in Vocabulary they expand their knowledge of verb phrases. In the video listening section, the language is pulled together, and Sts use picture prompts to retell the story so far. They then decide as a class whether they want to watch or hear a happy or a sad ending to the story, and then watch or listen to the one they have chosen. Finally, in the speaking activity, Sts answer some questions in pairs about the ending they watched or listened to.

More materials
For teachers
Photocopiables
Grammar time sequences and connectors *p.177*
Communicative Sentence race *p.222*
(instructions *p.209*)
Teacher's Resource Centre
Video One Dark October Evening
For students
Workbook 2C
Online Practice 2C

OPTIONAL LEAD-IN (BOOKS CLOSED)

Write the names of these bands / performers on the board and ask Sts if they can complete them with colours:

G___________ DAY
B___________ SABBATH
R___________ HOT CHILI PEPPERS
B___________ EYED PEAS
THE W___________ STRIPES
DEEP P___________
P___________

Green Day **Black** Sabbath **Red** Hot Chili Pepppers
Black Eyed Peas The **White** Stripes Deep **Purple** **Pink**

Then tell Sts that they are going to read a short story in which a song by Pink plays a part.

1 GRAMMAR time sequencers and connectors

a Books open. Focus on the story and tell Sts that they are going to read it, but that first they should look at the title and photos and guess what it is about.

Elicit ideas from the class.

b ◆ 2.16 Tell Sts to read the story and complete the gaps. Tell them that the end of the story is on audio, so the last paragraph here is not the end of the story. Point out that the first one (*Two minutes later*) has been done for them.

Get Sts to compare with a partner, and then play the audio for Sts to listen to the story and check.

Check answers.

> **2** When **3** The next day **4** After that **5** One evening in October **6** Suddenly

◆ 2.16

N = narrator, H = Hannah, J = Jamie

N *Hannah met Jamie last summer. It was Hannah's birthday, and she and her friends went to a club. They wanted to dance, but they didn't like the music, so Hannah went to speak to the DJ.*
H This music is awful.
N *…she said.*
H Could you play something else?
N *The DJ looked at her and said…*
J Don't worry – I have the perfect song for you.
N *Two minutes later, he said…*
J The next song is by Pink. It's called *Get the Party Started* and it's for a beautiful girl over there who's wearing a pink dress.
N *Hannah knew that the song was for her. When Hannah and her friends left the club, the DJ was waiting for her at the door.*
J Hi, I'm Jamie.
N *…he said to Hannah.*
J Can I see you again?
N *So Hannah gave him her phone number. The next day, Jamie phoned Hannah and invited her to dinner. He took her to a very romantic French restaurant and they talked all evening. Although the food wasn't very good, they had a wonderful time. After that, Jamie and Hannah saw each other every day. Every evening when Hannah finished work, they met at five thirty in a coffee bar in the high street. They were madly in love. One afternoon in October, Hannah was at work. As usual, she was going to meet Jamie at five thirty. It was dark and it was raining. She looked at her watch. It was five twenty! She was going to be late! She ran to her car and got in. At five twenty-five, she was driving along the high street. She was going very fast because she was in a hurry. Suddenly, a man ran across the road. He was wearing a dark coat, so Hannah didn't see him at first. Quickly, she put her foot on the brake…*

c Now give Sts time to read the story again.

Then put them in pairs to answer the questions. They can answer orally or in writing.

Check answers.

1 Because she didn't like the music.
2 Because it's by Pink, and Hannah was wearing a pink dress.
3 Jamie was waiting at the door and asked to see Hannah again.
4 It was very romantic, but the food wasn't very good.
5 To a coffee bar in the high street
6 It was dark and raining.
7 Because she was in a hurry.
8 Because he was wearing a dark coat.

EXTRA CHALLENGE Tell Sts to try to answer questions 1–8 from memory.

d Focus on the three sentences. Tell Sts <u>not</u> to look back at the story, but to try and complete the sentences from memory.

Check answers, and elicit / explain the meaning of the missing words or ask Sts how to say them in their L1. Model and drill the pronunciation of *so*, *because*, and *although*. Write them on the board and underline the stressed syllable, or write them up in phonetics (/səʊ/, /bɪ'kɒz/, and /ɔːl'ðəʊ/).

1 because   2 Although   3 so

e Tell Sts to go to **Grammar Bank 2C** on *p.128*.

Grammar notes

We usually put a comma before *so*, *although*, and *but*, e.g. *She was tired, so she went to bed.*

Sts may also ask you about *though*, which is a colloquial, abbreviated form of *although*. *Though* is not usually used at the beginning of a sentence. It is probably best at this level if Sts just learn *although*.

! *So* has another completely different meaning, which is to intensify adjectives, e.g. *He was so tired that he went to bed at 9.00.* You may want to point out this meaning too, in case Sts get confused.

Focus on the example sentences and play audio 2.17, 2.18 and 2.19 for Sts to listen and repeat. Encourage them to copy the rhythm. Then go through the rules with the class.

Focus on the **then, after that** box and go through it with the class.

Now focus on the exercises for **2C** on *p.129*. Sts do the exercises individually or in pairs.

Check answers, getting Sts to read the full sentences.

a
2 G   3 B   4 E   5 A   6 F   7 H   8 D

b
1 **Although** it was very cold, she wasn't wearing a coat.
2 I woke him up in the night **because** there was a noise.
3 I called him, **but** his mobile was turned off.
4 **Although** she's very nice, she doesn't have many friends.
5 There was nothing on TV, **so** I went to bed.
6 All the cafés were full **because** it was a public holiday.
7 She wanted to be a doctor, **but** she failed her exams.
8 The garden looked very beautiful, **so** I took a photograph.
9 **Although** the team played well, they didn't win.

Tell Sts to go back to the main lesson **2C**.

EXTRA SUPPORT If you think Sts need more practice, you may want to give them the **Grammar** photocopiable activity at this point.

f Tell Sts to look at the six sentence beginnings and to complete them with their own ideas.

When Sts have finished, get them to compare their sentences with a partner.

Get some feedback from the class. You could write some of the sentences on the board.

2 PRONUNCIATION word stress

a Focus on the **Stress in two-syllable words** box and go through it with the class.

Now focus on the task and give Sts time, in pairs, to underline the stressed syllable in the words.

b 2.20 Play the audio for Sts to listen and check.

Pause the audio after each word, elicit the answer, and write the word on the board with the stressed syllable underlined.

a<u>cross</u>   <u>af</u>ter   a<u>gain</u>   a<u>long</u>   al<u>though</u>   <u>aw</u>ful
be<u>cause</u>   <u>birth</u>day   <u>eve</u>ning   in<u>vite</u>   <u>per</u>fect   <u>quick</u>ly

2.20
See words in Student's Book on *p.19*

Play the audio again, pausing after each word for Sts to repeat.

Put Sts in pairs and get them to practise saying the words.

c Focus on the instructions and the example.

In pairs, Sts write a sentence using two or more of the words in **a**.

Get a few pairs to read their sentence to the class.

3 VOCABULARY & SPEAKING verb phrases

a Focus on the two boxes and the example. Tell Sts that by combining a verb from **1** with a phrase from **2**, they will make verb phrases from the story.

Put Sts in pairs and give them a few minutes to match the verbs and phrases. Tell them that sometimes two verbs may be possible with a phrase, but to try to remember the phrases from the story.

Check answers.

> have a great time
> drive along the high street
> meet in a coffee bar
> give somebody your phone number
> take somebody to a restaurant
> wait for somebody
> be in a hurry
> play a song
> leave the club (very late)
> run across the road

b Get Sts to test themselves by covering box **1** and remembering the verbs for each phrase.

EXTRA IDEA You could get Sts to close their books and say a phrase from box 2, e.g. *in a coffee bar*, for Sts to respond *meet in a coffee bar*.

c ◀)) **2.16** Play the audio for Sts to listen to the story again.

◀)) **2.16**
See script 2.16 on the previous page

---

d Re-telling a story gives Sts the opportunity for some extended oral practice, and in this case, to recycle the tenses and connectors they have been studying. Focus on the photos in **1** and the example, and tell Sts they are going to re-tell the story of Hannah and Jamie, but in first person (as either Jamie or Hannah). Tell Sts they should try to use the verb phrases from **a**.

Put Sts in pairs, **A** and **B**. Tell Sts **A** they are Jamie and Sts **B** they are Hannah. Get Sts **A** to cover the text and focus on the photos. Tell them to tell as much of the story as they can for photos 1–3 while Sts **B** look at the story to prompt / correct. They then swap roles for photos 4–6.

Get individual Sts to tell the class about each photo in their roles.

4 ▶ VIDEO LISTENING

This is the first of six video listenings, which are incorporated into the Student's Book. If you are unable to show the video in class, remind students that they can find the video on *Online Practice* and ask them to watch the video and do the activities for homework.

a Tell Sts they are now going to watch or listen to the end of the story. First, Sts have to vote with a show of hands on whether they want to hear a happy ending or a sad ending.

If Sts vote for the happy ending, play the video / audio ◀)) **2.21**. If they vote for the sad ending, play the video / audio ◀)) **2.22**.

b ◀)) **2.21 / 2.22** Before playing the ending chosen by Sts, elicit ideas from the class about what they think happens, but <u>don't</u> tell them if they are right or wrong, to help build suspense.

Play the video / audio once the whole way through for Sts to watch or listen.

EXTRA SUPPORT Read through the script and decide if you need to pre-teach any new lexis before Sts watch or listen.

At the end of the story, get Sts to tell you what happened. Then play the video / audio again.

◀)) **2.21**
Happy ending
N = narrator, H = Hannah, J = Jamie, W = waiter
N *Suddenly, a man ran across the road. He was wearing a dark coat, so Hannah didn't see him at first. Quickly, she put her foot on the brake. She stopped just in time. She got out of her car and shouted at the man.*
H Don't you usually look before you cross the road? I nearly hit you. I didn't see you until the last moment.
J Sorry! Hey, Hannah, it's me. It's Jamie.
H Jamie! What are you doing here? I nearly killed you!
J I was buying something. I was in a hurry and I crossed the road without looking.
H Come on. Get in!
N *Hannah and Jamie drove to the coffee bar. They sat down in their usual seats and ordered two cups of coffee.*
W Here you are. Two cappuccinos.
H and J Thanks.
H What an evening! I nearly killed you.
J Well, you didn't kill me, so what's the problem?
H But what were you doing in the high street? I thought you were here, in the café, waiting for me.
J I went to the theatre to buy these tickets for the Pink concert. I know you wanted to go. And it's on the fifteenth of October – next Saturday. Our anniversary.
H Our anniversary?
J Yes. Three months since we first met. We met on Saturday the fifteenth of July. Remember?
H Gosh, Jamie. I can't believe you remember the exact day! What a romantic! It's lucky I didn't hit you in the street…

 **2.22**

Sad ending

N = narrator, H = Hannah, P = policewoman

N *Suddenly, a man ran across the road. He was wearing a dark coat, so Hannah didn't see him at first. Quickly, she put her foot on the brake. Although Hannah tried to stop, she couldn't. She hit the man. Hannah panicked. She drove away as fast as she could. When she arrived at the coffee bar, Jamie wasn't there. She called him, but his phone was turned off. She waited for ten minutes and then she went home.*
Two hours later, a car arrived at Hannah's house. A policewoman knocked at the door.
P Good evening, Madam. Are you Hannah Davis?
H Yes, I am.
P I'd like to speak to you. Can I come in?
N *The policewoman came in and sat down on the sofa.*
P Are you a friend of Jamie Dixon?
H Yes.
N *…said Hannah.*
P Well, I'm afraid I have some bad news for you.
H What? What's happened?
P Jamie had an accident this evening.
H Oh no. What kind of accident?
P He was crossing the road and a car hit him.
H When…when did this happen? And where?
P This evening at twenty-five past five. He was crossing the road in the high street, by the theatre.
H Oh no! How is he?
P He's in hospital. He's got a bad injury to his head and two broken legs.
H But is he going to be OK?
P We don't know. He's in intensive care.
H Oh no. And the driver of the car?
P She didn't stop.
H She?
P Yes, it was a woman in a black car. Somebody saw the number of the car. You have a black car outside, don't you, Madam? Is your number plate G-Y fifty-six, R-Z-R?
H Yes…yes, it is.
P Can you tell me where you were at twenty-five past five this evening?

  If there's time and you are using the video, you could get Sts to watch again with subtitles, so they can see exactly what they understood / didn't understand. Translate / Explain any new words or phrases.

c If Sts chose the happy ending (2.21), tell them to go to **Communication Happy ending** on *p.103*.
If Sts chose the sad ending (2.22), tell them to go to **Communication Sad ending** on *p.109*.

Set a time limit for Sts to answer questions 1–8 in pairs.

Check answers.

Happy ending
1 Because he was wearing a dark coat.
2 Jamie
3 He was in a hurry.
4 To a coffee bar
5 Two cappuccinos
6 He was buying tickets for a concert.
7 It was the Pink concert on 15th October.
8 15th October is their three-month anniversary.

Sad ending
1 Because he was wearing a dark coat.
2 She hit him.
3 She went to the coffee bar and called Jamie.
4 The police / A policewoman
5 That Jamie was in a car accident.
6 He had a bad injury to his head and two broken legs. He's in intensive care.
7 The car was white and the driver was a woman.
8 She asked Hannah about the number plate of her car and where she was at 5.25 p.m.

EXTRA IDEA Ask Sts if they want to watch / listen to the ending they didn't choose (they almost always do). You could let them watch / listen to the other ending for pleasure, without doing the tasks.

There are two pages of revision and consolidation after every two Files. These exercises can be done individually or in pairs, in class or at home, depending on the needs of your Sts and the class time available.

The first page revises the **grammar**, **vocabulary**, and **pronunciation** of the two Files. The exercises add up to 50 (grammar = 15, vocabulary = 25, pronunciation = 10), so you can use the first page as a mini-test on Files 1 and 2. The **pronunciation** section sends Sts to the Sound Bank on *pp.166–167*. Explain that this is a reference section of the book, where they can check the symbols and see common sound–spelling patterns for each of the sounds. Highlight the video showing the mouth position for each sound. If you don't want to use this in class, tell Sts to look at it at home, and to practise making the sounds and saying the words.

The second page presents Sts with a series of skills-based challenges. First, there is a **reading** text which is of a slightly higher level than those in the File, but which revises grammar and vocabulary Sts have already learned. The **listening** is some unscripted street interviews, where people are asked questions related to the topics in the Files. Sts can either watch the interviews on video or listen to them on audio. You can find these on the *Class DVD*, *Classroom Presentation Tool*, and *Class Audio* (audio only). Finally, there is a **speaking** challenge which assesses Sts' ability to use the language of the Files orally. You could get Sts to do these activities in pairs, or Sts can tick the boxes if they feel confident that they can do them.

More materials
For teachers
Teacher's Resource Centre
Video Can you understand these people? 1&2
Quick Test 2
File 2 Test
For students
Online Practice Check your progress

GRAMMAR

1 c	2 b	3 a	4 c	5 a	6 c	7 c	8 b	9 b	10 c
11 a	12 c	13 a	14 b	15 c					

VOCABULARY

a
1 do 2 look 3 wear 4 take 5 stay 6 book 7 invite
8 drive 9 play 10 leave
b
1 on 2 in 3 in 4 on 5 at 6 at 7 in
c
1 beard (the others are adjectives to describe hair)
2 lazy (the others are positive adjectives)
3 clever (the others are negative adjectives)
4 dress (the others are worn by men)
5 gloves (the others are worn on your feet)
6 scarf (the others are pieces of jewellery)
7 noisy (the others are about the weather)
8 luxurious (the others are negative adjectives)

PRONUNCIATION

c
1 qu**ie**t /aɪ/   2 sk**ii**ng /iː/   3 book**ed** /t/   4 wait**ed** /ɪd/
5 noi**s**y /z/
d
1 extrovert   2 over**weight**   3 brace**let**   4 on**line**
5 **comfor**table

CAN YOU understand this text?

a
1 B   2 C   3 A
b
1 F   2 F   3 T   4 F   5 T   6 F

▶ CAN YOU understand these people?

1 c   2 a   3 b   4 c   5 c

◀))) 2.23
1
I = interviewer, L = Lewis
I   Who do you look like in your family?
L   Er, well people say I often look like my dad a lot. We've got the same sort of nose and the same face shape, but I've got my mum's hair colour and my mum's eyes.
I   Do you have a similar personality?
L   Er, again there is, there are quite a lot of similarities between me and my dad. We're both into German and speaking German, and also into architecture, which is why I'm here.
2
I = interviewer, S = Susie
I   Do you have a favourite painting?
S   Um, I think so. I'm not sure of the name of the painting, but I like Salvador Dali. I really like the painting with the dripping clocks.
I   Can you describe it?
S   Er, yes, like I said, there are dripping clocks. It's very, um, it's an interesting style. It's not something you see all the time, and it's very colourful.
3
I = interviewer, S = Shosanna
I   Where did you go for your last holiday?
S   My last vacation I went to Guyana, which is my parents' country in South America.
I   Did you have a good time?
S   I did. It was actually one of the best vacations I had. It was really educational, and I was able to see how my parents grew up, which was interesting.
4
I = interviewer, S = Susan
I   Do you take a lot of photos?
S   I take a lot of photos. My telephone is full of photos and I use Instagram.
I   What do you usually take photos of?
S   Mostly people, places, gardens, lots of flowers. I never post photos of people, but I take photos of family, but lots of gardens and flowers.
5
I = interviewer, S = Sam
I   Do you prefer films with a happy or sad ending?
S   Um, it just has to be a good film. I don't mind if it's a happy ending or a sad ending.

TripAside

G *be going to* (plans and predictions)
V airports
P the letter *g*

Lesson plan

In this lesson Sts revise *going to*, which they learned at Elementary level, to talk about plans and predictions. The context is a reading and listening based on TripAside, a company which helps travellers make the most of stopovers at airports. The lesson begins with vocabulary, and Sts learn useful vocabulary related to airports. They then focus on the pronunciation of the letter *g*. Sts read an article from the British press about TripAside and then listen to a traveller meeting his guide at the airport in Rome. This leads Sts into the grammar, which is revised and practised. Sts then ask and answer questions about their plans. The lesson ends with a speaking activity in pairs, in which Sts imagine they work for TripAside and plan a tour for travellers on a stopover at their nearest airport.

More materials	
For teachers	
Photocopiables	
Grammar *be going to* (plans and predictions) *p.178*	
Communicative A day in… *p.223* (instructions *p.209*)	
For students	
Workbook 3A	
Online Practice 3A	

OPTIONAL LEAD-IN (BOOKS CLOSED)
Write AIRPORT on the board. Put Sts in pairs and give them two minutes to think of five things people do at an airport, e.g. *catch a plane, leave, arrive, meet somebody, check in, board, fly*, etc.

Elicit answers and write some of their suggestions on the board.

1 VOCABULARY airports

a Books open. Focus on the questions, making sure Sts know the meaning of *to pick someone up* and *to drop someone off*. Sts can answer them in pairs or do it as a whole-class activity.

If Sts worked in pairs, get some feedback.

EXTRA CHALLENGE Tell Sts to ask for more information if possible. For example, if their partner says they were travelling somewhere, they should find out where, etc. If their partner says they were picking up or dropping off someone, they should find out who, etc.

b Focus on the instructions and tell Sts to look at the 12 signs and to match them to the words and phrases.

Get Sts to compare their answers with a partner.

c 🔊 **3.1** Play the audio for Sts to listen and check.
Check answers and make sure Sts know the meaning of all the words and phrases.

🔊 **3.1**
3 arrivals
7 bag drop
1 baggage reclaim
9 check-in
8 customs
2 departures
11 gates
5 lifts
10 passport control
12 security check
4 terminal
6 trolley

EXTRA SUPPORT Use the audio to drill the pronunciation of the words and phrases, or model and drill them yourself.

Then tell Sts to cover the words and look at the signs, and try to remember the words and phrases.

d 🔊 **3.2** Focus on the task and make sure Sts understand what they have to do. Point out that the first one (*a lift*) has been done for them.

Play the audio once the whole way through.

Get Sts to compare with a partner, and play the audio again if necessary.

Check answers.

2 baggage reclaim	**3** security check	**4** gates
5 passport control	**6** check-in	

🔊 **3.2**
1 Doors opening. Second floor. Departures. Check-in and bag drop.
2 **A** Excuse me. My suitcase hasn't arrived. Do you know where I can go to report it?
  B Yes, madam. Lost luggage is that window over there.
3 **A** Can you take your boots off, please?
  B Sorry?
  A Your boots. Take them off and put them on the belt, please.
4 Boarding for British Airways flight B-A-zero-five-six-four to Milan will begin in a few minutes. Passengers in rows fifteen to thirty are invited to board first. Please have your passport and boarding pass ready.
5 **A** Are you here on vacation?
  B Er, yes, I am.
  A How long are you staying?
  B Two weeks.
6 Passport and boarding pass, please. Thanks. How many bags are you checking in?

2 PRONUNCIATION the letter *g*

Pronunciation notes

The letter *g* can be pronounced in two different ways, /g/ or /dʒ/.

g before *a*, *o*, and *u*, and before a consonant, is pronounced /g/, e.g. *gas*, *go*, *gun*, *great*.

gu + vowel is also pronounced /g/, e.g. *guard*.

g is also always pronounced /g/ when it comes after a vowel at the end of a word, e.g. *bag*, *dog*.

ge and *gi* can be pronounced /g/ or /dʒ/, e.g. *get*, *give*, but also *generous*, *page*, *giraffe*.

gg is usually pronounced /g/, e.g. *bigger*, but there are two exceptions where it is pronounced /dʒ/: *suggest* and *exaggerate*.

You could also tell Sts that the letter *g* is sometimes silent, e.g. *foreign*, *sign*, etc.

a Do this as a whole-class activity.

gg = /g/   *ge* = /dʒ/

b Focus on the chart. Elicit the two sound-picture words (*girl* and *jazz*) and the sounds /g/ and /dʒ/.

Now tell Sts to put the words in the list in the correct row. Remind Sts that this kind of exercise is easier to do if they say the words aloud.

Get Sts to compare with a partner.

c 🔊 **3.3** Play the audio for Sts to listen and check. Check answers.

🔊 **3.3**
girl /g/ gate, foggy, forget, guide, guest, begin, gift, guarantee, organize
jazz /dʒ/ large, village, engineer, agent, region, emergency, general

Now play the audio again, pausing after each word or group of words for Sts to listen and repeat.

Put Sts in pairs and get them to practise saying the words. Finally, ask Sts *When can* g *be pronounced* /dʒ/?

When it is followed by the letter *e* or *i*.

 If these sounds are difficult for your Sts, it will help to show them the mouth position. You could model this yourself or use the Sound Bank videos on the *Teacher's Resource Centre*.

3 READING & LISTENING understanding text cohesion – connectors

a Focus on the task and give Sts time to read the article. Tell them not to worry about the gaps for the moment.

Elicit opinions from the class.

 Before Sts read the article the first time, check whether you need to pre-teach any vocabulary, but not the words or phrases in **c**.

b Tell Sts to read the article again and complete the gaps with phrases A–H.

Give Sts time to read the article and complete the task. Tell them to focus on the words that come before or after the gaps, which are mainly connectors like *and*, *or*, *so*, etc.

Get Sts to compare with a partner, and then check answers. You could tell Sts that you can say *look around* or *look round* (*a city*).

1 D **2** H **3** E **4** F **5** C **6** G **7** B **8** A

  To check comprehension, ask some more questions, e.g. *What is TripAside?* (a company that organizes short guided tours for people on stopovers), *Which airports offer trips with TripAside?* (Paris, Frankfurt, London, Brussels, Rome and Madrid), *Is TripAside unique?* (No, other small companies offer similar tours.), etc.

c Focus on the task and get Sts to work with a partner to say what the words and phrases mean. Encourage them to go back and look at the words in context if they can't remember their meaning.

Check answers, either explaining in English, translating into Sts' L1, or getting Sts to check in their dictionaries. Model and drill pronunciation.

stopover /ˈstɒpəʊvə/ = a short stay somewhere between two parts of a journey
connecting flight /kəˈnektɪŋ flaɪt/ = a second flight where you have had to change planes
departure lounge /dɪˈpɑːtʃə laʊndʒ/ = the place at an airport where you wait for your flight
duty-free shop /ˌdjuːti ˈfriː ʃɒp/ = a shop in an airport or on a ship, etc. that sells things like cigarettes, alcohol, perfume, etc. without tax on them
air traveller /eə ˈtrævələ/ = a passenger on a plane

Deal with any other new vocabulary. Model and drill the pronunciation of any tricky words.

d 🔊 **3.4** Focus on the task and question. Remind Sts that it will be one of the six cities mentioned in the article.

Play the audio once the whole way through.

Check the answer. Ask Sts how they knew (the Colosseum, the Forum, the Pantheon, *Via del Corso*, all the Italian food mentioned, etc.).

  Read through the script and decide if you need to pre-teach any new lexis before Sts listen.

Rome

🔊 **3.4**
(script in Student's Book on *p.121*)
A = Anna, J = Jake
A Hello, Mr Bevan. I'm Anna, your tour guide.
J Hi. Please, call me Jake.
A OK, Jake. Nice to meet you. How was the flight? Are you very tired?
J No, I'm fine.
A Great. Let's go to the car park, then. Is it your first time here?
J Yeah. I was in Europe when I was a student, but somehow I never got here.
A And your final destination is London, is that right?
J Yes. I'm going to give a talk at a conference in Oxford.
A So work, not pleasure?
J Yes – well, maybe some pleasure, too. I have a friend – well, an ex-girlfriend, really, who I was with when I was a student. She's British – she lives in Oxford – and we're planning to meet up.
A That's nice! OK, so now I'm going to tell you a bit about our tour today. We're going to drive to the centre – it takes about forty-five minutes – and then we're going to start at the Colosseum.
J Great. I've always wanted to see it.
A And then we're going to visit the Forum. After that, we're going to see the Pantheon – one of the oldest buildings in the city.

J Wow.
A So, then we are very near the *Via del Corso*, where all the best shops are. Would you like to maybe do some shopping?
J Well, I'd like to see the shops, but I'm probably not going to buy anything.
A Maybe a little present – a present for your friend in Oxford?
J Well, maybe.
A And then I'm sure you're going to be hungry, so I'm going to take you to a really nice restaurant for lunch. We can have pizza, or a good carbonara, a gelato – an ice cream, that is. Our typical dishes, but I promise you, very different from Italian food in America.
J Sounds great. And then back to the airport, I guess?
A That's right. We need to allow time for that.
J Yes, I don't want to miss my flight.
A Don't worry. We do this tour every day – and nobody has ever missed their flight.
J Is it going to be very hot today?
A No, not too hot. It's going to be nice: about twenty-two degrees.
J Perfect. It's going to be a fantastic day.
A Here we are. If you can just wait a minute while I pay for the parking. Oh, Mr Bevan – Jake – is this yours?
J My passport! Thanks, Anna. Typical me. I always lose things when I'm travelling.

e Focus on the task and give Sts time to read sentences 1–10. Make sure they understand all the lexis, e.g. *sites*, *looking forward to*, etc.

Play the audio for Sts to listen again and complete the task. Remind them to correct the *F* sentences.

Get Sts to compare with a partner, and then play again if necessary.

Check answers.

1 T
2 F (He **has** been to Europe before.)
3 F (His next flight is to **London**.)
4 T
5 F (He **has an old friend / ex-girlfriend** there.)
6 T
7 T
8 F (**They are going to have lunch at a nice restaurant.**)
9 F (The weather forecast **is** very good.)
10 T

 If there's time, you could get Sts to listen again with the script on *p.121*, so they can see exactly what they understood / didn't understand. Translate / Explain any new words or phrases.

f Do this as a whole-class activity. If you have ever had a long stopover at an airport, tell Sts about it.

4 GRAMMAR *be going to* (plans and predictions)

a ◆ **3.5** Focus on the instructions and give Sts time to complete the gaps with the correct form of *be going to*.

Get Sts to compare with a partner, then play the audio for them to listen and check.

Check answers.

◆ **3.5**
1 I'm **going to give** a talk at a conference.
2 We**'re going to drive** to the centre.
3 And then we**'re going to visit** the Forum.
4 I'm probably **not going to buy** anything.
5 Is it **going to be** very hot?
6 It's **going to be** a fantastic day.

b First, make sure that Sts are clear about what the difference is between *a plan* (something you intend to do) and *a prediction* (something that you think is going to happen).

Now, in pairs, Sts focus on whether sentences 1–6 in **a** are plans (*Pl*) or predictions (*Pr*).

Check answers.

1 Pl   2 Pl   3 Pl   4 Pr   5 Pr   6 Pr

c Tell Sts to go to **Grammar Bank 3A** on *p.130*.

Grammar notes

Be going to is revised here with its two main uses: plans (*I'm going to stay for six months.*) and predictions (*It's going to be a big surprise for him.*).

You may want to point out that when people speak fast, *going to* often sounds like *gonna*, and it is even sometimes written like that, for example, in song lyrics.

◆ **3.6** Focus on the example sentences and play the audio for Sts to listen and repeat. Encourage them to copy the rhythm. Then go through the rules with the class.

Now focus on the exercises for **3A** on *p.131*. Sts do the exercises individually or in pairs.

Check answers, getting Sts to read the full sentences.

a
1 Is…going to learn   2 aren't going to go, 're going to stay
3 're going to be   4 's going to get   5 'm going to cook
6 'm not going to listen   7 are…going to do , 'm going to study
b
1 's going to win   2 're going to be   3 're going to break

Tell Sts to go back to the main lesson **3A**.

 If you think Sts need more practice, you may want to give them the **Grammar** photocopiable activity at this point.

d Put Sts in pairs, **A** and **B**, and tell them to go to **Communication** What are your plans?, **A** on *p.103*, **B** on *p.109*.

Go through the instructions carefully and make sure Sts understand what they have to do.

 Get Sts to look at the prompts and give them time to write the questions.

Sit **A** and **B** face-to-face. **A** asks **B** his / her questions and, when possible, for more information. Then they swap roles.

When they have finished, elicit some answers from individual Sts.

Tell Sts to go back to the main lesson **3A**.

5 SPEAKING

a Focus on the task and make sure Sts understand what they have to do.

Put Sts in pairs and get them to discuss the questions.

Monitor and help, correcting any errors they make with *going to*.

 In a large class, you may prefer Sts to do the activity in groups of three or four.

b When Sts are ready, get each pair to present their tour to the class.

With a show of hands, get Sts to vote for the best tour.

G present continuous (future arrangements)
V verbs + prepositions, e.g. *arrive in*
P linking

Lesson plan

In this lesson Sts learn a new use of the present continuous: to talk about fixed arrangements. The context is the continuation of the story of Jake, the man who went on a guided tour in **3A**, who was going to a conference and hoping to meet up with an ex-girlfriend. Sts begin this lesson by doing a quiz to see how organized they are. They answer the questions individually, compare answers in pairs, calculate the score of their quiz, and then discuss the results. The lesson continues with a vocabulary focus on verbs which are normally followed by prepositions, and then there is a pronunciation focus on linking, to help Sts understand fast speech. Sts then listen to a conversation between Jake and Sarah, the ex-girlfriend, in which they make contact – Sts complete a calendar with Jake's appointments – and arrange to see each other. Finally, they listen to the meeting to find out how it went. After focusing on the grammar, Sts get more practice in a speaking activity where they try to make arrangements to go out with other Sts in the class. The lesson ends with Writing, where Sts use both the grammar and the vocabulary to write an email about travel arrangements.

More materials

For teachers

Photocopiables
Grammar present continuous (future arrangements) *p.179*
Vocabulary What's the preposition? *p.261*
(instructions *p.254*)
Communicative Come fly with me! *p.224*
(instructions *p.210*)

For students

Workbook 3B

Online Practice 3B

OPTIONAL LEAD-IN (BOOKS CLOSED)

Quickly revise months. Write SPRING, SUMMER, AUTUMN, and WINTER on the board and tell Sts, in pairs, to write the months in each season.

Check answers, and model and drill the pronunciation of any months which Sts find difficult, e.g. *February* /ˈfebruəri/, *July* /dʒuˈlaɪ/, etc.

1 READING & SPEAKING

a Books open. Focus on the quiz and give Sts time to read it and choose their answers. You may want to check that they know the meaning of some of the lexis, e.g. *Post-it note*, *list*, *pack*, etc.

b Get Sts to compare their answers with a partner.

c Tell Sts to go to **Communication How organized are you?** on *p.103*.

Give Sts time to calculate their score and then read the result.

Tell Sts to go back to the main lesson **3B**.

d Back in their same pairs, Sts compare their results and discuss whether or not they agree with them.

Get some feedback from various pairs.

Ask the class if they know anybody who is very organized or very disorganized.

2 VOCABULARY & PRONUNCIATION
verbs + prepositions; linking

Vocabulary notes

Certain verbs are often followed by a particular preposition, which may well be different in Sts' L1. When Sts learn these verbs, they should make a note of the preposition that follows each verb.

a Focus on the two extracts from the quiz and explain that in each sentence there is a preposition missing. Highlight the fact that certain verbs are often followed by a particular preposition, e.g. *It depends **on** the weather.*

Get Sts to complete the sentences, and then check answers.

1 at **2** for

b Tell Sts to go to **Vocabulary Bank Prepositions** on *p.153* and do **2 Verbs + prepositions**.

Focus on **a** and get Sts to complete the **Prepositions** column individually or in pairs.

🔊 **3.7** Now do **b**. Play the audio for Sts to listen and check.

Check answers. When looking at 13 and 14, you might want to highlight the difference between *think about* and *think of*: *think about* = action verb, e.g. *'Why are you so happy?' 'I'm thinking about my holiday'*, and *think of* = non-action verb, to have an opinion, e.g. *'What do you think of Coldplay?' 'I don't like them.'*

🔊 **3.7**
Prepositions 2 Verbs + prepositions
1 I arrived **in** Paris on Friday night.
2 I was very tired when I arrived **at** the hotel.
3 I hate waiting **for** people who are late.
4 **A** What are you going to do at the weekend?
   B I don't know. It depends **on** the weather.
5 I'm sorry, but I really don't agree **with** you.
6 I asked **for** a chicken sandwich, but this is tuna!
7 Please listen **to** what I'm saying.
8 Who's going to pay **for** the meal?
9 I need **to** speak to Martin **about** the meeting.
10 I don't spend much money **on** food.
11 Don't worry **about** the exam. It isn't very hard.
12 Do you believe **in** ghosts?
13 You're not listening! What are you thinking **about**?
14 **A** What do you think **of** this painting?
   B I really like it. I think it's beautiful.
15 Who does this bag belong **to**?

Now either use the audio to drill the pronunciation of the sentences, or model and drill them yourself. Give further practice of any words your Sts find difficult to pronounce.

Focus on the **arrive in or arrive at?** box and go through it with the class.

Focus on **a** in **Activation** and get Sts to cover the **Prepositions** column and say the sentences.

Finally, in **b**, get Sts to complete the gaps with a preposition, and then check answers.

1 on **2** about, to **3** in **4** to **5** for **6** for

 EXTRA SUPPORT Write the prepositions on the board in random order to help Sts.

Make sure Sts understand all the questions, e.g. *love at first sight*, etc.

Put Sts in pairs and get them to ask and answer the questions.

Get some feedback from various pairs.

Tell Sts to go back to the main lesson **3B**.

EXTRA SUPPORT If you think Sts need more practice, you may want to give them the **Vocabulary** photocopiable activity at this point.

c ◗ **3.8** Here Sts practise deciphering connected speech. Focus on the **Connected speech** box and go through it with the class. Highlight that this is an aspect of pronunciation that is particularly important to help them understand spoken English.

Tell Sts they are going to hear six sentences said at normal speed. The first time, tell them just to listen, not to write. Play the audio once the whole way through.

◗ **3.8**
1 We arrived at the airport.
2 It depends on the time.
3 Let's talk about it.
4 What does she think of him?
5 Don't think about the past.
6 How much did you spend on food?

Now play the audio again, pausing after each sentence to give Sts time to write.

Check answers, eliciting the sentences onto the board.

See sentences in script 3.8

Finally, play the audio again, pausing after each sentence for Sts to repeat and copy the rhythm.

EXTRA SUPPORT Repeat the activity, eliciting responses from individual Sts.

d Put Sts in pairs and get them to practise saying the sentences.

3 LISTENING understanding times, dates and appointments

a ◗ **3.9** Ask Sts if they can remember Jake Bevan from **3A**. If not, remind them that he is the American man who had a stopover in Rome with the tour guide Anna.

Now focus on the instructions and make sure Sts understand the situation.

EXTRA SUPPORT Before playing the audio, focus on the phone and ask Sts the times. Elicit both ways of telling the time where possible.

(a) quarter past eight / eight fifteen
eleven / eleven o'clock
two / two o'clock
four / four o'clock
half past seven / seven thirty

Play the audio for Sts to listen and complete the phone calendar.

Check the answer.

EXTRA SUPPORT Read through the script and decide if you need to pre-teach any new lexis before Sts listen.

Tuesday at 11.00

◗ **3.9**
(script in Student's Book on *p.121*)
S = Sarah, J = Jake
S Hello?
J Sarah?
S Hi, Jake.
J Hi. Great to hear your voice! How are things?
S Oh fine, fine. How was the journey? When did you arrive in the UK?
J Last night. The journey was fine. I got a cheap flight with Alitalia, but it meant a long stopover in Rome, but I went on a guided tour and I had a great time.
S That sounds like fun. What did you think of Rome?
J Fantastic. I loved it. So when can we meet?
S I'm afraid I'm really busy this week. The only possible day for me is Tuesday. I'm going to London from Wednesday to Friday…
J Tuesday. Let me look at my calendar.
S Wow, Jake, you put things in your calendar! You're much more organized than when we were going out.
J Well, I'm better than I was. But I nearly lost my passport when I was in Rome. OK, Tuesday. I'm not free in the evening. I'm having dinner with Mark Taylor, my old professor. Do you remember him? It's at seven thirty. I can't change that. How about lunch?
S It depends on the time. A late lunch would be OK, around one forty-five?
J The problem is I'm giving my talk at two. And I'm having a breakfast meeting at eight fifteen with some colleagues.
S Well, morning coffee, or tea in the afternoon, then. What are you doing then?
J Let's see…I'm going to a talk about climate change at four, so I think maybe morning coffee is best. And then we can try to arrange another time.
S OK. There's a nice coffee bar in the high street called The Grand Café. Meet there at eleven?
J Perfect. I'm really looking forward to it!
S Me too. Bye.

b Focus on the task and give Sts time to read all the appointments in the list. Make sure Sts realize that there are two appointments they do not need to use.

Play the audio again the whole way through.

Get Sts to compare with a partner, and then play the audio again if necessary.

Check answers.

> **8.15** breakfast meeting   **2.00** my talk   **4.00** talk: climate change   **7.30** dinner with Mark

EXTRA SUPPORT If there's time, you could get Sts to listen again with the script on *p.121*, so they can see exactly what they understood / didn't understand. Translate / Explain any new words or phrases.

c ◗ **3.10** Tell Sts they are now going to listen to Jake and Sarah talking. They must listen and decide if they think Jake and Sarah will meet again.

Play the audio once the whole way through.

Get Sts to compare with a partner, and then elicit opinions.

◗ **3.10**

J = Jake, S = Sarah

J   Sarah! Sorry I'm late!
S   Same old Jake. You were always late. Good to see you. You look really well.
J   You look fantastic.
S   Thank you. What would you like? I'm having a cappuccino.
J   The same for me. And a croissant or something. Excuse me…can we order some coffee please?

***

J   It's great to see you again, Sarah – just like old times. You really haven't changed. We need to meet again. Are you doing anything on Saturday?
S   Well, actually…
J   Lunch? Dinner? Breakfast?
S   Jake, there's something I need to tell you. I'm not single now. In fact, um…in fact, I'm with someone. He's called Mike, and… we're getting married on Saturday. That's why I'm so busy all this week…
J   Wow! That's…that's great news! I wish you all the best!
S   Thanks, Jake. Would you like another coffee, or a croissant?

---

4 GRAMMAR present continuous (future arrangements)

a ◗ **3.11** Focus on the instructions. Tell Sts the first time they listen they must complete the gaps in 1–5.

Play the audio, pausing after each extract to give Sts time to write.

Get Sts to compare with a partner, and then check answers.

◗ **3.11**

1   I'm **going** to London from Wednesday to Friday.
2   I'm **having** dinner with Mark Taylor.
3   I'm **giving** my talk at two o'clock.
4   Are you **doing** anything on Saturday?
5   We're **getting married** on Saturday.

Now ask Sts whether they refer to the present or the future.

> They all refer to b) the future.

b Tell Sts to go to **Grammar Bank 3B** on *p.130*.

Grammar notes

Sts already know how to use the present continuous to talk about things happening now, but may find this future use (*What are you doing this evening?*) quite strange. They may find it more natural to use the present simple tense for this because of L1 interference.

A typical mistake is: ~~What do you do this evening? I go to the cinema.~~

The difference between using *be going to* and the present continuous is quite subtle, so it is probably worth stressing that they can often be used as alternative forms when we talk about plans and arrangements, e.g. *What are you going to do tonight? / What are you doing tonight?*

You may want to point out that whereas it is very common to use the present continuous with verbs such as *leave*, *arrive*, *go*, and *come* because these often refer to previously-made travel arrangements, *be going to* is more common with actions for which you don't usually make special arrangements, e.g. *I'm going to wash my hair tonight* is more common than *I'm washing my hair tonight*.

It is also important to highlight that the present continuous is not used for predictions, e.g. *I'm sure you're going to find a job.* NOT ~~I'm sure you're finding a job.~~

◗ **3.12** Focus on the example sentences and play the audio for Sts to listen and repeat. Encourage them to copy the rhythm. Then go through the rules with the class.

Now focus on the **be going to or present continuous?** box and go through it with the class.

Focus on the exercises for **3B** on *p.131*. Sts do the exercises individually or in pairs.

Check answers, getting Sts to read the full sentences.

> **a**
> 1 N   2 F   3 F   4 N   5 N   6 F   7 F   8 N   9 N   10 F
> **b**
> 1   I'm **packing** my suitcase.
> 2   I'm **flying** to Vienna at eight o'clock tonight.
> 3   Why **are you going** to Vienna?
> 4   I'm **meeting** the boss of VTech Solutions tomorrow.
> 5   Why **are you seeing** him?
> 6   He**'s working** on a project with me at the moment…

Tell Sts to go back to the main lesson **3B**.

EXTRA SUPPORT If you think Sts need more practice, you may want to give them the **Grammar** photocopiable activity at this point.

c Focus on Jake's phone and the example.

Put Sts in pairs and get them to ask and answer questions about Jake's phone calendar.

5 SPEAKING

a ◗ **3.13** Focus on the task and tell Sts that the first time you play the audio, they should just listen and read at the same time. They should pay attention to **B**'s intonation in the highlighted phrases, which helps to show how she is feeling, e.g. enthusiastic, apologetic.

Play the audio once the whole way through.

◗ **3.13**
See the conversation in Student's Book *p.25*

Now tell Sts they must listen and repeat the conversation. Play the audio again, pausing after each line for Sts to listen and repeat. Encourage them to copy the intonation.

b Now put Sts in pairs and get them to practise the conversation.

You could get a few pairs to perform in front of the class.

c Focus on the instructions and give Sts time to complete their calendar with different activities for three evenings next week. Encourage them to write the activities with the verb in the infinitive, or without the verb, as this is how people normally put things in a diary, e.g. *(go to) cinema with friends* NOT ~~I'm going to the cinema with friends~~.

EXTRA SUPPORT Elicit some activities Sts could do in the evening and write them on the board, e.g. *study, do homework / housework, go to the cinema / a concert, go to a restaurant, cook dinner, watch a film at home*, etc.

d Focus on the instructions and make sure Sts know what they have to do. Read the example with a student.

Tell Sts to mingle and try to make arrangements with a different person for every free evening they have.

When time is up, find out who is doing what when.

6 WRITING an informal email

Tell Sts to go to **Writing An informal email** on *p.115*.

a Focus on the instructions. Get Sts to read the email, and help them with any vocabulary, e.g. *for some reason, to share a room, attaching*, etc.

Now get Sts to read the email again and answer questions 1–5. Tell them not to worry about the gaps.

Get Sts to compare with a partner, and then check answers.

> **1** Last August
> **2** By plane
> **3** Sally and her family
> **4** Because she doesn't have it; it isn't on her phone.
> **5** He needs to decide if he wants to share a bedroom, and if there's anything he'd like to do in the UK.

b Focus on the expressions in the list and give Sts a few minutes in pairs to complete the gaps.

Check answers.

> **1** Hi
> **2** Thanks for your email
> **3** Looking forward to hearing from you.
> **4** Best wishes
> **5** PS

Now either do questions 1–3 as a whole-class activity or put Sts in pairs.

If Sts worked in pairs, check answers.

> **1** a **2** b **3** Yes

c Now focus on the instructions and tell Sts they are going to write an email to Sally. Give them time to plan their email.

> **Details to give Sally:**
> The time the plane / flight arrives.   the flight number
> a (mobile) phone number
> Need to decide which room to sleep in and what to visit

d Go through the layout of the email with the class, pointing out the three different paragraphs.

Set the writing in class or for homework.

e Make sure Sts check their emails for mistakes before handing them in.

3C Word games

G defining relative clauses (*a person who…*, *a thing which…*)

V paraphrasing: *like, for example*, etc.

P silent *e*

Lesson plan

The topic of this lesson is word games. First, Sts are introduced to simple, defining relative clauses through the context of a TV game show where contestants have to complete the alphabet wheel by saying the correct word for definitions for each letter of the alphabet. This context shows Sts that relative clauses can help them with the essential language skill of paraphrasing. After practising the grammar, they go on to learn other useful phrases which will help them keep going in a conversation when they don't know the exact word for something. Sts then play the game with letters A–E only. The pronunciation focus is on how the silent letter *e* at the end of words, e.g. *site, fate*, etc., changes the preceding vowel sound. Finally, Sts define words to each other in order to complete a crossword.

More materials
For teachers
Photocopiables
Grammar defining relative clauses *p.180*
Communicative Can you explain the word? *p.225* (instructions *p.210*)
For students
Workbook 3C
Online Practice 3C

1 READING & LISTENING understanding rules of a game

a Books open. Focus on the questions. Do the first one as a whole-class activity and tell Sts if you like word games.

Now give Sts, in pairs, three minutes to find as many words as possible of four letters or more (not including the letters in the circle).

Get some possible answers.

fear, brother, bread, learn, angel, danger, etc.

EXTRA CHALLENGE You could play other word games with these letters, e.g. give Sts three minutes to try to make the longest word they can.

b Focus on the photo of the quiz show. Use it to elicit the word *wheel*, and ask Sts if any of them recognize the show.

Then give Sts time to read the text.

Elicit answers. The original show on TV in the UK was called *The Alphabet Game*, and it has been adapted in many countries around the world, e.g. in Spain, where it is called *Pasapalabra* and is very popular.

EXTRA SUPPORT Before Sts read the text the first time, check whether you need to pre-teach any vocabulary.

c Tell Sts to read the text again and then cover it.

Put Sts in pairs and get them to answer questions 1–5.

Check answers.

1 To complete the wheel by saying the correct word for each letter
2 Two minutes
3 The place where you catch a plane, airport
4 He or she says 'pass', and the presenter goes on to the next letter.
5 They get all 25 words correct.

Deal with any other new vocabulary. Model and drill the pronunciation of any tricky words.

d ◀ **3.14** Focus on the instructions and make sure Sts understand the situation. Explain that they are going to listen to the end of the show and they should try to write down the last six words the contestant needs to guess. Tell Sts <u>not</u> to call out the answers.

Play the audio, pausing after each 'ping' to give Sts time to write their answer.

Get Sts to compare with a partner, but <u>don't</u> check answers yet.

EXTRA SUPPORT Read through the scripts and decide if you need to pre-teach any new lexis before Sts listen.

P = presenter, V = Victoria

P OK. It begins with *B*. It's an adjective for a man who has no hair on his head!

V (*ping*)

P Right. It begins with *C*. It's an adjective. It describes a place where there are a lot of people, for example a restaurant or a beach in the summer.

V (*ping*)

P Right. It begins with *G*. They're things which people wear on their hands.

V (*ping*)

P Right. It begins with *K*. It's the room where people cook.

V (*ping*)

P Right. It begins with *L*. It's an adjective for a person who doesn't like studying or working, for example. It's the opposite of *hard-working*.

V (*ping*)

P Right. It begins with *T*. It's a thing which you use in an airport to help you with your cases, or in a supermarket to put your shopping in. Just three seconds left…

V (*ping*)

e 🔊 **3.15** Tell Sts that they are going to listen to Victoria again, but this time they will hear her answers. They must compare their answers to hers.

Play the audio the whole way through for Sts to compare their answers.

Check answers. Find out with a show of hands how many Sts got all six answers correct.

1 bald **2** crowded **3** gloves **4** kitchen **5** lazy **6** trolley

🔊 **3.15**

P OK. It begins with *B*. It's an adjective for a man who has no hair on his head!

V Bald.

P Right. It begins with *C*. It's an adjective. It describes a place where there are a lot of people, for example a restaurant or a beach in the summer.

V Crowded.

P Right. It begins with *G*. They're things which people wear on their hands.

V Gloves.

P Right. It begins with *K*. It's the room where people cook.

V Kitchen.

P Right. It begins with *L*. It's an adjective for someone who doesn't like studying or working, for example. It's the opposite of *hard-working*.

V Lazy.

P Right. It begins with *T*. It's a thing which you use in an airport to help you with your cases, or in a supermarket to put your shopping in…Just three seconds left.

V Trolley!

P Congratulations, Victoria! You've done it!

V Oh, great!

  If there's time, you could get Sts to listen again with script 3.14 on *p.121*, so they can see exactly what they understood / didn't understand. Translate / Explain any new words or phrases.

2 GRAMMAR defining relative clauses

a Focus on the three sentences from the game show and get Sts to complete the gaps.
Check answers.

1 where **2** who **3** which

  Get Sts to focus on the three sentences in **a** and elicit when the words *who*, *which*, and *where* are used.

We use *who* with people, *which* with things, and *where* with places.

b Tell Sts to go to **Grammar Bank 3C** on *p.130*.

Grammar notes

You may want to point out that in conversation and informal writing, native speakers often use *that* rather than *who* and *which*, e.g. *A waiter is somebody that works in a restaurant*.

The relative pronoun can be omitted in sentences like *This is the book I told you about*, where the subject of the relative clause changes. This is not actively focused on at this level, but is probably worth pointing out, as its omission sometimes causes comprehension problems when Sts are reading or listening, especially when they cannot leave it out in their L1.

🔊 **3.16** Focus on the example sentences and play the audio for Sts to listen and repeat. Encourage them to copy the rhythm. Then go through the rules with the class.

Now focus on the information box on *that* and go through it with the class.

Focus on the exercises for **3C** on *p.131*. Sts do the exercises individually or in pairs.

Check answers, getting Sts to read the full sentences.

  After checking the answers to **a**, you could tell Sts to close their books and then ask them *What's an octopus? What's a lawnmower?*, etc. and see if they can remember the definitions.

a

1 An octopus in an animal **which** lives in the sea

2 A lawnmower is a machine **which** cuts the grass.

3 A surgeon is a doctor **who** does operations.

4 A changing room is a room **where** people try on clothes.

5 A porter is the person **who** helps you with your luggage.

6 Garlic is a kind of food **which** keeps vampires away.

7 A garage is a place **where** mechanics repair cars.

b

1 That's the dog which always barks at night.

2 That's the shop where I bought my wedding dress.

3 He's the actor who was in the last James Bond film.

4 They're the children who live next door to me.

5 This is the restaurant where they make great pizza.

6 That's the switch which controls the air conditioning.

7 He's the teacher who teaches my sister.

8 That's the room where we have our meetings.

9 This is the light which is broken.

Tell Sts to go back to the main lesson **3C**.

  If you think Sts need more practice, you may want to give them the **Grammar** photocopiable activity at this point.

3 VOCABULARY & SPEAKING paraphrasing

Vocabulary notes

Native speakers often paraphrase when they can't think of the word they want. This is an essential skill for Sts at any level. Encourage Sts to get into the habit of paraphrasing whenever they need to. You can help them with this by giving definitions when they ask what a word means.

a Focus on the question and go through the possible answers a–c, making sure Sts understand them.

Elicit answers and try to get a mini discussion going about the relative merits of each one.

You may want to point out to Sts that the word to describe option c is *paraphrasing* (the subheading of this section).

b ◗ **3.17** Tell Sts that they are going to learn some useful expressions to help them explain words they don't know. In pairs, Sts complete the eight expressions with the words in the list.

Play the audio for Sts to listen and check.

Check answers.

> **1** somebody **2** something **3** somewhere **4** kind
> **5** opposite **6** like **7** similar **8** example

◗ **3.17**
1 It's somebody who shows you round a city or a museum.
2 It's something which we use to pay, instead of cash.
3 It's somewhere where people go when they want to send a parcel or a letter.
4 It's a kind of fruit. It's long and yellow.
5 It's the opposite of *expensive*.
6 It's like a sweater, but it has buttons.
7 It's similar to a wallet, but it's for a woman.
8 It's a verb. For example, you do this to the TV when you've finished watching something.

---

c Play the audio again, pausing after each sentence, and elicit the word being defined. You could point out that after *somewhere*, you can leave out the relative pronoun *where*.

EXTRA SUPPORT Give Sts time, in pairs, to read the expressions again and work out the word being defined.

> **1** guide
> **2** credit / debit / bank card
> **3** post office
> **4** banana
> **5** cheap
> **6** cardigan
> **7** purse
> **8** turn off

d Focus on the six words and give Sts time in pairs to write definitions.

Elicit some of their answers onto the board.

Possible answers
1 It's somebody who plays music on the radio or in a club.
2 It's somewhere where you can see paintings.
3 It's something which you use to take photos.
4 It's a kind of document which you need if you travel abroad / to another country.
5 For example, you do this when you are on the beach.
6 It's the opposite of *straight*.

e Focus on the instructions and make sure Sts only write five definitions – one for each letter from A to E.

EXTRA SUPPORT Put Sts in pairs to write their definitions. If they can't think of words, you could give them words to use, e.g.:

actor	apple	armchair	abroad
bag	builder	breakfast	bathroom
charger	cold	cook	cousin
dictionary	dangerous	dirty	drive
empty	easy	extrovert	earrings

Monitor and help Sts, correcting any errors with relative clauses.

When Sts are ready, put them in groups of three or four. If Sts wrote their definitions in pairs, then put two pairs together.

Sts read their definitions for their teammates to guess.

When they have finished, you could get a few Sts to read their definitions to the class.

4 PRONUNCIATION silent *e*

Pronunciation notes

Learning how a final *e* after a vowel often changes the pronunciation of this vowel will help Sts to predict the pronunciation of new words.

You may want to point out to Sts that a few common words are exceptions, e.g. *have*, *give*, and *live*, and that with two-syllable words the rule is usually true when the syllable with the silent *e* is stressed, e.g. *decide* and *arrive*, but not *practise*.

a Focus on the **Silent *e*** box and go through it with the class.

Now focus on the two definitions and elicit the words.

> **1** hat **2** hate

Ask the class how the pronunciation of the first word changes when you add the *e*.

> It changes from /æ/ to /eɪ/ (from short to a diphthong). With an *e*, it's the same sound as the letter *a*.

b Put Sts in pairs and get them to practise saying the words. Check answers and make sure Sts know the meaning of the words. Model and drill pronunciation.

bit /bɪt/ – bite /baɪt/
not /nɒt/ – note /nəʊt/
plan /plæn/ – plane /pleɪn/
cut /kʌt/ – cute /kjuːt/

EXTRA SUPPORT Write the words and phonetics on the board to help Sts.

c 3.18 Focus on the instructions, and then play the audio for Sts to listen to the definitions and write the pairs of words.

Get Sts to compare with a partner, and then play the audio again if necessary.

Now play the audio again, pausing after each definition, and elicit the words.

1	**a** win	**b** wine
2	**a** pet	**b** Pete
3	**a** mad	**b** made

3.18
1 **a** It's a verb. It's the opposite of *lose*.
  b It's something you drink. It's alcoholic and it can be red, white, or rosé.
2 **a** It's an animal which people have in their house, for example a cat.
  b It's the short form of the name *Peter*.
3 **a** It's an adjective similar to *crazy*.
  b It's the past tense of the verb *make*.

d Put Sts in pairs and get them to say the words to each other.

e 3.19 Play the audio for Sts to listen and check. Check answers.

kite /kaɪt/   bin /bɪn/   stone /stəʊn/
tap /tæp/   grapes /greɪps/   mug /mʌg/

3.19
See words in Student's Book on *p.27*

5 SPEAKING

Put Sts in pairs, **A** and **B**, and tell them to go to **Communication Split crossword**, **A** on *p.103*, **B** on *p.109*. Go through the instructions carefully and make sure Sts understand what they have to do. Before Sts start, check they understand the meaning of *down* and *across* when asking for the crossword clues.

EXTRA SUPPORT Put Sts in pairs, **A** and **B**. Then put two Sts **A** and two Sts **B** together. Get them to look at the words in their crossword and make sure they know the meanings. Now put Sts back in their original pairs to do the activity.

Sit **A** and **B** face-to-face. **A** asks **B** to define his / her missing words. Then **B** does the same, and they continue taking turns to ask for and give definitions.

When they have finished, get them to compare crosswords.

Function at the restaurant
Vocabulary restaurants: *menu*, *bill*, etc.

Lesson plan

In this lesson Sts practise ordering food and then explaining that there is a problem. The Rob and Jenny story develops. Jenny shows Rob around the New York office, and introduces him to Barbara, the boss. Jenny and Rob go out for lunch, and Holly, Jenny's colleague, joins them and takes over the conversation!

More materials
For teachers
Teacher's Resource Centre
Video Practical English Episode 2
Quick Test 3
File 3 Test
For students
Workbook Practical English 2
Can you remember...? 1–3
Online Practice Practical English 2
Check your progress

OPTIONAL LEAD-IN (BOOKS CLOSED)

Before starting Episode 2, elicit what Sts can remember about Episode 1. Ask *Who's Rob? Where does he work / live? Who's Jenny? Where is she from?*, etc.

Alternatively, you could play the last scene of Episode 1.

1 ▶ IN THE NEW YORK OFFICE

a 🔊 **3.20** Books open. Focus on the photo and ask Sts to guess where Rob is and who the woman is.

Now focus on the instructions and on sentences 1–6. Go through them with Sts and make sure they understand them.

Now play the video / audio once the whole way through, and get Sts to mark the sentences *T* (true) or *F* (false). Make it clear that they don't need to correct the false sentences yet.

Get Sts to compare with a partner, and then check answers.

1 F 2 T 3 F 4 F 5 T 6 F

🔊 **3.20**
J = Jenny, R = Rob, B = Barbara, H = Holly
J Well, I think that's everything. What do you think of the office?
R It's brilliant, and much bigger than our place in London.
J Oh, here's Barbara. Rob, this is Barbara, the editor of the magazine.
B It's good to finally meet you, Rob.
R It's great to be here.
B Is this your first time in New York?
R No, I came here when I was eighteen. But only for a few days.
B Well, I hope you get to know New York much better this time!
J Barbara, I'm going to take Rob out for lunch. Would you like to come with us?
B I'd love to, but unfortunately I have a meeting at one. So, I'll see you later. We're meeting at three, I think.
J That's right.
B Have a nice lunch.
***
H Hey, are you Rob Walker?
R Yes.
H Hi, I'm Holly. Holly Tyler.
R Hello, Holly.
H We're going to be working together.
J Really?
H Didn't Barbara tell you? I'm going to be Rob's photographer!
J Oh, well…We're just going for lunch.
H Cool! I can come with you. I mean, I had a sandwich earlier, so I don't need to eat, but Rob and I can talk. Is that OK?
J Sure.
H So, let's go.

b Play the video / audio again, so Sts can watch or listen a second time and correct the false sentences.

Get Sts to compare with a partner, and then check answers.

1 The New York office is **much bigger.**
3 Rob **has been** to New York before.
4 **Holly** is going to have lunch with Rob and Jenny.
6 Holly wants to go to the restaurant because she **wants to talk to Rob.**

EXTRA SUPPORT If there's time and you are using the video, you could get Sts to watch again with subtitles, so they can see exactly what they understood / didn't understand. Translate / Explain any new words or phrases.

2 ▶ VOCABULARY restaurants

a Put Sts in pairs and tell them to answer the questions in the restaurant quiz.

b 🔊 **3.21** Play the video / audio for Sts to watch or listen and check.

Check answers.

> **What do you call…?**
> 1 the menu
> 2 courses
> 3 a waiter / waitress
> 4 the bill
> 5 the tip
>
> **What do you say…?**
> 6 A table for four, please.
> 7 Can I have the pasta? Could I have the pasta? I'll have the pasta. I'd like the pasta.
> 8 Can I have the bill, please? Could I have the bill, please?

EXTRA IDEA You could do the quiz as a competition. Set a time limit, and the pair with the most correct answers are the winners.

3 ▶ AT THE RESTAURANT

a 🔊 **3.22** Focus on the photo and ask Sts *Where are they?* (at the restaurant) and *Who are the three people?* (Rob, the waitress, and Jenny).

Now either tell Sts to close their books, and write the questions on the board, or get Sts to focus on the two questions and cover the conversation on *p.29*.

Play the video / audio once the whole way through and then check answers. You might want to point out that the waitress has an Australian accent.

> 1 Jenny orders tuna and a green salad. Rob orders steak and fries. Holly doesn't order anything.
> 2 The waitress gives Jenny fries instead of a salad and Rob's steak is rare, not well done.

🔊 **3.22 3.23**
W = waitress, J = Jenny, R = Rob, H = Holly
W Are you ready to order?
J Yes, please. *(repeat)*
W Can I get you something to start with?
J No, thank you. *(repeat)* I'd like the tuna with a green salad. *(repeat)*
W And for you, sir?
R I'll have the steak, please. *(repeat)*
W Would you like that with fries or a baked potato?
R Fries, please. *(repeat)*
W How would you like your steak? Rare, medium, or well done?
R Well done. *(repeat)*
H Nothing for me. *(repeat)*
W OK. And to drink?
J Water, please. *(repeat)*
W Still or sparkling?
J Sparkling. *(repeat)*
***
W The tuna for you, ma'am, and the steak for you, sir.
J I'm sorry, but I asked for a green salad, not fries. *(repeat)*
W No problem. I'll change it.
R Excuse me. *(repeat)*
W Yes, sir?
R Sorry, I asked for my steak well done, and this is rare. *(repeat)*
W I'm really sorry. I'll take it back to the kitchen.

b Focus on the conversation in the chart. Elicit who says the **You hear** phrases (the waitress) and who says the **You say** phrases (the customer, or here Jenny, Rob, and Holly). These phrases will be useful for Sts if they need to order food / a drink, and if they then have problems. You might want to point out the difference between *madam* in British English, which Sts will have seen if they did Elementary, and *ma'am* in American English.

Give Sts a minute to read through the conversation and to think about what the missing words might be. Then play the video / audio again, and get Sts to complete the gaps. Play again if necessary.

Get Sts to compare with a partner, and then check answers.

> 1 order 2 start 3 potato 4 medium 5 drink 6 Still
> 7 sir 8 change 9 take

Go through the conversation line by line with Sts, helping them with any words or expressions they don't understand. Make sure Sts understand that *rare*, *medium*, and *well done* refer to the different ways a steak can be cooked. Also remind Sts of the two kinds of mineral water, *still* and *sparkling*.

c 🔊 **3.23** Now focus on the **You say** phrases and tell Sts they're going to hear the conversation again. They should repeat the **You say** phrases when they hear the beep. Elicit / Explain the two ways of ordering, e.g. *I'd like* (*I would like*) *the tuna with a green salad* or *I'll have the steak, please.* Elicit what Holly says (*Nothing for me.*) and ask Sts why she says that (she had a sandwich earlier).

Play the video / audio, pausing if necessary for Sts to repeat the phrases. Encourage them to copy the rhythm and intonation, but probably not to try to copy Jenny and Holly's American accents. When Jenny pronounces *water* as /ˈwɔːdər/, Sts should use the British English pronunciation of *water* /ˈwɔːtə/.

🔊 **3.23**
Same as script 3.22 with repeat pauses

d Put Sts in pairs, **A** and **B**. **A** is Jenny, Rob, and Holly, and **B** is the waiter / waitress. Get Sts to read the conversation aloud and then swap roles.

e Focus on the instructions. **B** (book open) is the waiter / waitress. **A** (book closed) should decide what to eat and then respond when **B** starts with *Are you ready to order?*. Sts now role-play the conversation.

f When they have finished, they should swap roles.

You could get a few pairs to perform in front of the class.

4 ▶ HOLLY AND ROB MAKE FRIENDS

a ◀)) **3.24** Focus on the question.

Play the video / audio once the whole way through, and then check the answer.

> Rob and Holly enjoy the lunch, but Jenny doesn't.

◀)) **3.24**

H = Holly, R = Rob, J = Jenny, W = waitress

H So tell me, Rob, what are you going to write about?
R Well, to start with, my first impressions of New York. You know, the nightlife, the music, things like that.
H Are you planning to do any interviews?
R I'd like to. Do you have any suggestions?
H Well, I know some great musicians.
R Musicians?
H You know, guys in bands. And I also have some contacts in the theatre and dance.
R That would be great.
H Maybe we could go to a show, and after you could talk to the actors.
R I really like that idea.
W Can I bring you anything else?
J Could we have the check, please?
W Yes, ma'am.
***
W Here's your check.
J Thanks.
***
J Excuse me. I think there's a mistake. We had two bottles of water, not three.
W You're right. I'm really sorry. It's not my day today! I'll get you a new check.
J Thank you.
H We're going to have a fun month, Rob.
R Yeah, I think it's going to be fantastic.
J OK, time to go. You have your meeting…with Barbara at three.
R Oh yeah, right.

b Focus on questions 1–6 and give Sts time to read them.

Before playing the video / audio again, focus on the **British and American English** box and go through it with the class.

Now play the video / audio again, so Sts can watch or listen a second time and answer the questions.

Get Sts to compare with a partner, and then check answers.

> 1 He's going to write about his first impressions of New York, the nightlife, and music.
> 2 Holly says she can introduce him to musicians, and she also knows people in the theatre and dance.
> 3 She says they could go to a show.
> 4 It says three bottles of water, but they only had two.
> 5 Because Rob has a meeting with Barbara (and maybe because she is getting tired of Holly).
> 6 No, she wanted to be alone with Rob.

  If there's time and you are using the video, you could get Sts to watch again with subtitles, so they can see exactly what they understood / didn't understand. Translate / Explain any new words or phrases.

c Focus on the **Social English** phrases. In pairs, get Sts to see if they can remember any of the missing words.

  In pairs, get Sts to complete the phrases before they listen.

d ◀)) **3.25** Play the video / audio for Sts to watch or listen and complete the phrases.

Check answers. If you know your Sts' L1, you could get them to translate the phrases.

> **1** So **2** start **3** suggestions **4** be **5** Could **6** mistake **7** time

◀)) **3.25**

1 So, tell me…
2 Well, to start with…
3 Do you have any suggestions?
4 That would be great.
5 Could we have the check, please?
6 Excuse me, I think there's a mistake.
7 OK, time to go.

Now play the video / audio again, pausing after each phrase, for Sts to watch or listen and repeat.

e Focus on the instructions and make sure Sts understand what they have to do.

Get Sts to compare with a partner, and then check answers.

> **A** 7 **B** 6 **C** 3 **D** 4 **E** 2 **F** 5 **G** 1

Now put Sts in pairs and get them to practise the conversations.

Finally, focus on the **CAN YOU…?** questions and ask Sts if they feel confident they can now do these things. If they feel that they need more practice, tell them to go to *Online Practice* to watch the episode again and practise the language.

G present perfect + *yet, just, already*
V housework, *make* or *do*?
P the letters *y* and *j*

Lesson plan

This lesson presents the present perfect to talk about the recent past, and Sts also learn to use it with *yet, just,* and *already*. Sts who completed *English File* Elementary will have seen the present perfect (though not *yet, just,* and *already*), but for other Sts this will be completely new. The context of the lesson is housework. Sts begin with two articles about housework to read and discuss. There is then a vocabulary focus on common verb phrases for housework, and collocations with *make* and *do*. In a speaking activity, Sts read a questionnaire and discuss who in their country does housework and whether they do any themselves. The grammar is then presented through three short conversations between family members about housework. The pronunciation focus is on the letters *y* and *j*, as in *yet* and *just*. The lesson ends with a listening which gives tips about how to clean quickly and efficiently.

More materials

For teachers

Photocopiables
Grammar present perfect + *yet, just, already* p.181
Vocabulary Housework, *make* and *do*? p.262
(instructions *p.254*)
Communicative Find the response *p.226*
(instructions *p.210*)

For students

Workbook 4A

Online Practice 4A

OPTIONAL LEAD-IN (BOOKS CLOSED)

Write these countries on the board:
CANADA ITALY NORWAY SPAIN UK

Ask Sts to rank them 1–5, with 1 = men do the most housework, and 5 = men do the least housework.

Now tell them the real order according to a 2016 survey.

1 Norway, where men do more housework than any other country in the world
2 Canada
3 Spain
4 UK
5 Italy

Ask Sts if they're surprised by the order.

1 READING & VOCABULARY housework, *make* or *do*?

a Books open. Focus on the task and read the two headlines. Explain / Elicit the meaning of the expression *as good as* (= equally good).

Elicit what the missing words might be.

b Tell Sts to read the two articles to check their answers to **a**. Then they should read the online comments after the articles and match comments A–F to either article 1 or 2. Point out that the first one (*1A*) has been done for them. When Sts have completed the task, get them to compare with a partner.

Check answers.

EXTRA SUPPORT Before Sts read the articles the first time, check whether you need to pre-teach any vocabulary.

a housework
b B 2   C 2   D 1   E 2   F 1

Now put Sts in pairs and get them to discuss which comments they agree with.

Get some feedback.

c Do this as a whole-class activity.

do (housework, sport, the cleaning,)

Deal with any other new vocabulary. Model and drill the pronunciation of any tricky words.

d Tell Sts to go to **Vocabulary Bank** Housework, *make* or *do*? on *p.154*.

Vocabulary notes

Housework

You may want to point out that *wash* and *wash up* are used as normal verbs, (e.g. *I'm going to wash my hair*, etc.), but that when we refer to the housework activity of washing clothes or washing up plates, etc., it is more common to use the phrases *do the washing* and *do the washing-up*.

This is similar to the difference between *swimming* and *go swimming*, focused on in **2A**.

You might also want to tell Sts that in British English *vacuuming* and *hoovering* are synonyms. The word *hoover* comes from the American vacuum cleaner company.

make or do

You could suggest that when Sts aren't sure whether to use *make* or *do*, to bear in mind that *make* often has the meaning of 'creating' something which wasn't there before, e.g. *make dinner, make a noise, make a cake*, etc., whereas *do* has the meaning of fulfilling a task which already exists, e.g. *do an exercise, do housework, do a course*, etc. This rule of thumb is generally true, although there are a few exceptions, e.g. *make the bed*.

Focus on **1 Housework** and get Sts to do **a** individually or in pairs.

4.1 Now do **b**. Play the audio for Sts to listen and check.

Check answers.

4.1

Housework, *make or do?* 1 Housework

7 clean the floor
6 do the ironing
3 do the shopping
10 do the vacuuming
2 do the washing
8 do the washing-up
13 dust the furniture
1 lay the table (opposite *clear*)
15 load the dishwasher (opposite *unload*)
14 make lunch
4 make the bed
11 pick up dirty clothes
5 put away your clothes
12 take out the rubbish
9 tidy your room

Now either use the audio to drill the pronunciation of the verb phrases, or model and drill them yourself. Give further practice of any words and phrases your Sts find difficult to pronounce.

Finally, do **c** and get Sts to cover the phrases and look at the photos. They can test themselves or a partner.

Now focus on **2 *make* or *do*** and get Sts to do **a** individually or in pairs.

4.2 Now do **b**. Play the audio for Sts to listen and check.

Check answers.

4.2

2 *make* or *do*

1 **do** a course
2 **make** a mistake
3 **do** an exam (an exercise, homework)
4 **make** a noise
5 **make** a phone call
6 **do** housework
7 **make** friends
8 **do** sport (or exercise)
9 **make** plans
10 **make** an excuse

Now either use the audio to drill the pronunciation of the phrases, or model and drill them yourself. Give further practice of any words and phrases your Sts find difficult to pronounce.

Finally, do **c** and get Sts to cover the phrases and look at the photos. They can test themselves or a partner.

Focus on **Activation** and put Sts in pairs to test each other. **A** (book open) says a noun and **B** (book closed) says the verb. Make sure they swap roles.

Tell Sts to go back to the main lesson **4A**.

EXTRA SUPPORT If you think Sts need more practice, you may want to give them the **Vocabulary** photocopiable activity at this point.

2 SPEAKING

Focus on the questionnaire and go through the questions, making sure Sts understand all the lexis, e.g. *fair, typical, teenager, argue*, etc.

Now put Sts in pairs and get them to answer the questions.

Get some feedback from various pairs.

3 GRAMMAR present perfect + *yet, just, already*

a Tell Sts to look at the pictures and read the conversations. Then they should complete them with the verbs from the list. Explain that these are past participles. Point out that the first one (*finished*) has been done for them.

EXTRA SUPPORT If your Sts haven't seen the present perfect before, or they've seen it only very briefly, tell them that the past participles are of regular and irregular verbs, and elicit which verbs they are.

Give Sts time to complete the three conversations.

b **4.3** Play the audio for Sts to listen and check.

Check answers, and if you didn't do this before, elicit the infinitive of each verb.

1 finished (finish), started (start), broken (break)
2 made (make), come (come), been (be)
3 done (do), put (put)

4.3

1 **A** Have you *finished* the washing-up?
   B Not yet.
   A Have you started it?
   B Er…yes.
   A What's that noise? Have you broken something?
   B Sorry. Only a glass.
2 **A** What's for dinner?
   B I don't know. I haven't made anything. I've just come home.
   A Is there anything in the fridge?
   B Not much. I haven't been to the supermarket yet.
   A Oh!
   B Maybe you can go?
3 **A** Are you going to take the rubbish out?
   B I've already done it.
   A And have you put a new bag in the bin?
   B No, I couldn't find the bags.

Ask the class the two questions and elicit some answers. You could also tell Sts if you have conversations like this, and who with.

c Focus on the instructions and then give Sts time to match sentences 1–4 to meanings A–D.

Check answers. If you know your Sts' L1, you could elicit the translation of *just, already*, and *yet*. Elicit / Explain that the verbs are in the present perfect.

1 d   2 c   3 b   4 a

! *Just* has other meanings in other contexts, e.g. *only*.

d Tell Sts to go to **Grammar Bank 4A** on *p.132*.

Grammar notes

For some Sts the present perfect may be new. They may have something similar in their L1 or they may not, and the use is likely to be different. It takes time for Sts to learn and use the present perfect correctly, but this use (for things that have happened recently, with no time mentioned) is probably the simplest to understand, and Sts will probably already be used to you asking them, e.g. *Have you finished?*, etc.

Yet / already may not have an exact equivalent in Sts' L1, and the meaning is not that easy to explain, as they are words which simply add emphasis. There is not much difference between *I haven't finished* and *I haven't finished yet*, but adding *yet* implies that you are going to finish.

just + present perfect: This use may be difficult for Sts to assimilate, as it may be expressed in a completely different way in Sts'L1, i.e. with another verb followed by the infinitive. Sts may also have previously met *just* with the meaning *only*. Tell them that the meaning is usually clear from the context.

Lesson **4B** focuses on the present perfect for past experience with *ever / never*, and contrasts it with the past simple. Later in the course (**9B**) Sts are introduced to the present perfect with *for* and *since* for unfinished actions, and this is again contrasted with the past simple in **9C**.

Focus on the example sentences and play both audio 4.4 and 4.5 for Sts to listen and repeat. Encourage them to copy the rhythm. Then go through the rules with the class.

If your Sts are new to the present perfect, when you go to the **Irregular verbs** list on *p.164*, get them to underline or highlight the verbs where the past participle is different from the past simple, e.g. *be, become*, etc.

EXTRA IDEA Get Sts to close their books, and test them on participles which are different from the past simple.

Focus on the exercises for **4A** on *p.133*. Sts do the exercises individually or in pairs.

Check answers, getting Sts to read the full sentences.

> **a** 1 She's bought a new jacket.
> 2 He hasn't found a job yet.
> 3 Have you spoken to Mr Jackson?
> 4 We've found a fantastic hotel.
> 5 They haven't finished eating.
> 6 Have you seen Peter recently?
> 7 Have you done your homework?
> 8 We haven't replied to their email yet.
> **b** 1 I've just had breakfast.
> 2 Have you finished your dinner yet?
> 3 The film has already started.
> 4 I haven't met his girlfriend yet.
> 5 They've just got married.
> 6 He's already gone home.
> 7 We've just spoken to him.
> 8 I haven't read his new book yet.

Tell Sts to go back to the main lesson **4A**.

EXTRA SUPPORT If you think Sts need more practice, you may want to give them the **Grammar** photocopiable activity at this point.

4 PRONUNCIATION & SPEAKING the letters *y* and *j*

> ### Pronunciation notes
> Remind Sts that:
> - the letter *y* at the beginning of a word is always pronounced /j/.
> - the letter *j* is always pronounced /dʒ/.

a 4.6 Focus on the sound pictures and elicit the words and sounds: *yacht* /jɒt/ and *jazz* /dʒæz/.
Play the audio for Sts to listen and repeat.

> **4.6**
> See words and sounds in Student's Book on *p.31*

b 4.7 Before playing the audio, make sure Sts know the meaning of all the words, especially *jaw* (= the parts of your face that move when you talk or eat).
Now play the audio once for Sts just to listen.

> **4.7**
> 1 a yet b jet
> 2 a yes b Jess
> 3 a yours b jaws

Play the audio again, pausing after each word or group of words for Sts to repeat.
Now ask Sts how the letters *y* and *j* are pronounced at the beginning of words.

> At the beginning of a word, *y* = /j/ and *j* = /dʒ/.

c 4.8 Tell Sts they are going to hear three words from **a**. Play the audio, pausing after each word to check the answer.

> **4.8**
> 1 a yet 2 b Jess 3 a yours

EXTRA SUPPORT If this sound is difficult for your Sts, it will help to show them the mouth position. You could model this yourself or use the the Sound Bank videos on the *Teacher's Resource Centre*.

d 4.9 Tell Sts they are going to hear five sentences and they must write them down.
Play the audio the whole way through for Sts just to listen.

> **4.9**
> 1 I've just bought some jeans and a jacket.
> 2 Have you used your new computer yet?
> 3 Jane's really enjoying her Japanese classes.
> 4 Do you usually argue about housework?
> 5 Is John's birthday in June or July?

Now play it again, pausing after each sentence to give Sts time to write.

Check answers by eliciting the sentences onto the board. You may want to point out the hidden /j/ sound in *new*, *computer*, and *argue*.

> See sentences in script 4.9

Finally, get Sts to practise saying the sentences in pairs.

e 4.10 Tell Sts they are going to hear six sound effects of things that have just happened. Point out the example. Put Sts in pairs and tell them first to listen only. Play the audio once the whole way through.

> **4.10**
> (Sound effects to illustrate the following sentences)
> 1 *She's just broken a glass.*
> 2 *They've just got married.*
> 3 *He's just taken a photo.*
> 4 *She's just seen a mouse.*
> 5 *The film has just finished.*
> 6 *A dog has just seen a cat.*

Now play the audio again, pausing after each sound effect for Sts to say a sentence with *just* and the present perfect.
Accept all correct and possible sentences.

> See sentences in script 4.10

 When Sts listen the first time, tell them to make notes only. Then play the audio again, pausing after each sound effect for Sts, in pairs, to write their sentences.

f Tell Sts to go to **Communication Has he done it yet?** on *p.104*. Give them one minute to look at and remember the picture.

Now tell Sts to go to *p.106*. Go through the instructions and point out the example. They should write their seven sentences with either *already* or *yet*.

When Sts have written their sentences, put them into pairs. They read their sentences aloud to each other to see if they have written the same. Monitor to check they are forming the present perfect correctly and are putting *already* and *yet* in the correct place.

Finally, Sts check with the picture to see how many of their sentences were correct.

Get feedback.

Things Max has already done
1 He's already made the bed.
2 He's already had breakfast.
3 He's already had a shower.

Things Max hasn't done yet
1 He hasn't tidied his desk yet.
2 He hasn't taken the dog for a walk yet.
3 He hasn't turned off his computer yet.
4 He hasn't put away his clothes yet.

You could do **c** as a whole-class activity.

Tell Sts to go back to the main lesson **4A**.

5 LISTENING checking hypotheses using background knowledge

a Do this as a whole-class activity.

b Focus on the task and make sure Sts understand all the lexis in the title of the video blog.

Put Sts in pairs and give them time to guess what the missing words in tips 1–7 are.

c 🔊 **4.11** Play the audio for Sts to listen and check.

Get Sts to compare with their partner, and play the audio again if necessary.

Check answers.

1 often   2 right   3 microwave   4 clean   5 their shoes
6 floor   7 to music

🔊 **4.11**

I'm lazy, but I like living in a clean tidy home. Maybe you're the same. It doesn't matter if you live by yourself, with a partner, or with a group of friends. You're always going to have to do some housework. Learn a few cleaning tricks and you can have a clean home – and still have plenty of time to relax and do nothing.
Tip one: Clean quickly, but often.
Clean for just ten minutes twice a day. This gives you time to, for example, load the dishwasher and do one other thing like vacuuming. Set an alarm on your phone to motivate yourself.
Tip two: Keep cleaning products in the right place.
Put cleaning products near the place where you need them. Keep bathroom cleaners in the bathroom, keep bin bags by the bin, and keep dishwasher tablets on top of the dishwasher. Sometimes you don't clean if you can't immediately see what you need, and you don't want to look for it.
Tip three: Clean the microwave regularly.

You probably use this every day and it gets dirty quickly, believe me. But cleaning it is super easy. All you need to do is pour a little water into a microwave-safe bowl, slice a lemon in half and squeeze the juice into the water. Then, put the two halves of the lemon in the bowl and microwave on high for three minutes. Leave the door closed for another five minutes, and then clean the inside with a cloth.
Tip four: Use your dishwasher to clean other things.
If you have a dishwasher, it's probably already your best friend. But did you know that it can clean much more than just kitchen things? You can use it to clean all kinds of things made of plastic like toys, or even flip flops or other plastic shoes, and also for things made of metal like tools, or keys.
Tip five: Tell people to take off their shoes when they come in.
If you hate vacuuming, but you also hate the floor because you don't do the vacuuming, there's an easy solution – tell your housemates and guests to take off their shoes at the front door. And if they forget or refuse, give them the vacuum cleaner.
Tip six: Use your socks to clean the floor.
If you have a hard floor, like wood or stone, for example, make your socks work for you. Take your shoes off, and slide across a different part of your floor each time you move across it. It'll soon be completely clean. Then, just throw your socks in the washing machine.
And finally tip seven: Listen to music while you clean.
Sometimes you really need to do some housework that you hate, like ironing or cleaning the bathroom. Put on your favourite playlist and focus on the music, not the boring housework.
And one last word – many people say that lazy people are often the best employees because they find the most efficient way to complete a task. That's the way you need to think when you're cleaning. Good luck!

d Now tell Sts they are going to listen again and they need to answer questions 1–7. Tell them that each question is linked to a tip in **b**, so for questions 6 and 7, they must quickly look at the tip again.

Give Sts time to read the questions and make sure they understand all the lexis, e.g. *flip-flops, tools*, etc.

Play the audio again, pausing after each tip to give Sts time to answer the question.

Get Sts to compare with a partner, and then play the audio again if necessary.

Check answers.

1 For ten minutes twice a day. Set an alarm on your phone to motivate yourself.
2 Near the place where you need them. If you don't know where the product is, you don't want to look for it.
3 Pour a little water into a microwave-safe bowl, slice a lemon in half and squeeze the juice into the water. Then, put the two halves of the lemon in the bowl and microwave on high for three minutes. Leave the door closed for another five minutes, and then clean the inside with a cloth.
4 Because you can clean them in the dishwasher.
5 Give them the vacuum cleaner.
6 Hard floors, like wood or stone. Throw your socks in the washing machine when you finish.
7 Ironing and cleaning the bathroom.

e Do this as a whole-class activity and answer the questions yourself.

G present perfect or past simple? (1)
V shopping
P *c* and *ch*

Lesson plan

In this lesson Sts look at the present perfect for past experience with *ever / never*, and contrast it with the past simple. The context of the lesson is shopping. Sts begin with a speaking activity about global chain stores, and a vocabulary focus on shopping. This is followed by a pronunciation focus on different ways of pronouncing the letters *c* and *ch*. Sts then listen to five people answering questions about shopping, and through this the grammar is presented. Then in speaking, Sts have a mingle activity where they ask other Sts some shopping-related *Have you ever…?* questions, which they then follow up with past simple questions. Finally, the lesson ends with an article explaining why we often find areas where there are a lot of the same kinds of shops.

More materials
For teachers
Photocopiables
Grammar present perfect or past simple? (1) *p.182*
Vocabulary Shopping *p.263* (instructions *p.254*)
Communicative Have you ever…? *p.227*
(instructions *p.210*)
For students
Workbook 4B
Online Practice 4B

OPTIONAL LEAD-IN (BOOKS CLOSED)

Quickly revise vocabulary for clothes. Tell Sts to describe what other Sts are wearing or to test each other using the **Vocabulary Bank** on *p.151*.

1 SPEAKING & VOCABULARY shopping

a Books open. Focus on the task and make sure Sts understand what a *global chain store* is.

Put Sts in pairs and get them to discuss questions 1–7.

Check answers for questions 1 and 2, and get some feedback from various pairs for questions 3–7.

1 Zara sells clothes and accessories (also Zara Home, which sells things for the house); Apple sells technology; Topshop sells clothes and accessories; The Body Shop sells products for skin and body (e.g. face cream); H&M sells clothes and accessories; Nike sells sportswear; IKEA sells things for the house; Uniqlo sells clothes and accessories.

2 Zara is from Spain; Apple is from the USA; Topshop is from the UK; The Body Shop is from the UK; H&M is from Sweden; Nike is from the USA; IKEA is from Sweden; Uniqlo is from Japan.

b Tell Sts to go to **Vocabulary Bank Shopping** on *p.155* and do **1 In a shop or store**.

Focus on **a** and get Sts to do it individually or in pairs.

4.12   Now do **b**. Play the audio for Sts to listen and check. Check answers.

4.12
Shopping 1 In a shop or store
3   basket
1   changing rooms
10   (self-service) checkout
5   customer
11   receipt
9   shelves
7   shop assistant
4   shopping bag
2   the sales
6   till
8   trolley

Now either use the audio to drill the pronunciation of the words, or model and drill them yourself. Point out to Sts that the *p* in *receipt* is silent. Give further practice of any words your Sts find difficult to pronounce.

EXTRA SUPPORT   Get Sts to cover the words and look at the photos. They can test themselves or each other.

Focus on **c** and get Sts to match the sentences.

4.13   Now do **d**. Play the audio for Sts to listen and check.

Check answers. Model and drill the pronunciation of *suit* /suːt/.

1 d   2 e   3 a   4 b   5 c   6 f

4.13
2 Shopping online
1   Can I help you?
    I'm just looking, thank you.
2   What size are you?
    I'm a medium.
3   Can I try on this shirt?
    Yes, the changing rooms are over there.
4   This shirt doesn't fit me.
    It's too big for me.
5   That jacket really suits you!
    You always look good in red.
6   I'm going to take these trousers back. They're too short.

Now do **2 Online**. Focus on **a** and get Sts to read the text and complete the gaps.

4.14 Now do **b**. Play the audio for Sts to listen and check.

Check answers. Give further practice of any words your Sts find difficult to pronounce.

2 account   3 item   4 basket   5 checkout   6 delivery
7 next-day   8 debit   9 payment   10 auction

4.14

2 Shopping online
All major chain stores and many other shops sell online, and a lot of people prefer going to their website than the actual shop. The first time you use a site, you usually have to create an account, where you give your personal details. Then you choose what you want to buy, and click on each item. Everything you buy goes in your basket, usually at the top right of the page. When you are ready to pay, you click on 'proceed to payment'. You then have to give the delivery address where you want them to send your things. You can usually pay extra for next-day delivery – standard delivery is sometimes free. Then you choose how you want to pay, for example with a credit or debit card or with PayPal, and give your payment details, for example your credit card number and expiry date. Finally, you confirm your payment and receive a reference number and a confirmation email. And then you wait! Many people also buy and sell things online at auction sites, like eBay.

Finally, focus on **Activation**. Put Sts in pairs to discuss the questions.

Get some feedback from various pairs.

Tell Sts to go back to the main lesson **4B**.

EXTRA SUPPORT If you think Sts need more practice, you may want to give them the **Vocabulary** photocopiable activity at this point.

2 PRONUNCIATION *c and ch*

a Write on the board CUT and CENT and elicit their pronunciations. Highlight that *c* can be pronounced /k/ or /s/.

Focus on the two sound pictures and elicit the words and sounds: *key* /kiː/ and *snake* /sneɪk/. Give Sts a few minutes to put the words in the correct row. Encourage them to say the words aloud as they do this.

Get Sts to compare with a partner.

b **4.15** Play the audio for Sts to listen and check. Check answers.

4.15
key /k/ account, auction, click, clothes, credit card, customer
snake /s/ city, proceed, receipt, shopping centre

Play the audio again, pausing after each word or group of words for Sts to repeat.

Then focus on the question and check the answer.

c is usually /s/ before *e* and *i*, e.g. *centre, city*, etc.

c **4.16** Focus on the first question and elicit the answer.

The letters *ch* are usually pronounced /tʃ/.

Now play the audio for Sts to listen to the words and circle the ones that are pronounced differently.

Check answers.

chemist's and *cash machine* are pronounced differently. In *chemist's* the letters *ch* are pronounced /k/ and in *machine* they are pronounced /ʃ/.

4.16
See words in Student's Book on *p.32*

EXTRA CHALLENGE Elicit some more words where *ch* is pronounced /k/ or /ʃ/. Sts should know, e.g. *architect, mechanic, Christmas* (*ch* = /k/), and *chef, moustache* (*ch* = /ʃ/). You may want to tell them that words where *ch* is pronounced /ʃ/ are mostly of French origin.

d Get Sts to practise saying all the words in **a** and **c**.

EXTRA SUPPORT If these sounds are difficult for your Sts, it will help to show them the mouth position. You could model this yourself or use the the Sound Bank videos on the *Teacher's Resource Centre*.

3 GRAMMAR present perfect or past simple? (1)

a **4.17** Tell Sts that they're going to listen to three people being interviewed about shopping. Tell them the first time they listen they just need to write down the names of shops in **1a** that the people mention.

Play the audio once the whole way through.

Check answers.

EXTRA SUPPORT Read through the script and decide if you need to pre-teach any new lexis before Sts listen.

Kate: H&M
Rosie: Top Shop and The Body Shop
John: Uniqlo

4.17
I = interviewer, K = Kate
I   Have you been to a chain store recently?
K   Yes, I have. I went to H&M three weeks ago.
I   And what did you buy?
K   I bought a skirt. It's a long, black skirt.
I   Are you happy with it?
K   Yes, yes, and er...it was very cheap because it was in the sale. And it suits me.
I = interviewer, R = Rosie
I   Have you been shopping for clothes recently?
R   Yes, I went shopping at the weekend with my friends.
I   Where did you go?
R   We went to the city centre, to Princes Street – that's where we always go.
I   Did you buy anything?
R   I tried on a few things in Topshop, but in the end there wasn't anything I liked. But I did get something in The Body Shop. There's a shopping centre just off Princes Street, and there's a Body Shop there, and I bought some strawberry shower gel. I really like it.
I = interviewer, J = John
I   Have you ever bought anything from Uniqlo?
J   Not from the shop, because there isn't one where I live, but I sometimes buy stuff on their website.
I   What was the last thing you bought there?
J   It was a few months ago. I got some T-shirts. I always get them there; they do really good, cheap T-shirts.
I   How many did you get?
J   Five, I think. Yes, five.
I   And are you happy with them?
J   Yes. They were about five pounds each, and delivery was another five pounds, so that was thirty pounds for five T-shirts.

b Before playing the audio again, get Sts, in pairs, to talk about what they can remember for the two questions.

Play the audio again. Pause it after each speaker to give Sts time to answer the questions.

Get Sts to compare with a partner, and then check answers.

> **Speaker 1 (Kate):** a skirt; yes
> **Speaker 2 (Rosie):** strawberry shower gel; yes
> **Speaker 3 (John):** five T-shirts; yes

c ◆ **4.18** Tell Sts to look at the beginning of Kate's interview and think what the missing verbs might be.

Play the audio for Sts to listen and complete the task.

Check answers.

> **1** Have…been **2** have **3** went **4** did…buy **5** bought

◆ **4.18**
A Have you been to a chain store recently?
B Yes, I have. I went to H&M three weeks ago.
A And what did you buy?
B I bought a skirt.

d Do this as a whole-class activity.

> present perfect; past simple

e Tell Sts to go to **Grammar Bank 4B** on *p.132*.

> ### Grammar notes
>
> This use of the present perfect, to talk about past experiences when we don't mention a time, is usually quite easy for Sts to understand. However, they may have problems with the switch to the past simple to talk about the specific experience / time, as in some Sts' L1, they may be able to continue with the present perfect.
>
> If this is your Sts' first exposure to the contrast, don't expect too much oral accuracy yet. The contrast between present perfect and past simple for unfinished and finished actions is also studied in **9C**.

Focus on the example sentences and play both audio ◆ **4.19** and ◆ **4.20** for Sts to listen and repeat. Encourage them to copy the rhythm. Then go through the rules with the class.

Now focus on the ***been* and *gone*** box and go through it with the class.

Then focus on the exercises for **4B** on *p.133*. Sts do the exercises individually or in pairs.

Check answers, getting Sts to read the full sentences.

> **a 1** Have…bought **2** 've…wanted **3** haven't read
> **4** haven't been **5** Has… lived **6** 've been **7** hasn't flown
> **8** hasn't met **9** Have…eaten **10** has…told
> **b 1** went **2** was **3** Did…buy **4** got **5** Were
> **6** Have…bought **7** gave
> **c 1** gone **2** been **3** been **4** gone **5** been

Tell Sts to go back to the main lesson **4B**.

 If you think Sts need more practice, you may want to give them the **Grammar** photocopiable activity at this point.

f Tell Sts they are now going to answer the same questions as the people in the interview in **3a**.

Put Sts in pairs and get them to interview each other.

Get some feedback from various pairs.

4 SPEAKING

a Focus on the instructions. Do question 1 with the whole class and elicit the missing past participles (*bought* and *sold*). Sts should complete questions 2–6 with the missing participles.

Check answers.

> **2** bought **3** got **4** lost **5** tried **6** had

b Focus on the follow-up question(s) after each present perfect question in **a** and point out that they are in the past simple.

Get Sts to interview you with the first two or three questions.

Finally, get Sts to stand up and move round the class. When somebody answers *Yes, I have* to the present perfect question, Sts should ask the follow-up questions.

Get some feedback from the class.

5 READING understanding a theory

a Focus on the instructions. Then read the introduction as a class and elicit some answers.

b Do this as a whole-class activity.

Elicit some ideas from the class, but <u>don't</u> tell them if they are correct.

c Tell Sts to read the article and check their answer to **b**. Tell them not to worry about the gaps.

Check the answer.

 Before Sts read the article the first time, check whether you need to pre-teach any vocabulary.

> The second situation because nobody needs to walk more than 250 metres for an ice cream.

d Now tell Sts to read the article again and complete the gaps with phrases A–D.

Get Sts to compare with a partner, and then check answers.

> **1** B **2** C **3** D **4** A

Deal with any other new vocabulary. Model and drill the pronunciation of any tricky words.

e Do the first question as a whole-class activity. Focus on the pronunciation of *half* /hɑːf/ and *halves* /hɑːvz/.

> half

Now put Sts in pairs and get them to work out the plural of the nouns in the list.

Check answers, making sure Sts know what all the words mean.

> leaves, lives, knives, shelves, wives

f Do this as a whole-class activity.

G *something, anything, nothing,* etc.
V adjectives ending *-ed* and *-ing: bored, boring,* etc.
P /e/, /əʊ/, and /ʌ/

Lesson plan

In this lesson Sts learn how to use *something, anything, nothing,* etc. These words will be familiar to Sts by this stage, but here their grammar is focused on in detail. The context is the weekend. The lesson begins with Sts reading an article about the fact that many people on social media invent what they did at the weekend in order to make it sound more exciting. Then in Vocabulary, Sts focus on the difference between *-ed* and *-ing* adjectives. This is followed by the grammar focus, and then Sts focus on three vowel sounds in order to be able to pronounce the key grammar expressions correctly. Sts then answer questions about their own weekends, with one of their answers being invented. The lesson ends with a video listening about the history and possible future of the weekend.

More materials
For teachers
Photocopiables
Grammar something, anything, nothing, etc. *p.183*
Communicative The same or different? *p.228*
(instructions *p.211*)
Teacher's Resource Centre
Video The history of the weekend
For students
Workbook 4C
Online Practice 4C

OPTIONAL LEAD-IN (BOOKS CLOSED)
Tell Sts that you're going to describe your last weekend, but that one detail will be false, and that they have to guess which detail it is. The detail can be as easy or hard to spot as you like. (Sts do this themselves later in the lesson, so don't ask them to do it now.)

1 READING

a Books open. Focus on the instructions and make sure Sts understand the word *tweet* (= a message sent using Twitter).

Give Sts time to read the four tweets and then ask them the question as a whole class.

b Focus on the article and tell Sts to read it first, then read the tweets again, and answer the questions.

Get Sts to compare with a partner, and elicit some opinions on which tweets probably aren't true.

EXTRA SUPPORT Before Sts read the article the first time, check whether you need to pre-teach any vocabulary.

c Go through 1–6 with the class, making sure Sts understand all the lexis, e.g. *fake tan.*

Get Sts to read the article again and correct the wrong information.

Get Sts to compare with a partner, and then check answers.

1 One in **five** people sometimes lie about their lives on social media.
2 When people read about what their friends are doing, they are **jealous of** them.
3 People invent stories about their weekend because they want their **colleagues or school friends** to think they have exciting lives.
4 Some people put on fake tan on Sundays so that people at work think **they've had a weekend away in the sun**.
5 Young **men** are the biggest liars.
6 People's online lives are **different from** their real lives.

Deal with any other new vocabulary. Model and drill the pronunciation of any tricky words.

d Put Sts in pairs and get them to discuss the two questions. Get some feedback from various pairs.

2 VOCABULARY adjectives ending *-ed* and *-ing*

Vocabulary notes

Several common adjectives in English have two forms with different meanings, e.g. *tired* and *tiring*. The *-ed* form has a passive meaning, and describes a person who feels this way. The *-ing* form has an active meaning, and describes the person or thing that produces the feeling.

It is important to highlight that we use *-ed* adjectives mainly for people because they refer to feelings, e.g. *I'm tired.* We use *-ing* adjectives for things (and sometimes people) which produce the feeling, e.g. *Driving at night is tiring.*

It is also useful to point out that although the majority of adjectives that end in *-ed* also exist ending in *-ing*, there are some which don't, e.g. *I'm feeling stressed. My job is very stressful.* NOT *My job is very stressing.*

a Focus on the two highlighted words in the article and elicit the answers to the questions. You could tell Sts that a person can also be boring, e.g. *My neighbour is a very boring man.*

1 bored   2 boring

b 🔊 **4.21** Get Sts to read questions 1–6 and circle the correct adjective.

Play the audio for Sts to listen and check.

Check answers, making sure that Sts understand the meaning of all the adjectives.

! Be careful with *excited / exciting.* It is a false friend in some languages.

1 **a** boring   **b** bored
2 **a** depressed   **b** depressing
3 **a** relaxing   **b** relaxed
4 **a** interesting   **b** interested
5 **a** excited   **b** exciting
6 **a** frightened   **b** frightening

🔊 **4.21**

1 a Do you think Sundays are usually boring?
  b Are you bored with your job or studies?
2 a What kind of weather makes you feel depressed?
  b Do you think the news is always depressing?
3 a What activities do you find relaxing?
  b Do you usually feel relaxed at the end of the weekend?
4 a Have you read any interesting articles or books recently?
  b What sports are you interested in?
5 a Are you excited about your next holiday?
  b Are you doing anything exciting next weekend?
6 a What were you frightened of when you were a child?
  b Do you find storms frightening?

Drill the pronunciation of the adjectives. Remind Sts that the *-ed* is pronounced in the same way as regular past verbs, i.e. /t/, /d/, or /ɪd/.

EXTRA CHALLENGE You could elicit / teach some more *-ed* / *-ing* adjectives, e.g. *surprised* / *surprising*, *disappointed* / *disappointing*, etc.

c Now put Sts in pairs and get them to ask and answer the questions in **b**. They should give extra information when possible.
Get some feedback from the class.

3 GRAMMAR *something, anything, nothing,* etc.

a Focus on the instructions and make sure Sts know what a *hashtag* is (= a word or phrase with the symbol # in front of it, included in some messages sent using Twitter so that you can search for all messages with the same subject). You might want to point out that in tweets, words like articles, prepositions, and subjects are often left out.
Give Sts time to complete the hashtags.
Check answers.

> 1 badweekend 2 goodweekend 3 badweekend

b Focus on the instructions and give Sts a few moments to complete the rules.
Check answers.

> 1 things 2 places 3 people

c Tell Sts to go to **Grammar Bank 4C** on *p.132*.

Grammar notes

Sts may have problems with the negative form. The typical mistakes are:

1 using *nobody* / *nothing* / *nowhere* with a negative verb, e.g. ~~I didn't see nobody~~. Highlight that you cannot use a 'double negative' in English.
2 using *anybody* / *anything* / *anywhere* in one-word answers to convey a negative meaning, e.g. *Who did you see?* ~~Anybody~~.
3 using *anybody* / *anything* / *anywhere* as the subject of a negative verb, e.g. ~~Anybody didn't invite him~~.

To talk about people there are two alternative forms: *-body* and *-one*, e.g. *somebody* / *someone*. They are identical in meaning. You could point out that *no one* is usually written as two words.

Something (like *some*) is also used in questions to make an offer or request, e.g. *Would you like something to drink? Could you ask somebody to help me?* To avoid overloading Sts, it may be best to focus on this rule only if Sts ask.:

🔊 **4.22** Focus on the example sentences and play the audio for Sts to listen and repeat. Encourage them to copy the rhythm. Then go through the rules with the class.
Now focus on the ***any, anything,* etc. + positive verb** box and go through it with the class.
Then focus on the exercises for **4C** on *p.133*. Sts do the exercsies individually or in pairs.
Check answers, getting Sts to read full sentences in **a** and **c**.

> a
> 1 anybody 2 Somebody 3 somewhere 4 nothing
> 5 anybody 6 somewhere 7 something 8 nobody
> 9 Anything 10 nowhere
> b
> 1 Nothing 2 Nowhere 3 Nobody
> c
> 1 I didn't do anything. 2 I didn't go anywhere.
> 3 I didn't see anybody.

Tell Sts to go back to the main lesson **4C**.

EXTRA SUPPORT If you think Sts need more practice, you may want to give them the **Grammar** photocopiable activity at this point.

4 PRONUNCIATION /e/, /əʊ/, and /ʌ/

a Focus on the three sound pictures and elicit the words and sounds: *egg* /e/, *phone* /əʊ/, and *up* /ʌ/.
Focus on sentences 1–6 and the pink letters. Give Sts, in pairs, a few minutes to say them out loud to each other and decide which sound they are (a, b, or c). You could do the first one as a class.

b 🔊 **4.23** Play the audio for Sts to listen and check.
Check answers.

> 1 b 2 c 3 a 4 c 5 a 6 b

🔊 **4.23**

1 b Nobody knows where he goes.
2 c Somebody's coming to lunch.
3 a I never said anything.
4 c I've done nothing since Sunday.
5 a Don't tell anybody about the message.
6 b There's nowhere to go except home.

Play the audio again, pausing after each sentence for Sts to listen and repeat.
Give Sts time to practise saying the sentences.
Finally, get individual Sts to say them out loud.

EXTRA SUPPORT If these sounds are difficult for your Sts, it will help to show them the mouth position. You could model this yourself or use the the Sound Bank videos on the *Teacher's Resource Centre*.

c 🔊 **4.24** Tell Sts they are going to hear a question and they must answer it first with a one-word negative answer with *No-*, and then with a full sentence using a negative verb. Point out the example. You might want to stress that this is a drill, so Sts must always answer in the negative and not think about themselves.

Play the audio, pausing after each question to give Sts time to respond.

1 What did you buy? (*pause*) Nothing. I didn't buy anything.
2 Where did you go? (*pause*) Nowhere. I didn't go anywhere.
3 Who did you see? (*pause*) Nobody. I didn't see anybody.
4 What did you eat? (*pause*) Nothing. I didn't eat anything.
5 Who did you speak to? (*pause*) Nobody. I didn't speak to anybody.
6 Where did you walk? (*pause*) Nowhere. I didn't walk anywhere.
7 Who did you meet? (*pause*) Nobody. I didn't meet anybody.
8 What did you say? (*pause*) Nothing. I didn't say anything.

Then repeat the activity, eliciting responses from individual Sts.

EXTRA SUPPORT Write NOTHING, NOBODY, NOWHERE, and I DIDN'T…ANY- on the board to give Sts something to focus on and to help elicit the response.

5 SPEAKING

a Tell Sts to look at all the questions in *Did you have a good weekend?*. They must think about their answers, and they must tell the truth when answering all the questions except for one. This 'lie' must make their weekend sound very exciting.

b Now put Sts in pairs and get them to interview each other.

Monitor and help when necessary. Before Sts swap roles, the student asking the questions should try to guess the lie.

Get feedback from the class.

6 ▶ VIDEO LISTENING

a Tell Sts they are going to watch a documentary *The history of the weekend*.

Give Sts time to read questions 1–10, making sure they understand all the lexis.

Tell Sts they will watch twice. The first time they just need to mark each sentence *T* (true) or *F* (false).

Now play the video once the whole way through.

Get Sts to compare with a partner, and then play the video again for Sts to correct the false sentences. Check answers.

EXTRA SUPPORT Read through the script and decide if you need to pre-teach any new lexis before Sts watch.

1 T
2 T
3 F (They asked factory owners for **half** of Saturday off.)
4 T
5 F (They closed their factories at **2** o'clock on Saturdays)
6 T
7 F (St Mark's football club became Manchester **City**.)
8 F (By the **1960s** most people had a two-day weekend.)
9 T
10 F (Most British workers think a three-day weekend **would** make people happier.)

The history of the weekend

Hi, I'm Karen. Welcome to my home town, Manchester. Manchester is a city in the north west of England.

When you think of Manchester, you probably think of our football teams, but there is a lot more to the city.

This is the Manchester Museum of Science and Industry. I've come here today, because I'm going to find out about the city's link to the British weekend. Like many good ideas, it started right here in Manchester.

To us, the weekend is part of our routine and we can't imagine life without it. But, there was a time when working people didn't really get a weekend.

In the nineteenth century, thousands of people left their homes in the country to find work in the city. Manchester became the first industrial city and it was the home of the cotton industry.

Until eighteen forty-three, people worked for six days – from Monday to Saturday – and had a day of rest on Sunday, when they went to church. The work – like here in a cotton mill – was hard and often dangerous. But in the eighteen forties, a group of men began to ask local factory owners to give people an extra half day off on Saturday afternoon.

One of these men, Robert Lowes, was the great, great grandfather of the British actor, Sir Ian McKellen. Lowes and his colleagues had three reasons for this change.

The first reason was commercial. When people worked from Monday to Saturday, they had no time to spend their money, because shops were shut on Sunday. The second reason was religious. People were tired from the working week, so they didn't always go to church on Sundays. The last reason was economic. When people had more time off, they could rest more, be healthier and work harder during the week.

In eighteen forty-three, Lowes and his colleagues persuaded many of Manchester's factory owners to close their factories at two o'clock on Saturday. By the eighteen seventies, all workers had the same one-and-a-half-day weekend.

The extra half day made a big difference to people and to society. With more free time, people could relax, shop and watch and play sports.

In fact, Manchester's love of football began at this time; in eighteen seventy-eight Newton Heath football club began and two years later St Mark's Football club was formed. Newton Heath became Manchester United. And St Mark's became Manchester City.

The British weekend has continued to change and, by the nineteen sixties, we had a two-day weekend.

Today we enjoy a very different weekend to our ancestors. We now watch and play sports. We go to the cinema. We eat out in restaurants. Or we go to shopping centres like this one – the Arndale Centre – because in the nineteen nineties the law changed and shops started to open on Sundays.

But all these changes haven't been good for everyone. Some people, shop assistants for example, have to work at the weekend and are not paid any extra.

Maybe our working week is going to change again to improve our quality of life. One suggestion is that we make the working week four days and increase the weekend to three days. In theory, this would be better for the economy, because more people would have a job, and we would also spend more time with our families.

Seventy-one percent of British workers think Britain would be a happier place with a three-day weekend.

Until that happens, have a good weekend – a two-day weekend!

EXTRA SUPPORT If there's time, you could get Sts to watch again with subtitles, so they can see exactly what they understood / didn't understand. Translate / Explain any new words or phrases.

b Put Sts in pairs or small groups and get them to discuss the questions. Make sure they understand what a 'four-day week' is. Monitor and help if necessary.

Get some feedback. You could tell the class what you think of the idea of a 'four-day week'.

EXTRA IDEA Do the last question as a whole-class activity.

For instructions on how to use these pages, see *p.40*.

More materials
For teachers
Teacher's Resource Centre
Video Can you understand these people? 3&4
Quick Test 4
File 4 Test
For students
Online Practice Check your progress

GRAMMAR

1 b   2 c   3 a   4 b   5 c   6 a   7 b   8 a   9 a   10 c
11 a   12 c   13 b   14 b   15 b

VOCABULARY

a
1 in   2 for   3 for   4 on   5 for
b
1 do   2 make   3 do   4 do   5 make
c
1 lay   2 washing   3 try on   4 receipt   5 fit   6 Gate
7 trolley   8 check-in   9 Terminal   10 lifts
d
1 boring   2 relaxed   3 exciting   4 depressed   5 interested

PRONUNCIATION

c
1 trolley /ɒ/   2 guide /g/   3 who /h/
4 clothes /əʊ/   5 chain /eɪ/
d
1 departures   2 arrive   3 opposite   4 somebody
5 exciting

CAN YOU understand this text?

a
seven ways
b
1 Every three months
2 It's a combination of *video* and *blog*.
3 A noun
4 Italian
5 To describe new technology
6 Newspaper

▶ CAN YOU understand these people?

1 b   2 c   3 c   4 a   5 c

◀) 4.25
1
I = interviewer, S = Sean
I   When was the last time you were at an airport?
S   Um, about a month ago.
I   Were you going somewhere or meeting someone?
S   I was meeting, um, my mother, who was, er, she arrived at midnight, coming back from Tenerife.
2
I = interviewer, Su = Susie
I   Do you have any plans for tonight?
Su Er, yes, I do have plans for tonight. I'm going to a party with some friends.
3
I = interviewer, C = Caroline
I   What housework do you hate doing?
C   I hate cleaning the bathroom, that's my least favourite job around the house.
I   Is there anything you don't mind doing?
C   I don't mind cleaning the kitchen, because there's usually a lot of food to eat.
4
I = interviewer, A = Albert
I   Have you ever bought something online and had a problem?
A   I, I bought clothes online that didn't fit, but that's about it.
5
I = interviewer, M = Mick
I   How organized are you?
M   Er, not very. Um, I tend to be fairly disorganized, but still get things done.
I   Have you ever missed a train or a flight?
M   Yes, yes. I was flying to Poland and didn't wake up in the morning, and got to the gate as the flight was leaving.

5A I want it NOW!

Lesson plan

In this lesson Sts revise comparative adjectives, and learn to use comparative adverbs and the structure (*not*) *as…as* to compare things. The context is some new information based on recent research which shows how fast the pace of life has become in recent years. Sts start by answering a questionnaire about how fast their life is and then read an article and infographic about the effect on us of the increase in the pace of life. This is followed by Vocabulary, which focuses on types of numbers, such as fractions, dates, percentages, etc., which Sts have just seen in the infographic. The grammar is then presented and practised, and there is a pronunciation focus on the /ə/ sound in unstressed syllables and words. Sts then listen to five people talking about one aspect of their lives that has changed over the last three years as they either spend more or less time on it. Sts then answer the same questions about their own lives.

More materials
For teachers
Photocopiables
Grammar comparative adjectives and adverbs, *as…as p.184*
Communicative Which do you prefer? Why? *p.229* (instructions *p.211*)
For students
Workbook 5A
Online Practice 5A

OPTIONAL LEAD-IN (BOOKS CLOSED)

Write on the board:

WORKING / STUDYING   EATING   SLEEPING   RELAXING

In pairs, Sts say how long they spend doing these things in a typical day.

Get feedback and ask Sts if they think they have enough free time.

1 READING & SPEAKING scanning for data (facts and numbers)

a Books open. Focus on the questionnaire and make sure Sts understand the title. Then go through the questions. Check that Sts understand *get impatient, feel frustrated*, and *get irritable*.

Focus on the task. Tell Sts to answer with *Yes, often / sometimes*, or *No, never*, and then explain why, or give examples if they can. They should also make a note of their partner's answers, as they will need them later.

Put Sts in pairs and get them to ask and answer the questions.

Get some feedback from various pairs.

EXTRA SUPPORT Get Sts to interview you first, so you can model how you want them to answer.

b Tell Sts to go to **Communication How fast is your life?** on *p.109*.

Sts calculate their partner's score and then tell him / her what it is.

Sts then read the meaning of their own result. While they read, go round monitoring and helping with any vocabulary problems, e.g. *in the slow lane, pace of life, rushing*, etc.

When Sts have read their result, they tell their partner if they agree with it.

Get some feedback from various pairs.

Finally, with a show of hands, find out how many people belong to each category (slow, medium, and fast).

Tell Sts to go back to the main lesson **5A**.

c Focus on the article and the task. Give Sts time to read the article, including all the information in the infographic, and answer the question.

Get Sts to compare with a partner, and then check the answer.

technology / the internet

EXTRA SUPPORT Before Sts read the article the first time, check whether you need to pre-teach any vocabulary.

d Focus on the instructions and stress that Sts have exactly two minutes to complete the task.

When the two minutes are up, get Sts to compare with a partner, and then check answers.

1	Impatient
2	Mobile phone apps like Tinder
3	10%
4	More than 125 million
5	Three out of five
6	A 'like'
7	Six minutes
8	Waiting for a replacement credit card

Deal with any new vocabulary. Model and drill the pronunciation of any tricky words.

e Give Sts time to find six technology words in the article. Tell them there are more than six possible answers.

Check answers.

Possible answers
broadband, searches, downloads, apps, Google, web page, site, a 'like', posting

EXTRA CHALLENGE Ask Sts if they know any more words on the topic of technology, e.g. *USB, a mouse, a laptop*, etc.

Deal with any other new vocabulary. Model and drill the pronunciation of any tricky words.

f Focus on the three questions and make sure Sts understand all the lexis, e.g. *statistics*, *time-wasting*, and *annoy*.

Put Sts in pairs and give them time to ask and answer the questions.

You might want to remind Sts to use *fewer* with countable nouns and *less*, with uncountable nouns e.g. *fewer people*, *less time*, etc.

Get feedback from various pairs. You could have a class discussion for question 3.

2 VOCABULARY types of numbers

Vocabulary notes

You might want to highlight that:

- we can use the article *a* or the number *one* when saying numbers, e.g. *one hundred / a hundred*
- the same is true with fractions, e.g. you can say *a third* or *one third*. All fractions are expressed with ordinal numbers, except *a half* and *a quarter* (not a *second* or a *fourth*)
- we don't add an *-s* to *hundred*, *thousand*, or *million*
- with decimals, e.g. *3.14*, we use *point*, not *dot* (unlike with email addresses)

a Focus on the instructions and elicit / explain what an *infographic* is (= information or data that is shown in a chart, diagram, etc. so that it is easy to understand).

Put Sts in pairs and get them to tell each other the green numbers in the top row only.

b **5.1** Tell Sts they will now hear the whole sentence, not just the numbers. Play the audio for Sts to listen and check.

Check answers by eliciting the numbers.

1 a hundred and twenty-five million
2 fifty per cent
3 a third

5.1

More than **a hundred and twenty-five million** Google searches are made every hour.
Fifty per cent of users leave a web page that doesn't load in ten seconds. Three out of five people don't return to that site.
A third of British people expect a 'like' on a Facebook picture in less than a minute after posting it.

c Focus on the numbers and dates, and get Sts, in pairs, to decide how they think you say them.

d **5.2** Play the audio for Sts to listen and check.

Check answers, making sure Sts also know how to say $ (dollar), % (per cent), and . (point).

5.2

a hundred and eighty-four
three thousand and twenty-five
two thousand five hundred
the twenty-fifth of May
six million dollars
seventy-five per cent
two thirds
nine point two

EXTRA IDEA As an alternative to just getting Sts to say the numbers in **c**, copy the following on the board and ask Sts to identify a typical mistake in each one:

1 A HUNDRED EIGHTY-FOUR (184)
2 THREE THOUSAND TWENTY-FIVE (3,025)
3 TWO THOUSAND AND FIVE HUNDRED (2,500)
4 THE TWENTY-FIVE OF MAY (25TH MAY)
5 SIX MILLIONS DOLLARS ($6,000,000)
6 SEVENTY-FIVE POR CENT (75%)
7 TWO THIRD ($\frac{2}{3}$)
8 NINE DOT TWO (9.2)

EXTRA SUPPORT If you think your Sts need more practice, write some more numbers and dates on the board for them to say.

e **5.3** Tell Sts they are going to hear six conversations in which some numbers are mentioned. They need to write the numbers only. Point out that the first one (*213*) has been done for them.

Play the audio the whole way through for Sts just to listen.

Now play it again, pausing after each conversation to give Sts time to write their answers.

Get Sts to compare with a partner, and then play the audio again if necessary.

Check answers.

2 20th **3** 120,000 **4** $795,000 **5** $\frac{1}{3}$ **6** 60–70%

5.3

1 **A** What's your address?
B Two hundred and thirteen Station Road.
2 **A** When's your birthday?
B The twentieth of June.
3 **A** So how many people live here?
B About a hundred and twenty thousand, I think.
4 **A** How much did the house cost?
B A lot. Seven hundred and ninety-five thousand.
A Is that in pounds or dollars?
B Dollars.
5 **A** How much of your salary do you spend on rent?
B Er, at least a third, I think.
6 **A** What percentage of your day do you spend working or studying?
B I'm not sure. Between sixty and seventy per cent, maybe?

f Focus on the **Saying approximate numbers** box and go through it with the class.

Now put Sts in pairs and get them to answer questions 1–5.

Monitor and help if necessary.

Get some feedback from various pairs.

3 GRAMMAR & PRONUNCIATION

comparative adjectives and adverbs, *as…as; /ə/*

a Tell Sts to look at the highlighted words in the sentences and decide if they are adjectives or adverbs.

Check answers.

> **1** busy, stressed = adjectives **2** quickly = adverb
> **3** fast = adjective **4** fast = adverb, impatient = adjective
> **5** bad = adjective **6** well = adverb

b Focus on the instructions. Give Sts a few minutes to read sentences 1–6 and circle the correct forms.

Get Sts to compare with a partner, and then check answers.

> **1** faster **2** worse **3** busier **4** more stressed **5** more quickly **6** as patient as

c Tell Sts to go to **Grammar Bank 5A** on *p.134*.

Grammar notes

Although Pre-intermediate Sts will usually have studied comparative adjectives before, they will probably need reminding of the rules, especially for one-syllable adjectives and two-syllable adjectives ending in *-y*. Typical mistakes are: ~~more big~~, ~~more easy~~, etc.

Point out that the rules for adverbs are very similar. The only difference is that whereas two-syllable adjectives ending in *y* make the comparative with *-ier*, e.g. *heavy – heavier*, two-syllable adverbs ending in *y* form the comparative with *more*, e.g. *more slowly* NOT ~~slowlier~~.

The structure *as…as* is more common in the negative, but can also be used in the affirmative, e.g. *She's as tall as I am*. It is also very common with *much* and *many*, e.g. *I don't eat as much as you*.

You may also want to teach *the same as…*, e.g. *Your book is the same as mine*.

Focus on the example sentences and play both audio ◗ **5.4** and ◗ **5.5** for Sts to listen and repeat. Encourage them to copy the rhythm. Then go through the rules with the class.

Now focus on the **Comparatives with pronouns** box and go through it with the class.

Then focus on the exercises for **5A** on *p.135*. Sts do the exercises individually or in pairs.

Check answers, getting Sts to read the full sentences.

> **a**
> **1** Modern computers are much **faster than** the early ones.
> **2** My sister is **shorter than** me.
> **3** This exercise is **easier than** the last one.
> **4** Newcastle is **further** from London **than** Leeds.
> **5** I thought the third Bridget Jones film was **worse than** the first two.
> **6** Manchester United played **better than** Arsenal.
> **7** I'm **more stressed** this year **than** I was last year.
> **8** I'm working **harder** this year **than** last year.
> **9** The new airport is **bigger than** the old one.
> **10** I'm not lazy – I just work **more slowly** than you!

> **b**
> **1** Jerry isn't **as short as** Adam.
> **2** My bag isn't **as nice as** yours.
> **3** London isn't **as big as** Tokyo.
> **4** Cricket isn't **as popular as** tennis.
> **5** Adults don't **learn languages as fast as** children.
> **6** You don't **work as hard as** me.
> **7** France didn't **play as well as** England.

Tell Sts to go back to the main lesson **5A**.

 If you think Sts need more practice, you may want to give them the **Grammar** photocopiable activity at this point.

Pronunciation notes

At this level it is important to focus on the weak forms of *as* and *than* more for comprehension than production. However, if you encourage Sts to get the stress correct both in words and sentences, then this will help them to produce the /ə/ sound in these words.

With the *-er* ending, this is such a common feature of English that it is really worth making an effort to correct Sts and to encourage them to pronounce it as the /ə/ sound.

d ◗ **5.6** Focus on the task.

Play the audio the whole way though for Sts to listen and read the sentences in **b**.

Check answers. Remind Sts that it is the most common sound in English.

> Both a schwa /ə/

◗ **5.6**
See sentences in Student's Book on *p.39*

e Now play the audio again, pausing after each sentence for Sts to repeat and copy the rhythm.

Then repeat the activity, eliciting responses from individual Sts.

 If this sound is difficult for your Sts, it will help to show them the mouth position. You could model this yourself or use the the Sound Bank videos on the *Teacher's Resource Centre*.

4 LISTENING & SPEAKING

a ◀)) **5.7** Focus on the instructions and tell Sts to look at the title, question 1, and the ten activities. Make sure Sts understand that each speaker is speaking about a different activity. Tell Sts that they won't hear the question, and when the speaker names the activity, they will hear a beep (see script 5.7).

Play the audio, pausing after each speaker to give Sts time to number the question the speaker answered.

Get Sts to compare with a partner, and then play again if necessary.

EXTRA SUPPORT Read through the script and decide if you need to pre-teach any new lexis before Sts listen.

◀)) **5.7**

1 I spend much less time (*beep*) – that is, going to real shops – than in the past, because now I get so much online. I buy most of my food online – everything except fresh things like meat or fruit and vegetables. Er, I get books from Amazon. I buy a lot of clothes online. And it's so quick. You don't have to go there; you don't spend as long looking for what you want. It's just much, much quicker. I definitely prefer it.

2 One of the things that has changed for me is (*beep*). It takes me much longer now because I cycle. A few years ago, I drove – I took the car – but then I decided to cycle, not always because I enjoy it, but because I know it's healthier. It takes me about half an hour to get to work now. Actually, when the weather's good I really enjoy it, but when it's raining or just cold and horrible, I get up and I think *oh no!*

3 I definitely spend a lot more time (*beep*) now than I did before, I think because, er, about a year ago, I started living with my boyfriend. When I lived alone, in the evening I was tired and I just got a takeaway, or made something really quickly, or just had some bread and cheese or whatever was in the fridge – whatever was easier. But when you have someone else in the house, you feel more like cooking. And also my boyfriend's a vegetarian, so it's a bit more complicated to do something very quick. So before, I spent about twenty minutes a day, and now I spend about an hour. But I'm quite happy with that – I enjoy it.

4 I probably spend about the same amount of time (*beep*) as I did three years ago. I'm a freelance writer now, and three years ago I had an office job, so I was doing, you know, thirty-five hours a week. Now, some weeks I probably work about fifty hours, and others twenty hours, but on average, I think it's about the same.

5 I definitely spend less time (*beep*), because two years ago we moved to the country from the city – and most of our friends are in the city and they're quite a long way away from us now. Sometimes they come and spend the weekend with us, or we go and spend the weekend with them, but on average, I definitely spend less time with them.

---

b ◀)) **5.8** Elicit answers, but <u>don't</u> tell Sts if they are correct yet or not.

Now play the audio (where the speakers now name the activities) for Sts to listen and check.

Check answers.

> **1** shopping   **2** getting to work   **3** cooking   **4** working
> **5** seeing friends

◀)) **5.8**
(script in Student's Book on *p.121*)

1 I spend much less time shopping – that is, going to real shops – than in the past, because now I get so much online. I buy most of my food online – everything except fresh things like meat or fruit and vegetables. Er, I get books from Amazon. I buy a lot of clothes online. And it's so quick. You don't have to go there; you don't spend as long looking for what you want. It's just much, much quicker. I definitely prefer it.

2 One of the things that has changed for me is getting to work. It takes me much longer now because I cycle. A few years ago, I drove – I took the car – but then I decided to cycle, not always because I enjoy it, but because I know it's healthier. It takes me about half an hour to get to work now. Actually, when the weather's good, I really enjoy it, but when it's raining or just cold and horrible, I get up and I think *oh no!*

3 I definitely spend a lot more time cooking now than I did before, I think because, er, about a year ago, I started living with my boyfriend. When I lived alone, in the evening I was tired and I just got a takeaway, or made something really quickly, or just had some bread and cheese or whatever was in the fridge – whatever was easier. But when you have someone else in the house, you feel more like cooking. And also my boyfriend's a vegetarian, so it's a bit more complicated to do something very quick. So before, I spent about twenty minutes a day, and now I spend about an hour. But I'm quite happy with that – I enjoy it.

4 I probably spend about the same amount of time working as I did three years ago. I'm a freelance writer now, and three years ago I had an office job, so I was doing, you know, thirty-five hours a week. Now, some weeks I probably work about fifty hours, and others twenty hours, but on average, I think it's about the same.

5 I definitely spend less time seeing friends, because two years ago we moved to the country from the city – and most of our friends are in the city and they're quite a long way away from us now. Sometimes they come and spend the weekend with us, or we go and spend the weekend with them, but on average, I definitely spend less time with them.

Give Sts time to answer questions A–E. If necessary, play the audio again.

Check answers.

> **a** Speaker 4   **b** Speaker 1   **c** Speaker 5
> **d** Speaker 2   **e** Speaker 3

EXTRA SUPPORT If there's time, you could get Sts to listen again with the script on *p.121*, so they can see exactly what they understood / didn't understand. Translate / Explain any new words or phrases.

c Focus on the task and the example. Put Sts in small groups and give them time to discuss the three questions in **a**.

When Sts have finished discussing all three questions, they should decide whose life has changed the most.

Get some feedback from each group.

G superlatives (+ *ever* + present perfect)
V describing a town or city
P sentence stress

Lesson plan

In this lesson Sts move from comparatives to superlatives. Sts who did not use *English File* Elementary may not have studied superlatives before, in which case you will probably need to spend more time on them. The context is a TripAdvisor survey of cities around the world, and an experiment carried out by the *Reader's Digest* to find out how honest 16 cities around the world were. The present perfect is also recycled in expressions like *the most beautiful place I've ever been to*.

The lesson begins with a vocabulary focus on language used to describe a city. Then the grammar presentation through the TripAdvisor survey is followed by a listening on the most honest cities in the world. In Pronunciation and Speaking, Sts look at sentence stress in superlative questions and then ask and answer some superlative questions. Finally, the lesson ends with Sts writing a description of where they live.

More materials

For teachers

Photocopiables
Grammar superlatives (+ *ever* + present perfect) p.185
Vocabulary Describing a town or city p.264
(instructions p.254)
Communicative Superlative questions p.230
(instructions p.211)

For students
Workbook 5B
Online Practice 5B

OPTIONAL LEAD-IN (BOOKS CLOSED)

Ask Sts *What are the biggest cities in your country?* and write them on the board.

Then get Sts to ask each other in pairs *Have you been to ___? When did you go there? Did you like it? Why (not)?*

1 VOCABULARY describing a town or city

Vocabulary notes

Sts are sometimes confused about whether to describe the place where they live as a village, a town, or a city. A city is a large town (in the UK, historically, anywhere with a cathedral is a city); a town is medium-sized; and a village is a very small town located in a country area.

Sts often use the word *monument* to describe any historic building. You may want to point out that a monument is only a building, statue, or column built to remind people of a famous person or event.

You may want to explain the difference between *crowded* and *full* (*crowded* = full of people), and *polluted* and *dirty* (*polluted* = dirty because of contamination).

a Books open. Focus on the task and give Sts time to think about their answers.

Put Sts in pairs and get them to compare their answers. If your Sts live in the same town or city, do this as a whole-class activity.

If Sts worked in pairs, get some feedback.

b Tell Sts to go to **Vocabulary Bank Describing a town or city** on *p.156*.

Focus on **1 Where is it? How big is it?** In **a**, tell Sts they are going to read about a city called York. They might remember Anya talking about it in Lesson **2B**. Get Sts to circle the correct words or phrases.

 **5.9** Now do **b**. Play the audio for Sts to listen and check.

Check answers.

5.9
Describing a town or city 1 Where is it? How big is it?
York is a city in the **north** of England, on **the River Ouse**. It's about twenty-five miles **east** of Leeds. It's a **medium-sized** city and it has a population of about two hundred thousand. It's famous for its cathedral, York Minster, and its historic city centre.

Now do **2 What's it like?**. Remind Sts what the question means and then focus on **a**, where Sts match the adjectives and sentences.

EXTRA SUPPORT Check Sts' answers to **a** before they match the opposites in **b**.

3 crowded **6** dangerous **4** modern **1** noisy **2** polluted

Now do **b** and get Sts to match the adjectives in the list to their opposites in **a**.

5.10 Then do **c**. Play the audio for Sts to listen and check answers to **a** and **b**.

Check answers.

5.10
2 What's it like?
5 boring, exciting, interesting
3 crowded, empty
6 dangerous, safe
4 modern, historic
1 noisy, quiet
2 polluted, clean

Now either use the audio to drill the pronunciation of the adjectives, or model and drill them yourself. Give further practice of any words your Sts find difficult to pronounce.

Finally, do **d** and get Sts to cover the words and look at sentences 1–6. They can test themselves or each other.

Now do **3 What is there to see?** and tell Sts to look at the photos, and ask them what they can see.

Tell Sts to do **a** individually or in pairs. Point out that each column already has one answer in it.

🔊 **5.11**   Then do **b**. Play the audio for Sts to listen and check.

Check answers.

🔊 **5.11**
3 What is there to see?
Religious buildings: *cathedral*, church, mosque, synagogue, temple
Places where you can buy things: *department store*, market, shopping centre
Historic buildings and monuments: *castle*, city walls, museum, palace, ruins, statue, town hall, ruins
Others: *bridge*, canal, harbour, hill, lake

Now either use the audio to drill the pronunciation of the words, or model and drill them yourself. Give further practice of any words your Sts find difficult to pronounce.

EXTRA CHALLENGE   Elicit more words for each column, e.g. *synagogue, (clock) tower*, etc.

Finally, get Sts to do **Activation** in pairs.

Then get some feedback from individual Sts.

Tell Sts to go back to the main lesson **5B**.

EXTRA SUPPORT   If you think Sts need more practice, you may want to give them the **Vocabulary** photocopiable activity at this point.

2 GRAMMAR superlatives (+ *ever* + present perfect)

a Do this as a whole-class activity.

Stockholm is in Sweden.   Rome is in Italy.   New York is in the USA.   Dubrovnik is in Croatia.   Vienna is in Austria.   Budapest is in Hungary.   Tokyo is in Japan.

Then ask Sts what they know about each city and if anyone has been there. You could then tell Sts what you know about these places, and if you've been to any of them.

b Focus on the text and the instructions, and make sure Sts understand the situation.

Before Sts read the text, ask them if they know the website TripAdvisor, and if so, what they think of it.

Read the text with the class and go through the seven different categories.

Put Sts in pairs and get them to guess which city was the winner in each category. Tell them the photos will help them answer.

Elicit opinions and then tell Sts the answers. If your Sts have been to any of these cities, ask them if they agree with the survey. You could ask if they found any of the answers surprising.

1 Tokyo   **2** Vienna   **3** Budapest   **4** Dubrovnik
5 New York City   **6** Stockholm   **7** Rome

c Tell Sts to look at the categories in **b** and think about their city. Would it do well in any of the categories?

Get some feedback from the class, and tell them what you think.

---

d Focus on the instructions and get Sts to work out the rules.

Get Sts to compare with a partner, and then check answers.

1 Add *-est*
2 Change the *y* to *i* and add *-est*
3 Put *more* before the adjective
4 *best*

e Tell Sts to go to **Grammar Bank 5B** on *p.134*.

Grammar notes

Remind Sts that the rules for making superlatives are similar to comparatives, but adding *-est* instead of *-er*, or using *most* instead of *more*. Remind them to use *the* before superlatives.

Sts sometimes use comparatives where they should use superlatives. A typical mistake is: ~~the more expensive city in Europe~~, etc.

Highlight that Sts must always think if they are comparing two things (comparative), or more than two (superlative) when deciding which form to use, e.g. *The most beautiful city I've ever been to.*

Some languages use *never* (not *ever*) in this structure. A typical mistake is: ~~The most beautiful city I've never been to.~~

Adverbs can also be used in the superlative, e.g. *He drives the fastest.*

🔊 **5.12**   Focus on the example sentences and play the audio for Sts to listen and repeat. Encourage them to copy the rhythm. Then go through the rules with the class.

Now focus on the exercises for **5B** on *p.135*. Sts do the exercises individually or in pairs.

Check answers, getting Sts to read the full sentences.

a
1 The Polish are **the most generous** people I've ever met.
2 Yesterday was **the hottest** day of the year.
3 Early morning is **the worst** time to drive in the city centre.
4 She's **the friendliest** girl at school.
5 This is **the most important** part of the exam.
6 **The best** time to visit New England is autumn.
7 Delhi in India is one of **the most polluted** cities in the world.
8 **The furthest** (or **The farthest**) I've ever flown is to Bali.
9 It was **the funniest** film I've ever seen.
10 Rob's daughters are all pretty, but I think Emily is **the prettiest**.
b
1 It's the windiest place I've ever been to.
2 She's the most unfriendly person I've ever met.
3 It's the easiest exam we've ever done.
4 They're the most expensive trousers I've ever bought.
5 This is the longest book I've ever read.
6 He's the most attractive man I've ever seen.
7 It's the worst meal I've ever eaten.
8 He's the most interesting teacher we've ever had.
9 It's the most exciting job I've ever done.

Tell Sts to go back to the main lesson **5B**.

EXTRA SUPPORT   If you think Sts need more practice, you may want to give them the **Grammar** photocopiable activity at this point.

3 LISTENING understanding ranking

a Focus on the title of the article and make sure Sts know the meaning of *honest* (= always telling the truth, and never stealing or cheating).

Now focus on the task and give Sts time to read about the experiment.

When Sts have finished reading, get them to cover the text or close their books. Elicit from the class how the experiment worked.

EXTRA SUPPORT Get Sts to explain how the experiment worked in pairs, and then get feedback.

b Focus on the task. You might first want to get Sts to name the countries where all these cities are (Amsterdam is in the Netherlands, Berlin is in Germany, Budapest is in Hungary, Bucharest is in Romania, Helsinki is in Finland, Lisbon is in Portugal, Ljubljana is in Slovenia, London is in England, Madrid is in Spain, Moscow is in Russia, Mumbai is in India, New York is in the USA, Prague is in the Czech Republic, Rio de Janeiro is in Brazil, Warsaw is in Poland, and Zurich is in Switzerland).

Put Sts in pairs and give them time to discuss their choices.

c ◀)) **5.13** Before playing the audio, focus on the **Ranking things in order** box and go through it with the class.

Now tell Sts they are going to listen to a reporter talking about the results of the experiment. They must listen and rank nine of the cities in **b** in the correct order.

Play the audio the whole way through for Sts just to listen.

Now play it again and get Sts to complete the task.

Check answers.

EXTRA SUPPORT Tell Sts that the first time they listen, they should just tick the nine cities that are mentioned.

EXTRA SUPPORT Read through the script and decide if you need to pre-teach any new lexis before Sts listen.

> **1** Helsinki   **2** Mumbai   **3** Budapest, New York
> **5** Moscow, Amsterdam   **9** London, Warsaw   **16** Lisbon

◀)) **5.13**
(script in Student's Book on *pp.121–122*)
I = **interviewer**, O= **Oliver**

I Today, we're talking about a very interesting experiment to find the most and least honest cities in the world. It involved journalists travelling to sixteen cities and 'losing' twelve wallets in each city, then waiting to see how many people returned them in each place. Our presenter, Oliver, has got the results. So, Oliver, which was the most honest city?

O Well, in first place was Helsinki, in Finland. People returned eleven of the twelve wallets. A businessman who found the wallet in the city centre said that Finnish people were naturally honest. He said there was very little corruption in Finland, and that people didn't even drive through red traffic lights!

I Really? And the least honest?

O Well, I was quite surprised by this, but the least honest city, in sixteenth place, was Lisbon, in Portugal. Only one person phoned to say they'd found the wallet. And he wasn't Portuguese: he was a sixty-year-old tourist from Holland.

I Interesting! What other results surprised you?

O Well, I expected richer cities – cities with a higher standard of living – to be more honest than poorer ones, but this wasn't necessarily true. The city that came second in the experiment was Mumbai, in India – people returned nine out of the twelve wallets. One of them was a young mother. She took it to a post office and she said, 'I teach my children to be honest, just like my parents taught me.'

I And which city came next?

O In joint third place were New York and Budapest. People gave back eight wallets in both places.

I And then?

O Moscow and Amsterdam came joint fifth. In both places, seven out of twelve wallets were returned. And people gave lovely reasons for returning them. In Moscow, a woman said, 'I think that people need to help each other, and if I can make someone a little happier, I want to do it.' And in Amsterdam, a man said 'My wife once lost her wallet. It was found and returned. So I wanted to do the same.'

I I notice my home city, London, is on the list. How did it do?

O London was somewhere in the middle: joint ninth with Warsaw. Just five of the wallets were returned in each place. Interestingly, one of the people who returned a wallet in London was a Polish woman. When she found the wallet, she gave it to her boss. He – her boss – said to her, 'If you find money, you can't be sure it belongs to a rich man – it might be the last bit of money a mother has to feed her family.'

I I think that's fantastic advice. So were there any general conclusions? What did the experiment prove?

O Forty-seven per cent of the wallets were returned, so that's nearly half. And when we looked through the results, we found that you couldn't predict who was going to be honest or dishonest. There was no common factor. Young people and old people both kept or returned wallets; men and women both kept or returned wallets; and as I said before, it didn't make any difference whether a city was rich or poor. So our conclusion was that there are honest and dishonest people everywhere.

d Tell Sts they are going to listen to the interview again, but this time they need to answer questions 1 and 2. Point out situations a–e in question 1.

Play the audio again.

Get Sts to compare with a partner, and then play it again if necessary.

Check answers. You could ask Sts if they found anything surprising.

> **1 a** Amsterdam   **b** Helsinki   **c** Moscow   **d** Mumbai
>   **e** London
> **2** 47%; No, there was no common factor.

e If your Sts are all from the same town or city, do this as a whole-class activity and elicit opinions.

If they are from different places, get them to answer in pairs, and then get some feedback.

4 PRONUNCIATION & SPEAKING
sentence stress

Pronunciation notes
Remind Sts that information words are the ones which are usually stressed in a sentence. These are the words which you hear more clearly when somebody speaks to you. The unstressed words are heard much less clearly, or sometimes hardly at all.

You may want to tell Sts that when native speakers use superlatives with *most*, they often link the two words together and don't pronounce the final *t* in *most*.

a ◑ **5.14** Focus on the task and give Sts time to look at questions 1–8. Point out that the first one (*most beautiful*) has been done for them.

Play the audio for Sts to listen and complete the gaps.

Check answers.

> **2** most relaxing   **3** most frightening   **4** most exciting
> **5** most expensive   **6** most generous   **7** most dangerous
> **8** most difficult

◑ **5.14**
1 What's the most beautiful city you've ever been to?
2 What's the most relaxing holiday you've ever had?
3 What's the most frightening film you've ever seen?
4 What's the most exciting sporting event you've ever watched?
5 What's the most expensive thing you've ever bought?
6 Who's the most generous person you've ever met?
7 What's the most dangerous sport you've ever done?
8 What's the most difficult subject you've ever studied?

---

b Play the audio again for Sts to listen to the questions and hear which words are stressed. You might want to highlight that the preposition *to*, which is not normally stressed, is stressed here because it comes at the end of the question.

Now play the audio again, pausing after each question for Sts to copy the rhythm.

Then repeat the activity, eliciting responses from individual Sts.

> **1** What's the most beautiful city you've ever been to?
> **2** What's the most relaxing holiday you've ever had?
> **3** What's the most frightening film you've ever seen?
> **4** What's the most exciting sporting event you've ever watched?
> **5** What's the most expensive thing you've ever bought?
> **6** Who's the most generous person you've ever met?
> **7** What's the most dangerous sport you've ever done?
> **8** What's the most difficult subject you've ever studied?

c Focus on the instructions and speech bubbles. Do 1 yourself with Sts as an example, and elicit follow-up questions. Put Sts in pairs, **A** and **B**. Tell **A** to answer 1 with a full sentence, and **B** to ask extra questions. Then they swap roles before moving on to 2.

Get some feedback from the class.

5 WRITING describing where you live
Tell Sts to go to **Writing Describing where you live** on *p.116*.

a Tell Sts to read the description and complete the gaps with the words in the list. Point out that the first one (*city*) has been done for them.

Check answers.

> **2** population   **3** area   **4** historic   **5** modern   **6** weather
> **7** food   **8** nature   **9** rivers

b Now tell Sts to match the questions to paragraphs 1–5.

Check answers.

> **1** Where do you live? Where is it? How big is it?
> **2** What's your town like? What is there to see there?
> **3** What's the weather like?
> **4** What's it famous for?
> **5** What's the best thing about it? Do you like living there?

c Tell Sts they are now going to plan a description of where they live. They should look at the questions in **b** and make notes of their answers.

d You may like to get Sts to do the writing in class or you could set it as homework. Make sure they write five paragraphs by answering the questions in **b** in the correct order.

e Sts should check for mistakes, and if they can, attach a photo or photos.

5C How much is enough?

G quantifiers, *too*, *(not) enough*
V health and the body
P /ʌ/

Lesson plan

In this lesson Sts revise quantifiers and learn to use *too much / many*, and *(not) enough*. The context is a magazine article about the latest medical research into drinks. The lesson begins with a questionnaire focusing on drinks, and what Sts drink when. Sts then go on to listen to a nutritionist talking about what kind of liquids we should drink. In Reading, the topic of the article is about confusing health advice regarding drinks. There is also a vocabulary focus on health and the body. Sts then work on the grammar, followed by a pronunciation focus on the /ʌ/ sound. The lesson ends with a speaking activity where Sts discuss more general lifestyle habits using the new quantifiers. Depending on the level of your class, you may want to do more or less revision of countability and basic quantifiers (see **Optional lead-in**).

More materials
For teachers
Photocopiables
Grammar quantifiers, *too, (not) enough* p.186
Communicative How much / How many…? p.231
(instructions p.211)
For students
Workbook 5C
Online Practice 5C

OPTIONAL LEAD-IN (BOOKS CLOSED)

Revise countability. Write on the board in two columns:

1	2
WATER	VEGETABLES
BREAD	BISCUITS
CHOCOLATE	SWEETS

Ask Sts *What's the difference between the words in columns 1 and 2?* and elicit that the words in column 1 are uncountable, and normally used in the singular, but the words in column 2 are countable and can be used in singular and plural. Elicit a few more words for each column, e.g. *wine, rice, apples*, etc.

Ask Sts *When do we use* a, some, *and* any? and elicit that you use *a* with singular countable nouns and *some / any* with plural countable nouns and uncountable nouns – *some* in positive sentences and *any* in negatives and questions, e.g. *I ate a biscuit and some bread. I didn't eat any vegetables or any fruit*.

1 SPEAKING & LISTENING

a Books open. Focus on the questionnaire and its title. Make sure Sts know what *a can* is.

Put Sts in pairs and give them time to answer the questions.

Get some feedback.

EXTRA SUPPORT Get Sts to interview you first.

b ◀)) **5.15** Focus on the drawing of the jug. Go through the instructions, making sure Sts know the meaning of *a nutritionist, a liquid, a jug, alcohol*, and *low-fat*. Model and drill pronunciation.

Play the audio once the whole way through for Sts to listen and complete the task.

Play it again if necessary.

Check answers.

EXTRA CHALLENGE Get Sts, in pairs, to predict which liquid goes where before they listen.

EXTRA SUPPORT Read through the script and decide if you need to pre-teach any new lexis before Sts listen.

1 water	**2** tea and coffee	**3** low-fat milk	**4** alcohol
5 diet coke	**6** fruit juice		
We should never drink sweet, fizzy drinks.			

◀)) **5.15**
(script in Student's Book on *p.122*)
At least half of your daily liquids should come from water. About one third – or three to four cups – can come from coffee or tea – but with no sugar. Low-fat milk can make up another twenty per cent. If you drink less milk, just try to get your calcium from another type of food or drink, for example green vegetables. You can have one small glass of fruit juice a day, and no more than one to two alcoholic drinks for men, or one for women. However, some doctors now think that it's a good idea to have several alcohol-free days a week. Diet drinks which use artificial sweeteners are not good for you, but up to one to two glasses a day is OK. But try not to have any drinks with a lot of sugar, for example, sweet fizzy drinks.

EXTRA CHALLENGE Get Sts to listen for the recommended quantities of each drink.

1 water (half of daily liquids)
2 tea and coffee (3 to 4 cups)
3 low-fat milk (20% of daily liquids)
4 alcohol (1 or 2 drinks for men, 1 for women)
5 diet coke (1 or 2 glasses)
6 fruit juice (1 small glass)

EXTRA SUPPORT If there's time, you could get Sts to listen again with the script on *p.122*, so they can see exactly what they understood / didn't understand. Translate / Explain any new words or phrases.

c Do this as a whole-class activity.

2 READING & VOCABULARY
health and the body

a Do this as a whole-class activity.

b Focus on the task and make sure Sts understand what the article is about. Pre-teach the verbs *increase*, *improve*, *reduce*, and *cause*.

Now get Sts to read the article and match the highlighted words to pictures 1–6.

Get Sts to compare their answers with a partner.

 Apart from the highlighted words, this article contains other medical vocabulary. Before Sts read it, check whether you need to pre-teach any other items, e.g. *heart attack*, *cancer*, *arthritis*, etc., or whether you think Sts will be able to guess their meaning. In many languages they are similar words, but pronounced differently.

c **5.16** Play the audio for Sts to listen and check their answers to **b**.

Check answers.

5.16

1 liver 2 heart 3 teeth 4 muscles 5 bones 6 blood

Then play it again, pausing after each word for Sts to listen and repeat.

Now get Sts to practise saying the words.

Finally, ask Sts what they think *heart attack* /'hɑːt ətæk/ and *blood pressure* /'blʌd preʃə/ mean. Model and drill pronunciation.

heart attack = a sudden, serious medical condition in which the heart stops working normally, sometimes causing death
blood pressure = the pressure of blood as it travels around the body

Deal with any other new vocabulary. Model and drill the pronunciation of any tricky words.

d Focus on the instructions and put Sts in pairs. Tell them to read about each drink again and answer the two questions.

Get some feedback. Sts might have a different opinion, but if so, ask them to justify it.

a tea, water **b** alcohol, coffee, juice, milk

e Do this as a whole-class activity.

3 GRAMMAR quantifiers, *too*, *(not) enough*

 If you didn't do the **Optional lead-in**, you could do it here.

a This exercise revises what Sts should already know. Focus on the instructions and give Sts time to decide if the words are countable or uncountable.

Check answers.

(C = countable, U = uncountable)
juice U   bottle C   can C   milk U   carton C   water U
wine U   cup C   glass C

b Focus on the instructions and get Sts, in pairs, to circle the correct word or phrase and say why the other one is wrong.

Check answers.

1 many (You can't use *much* with plural countable nouns.)
2 much (You can't use *many* with uncountable nouns.)
3 a lot of (You can't use *many* with uncountable nouns.)
4 a little (You can't use *a few* with uncountable nouns.)
5 a few (You can't use *a little* with countable nouns.)
6 a lot (You can't use *a lot of* without a noun.)

c Here the new language of the lesson is introduced. Tell Sts to look at the paragraphs about water in the article, and to focus on words or phrases which mean *the right amount* and *more than you need*.

Check answers.

1 enough   2 too much

d Now tell Sts to go to **Grammar Bank 5C** on *p.134*.

Grammar notes
too much, too many, too

Some Sts often use *too much* + adjective. A typical mistake is: *It's too much big*.

It is also important to highlight the difference between *too* and *very*:

It's very big. (= a statement of fact, neither good nor bad)
It's too big. (= more than it should be / more than you want)

(not) enough

The main problem here is the pronunciation of *enough* /ɪ'nʌf/ and the different positions: before nouns, but after adjectives. Some Sts may confuse *quite* and *enough* because of L1 interference.

Focus on the example sentences and play both audio **5.17** and **5.18** for Sts to listen and repeat. Encourage them to copy the rhythm. Then go through the rules with the class.

Now focus on the exercises for **5C** on *p.135*. Sts do them individually or in pairs.

Check answers, getting Sts to read the full sentences.

a
1 I eat **too much** chocolate.
2 I eat **too many** crisps.
3 Do you drink **enough water**?
4 I'm **too busy**.
5 This suitcase isn't **big enough**.
6 I worry **too much**.
7 You don't **go out enough**.
8 I don't eat **enough vegetables**.
b
1 I don't do **enough** exercsie.
2 It's **too** far.
3 There are **too many** cars on the roads today.
4 I spend **too much** time on the computer…
5 I don't read **enough**…
6 I didn't buy the coat because it was **too** expensive.
7 There were **too many** people at the hospital…
8 I don't like watching films on my phone because the screen isn't big **enough**.

Tell Sts to go back to the main lesson **5C**.

 If you think Sts need more practice, you may want to give them the **Grammar** photocopiable activity at this point.

4 PRONUNCIATION & SPEAKING /ʌ/

a 🔊 **5.19** This exercise helps Sts with the pronunciation of some of the words from the lesson.

Focus on the sound picture and elicit the word, and sound: *up* /ʌ/.

Give Sts time to read the **Typical spelling** chart. Make sure they know the meaning of *rare* (= not seen very often).

Play the audio once the whole way through for Sts just to listen.

🔊 **5.19**
See words in Student's Book on *p.43*

Now play the audio again, pausing after each word for Sts to repeat.

EXTRA SUPPORT If this sound is difficult for your Sts, or you want to contrast it with the /æ/ sound, it will help to show them the mouth position. You could model this yourself or use the the Sound Bank videos on the *Teacher's Resource Centre*.

b 🔊 **5.20** Tell Sts they are going to hear 12 sentences and they must write the last word in each one.

Play the audio, pausing after each item to give Sts time to write.

Check answers by playing the audio again and pausing after each item to elicit the word onto the board.

1 butter	**2** study	**3** worry	**4** young	**5** money
6 rubbish	**7** sunny	**8** lovely	**9** double	
10 lunch	**11** country	**12** funny		

🔊 **5.20**
1 Can you pass me the butter?
2 Do you work or study?
3 Everything's going to be fine – don't worry!
4 Your sister's very young!
5 I don't have any money.
6 Please can you take out the rubbish?
7 Is today going to be sunny?
8 The weather's going to be lovely.
9 Two single rooms, please, and one double.
10 What do you want for lunch?
11 What's the biggest city in your country?
12 She's usually serious, but she can be very funny.

EXTRA SUPPORT Elicit the whole sentences / questions, not just the last word, and write them on the board.

EXTRA IDEA Some Sts have a problem pronouncing *money* and tend to say /mʌneɪ/. To help them, you could tell them that *money* rhymes with *funny* and *sunny*.

c Play the audio again, pausing after each item for Sts to listen and repeat. Make sure they repeat the whole sentence and not just the last word.

d Focus on the speech bubbles, and then demonstrate the activity yourself by answering a couple of questions and explaining your reasons.

Now put Sts in pairs and get them to answer the questions, giving their reasons, too.

Get some feedback from various pairs.

Function taking something back to a shop
Vocabulary shopping

Lesson plan

In this third Practical English lesson Sts revise some basic shopping vocabulary, and learn some key phrases for taking things back to a shop. The story develops: Rob decides that he is unfit and needs to do some exercise. Holly invites him to join her and some friends in a game of basketball. Rob accepts, but first needs to buy some trainers. He buys a pair, without trying them on, and then realizes they are too small. He takes them back to the shop and manages to exchange them. Later, he accepts an invitation to go running with Jenny very early in the morning in Central Park.

More materials
For teachers
Teacher's Resource Centre
Video Practical English Episode 3
Quick Test 5
File 5 Test
For students
Workbook Practical English 3
Can you remember...? 1–5
Online Practice Practical English 3
Check your progress

OPTIONAL LEAD-IN (BOOKS CLOSED)
Before starting Episode 3, elicit what Sts can remember about Episode 2. Ask *Who's Holly? Where does she work / live? Who's Barbara?*, etc.

Alternatively, you could play the last scene of Episode 2.

1 ▶ ROB HAS A PROBLEM

a 🔊 **5.21** Focus on questions 1–8 and give Sts time to read them. Sts may not know the expression *to be in shape* (= in a good physical condition) and *to keep fit* (= stay healthy).

Play the video / audio once the whole way through. Play again if necessary.

Get Sts to compare with a partner, and then check answers.

1	He says he's eating too much.
2	Because he eats out all the time in New York and the portions are very big.
3	He cycles in London.
4	Because he doesn't have a bike (he lives near the office and is only going to stay for another three weeks).
5	She goes running before and after work.
6	Holly thinks running is very boring.
7	He could play basketball with Holly and her friends.
8	He needs to buy some trainers (*sneakers* in American English).

🔊 **5.21**
H = Holly, R = Rob
H Hey, Rob, come on. Keep up.
R Sorry. I'm a bit tired this morning.
H You aren't exactly in good shape, are you?
R I know, I know. I think I'm eating too much.
H Then eat less!
R It isn't easy. I eat out all the time. And the portions in American restaurants are enormous.
H You don't do enough exercise.
R I walk a lot.
H Walking isn't enough, Rob. Do you do anything to keep fit?
R I cycle when I'm in London...
H So why don't you get a bike here?
R I'm only here for another three weeks. Anyway, my hotel's near the office. I don't need a bike.
H You know, Jennifer goes running all the time. Before and after work. But I just think that running is so boring. I mean, where's the fun?
R Yeah, I'm not very keen on running.
H So why don't you play basketball with me and my friends?
R OK. That's a great idea! But I don't have any trainers.
H Trainers? Sneakers! You can buy some.
R Is there a sports shop near here?
H Sure, there's one across the street.

Now focus on the **British and American English** box and go through it with the class.

EXTRA SUPPORT If there's time and you are using the video, you could get Sts to watch again with subtitles, so they can see exactly what they understood / didn't understand. Translate / Explain any new words or phrases.

b 🔊 **5.22** Focus on the **Making suggestions with *Why don't you…?*** box and go through it with the class.

Now play the video / audio and get Sts just to watch or listen.

🔊 **5.22**
See the phrases in Student's Book on *p.44*

Play the video / audio again, pausing after each phrase, and get Sts to repeat it.

c Put Sts in pairs, **A** and **B**, and focus on the instructions. Make sure Sts understand the situation.

Tell Sts **A** to start.

When Sts have finished, ask a few Sts **A** what suggestions Sts **B** made and if they thought the suggestions were good or not.

d Sts stay in their pairs and focus on the new situation.

Tell Sts **B** to start.

When Sts have finished, ask a few Sts **B** what suggestions Sts **A** made and if they thought the suggestions were good or not.

EXTRA IDEA As a round-up, ask Sts for good suggestions for both situations and write them on the board.

2 ▶ VOCABULARY shopping

a Put Sts in pairs and tell them to answer the questions in the shopping quiz.

b ◀)) **5.23** Play the video / audio for Sts to watch or listen and check.

Check answers. For 1, you could also elicit *XS* and *XXL*.

◀)) **5.23**
1 S, M, L, and XL.
2 S is small, M is medium, L is large, XL is extra large
3 a changing room
4 a receipt
5 £25.99 = twenty-five pounds ninety-nine
   75p = seventy-five p / pence
   $45 = forty-five dollars
   15c = fifteen cents
   €12.50 = twelve euros fifty

3 ▶ TAKING SOMETHING BACK TO A SHOP

a ◀)) **5.24** Focus on the photo and ask Sts some questions, e.g. *Where is Rob? Who is he talking to?*, etc.

Now either tell Sts to close their books and write the two questions on the board, or get Sts to focus on the questions and cover the conversation on *p.45*.

Play the video / audio once the whole way through and then check answers.

---

1 They are too small.
2 He changes them for another pair.

◀)) **5.24** ◀)) **5.25**
S = shop assistant, R = Rob
S Can I help you, sir?
R Yes. Do you have these in an eight? (*repeat*)
S Just a minute. I'll go and check.
***
S Here you are, these are an eight. Do you want to try them on?
R No, thanks. I'm sure they'll be fine. (*repeat*) How much are they? (*repeat*)
S They're $83.94.
R Oh, it says $72.99. (*repeat*)
S Yes, but there's an added sales tax of fifteen per cent.
R Oh, OK. Do you take Mastercard? (*repeat*)
S Sure.
***
S Can I help you?
R Yes, I bought these about half an hour ago. (*repeat*)
S Yes, I remember. Is there a problem?
R Yes, I'm afraid they're too small. (*repeat*)
S What size are they?
R They're an eight. (*repeat*) But I take a UK eight. (*repeat*)
S Oh, right. Yes, a UK eight is a US nine.
R Do you have a pair? (*repeat*)
S I'll go and check. Just a minute.
***
S I'm sorry, but we don't have these in a nine. But we do have these, and they're the same price. Or you can have a refund.
R Erm…I'll take this pair, then, please. (*repeat*)
S No problem. Do you have the receipt?
R Yes, here you are. (*repeat*)
S Brilliant.

You might want to check Sts know what *Mastercard* is (same as *Visa card*) and that *erm* is a sound we use to give ourselves time to think. Also check they understand *a refund*. Model and drill the pronunciation /ˈriːfʌnd/.

b Focus on the conversation in the chart. Elicit who says the **You hear** phrases (the shop assistant) and who says the **You say** phrases (the customer, here Rob). These phrases will be useful for Sts if they need to buy something and then take it back if they have a problem.

Give Sts a minute to read through the conversation and think what the missing words might be. Then play the video / audio again and get Sts to complete the gaps. Play again if necessary.

Get Sts to compare with a partner, and then check answers.

---

1 minute   2 try   3 15   4 problem   5 size   6 sorry
7 same   8 receipt

Go through the conversation line by line with Sts, helping them with any words or expressions they don't understand. You may want to highlight the meaning of the phrasal verb *try on*. You could also remind Sts that we often use *a pair* to talk about plural clothes.

c ◀)) **5.25** Now focus on the **You say** phrases and tell Sts they're going to hear the conversation again. They should repeat the **You say** phrases when they hear the beep. Encourage them to copy the rhythm and intonation.

Play the video / audio, pausing if necessary for Sts to repeat the phrases.

◀)) **5.25**
Same as script 5.24 with repeat pauses

---

d Now put Sts in pairs, **A** and **B**. **A** is the shop assistant. Get Sts to read the conversation aloud, and then swap roles.

e Focus on the instructions. **A** is the customer and **B** the shop assistant. Make sure Sts understand the situation. **B** keeps his / her book open and starts with *Can I help you, sir / madam?*.

Sts now role-play the conversation. Monitor and help.

f Now focus on the new situation and make sure Sts know what *boots* are. **A** is now the shop assistant.

Sts role-play the conversation. Monitor and help.

You could get a few pairs to perform in front of the class.

4 ▶ ROB DECIDES TO DO SOME EXERCISE

a ◀)) **5.26** Focus on sentences 1–7 and go through them with Sts.

Then play the video / audio once the whole way through for Sts to just watch or listen.

Now play it again for Sts to circle the correct answer.

Get Sts to compare with a partner, and then check answers.

---

1 Brooklyn   2 shows   3 morning   4 6.45   5 early
6 7.15   7 has

◀) **5.26**
R = Rob, J = Jenny
R Hi, Jenny.
J Oh, hi.
R Have you had a good day?
J Oh, you know. Meetings! What about you?
R It was great. I went to Brooklyn and met some really
   interesting people.
J And you had time to go shopping, too.
R What? Oh yeah. I've just bought these.
J What are they?
R A pair of trainers – er, sneakers.
J Nice. Why did you buy sneakers?
R I think I need to get a bit fitter.
J Oh, I'm impressed. You know, I go running every morning in
   Central Park.
R Do you?
J It's so beautiful early in the morning. Why don't you come
   with me?
R Er…sure. Why not?
J Great! I'll come by your hotel tomorrow morning.
R OK. What time?
J Six forty-five?
R Six…?
J Forty-five.
R Can we make it a bit later? Say, seven forty-five?
J That's too late, Rob. Let's make it seven fifteen.
R OK.
J Excellent. See you later.
R Great.
H Basketball and running, Rob? You must have a lot of energy.
R Er…yeah.

 If there's time and you are using the video,
you could get Sts to watch again with subtitles, so they
can see exactly what they understood / didn't understand.
Translate / Explain any new words or phrases.

b Focus on the **Social English** phrases. In pairs, get Sts to
see if they can remember any of the missing words.

 In pairs, get Sts to complete the phrases
before they listen.

c ◀) **5.27** Play the video / audio for Sts to watch or listen
and complete the phrases.

Check answers. If you know your Sts' L1, you could get
them to translate the phrases.

1 had **2** know **3** don't **4** make **5** Let's

◀) **5.27**
1 Have you had a good day?
2 Oh, you know. Meetings!
3 Why don't you come with me?
4 Can we make it a bit later?
5 Let's make it seven fifteen.

Now play the video / audio again, pausing after each
phrase for Sts to watch or listen and repeat.

d Focus on the instructions and make sure Sts understand
what they have to do.

Get Sts to compare with a partner, and then check
answers.

A 3 **B** 4 **C** 1 **D** 5 **E** 2

Now put Sts in pairs and get them to practise the
conversations.

Finally, focus on the **CAN YOU…?** questions and ask Sts
if they feel confident they can now do these things. If
they feel that they need more practice, tell them to go to
Online Practice to watch the episode again and practise
the language.

G will / won't (predictions)
V opposite verbs: pass – fail, etc.
P 'll, won't

Lesson plan

In this lesson Sts are introduced to the future forms will and won't for the first time. They learn a specific use of these forms, which is to make predictions about the future, here particularly in response to what somebody says to you.

The context of the lesson is pessimists and optimists. The lesson begins with a vocabulary focus on common opposite verbs, e.g. pass – fail, buy – sell. The grammar is then presented through eight situations, looking at the typical predictions an optimist or pessimist might make, e.g. You won't like it, That'll be interesting, etc. In Pronunciation, Sts practise the contracted forms of will / won't. Sts then listen to a radio programme about positive thinking. They then read an article which states that negative thinking can be good for you, and they discuss the findings. Finally, Sts answer a questionnaire to find out whether they are a positive or negative thinker.

More materials
For teachers
Photocopiables
Grammar will / won't (predictions) p.187
Vocabulary Opposite verbs p.265 (instructions p.255)
Communicative Positive or negative? p.232 (instructions p.211)
For students
Workbook 6A
Online Practice 6A

Draw a big glass which is exactly half full of water on the board. Underneath, write THE GLASS IS HALF ______. Tell Sts to complete the sentence with one word, but they mustn't tell anybody which word they have written.

Now elicit from the class how to finish the sentence (full / empty).

Ask Sts who have written empty to put up their hands. Tell them that they are pessimists (explain / translate if necessary).

Now ask who wrote full and tell these Sts that they are optimists.

1 VOCABULARY opposite verbs

a 🔊 **6.1** Books open. Tell Sts they are going to hear five sentences or questions, and they have to write down the main verb from each sentence.

Play the audio, pausing after each sentence to give Sts time to write.

Check answers.

1 find	2 send	3 remember	4 start	5 turn on

🔊 **6.1**
1 Did you find your keys?
2 Did you send the email?
3 I never remember people's names.
4 What time does the film start?
5 Please turn on the air conditioning.

Elicit from the class the opposite verbs.

1 lose	2 get / receive	3 forget	4 finish / end	5 turn off

b Tell Sts to go to **Vocabulary Bank Opposite verbs** on p.157.

Vocabulary notes

You may want to highlight:

- the difference between lend and borrow, i.e. I lend money to you / you borrow money from me
- that the opposite of start is finish or end when referring to, e.g. a film or a book, but stop when referring to, e.g. an activity, a car, etc.
- the other meaning of miss, e.g. miss your family (= feel sad because you are not with them)

Focus on **a** and get Sts to match the verbs and photos. Check answers, but don't drill pronunciation yet.

10 arrive	6 break	4 buy	15 download	3 find
7 forget	2 lend	16 love	14 miss	8 pass
17 pick up	1 push	12 send	5 start	11 teach
9 turn on	13 win			

Then get Sts to do **b** by writing the verbs in the **Opposite** column in **a**. The first one (leave) has been done for them.

🔊 **6.2** Now do **c**. Play the audio for Sts to check answers to **b** and to drill the pronunciation of the verbs in **a** and **b**.

🔊 **6.2**
Opposite verbs

10	arrive	leave
6	break	mend / repair
4	buy	sell
15	download	upload
3	find	lose
7	forget	remember
2	lend	borrow
16	love	hate
14	miss	catch
8	pass	fail
17	pick up	drop off
1	push	pull
12	send	get / receive
5	start	finish
11	teach	learn
9	turn on	turn off
13	win	lose

Now either use the audio, pausing after each pair of opposite verbs, or model and drill them yourself. Give further practice of any verbs your Sts find difficult to pronounce.

Focus on **Activation**. In pairs, Sts try to remember the verbs and their opposites. **A** (book open) says a verb and **B** (book closed) says the opposite. Make sure they swap roles.

Tell Sts to go back to the main lesson **6A**.

EXTRA CHALLENGE   If you think Sts need more practice, you may want to give them the **Vocabulary** photocopiable activity at this point.

2 GRAMMAR *will / won't* (predictions)

a Tell Sts to look at the cartoon and if you didn't do the **Optional lead-in**, check Sts know what *an optimist* and *a pessimist* are.

Now focus on the eight conversations and go through the **Your friend says** phrases with the class.

Then focus on the **You say** responses and point out that each one has two options, a and b. Tell Sts to label each response with *O* for *optimist* and *P* for *pessimist*.

b 🔊 **6.3**   Play the audio for Sts to listen and check. Check answers.

1 a O	**b** P	**2 a** P	**b** O	**3 a** O	**b** P	**4 a** O	**b** P
5 a O	**b** P	**6 a** P	**b** O	**7 a** O	**b** P	**8 a** P	**b** O

🔊 **6.3**

1 This check-in queue is really slow!
optimist
Don't worry. It'll start moving soon.
pessimist
I know. We'll miss the flight.

2 Let's drive to the restaurant.
pessimist
We'll never find anywhere to park.
optimist
Yes, it'll be quicker.

3 I've lent my brother some money.
optimist
I'm sure he'll pay you back.
pessimist
You won't see it again.

4 I'm taking my driving test tomorrow.
optimist
It'll go well, you'll see.
pessimist
You won't pass.

5 I'm selling my old laptop on eBay.
optimist
You'll sell it easily.
pessimist
Nobody will buy it.

6 Hooray! We're in the final!
pessimist
Yes! But we'll lose.
optimist
Yes! I'm sure we'll win!

7 I'm having Japanese classes next week.
optimist
That'll be interesting!
pessimist
You'll never learn it.

8 We're going to see the film in English.
pessimist
You won't understand a word.
optimist
You'll love it. And it'll be good practice.

c Put Sts in pairs and get them to look at the eight situations in **a** and decide which response they would probably give.

If you didn't do the **Optional lead-in**, get Sts to say whether they are an optimist or a pessimist.

Get some feedback about various situations. With a show of hands, you could also see if there are more optimists or pessimists in the class.

d Focus on the **You say** responses in **a** and elicit the answer to the question.

the future

e Tell Sts to go to **Grammar Bank 6A** on *p.136*.

Grammar notes

In *English File* Elementary Sts learned that *be going to* can be used to make predictions, e.g. *You're going to be very happy*. This use was revised in **3A**.

In this lesson Sts learn the future form *will / won't* + infinitive, and that it can also be used to make predictions. Sometimes both forms are possible, e.g. *I think the government will lose the election. / I think the government is going to lose the election*.

However, there is often a difference in usage: *will / won't* tends to be used more than *be going to* to make instant, on-the-spot predictions in reaction to what another person says, e.g.:

A *I'm going to try that new restaurant tonight.*

B *You won't like it.*

At this level you may prefer to simplify things by telling Sts that both *be going to* and *will / won't* can be used to make predictions.

Sts will learn other uses of the future (*will / won't*) in **6B** (promises, offers, and decisions) and will study the use of *will / won't* in conditional sentences with *if* in **8B**.

🔊 **6.4**   Focus on the example sentences and play the audio for Sts to listen and repeat. Encourage them to copy the rhythm. Then go through the rules with the class.

Now focus on the ***be going to* for predictions** box and go through it with the class.

Then focus on the exercises for **6A** on *p.137*. Sts do the exercises individually or in pairs.

Check answers, getting Sts to read the full sentences.

a

1 I think they'll lose the match.
2 Will the meeting be long?
3 She won't get the job.
4 Will you see him at work later?
5 It'll be impossible to park.
6 You won't like that book.
7 I'm sure she'll love the present I bought her.
8 There won't be a lot of traffic in the morning.
9 You'll find a good job, I'm sure.
10 Everything will be OK, so there's no need to worry.

b

1 will be
2 will like
3 will snow
4 will get
5 will pass

Tell Sts to go back to the main lesson **6A**.

 If you think Sts need more practice, you may want to give them the **Grammar** photocopiable activity at this point.

3 PRONUNCIATION *'ll, won't*

> **Pronunciation notes**
>
> An important aspect of *will / won't* is the pronunciation of the contractions and Sts get some intensive practice here. Remind Sts that contractions are very common in conversation, but that it is not wrong to use the full uncontracted form.
>
> Sts often confuse the pronunciation of the contracted form of *will not* (*won't* /wəʊnt/) with the verb *want* /wɒnt/ when speaking and listening, so there is also a special focus on this.

a ◗ **6.5** Focus on **a** and play the audio for Sts to listen and repeat. Encourage them to copy the rhythm. Sts often find the contracted form of *it will* (*it'll*) difficult to say.

◗ **6.5**
See words and phrases in Student's Book on *p.46*

b ◗ **6.6** Tell Sts that they are going to hear six sentences and that they have to write them down. Explain that they all include either *won't* or *want to*. Tell Sts that they will hear each sentence twice.

Play the audio once for Sts just to listen.

Now play the audio again, pausing after each sentence to give Sts time to write down what they hear.

Then elicit answers and write them on the board. Get them to spell *want* or *won't* to make sure they have written the correct word.

◗ **6.6**
1 I want to go with you.
2 They won't come tonight.
3 You won't find a job.
4 We want to learn Russian.
5 They want to sell their house.
6 I'm sure she won't win.

Now ask Sts what sound the pink letters have. Highlight that *want* is always followed by *to* before another verb, which will always help them to be sure which form they have heard.

```
won't = /wəʊnt/
want = /wɒnt/
```

 Put Sts in pairs and get them to practise saying the sentences.

 Play the audio again, pausing after each sentence for Sts to listen and repeat.

c Focus on the instructions and make sure Sts know what they have to do.

Put Sts in pairs. Tell Sts **A** to start by reading the first line of conversation 1 in **2a**. Sts **B** should respond as an optimist. When Sts **A** have read all eight conversations, they swap roles, and this time Sts **A** respond to the situations as pessimists. Encourage them to use optimistic or pessimistic intonation.

Monitor and help, correcting any errors with *'ll* or *won't*.

d Put Sts in pairs, **A** and **B**, and tell them to go to **Communication You're a pessimist!**, **A** on *p.104*, **B** on *p.109*.

Go through the instructions carefully. Now make sure Sts understand what they have to do.

 Get a student to read you his / her first sentence, and give an example of a pessimistic response.

Sit **A** and **B** face-to-face. **A** says his / her first sentence and **B** responds in a pessimistic way. Then they swap roles.

When they have finished, you could get a few Sts to read a sentence and get others to respond.

Tell Sts to go back to the main lesson **6A**.

4 LISTENING using existing knowledge to predict content

a ◗ **6.7** Focus on the instructions and question. Tell Sts that the radio programme is a chat show where one of the guests is an expert on positive thinking.

Play the audio for Sts to listen and answer the question.

Check the answer.

 Read through the script and decide if you need to pre-teach any new lexis before Sts listen.

It helps you enjoy life more. Positive people are healthier and live longer.

◗ **6.7**
(script in Student's Book on *p.122*)
Presenter
Today's topic is 'positive thinking'. We all know that people who are positive enjoy life more than people who are negative and pessimistic. But scientific studies show that positive people are also healthier. They get better more quickly when they are ill, and they live longer. A recent study has shown that people who are optimistic and think positively live, on average, nine years longer than pessimistic people. So, let's hear what you, the listeners, think. Do you have any ideas to help us be more positive in our lives?

 Before playing the audio, elicit some ideas from the class why positive thinking is good for you.

b Now explain that five people have called the radio programme to give some tips (useful suggestions) to help people be more positive.

Get Sts, in pairs, to try and guess what the missing words in the sentences could be. Tell them <u>not</u> to write them in the sentences, but on a separate piece of paper.

You could elicit some ideas, but <u>don't</u> check answers yet.

c 🔊 **6.8** Play the audio once for Sts to listen and check their guesses and complete the gaps.

Check answers.

> 1 Live in the **present**, not in the **past**.
> 2 Think **positive** thoughts, not **negative** ones.
> 3 Don't spend a lot of time following the **news** online or on TV.
> 4 Every week, make a list of all the **good things** that happened to you.
> 5 Try to use positive **language** when you speak to other people.

🔊 **6.8**
(script in Student's Book on *p.122*)

P = presenter, C = caller

P Our first caller this evening is Andy. Hi, Andy. What's your tip for being positive?

C1 Hello. Well, I think it's very important to live in the present and not in the past. Don't think about mistakes you made in the past – you can't change things now. The important thing is to think about how you can do things better now and in the future.

P Thank you, Andy. And now we have another caller. What's your name, please?

C2 Hi, my name's Julie. My tip is think positive thoughts, not negative ones. We all have negative thoughts sometimes, but when we start having them, we need to stop and try to change them into positive ones. Like, if you have an exam tomorrow and you start thinking, 'I'm sure I'll fail,' then you'll fail the exam. So you need to change that negative thought to a positive thought. Just think to yourself, 'I'll pass. that exam' I do this and it usually works.

P Thank you, Julie. And our next caller is Martin. Hi, Martin.

C3 Hi. My tip is don't spend a lot of time following the news online or on TV. It's always bad news and it just makes you feel depressed. Read a book or listen to your favourite music instead, and you won't feel so bad.

P Thanks, Martin. Good tip! And our next caller is Miriam. Miriam?

C4 Hi.

P Hi, Miriam. What's your tip?

C4 Every week, make a list of all the good things that happened to you, on your phone or on a piece of paper. Then if you're feeling a bit sad or depressed, read the list and it'll make you feel better.

P Thanks, Miriam. And our last call is from Michael. Hi, Michael. We're listening.

C5 Hi. I think it's good to try to use positive language when you speak to other people. You know, if your friend has a problem, don't say, 'I'm sorry' or 'Oh, poor you.' Say something positive, like 'Don't worry! Everything'll be OK.' That way, you'll make the other person think more positively about their problem.

P Thank you, Michael. Well that's all we've got time for. A big thank you to all our callers.

---

d Play the audio again for Sts to write down extra information, e.g. a reason or an example.

Get Sts to compare with a partner, and then play the audio again.

Check answers (see script 6.8).

Finally, in pairs, small groups, or as a whole class, answer the two questions. For the question *Which tips do you think are the most useful?*, you could get Sts to vote for the best tip with a show of hands.

EXTRA SUPPORT If there's time, you could get Sts to listen again with the scripts on *p.122*, so they can see exactly what they understood / didn't understand. Translate / Explain any new words or phrases.

5 READING

a Focus on the cartoon of the girl studying and, with a show of hands, find out if Sts think the girl is an optimist or a pessimist.

b Give Sts time to read the article and check their answer to **a**. They should also answer the question *What is 'defensive pessimism'?*.

Check answers.

EXTRA SUPPORT Before Sts read the article the first time, check whether you need to pre-teach any vocabulary.

> She is a pessimist.
> It's a strategy which we use to control anxiety, fear, and worry.

Deal with any other new vocabulary. Model and drill the pronunciation of any tricky words.

c Now tell Sts to complete the two sentences from the article with the same word.

Check the answer.

> wrong

d Do this as a whole-class activity.

> 1 The printer isn't working.
> 2 You've got the incorrect number.
> 3 There were no problems on our journey.

e Focus on the task and make sure Sts understand what they have to do.

When Sts have finished reading the article again, either put them in pairs or do it as a whole-class activity.

If Sts worked in pairs, get some feedback.

> **Possible answers**
> He can leave home early / check what time the bus leaves.
> He can check which terminal the flight leaves from in advance.
> He can pack carefully / weigh the luggage before they leave home.
> He can take a jumper or jacket to wear on the plane.
> He can take some food of his own or buy food at the airport.

f Do this as a whole-class activity and elicit answers from Sts.

6 SPEAKING

Focus on the activity and on the seven questions.

Then go through the expressions in the **Responding to predictions** box with the class. Drill the pronunciation, making sure Sts do not over-stress the word *so* and are clear about the meaning. Point out that the word *so* in *I hope so*, etc. means *yes*, and that *maybe* and *perhaps* have the same meaning.

In pairs, Sts take it in turns to ask and answer each question, giving reasons for their predictions. They should then decide who is more optimistic.

Finally, get some feedback, e.g. ask how many people in the class think they will pass their next English exam.

I'll always love you

G *will / won't / shall* (other uses)
V verb + *back*: *come back*, *call back*, etc.
P word stress: two-syllable verbs

Lesson plan

Sts continue their work on the uses of *will*. In this lesson they learn that as well as making predictions, *will* can be used for making promises, offers, and decisions. The presentation context is an article and a listening about the true story of a couple whose promise to love each other was only kept after a chain of strange circumstances. This is followed by the grammar, presented through some humorous typical offers, promises, and decisions, and a pronunciation focus on stress in two-syllable verbs, e.g. *promise*, *decide*. Next, in Vocabulary, Sts focus on the use of certain verbs with *back* (*come back*, *take back*, etc.), which they then put into practice with a final speaking activity.

More materials
For teachers
Photocopiables
Grammar will / won't / shall (other uses) *p.188*
Communicative Guess my sentence *p.233* (instructions *p.212*)
For students
Workbook 6B
Online Practice 6B

OPTIONAL LEAD-IN (BOOKS CLOSED)

Write the word PROMISES on the board and elicit its meaning. Teach / Elicit that you can *make a promise* and then *keep* or *break a promise*.

Ask Sts *What promises do people in love often make?*. Try to elicit some promises and write them on the board, e.g. *I'll always love you / I'll never leave you / I'll marry you*, etc. Then ask Sts if they think people keep or break these promises.

1 READING & LISTENING understanding the order of events

a Books open. Focus on the task and the two photos. Elicit answers for the two questions from the class. They will find out if they were right later in the lesson.

b Tell Sts to read the article and complete it with the four time expressions.

Check answers.

EXTRA SUPPORT Before Sts read the article the first time, check whether you need to pre-teach any vocabulary.

1 17 years ago   **2** a year after   **3** a few years later   **4** for ten years

c Now tell Sts to read the article again and answer questions 1–3.

Get Sts to compare with a partner, and then check answers.

1 Carmen was studying English and Steve was living there.
2 Because Carmen moved to France, and the long-distance relationship didn't work.
3 Because Carmen's mother didn't send it to her.

Deal with any other new vocabulary. Model and drill the pronunciation of any tricky words.

d ◑ **6.9** Focus on the task and tell Sts they are now going to find out what happened to Steve and Carmen between the two photos. Tell Sts to look at questions 1–5.

Play the audio for Sts to listen and answer the questions. Then play it again if necessary.

Get Sts to compare with a partner, and then check answers. You could also check here the answer to **a**, i.e. that in the first photo they are both 25, and in the second they are 42.

EXTRA SUPPORT Read through the script and decide if you need to pre-teach any new lexis before Sts listen.

1 Some builders found it and gave it to Carmen's sister.
2 She phoned Steve.
3 They arranged to meet in Paris a few days later.
4 They kissed at the airport and fell in love again.
5 They got married.

◑ **6.9**

P = presenter, S = Steve, C = Carmen

P Earlier this year, ten years after Steve sent the letter, some builders were renovating the living room in Carmen's mother's house in Spain. When they were working on the fireplace, they found Steve's letter. They gave it to Carmen's sister, and she sent the letter to Carmen in Paris. Carmen was now forty-two, and she was still single.

C When I got the letter, I didn't call Steve immediately, because I was so nervous. I kept picking up the phone and putting it down again. I nearly didn't phone him at all. But I knew that I had to make the call.

P Carmen finally made the call and Steve answered the phone. He was also now forty-two and he was also single.

S I couldn't believe it when she phoned. I've just moved house, but luckily I kept my old phone number.

P Steve and Carmen arranged to meet in Paris a few days later.

S When we met, it was like a film. We ran across the airport and into each other's arms. Within thirty seconds of seeing each other again, we were kissing. We fell in love all over again.

P Last week the couple got married, seventeen years after they first met.

C I never got married in all those years, but now I have married the man I've always loved.

EXTRA SUPPORT If there's time, you could get Sts to listen again, so they can see exactly what they understood / didn't understand. Translate / Explain any new words or phrases.

e Do this as a whole-class activity.

 Get Sts to retell the story from Steve or Carmen's point of view.

2 GRAMMAR *will / won't / shall* (other uses)

a Focus on the sentences and the photos on **p.49**. Elicit / Explain any new words or phrases, e.g. *hurt*. Now tell Sts to match the sentences to the people who are saying them.

Check answers. Ask Sts if they have had experience of people saying these things to them, and if they were true or not.

> **A** This won't hurt.
> **B** I'll tidy my room now.
> **C** Shall I drive?
> **D** I won't have any more.
> **E**   I'll come back tomorrow and finish it.
> **F** I'll have what she's having.

b Focus on the instructions and make sure Sts understand *offer* and *promise*. Highlight that they should write the letter of the people. Point out that the first one (*B*) has been done for them.

Check answers.

> **offering to do something:** C
> **deciding to do something:** D, F
> **promising to do something:** A, E

c Tell Sts to go to **Grammar Bank 6B** on *p.136*.

Grammar notes

Sts shouldn't worry about being able to distinguish between an offer, a promise, or a decision. Depending on the context, *I'll help you tomorrow* could be an offer, a promise, or a decision.

In some languages the present tense is used for offers and decisions. Highlight that in English you say *I'll help you* NOT ~~I help you~~.

Shall I…? is only used when an offer to do something is asked as a question, e.g. *Shall I make you a cup of coffee?* NOT ~~Will I make you a cup of coffee?~~

In other future contexts *Will I…?* is used, e.g. *Will I need my passport?* NOT ~~Shall I need my passport?~~

In the past, *shall* was always used instead of *will* in the first person singular and plural. Today, *will* is commonly used for all persons, and *shall* is mainly used in offers (*Shall I turn on the heating?*) and suggestions (*Shall we get a taxi?*).

◗) 6.10 Focus on the example sentences and play the audio for Sts to listen and repeat. Encourage them to copy the rhythm. Then go through the rules with the class.

Now focus on the exercises for **6B** on *p.137*. Sts do the exercises individually or in pairs.

Check answers, getting Sts, in pairs, to read the full sentences.

> **a 1** C **2** H **3** D **4** B **5** I **6** A **7** F **8** E
> **b**
> **1** **Shall I help** you?
> **2** I **won't tell** anyone, I promise.
> **3** **I'll call** you tonight.
> **4** When **will** you **pay** me back?
> **5** Don't worry. I **won't forget**.
> **6** **Shall I take** you home?
> **7** **I'll get** a bigger pair for you, madam.
> **8** Yes, I know. I **won't buy** it again.

Tell Sts to go back to the main lesson **6B**.

 If you think Sts need more practice, you may want to give them the **Grammar** photocopiable activity at this point.

d Focus on the task and give Sts time to write their sentences. Monitor and help. Correct any errors with *will*, *won't*, and *shall*.

Now put Sts in pairs and get them to read their sentences to each other.

Find out if anyone wrote exactly the same as their partner.

3 PRONUNCIATION word stress: two-syllable verbs

a Focus on the activity and give Sts, in pairs, time to put the two-syllable verbs in the correct columns.

b ◗) 6.11 Tell Sts they are going to hear the verbs being used in sentences. First, they will hear all the verbs that are stressed on the first syllable.

Play the audio for Sts to listen and check.

Check answers. You might want to point out that most two-syllable verbs are stressed on the second syllable.

> **1st syllable:** offer, promise, borrow, happen, practise
> **2nd syllable:** decide, agree, arrive, complain, depend, forget, invite, prefer, receive, repair

---

◗) 6.11
First syllable
We'll offer him the job.
I promise to come.
Can I borrow your car?
It'll never happen.
Please practise the sentences.
Second syllable
We'll decide later.
I don't agree.
When do you arrive?
They complain about everything.
It'll depend on the weather.
Don't forget your keys.
Let's invite her.
Which do you prefer?
You'll receive it in a week.
Can you repair this, please?

c 🔊 **6.12** Tell Sts that this time they will only hear the verbs and they must listen and repeat them. Either tell Sts to look at the list of verbs in **a**, or get them to close their books.

Play the audio for Sts to practise saying the verbs, making sure they stress them clearly.

🔊 **6.12**

decide, offer, promise, agree, arrive, borrow, complain, depend, forget, happen, invite, practise, prefer, receive, repair

---

EXTRA CHALLENGE Divide the class into small groups. Tell Sts you are going to give them a verb from **a**, and in their groups they must write a sentence as quickly as possible, using the verb. The sentence must have a minimum of five words in it. When they are ready, they should read the sentence out loud. If the sentence is correct and their pronunciation is good, they get a point.

d Give Sts time to complete sentences 1–5 in their own words.

Now put Sts in pairs and get them to read their sentences to each other.

Find out if anyone wrote exactly the same as their partner.

4 VOCABULARY & SPEAKING verb + *back*

a Here Sts learn / revise some common verbs with *back*, e.g. *go back, pay (somebody) back*. Focus on the question and elicit the answer.

> *come back* = to return to a place

> ### Vocabulary notes
> The key thing for Sts to understand is that by adding *back* to a verb, they are adding the sense of 'returning' an action.
>
> You may want to point out that the object pronoun (*it, them*, etc.) goes between the verb and *back*, e.g. *give it back, send them back*. Word order with these kinds of verbs + prepositions / adverbs (phrasal verbs) is dealt with in detail in **10B.**
>
> Other verbs + *back* that you could also teach are *get back* (*get to somewhere* = arrive; *get back somewhere* = return to where you started from), *write back, walk back*, etc.

b Focus on the phrases in the list. Demonstrate *give back* by giving something to a student and then saying *Give it back, please*.

Give Sts a couple of minutes to read 1–6 and complete them with a phrase from the list.

c 🔊 **6.13** Play the audio for Sts to listen and check.

Check answers.

> **1** go back **2** take it back **3** call you back **4** give it back
> **5** pay you back **6** send them back

🔊 **6.13**

1 **A** Are you feeling better?
  B Yes, I think I'll go back to work tomorrow.
2 **A** The shirt you bought me is too small.
  B Don't worry. I'll take it back to the shop and change it. I still have the receipt.
3 **A** Hi, Jack. It's me, Karen.
  B I can't talk now, I'm driving. I'll call you back in fifteen minutes.
4 **A** That's my pen you're using!
  B Is it? Sorry. I'll give it back in a minute.
5 **A** Can you lend me twenty pounds? I'll pay you back next week.
  B OK – here you are.
6 **A** Where did you buy those shoes?
  B I got them online, but they're too big. I think I'll send them back.

Get Sts to practise the conversations in pairs.

d Focus on the **Giving examples and reasons** box and go through it with the class.

Now focus on the task and make sure that Sts understand the questions.

Put Sts into groups of three or four and get them to discuss 1–6.

Monitor and help while Sts are talking.

Get some feedback from the class.

EXTRA SUPPORT Demonstrate the activity by answering a couple of questions yourself.

6C The meaning of dreaming

G review of verb forms: present, past, and future
V modifiers
P the letters *ea*

Lesson plan

The final lesson in File 6 provides a consolidation of the verb forms studied in the first half of the book. Present, past, and future forms are revised through the context of interpreting dreams. Although the lesson provides a light-hearted look at dreams, the symbols and their interpretations have been taken from serious sources. Sts begin by listening to a psychoanalyst interpreting a patient's dream. After focusing on and revising different forms which are used in the conversation, Sts get the chance to ask and answer questions using all the verb forms they have studied. Then there is a vocabulary focus on modifiers like *quite*, *really*, and *incredibly*. In Pronunciation Sts look at the possible pronunciations of the letters *ea*, and the lesson ends with a video listening about the meaning of dreams.

More materials
For teachers
Photocopiables
Grammar review of verb forms: present, past, and future *p.189*
Communicative Talk about it *p.234* (instructions *p.212*)
Teacher's Resource Centre
Video What do our dreams really mean?
For students
Workbook 6C
Online Practice 6C

OPTIONAL LEAD-IN (BOOKS CLOSED)
Ask Sts if they had any dreams last night. If they say *Yes*, elicit from three or four Sts what they dreamed about (just the subject, not the details), e.g. *I dreamed I was falling / about my exams*. Write the dreams on the board and quickly ask the class if they know what the dreams mean. Accept any reasonable explanations, and tell them they are going to find out more about the meaning of dreams in the lesson.

1 LISTENING

a Books open. Focus on the four questions. Put Sts in pairs and get them to discuss the questions.

Get some feedback from various pairs. You could answer a couple of questions too.

b 🔊 **6.14** Focus on the instructions. Check Sts know the meaning of *psychoanalyst* and *patient*. Model and drill their pronunciation /ˌsaɪkəʊˈænəlɪst/ and /ˈpeɪʃnt/.

Focus on the pictures and ask Sts what they can see. Elicit that the pictures show an owl, champagne, a woman playing the violin, feet, people at a party, and flowers.

Play the audio and get Sts to number the pictures 1–6 in the correct order.

Get Sts to compare with a partner, and then check answers.

EXTRA SUPPORT Read through the scripts and decide if you need to pre-teach any new lexis before Sts listen.

1 party	**2** champagne	**3** flowers	**4** violin player	**5** owl
6 feet				

🔊 **6.14**
Dr = Dr Melloni, **P** = patient
Dr So, tell me, what did you dream about?
P I was at a party. The room was full of people.
Dr What were they doing?
P They were drinking and talking.
Dr Were you drinking?
P Yes, I was drinking champagne.
Dr And then what happened?
P Then suddenly I was in a garden. There were a lot of flowers.
Dr Flowers, yes…What kind of flowers?
P I couldn't see – it was a bit dark. And I could hear music – somebody was playing the violin.
Dr The violin? Go on.
P And then I saw an owl, a really big owl in a tree…
Dr How did you feel? Were you frightened of it?
P No, not frightened, really, no – but I remember I felt incredibly cold. Especially my feet – they were freezing. And then I woke up.
Dr Your feet? Mmm, very interesting, very interesting. Were you wearing any shoes?
P No. No, I wasn't.
Dr Tell me, have you ever had this dream before?
P No, never. So what does it mean, Doctor?

c Focus on the conversation and give Sts a few minutes to read it.

Play the audio again for Sts to complete the gaps. You may need to pause the audio to give Sts time to write the missing words.

Check answers.

1 doing	**2** talking	**3** drinking	**4** were	**5** couldn't
6 playing	**7** saw	**8** feel	**9** remember	**10** woke up
11 wearing	**12** had	**13** mean		

EXTRA CHALLENGE Get Sts to try to complete the missing words before they listen. <u>Don't</u> tell them whether their guesses are right or wrong.

d Tell Sts that they are going to try to understand the man's dream. In pairs, they must match the things in his dream in the **You dream…** column to interpretations 1–5 in **This means…**.

Get Sts to compare with a partner.

e **6.15** Focus on the task and play the audio for Sts to listen and check.

Check answers.

> that you are at a party 2
> that you are drinking champagne 5
> about flowers 1
> that somebody is playing the violin 3
> about an owl 4

6.15
(script in Student's Book on *p.122*)
Dr = Dr Melloni, P = patient
P So what does it mean, Doctor?
Dr Well, first the party. A party is a group of people. This means that you're going to meet a lot of people. I think you're going to be very busy.
P At work?
Dr Yes, at work…You work in an office, I think?
P Yes, that's right.
Dr I think the party means you're going to have a lot of meetings.
P What about the champagne?
Dr Let me look at my notes again. Ah yes, you were drinking champagne. Champagne means a celebration. It's a symbol of success. So we have a meeting or meetings, and then a celebration. Maybe in the future, you'll have a meeting with your boss, about a possible promotion?
P Well, it's possible. I hope so…What about the garden and the flowers? Do they mean anything?
Dr Yes. Flowers are a positive symbol. So, the flowers mean that you are feeling positive about the future. So perhaps you already knew about this possible promotion?
P No, I didn't. But it's true – I am very happy at work and I feel very positive about my future. That's not where my problems are. My problems are with my love life. Does my dream tell you anything about that?
Dr Mmm, yes, it does. You're single, aren't you?
P Yes – well, divorced.
Dr Because the violin music tells me you want some romance in your life – you're looking for a partner, perhaps?
P Yes, yes, I am. In fact, I met a woman last month – I really like her…I think I'm in love with her. I'm meeting her tonight.
Dr In your dream you saw an owl in a tree?
P Yes, an owl…a big owl.
Dr The owl represents an older person. I think you'll need to ask this older person for help. Maybe this 'older person' is me? Maybe you need my help?
P Well, yes, what I really want to know is: does this person, this woman…love me?

 Play the audio again, pausing after each bit of interpretation, and elicit as much information as possible from the class.

f **6.16** Elicit a few ideas from Sts about the meaning of picture 6 (the feet). You could write some of the ideas on the board.

Now play the audio for Sts to listen.

Check the answer.

> The woman doesn't love him.

6.16
P Well, yes, what I really want to know is: does this person, this woman…love me?
Dr You remember the end of your dream? You were feeling cold?
P Yes, my feet were very cold.
Dr Well…I think perhaps you already know the answer to your question.
P You mean she doesn't love me.
Dr No, I don't think so. I think you will need to find another woman. I'm sorry. Perhaps you can find someone…

 If there's time, you could get Sts to listen again to both parts with the scripts on *p.123*, so they can see exactly what they understood / didn't understand. Translate / Explain any new words or phrases.

2 GRAMMAR review of verb forms

a Look at the sentences and explain that they come from the listening, and are examples of the different tenses and forms Sts have studied so far.

Elicit which one is in the present perfect (3). Then give Sts, in pairs, a few minutes to decide what time the other sentences refer to.

Check answers.

> 1 P 2 P 3 PP 4 F 5 PR 6 F 7 PR 8 F

b Tell Sts to go to **Grammar Bank 6C** on *p.136*.

> ### Grammar notes
> Sts should by now be reasonably confident with the present simple and continuous, the past simple, and *be going to*. With the new forms and tenses, how quickly they assimilate them will depend to a large extent on whether they have a similar form in their L1. Don't over-correct mistakes, but encourage Sts to use these tenses where appropriate and to get the form correct.

6.17 Focus on the example sentences and play the audio for Sts to listen and repeat. Encourage them to copy the rhythm. Then go through the rules with the class.

Now focus on the exercises for **6C** on *p.137*. Sts do the exercises individually or in pairs.

Check answers, getting Sts to read the full sentences.

> a 1 **Do** you often remember your dreams?
>   2 **Did** you watch the match last night?
>   3 Who do you think **will** win the election next year?
>   4 **Have** you been to the supermarket?
>   5 **Does** your brother like rock music?
>   6 What **are** you going to watch on TV tonight?
>   7 **Was** it snowing when you left?
>   8 **Were** you at the party last night?
>   9 **Has** the film finished yet?
> b 1 We**'re having** dinner with Jack and Mary.
>   2 But we **had** dinner with them last week!
>   3 Yes, but they **want** to tell us some good news.
>   4 **Shall** I **buy** some champagne?
>   5 Where **have** you **been**?
>   6 When I **was walking** home…
>   7 I **decided** to buy…
>   8 And then I **saw** Mark in the shop…
>   9 We**'re going to be / are** late!
>   10 I**'ve already booked** a taxi…
>   11 I**'ll be** ready in five minutes.

Tell Sts to go back to the main lesson **6C**.

 If you think Sts need more practice, you may want to give them the **Grammar** photocopiable activity at this point.

3 SPEAKING

Put Sts in pairs, **A** and **B**. Tell Sts to go to **Communication Revision questionnaire**, **A** on *p.104*, **B** on *p.111*.

Go through the instructions with them carefully and make sure Sts know what they have to do. You could tell Sts that the questions practise all the tenses they have studied so far, and that each student has one question for each tense.

Give Sts time to interview each other, making sure they ask for more information.

Monitor and help while Sts are talking.

Get some feedback from the class.

Tell Sts to go back to the main lesson **6C**.

4 VOCABULARY modifiers

a In this activity Sts revise / learn some useful modifiers. Focus on the two examples in the chart.

Now make sure Sts understand that they have to complete the chart with the words in the list in order. Elicit the first one (*incredibly*) from the whole class.

b 🔊 **6.18** Play the audio for Sts to listen and check.

Check answers.

The room was	incredibly	
	really	
	very	dark.
	quite	
	a bit	
	not very	

🔊 **6.18**
1 The room was incredibly dark.
2 The room was really dark.
3 The room was very dark.
4 The room was quite dark.
5 The room was a bit dark.
6 The room was not very dark.

Focus on the **a bit** information box and go through it with the class.

Vocabulary notes
You may want to highlight that:

- *incredibly* /ɪnˈkredəbli/ has the stress on the second syllable
- *really* is a little stronger than *very*. Compare *She's very well* and *She's really well*
- *quite* means an intermediate amount – neither a lot nor a little

c Give Sts time to complete the sentences so that they are true for them, and then get them to compare their answers with a partner.

Get some feedback from the class.

5 PRONUNCIATION the letters *ea*

Pronunciation notes
The combination of vowels *ea* has several possible pronunciations.
The most common is /iː/, e.g. *speak*. /e/ is less common, e.g. *breakfast*. /eɪ/ is very rare, and the only common *ea* words with this sound are *great*, *break*, and *steak*.

a Focus on the activity and the chart. Elicit the six sound picture words and the sounds: *tree* /iː/, *egg* /e/, *train* /eɪ/, *chair* /eə/, *ear* /ɪə/, and *bird* /ɜː/.

Now tell Sts to put the words in the list in the correct column. Remind Sts that this kind of exercise is easier to do if they say the words aloud.

Get Sts to compare with a partner.

b 🔊 **6.19** Play the audio for Sts to listen and check. Check answers.

🔊 **6.19**

tree /iː/	dream, mean, beach, clean, easy, jeans, meat, speak
egg /e/	already, breakfast, sweater, weather
train /eɪ/	break, great
chair /eə/	wear
ear /ɪə/	really, clear, dear, hear, idea, near, theatre
bird /ɜː/	earn, learn

Then play it again, pausing after each word or group of words for Sts to listen and repeat.

Now ask Sts what the most common pronunciation of the letters *ea* is.

/iː/

Finally, ask them what the most common pronunciation of the letters *ear* is.

/ɪə/

 If these sounds are difficult for your Sts, it will help to show them the mouth position. You could model this yourself or use the the Sound Bank videos on the *Teacher's Resource Centre*.

c 🔊 **6.20** Tell Sts they are going to hear four sentences and they must write them down.

Play the audio once the whole way through for Sts just to listen.

Now play the audio again, pausing after each sentence to give Sts time to write.

Check answers.

🔊 **6.20**
1 What does my dream about the beach mean?
2 We've already had breakfast.
3 Great – it's time for a break!
4 Oh dear! I hear nobody likes your idea.

Finally, put Sts in pairs and get them to practise saying the sentences.

 Put Sts in pairs and get them to write three more sentences with the words in **a**. They should then practise saying the sentences. You could then get pairs to swap sentences and practise saying the new sentences.

6 ▶ VIDEO LISTENING

a Tell Sts that they're going to watch a film about common dreams and what they mean.

Play the video once the whole way through.

Get Sts to compare their ideas with a partner, and then check the answers.

 Read through the script and decide if you need to pre-teach any new lexis before Sts watch.

> The dreams with a good meaning are:
> - Dream 4, your life is successful (this dream can also have a bad meaning).
> - Dream 5, you're in love.
> - Dream 7, you're having an exciting time in your life.

What do our dreams really mean?

Meet Tom. Like everyone, Tom likes to get a good night's sleep. And like us all, Tom has about five separate dreams every night. These dreams can last between fifteen and forty minutes. According to experts, our dreams tell us who we are, what we need, and what we believe in, so, for Tom and for everyone else, here is a guide to the most common dreams and their meanings.

Dream one: someone is running after you.

If you have this dream, it means something is worrying you in real life. Something like a difficult decision or a difficult situation with a friend or a colleague. People often have this dream again and again until they make the decision or deal with the situation that is worrying them.

Dream two: you can't find something you need.

Dreaming about losing something and trying to find it again is surprisingly common. It usually means that you're worried about something stressful that you need to do soon, like going on a long journey or giving a talk in public. In these situations, people sometimes dream about losing their passport or tickets, or losing their notes or memory stick.

Dream three: you're unprepared for an exam.

This one is common for young adults or children who are under stress, and it can feel very real – sometimes you can wake up sure that you've just failed an important exam or test. If you're not doing any exams in real life, this dream could mean that you don't have enough confidence in your ability to do something.

Dream four: you're flying or falling.

Another very common dream is the flying dream. Sometimes people dream that they are in control. If you feel in control, it means that your life is successful – perhaps you've just passed an important exam, or your boss has given you a promotion.

But usually, people dream that they're out of control, and falling. This means the opposite – your life isn't going well, and you're worried about what's going to happen in the future.

Dream five: you're underwater.

If you dream that you're underwater, but you're feeling happy and comfortable and you can still breathe, it could mean you have very strong feelings for someone. You're probably in love!

Dream six: you're in an out of control vehicle.

A dream about cars is a dream about your direction in life. If you dream that you're driving, and you lose control of your car, you probably feel that your life is out of control.

If somebody you know is driving, then perhaps you feel that they have problems in their life, and need your help.

Dream seven: you find a new room in your house.

This dream means that you're having an exciting time in your life, and you're discovering new possibilities. If the room is white, it means you want to make a new beginning in your life.

Dream eight: You're late for a meeting or appointment.

Dreaming that you're late for a meeting represents your worry about taking a different direction in your life. Perhaps you're not one hundred per cent confident about making a change. This dream can also mean that you feel like you don't have enough time to get something done.

Sometimes, dreams come true, but more often, they don't.

Sweet dreams!

---

b Give Sts time to read the sentences, making sure they understand them.

Then play the video again for Sts to complete the sentences. You could pause after each dream to check answers.

 First put Sts in pairs and ask them to try to complete the meanings of the dreams from memory. Then play the video again. Ask students to check there answers and make a note of any extra information about each dream.

Get some feedback from various pairs.

> Dream 1 decision, friend
> Dream 2 journey, talk
> Dream 3 confidence, ability
> Dream 4 successful, future
> Dream 5 strong, love
> Dream 6 life, help
> Dream 7 exciting, possibilities
> Dream 8 direction, time

 If there's time, you could get Sts to watch again with subtitles, so they can see exactly what they understood / didn't understand. Translate / Explain any new words or phrases.

c Ask Sts to discuss the questions in groups or as a class.

Get some feedback from various Sts.

For instructions on how to use these pages, see *p.40*.

More materials
For teachers
Teacher's Resource Centre
Video Can you understand these people? 5&6
Quick Test 6
File 6 Test
Progress Test Files 1–6
For students
Online Practice Check your progress

GRAMMAR

1 a 2 c 3 a 4 b 5 c 6 c 7 b 8 a 9 b 10 b
11 a 12 c 13 a 14 b 15 b

VOCABULARY

a
1 Two thirds 2 five hundred and fifty 3 lend
4 coming back 5 teaching
b
1 sell 2 pull 3 forget 4 fail 5 lose
c
1 crowded 2 safe 3 noisy 4 south 5 museum
6 palace 7 harbour 8 bones 9 heart 10 disease
d
1 Very 2 incredibly 3 bit 4 really 5 quite

PRONUNCIATION

c
1 bett**er** /ə/ 2 m**a**ny /e/ 3 enou**gh** /f/ 4 **wh**y /w/
5 w**ear** /eə/
d
1 imp**a**tient 2 **ea**siest 3 **o**ptimist 4 de**pe**nd 5 for**ge**t

CAN YOU understand this text?

a
She shouted 'Tell them about the dream' when he was speaking in Washington.
b
1 E 2 A 3 C 4 F 5 B 6 D

CAN YOU understand these people?

1 b 2 c 3 c 4 b 5 a

🔊 6.21

1
I = interviewer, K = Katelyn
I Do you have more free time than three years ago?
K I actually definitely do have more free time than I did a couple of years ago, so I actually just graduated from college. This is my first year working full time, so working nine to five frees up your evenings, so definitely more free time than before.

2
I = interviewer, S = Susie
I What's the most beautiful city you've ever been to?
S That's such a good question. Um, I think probably Athens.
I Why?
S It's, it's just, it's absolutely gorgeous – the Acropolis, the Parthenon, the sights are beautiful. Yeah, it's the best place to go.

3
I = interviewer, A = Anna
I What do you drink in a typical day?
A In a typical day I usually just drink, er, a lot of coffee and water, sometimes juice.
I Is there anything you drink too much of?
A I probably drink too much coffee.
I Is there anything you don't drink enough of?
A I don't drink enough water most days, but I'm trying to get better.

4
I = interviewer, L = Laura
I Are you an optimist or a pessimist?
C I am a realist. Um, yeah, more pessimistic than optimistic.

5
I = interviewer, P = Paula
I Do you often dream about the same thing?
P Yes, I do. I had a really, really awful teacher at high school for history, and she was always really mean. And when I finished high school, I always dreamed that she would say, 'You will never pass your A levels'. And now I always dream of the same teacher from high school telling me, 'You will never finish your degree,' so that's kind of weird, yeah.

G uses of the infinitive with *to*
V verbs + infinitive: *try to*, *forget to*, etc.
P weak form of *to*, linking

Lesson plan

The context of this lesson is advice on how to 'survive' stressful situations such as the first day in a new job. The material is based on information on a website called *lifehack* which gives 'tips for life'. The lesson begins with Sts reading some useful advice on what to do and say (and not do and say) when you start a new office job. They then listen to two people describing their first day at work and see how they got on. In Vocabulary, the focus is on some high frequency verbs which are followed by the infinitive form, and in Grammar, Sts learn when to use the infinitive form with *to* (after certain verbs, after adjectives, etc.). Sts also read and re-tell two more *How to…* texts (surviving meeting your partner's parents for the first time and surviving a first date). In Pronunciation and Speaking, Sts practise the weak form of *to* in phrases using an infinitive and linking. Finally, in Writing they write some tips of their own on a different subject.

More materials		
For teachers		
Photocopiables		
Grammar uses of the infinitive with *to p.190*		
Communicative I'm going to tell you about… p.235		
(instructions *p.212*)		
For students		
Workbook 7A		
Online Practice 7A		

Write HOW TO SURVIVE… on the board in big letters. Tell Sts that there are websites giving people advice about how to survive stressful situations in daily life. Then elicit from Sts stressful situations that they would like to read advice for, and write them on the board.

You may want to give them a few ideas to start them off, e.g. *a week of exams*, *a first date*, etc.

Continue until you have five or six situations. Then ask Sts *What advice would you give?* and elicit ideas.

1 READING text coherence / understanding content words

a Books open. Focus on the task and the two sentence beginnings. Give Sts time to think, then either put Sts in pairs or do this as a whole-class activity.

If Sts worked in pairs, get some feedback and write it on the board in two columns.

b If you didn't do the **Optional lead-in**, focus on the title of the article and make sure Sts know the meaning of *survive* (= to continue to live in or after a difficult time).

Now tell Sts to read the article from a newspaper to see if their advice is included in the article. Tell them not to worry about the gaps.

Elicit from the class which tips on the board are mentioned in the article.

EXTRA SUPPORT Before Sts read the article the first time, check whether you need to pre-teach any vocabulary.

c Get Sts to read the article again and this time to complete gaps 1–7 with tips A–G. You could quickly go through the tips to make sure Sts understand all the lexis.

Get Sts to compare with a partner, and then check answers.

1 D	2 B	3 A	4 C	5 G	6 F	7 E

Deal with any other new vocabulary. Model and drill the pronunciation of any tricky words.

EXTRA IDEA Get Sts to underline the important content words in A–G, i.e. nouns and verbs. Then quickly read the article again and match the tips to the correct section.

d Do this as a whole-class activity.

2 LISTENING

! Track 7.1 is a long listening with two stories. You could do each story separately if you prefer.

a 🔊 **7.1** Tell Sts they are now going to listen to two people, Simon and Claire, describing their first day at a new job. They must listen to see what problems they had.

Play the audio once the whole way through.

Get Sts to compare with a partner, and then check answers.

EXTRA SUPPORT Read through the script and decide if you need to pre-teach any new lexis before Sts listen.

> Simon was wearing the wrong clothes (a suit).
> Claire had to teach three-year-olds and couldn't control them.

Simon

When I was about thirty, I got a job as an editor in a publishing company. It was my first office job, and um I didn't really know what to wear, but um for the interview I wore a suit, in fact I bought the suit specially for the interview. I got the job, so I thought that must be OK, so um on the first day I went to work wearing a suit and a tie. I got to work early, um, I wanted to make a good impression, and I was the first person in the office, so I went in, I found my desk, with my name on it, and I sat down and there were a few papers and documents for me to read, so I started reading those. I turned on my computer, and after about ten, fifteen minutes the other people in the office started to arrive and I noticed that nobody else was wearing a suit, and I thought, 'OK it's not a big problem'. So I introduced myself to the other people, I said, 'Hello, how are you? Hello, pleased to meet you' and the next thing someone said to me was 'My computer's really slow, do you think you know what the problem is?' and I said, 'No, no, not really.' So then I introduced myself to somebody else and said, 'Hello, nice to meet you' and she replied, 'Hello, nice to meet you' and then she said, 'Do you know how I can connect my computer to the printer?' and I said, 'No, I have no idea how to do that.' Anyway I went back to work and about half an hour later I had a meeting with my boss, and she said, 'How's it going?' and I said, 'Yeah, it's all good, everybody seems really nice. Just one thing, why does everybody think I can fix their computer?' and she looked at me and what I was wearing and she said, 'It's your suit. Nobody in this office ever wears a suit, so they think you're from the IT department and you've come to help with a computer problem. They're the only ones who wear suits!' So I never wore it again. To this day.

Claire

It was my first day at work as a teacher at a language school, and they asked me to come the first week of term to observe some teachers, to watch their lessons, and then I was going to start teaching the following week. But when I arrived there they told me that one of the teachers was ill and they asked me to take the class, and it was three-year-old kids! So I was in a class with about ten three-year-olds, who were running around – my boss gave me a story book to read to them, but the kids couldn't speak any English. I'd never taught – never been trained to teach children that small. I tried to read the book to two of them, but the others were running around shouting and hitting each other, and at the worst possible moment, just when all of them were being really noisy and not doing anything I was telling them to, my boss – the director of the school – opened the door and just looked at me. I felt terrible, but then she said, 'These children are too young for you, aren't they?' and I said, 'Yes' – I was nearly crying. Luckily after that she never gave me any classes with really young children, but it was the most stressful class I've ever tried to teach.

Now ask Sts which tip from the article in **1** they would give Simon and Claire.

Simon Wear smart work clothes, but not too smart.

Claire Be prepared to have problems. Don't be afraid to ask for help.

b Tell Sts they are going to listen again and this time they must answer questions 1–6. Go through the questions, making sure Sts understand all the lexis.

Play the audio, pausing after Simon's story. Then play Claire's story.

Get Sts to compare with a partner, and then check answers.

1 C **2** C **3** S **4** S **5** C **6** B

  If there's time, you could get Sts to listen again with the script on *p.122*, so they can see exactly what they understood / didn't understand. Translate / Explain any new words or phrases.

c Do this as a whole-class activity. You could tell Sts about your own experience if you have ever had a problem on your first day.

3 VOCABULARY & GRAMMAR
verbs + infinitive; uses of the infinitive with *to*

> **Vocabulary notes**
> Although Sts are learning these verbs partly in a grammar context, it's important to make sure that they're clear about what they all mean, e.g. *pretend*, *try*, *decide*, etc., and are also clear about the difference in meaning between *would like* and *like*.

a Here Sts focus on the verbs before the infinitives. Tell Sts <u>not</u> to look at the article and to complete the gaps in 1–4. Check answers.

1 Plan **2** Offer **3** want **4** Try

b Tell Sts to go to **Vocabulary Bank Verb forms** on *p.158*. Focus on **1 Verbs + infinitive**.

Focus on **a** and get Sts to complete the ***to + verb*** column with the verbs from the list.

◗) 7.2 Now do **b**. Play the audio for Sts to listen and check.

Check answers.

◗) 7.2
Verb forms 1 Verbs + infinitive
1 We've decided **to go** to France for our holiday.
2 Don't forget **to turn off** all the lights.
3 We hope **to see** you again soon.
4 I'm learning **to drive**. My test is next month.
5 I need **to go** to the supermarket. We don't have any milk. 6 **He offered to help** me with my case.
7 They're planning **to get married** soon.
8 He pretended **to be** ill, but he wasn't really.
9 He's promised **to pay** me back when he gets a job.
10 Remember **to bring** your dictionaries to class tomorrow.
11 It was very cloudy and it started **to rain**.
12 I'm trying **to find** a job, but it's very hard.
13 I want **to catch** the six o'clock train.
14 I'd like **to buy** a new car next month.

Either use the audio to drill the pronunciation of the sentences, or model and drill them yourself. Give further practice of any verbs your Sts find difficult to pronounce.

Now do **Activation** and tell Sts, in pairs, to cover the ***to + verb*** column. They must try to remember and say the full sentences.

Tell Sts to go back to the main lesson **7A**.

! The photocopiable vocabulary activity revises both verbs + infinitive and verbs + gerund, so wait until after the **Vocabulary Bank** in **7B** before using it.

c Tell Sts to focus on sentences A–C from the article and rules 1–3. They must match a sentence with a rule.

Get Sts to compare with a partner, and then check answers.

a 2   **b** 3   **c** 1

d Tell Sts to go to **Grammar Bank 7A** on *p.138*.

Grammar notes

The infinitive has two forms in English:

1 **work** is the form which is given in a dictionary. Sts have seen this used in present simple questions and negatives, e.g. *Do you work?*, *I didn't work*, and after the modal verb *can*.

2 **to work** Sts should already be familiar with the infinitive with *to* used after some verbs such as *want* and *would like*, e.g. *I want to come with you.*

! The infinitive of purpose is only used to express a positive reason. To express a negative reason we use *in order not to* or *so as not to*, e.g. *We took a taxi so as not to be late* NOT ~~We took a taxi not to be late~~. At this level it is better not to point this out unless it comes up.

7.3 Focus on the example sentences and play the audio for Sts to listen and repeat. Encourage them to copy the rhythm. Then go through the rules with the class.

Now focus on the **Infinitive without *to*** box and go through it with the class.

Then focus on the exercises in **7A** on *p.139*. Sts do the exercises individually or in pairs.

Check answers, getting Sts to read the full sentences.

a
1 F   2 D   3 E   4 A   5 C
b
1 Nice **to meet** you
2 What do you want **to do** tonight?
3 I promise **not to be** late.
4 Try **not to make** a noise.
5 I'd really like **to learn** a new language.
6 Be careful **not to drive** too fast – the roads are icy.
7 My brother has decided **to look for** a new job.
8 You don't **need to pay** to go in.

 Put Sts into small groups. Get them to try to think of at least two answers to each of the questions below, using *to* + infinitive.
Why do people...?

– go to parties   – go on holidays   – go to a gym
– get married   – learn English

Tell Sts to go back to the main lesson **7A**.

 If you think Sts need more practice, you may want to give them the **Grammar** photocopiable activity at this point.

e Put Sts in pairs, **A** and **B**. Tell Sts to go to **Communication How to survive…**, **A** on *p.104*, **B** on *p.110*.

Go through the instructions with them carefully, and make sure Sts know what they have to do.

A and **B** read their *How to survive…* articles. Give them time to try to memorize the information and deal with any vocabulary problems.

A then tells **B** the five tips. Then **A** and **B** decide together which they think is the most important tip.

B now tells **A** the five tips in his / her article and they again decide together which is the most important one.

When Sts have finished, get feedback from some pairs about which tip they thought was the most important.

 Tell Sts that they can look at the headings, but encourage them to give as much of the extra information as they can from memory.

Tell Sts to go back to the main lesson **7A**.

f Focus on the task and make sure Sts know the meaning of *appropriate* (= suitable, acceptable, or correct for the particular circumstances). Model and drill pronunciation. Then give Sts time to think about the tips they read or heard about in **Communication**.

Now ask the class if they think the tips they have read are appropriate in their country. If not, why not?

4 PRONUNCIATION & SPEAKING
weak form of *to*, linking

Pronunciation notes
Weak form of to
The word *to* is usually unstressed in a sentence (unless it comes at the end of a question, e.g. *Who are you talking to?*) and is pronounced as a weak form /tə/, e.g. *I never speak to* /tə/ *Jane.*

Linking
It's important for Sts to be aware of the way two consonant sounds are linked (see information box in the Student's Book) as this will help them to understand spoken language when this linking occurs.

a **7.4** Tell Sts to listen to the three sentences and especially to how the word *to* is pronounced.

Play the audio once for Sts just to listen.

Check answers.

to isn't stressed and is pronounced /tə/

7.4
See sentences in Student's Book on *p.55*

b 🔊 **7.5** Focus on the **Linking words with the same consonant sound** box and go through it with the class.

Now tell Sts they are going to hear ten questions and they must complete each gap with three or four words.

Play the audio, pausing after each question to give Sts time to write. Play again if necessary.

Get Sts to compare with a partner, and then check answers, making sure Sts understand the questions.

1 tried to learn
2 how to drive
3 what to wear
4 forgotten to turn off
5 hoping to go
6 planning to go anywhere
7 to work or study
8 pretended to be ill
9 to learn to cook
10 to stay friends

🔊 **7.5**
1 Have you ever tried to learn something new and failed?
2 How important is it to know how to drive?
3 How long do you usually spend deciding what to wear in the morning?
4 Have you ever forgotten to turn off your phone during a class or concert?
5 Where are you hoping to go for your next holiday?
6 Are you planning to go anywhere next weekend?
7 Would you like to work or study in another country?
8 Have you ever pretended to be ill (when you weren't)?
9 Do you think it's important to learn to cook at school?
10 Do you think it's possible to stay friends with an ex-boyfriend or girlfriend?

c This speaking activity reinforces the pronunciation presented in **a**, as well as the grammar.

Put Sts in pairs, **A** and **B**. **A** asks the first five questions to **B**, who answers giving as much information as possible. Then **B** asks the next five questions to **A**.

Get feedback from the class.

EXTRA SUPPORT Get Sts to choose questions to ask you first. Encourage them to ask follow-up questions for more information. You could write a few question words, e.g. WHY? WHEN?, etc. on the board to remind them.

5 WRITING

In pairs, Sts now write their own *How to survive…* article. First, they must choose one of the three titles and then they must write at least four tips.

When Sts have finished, make sure they check their work for mistakes.

Then they could swap articles with another pair.

EXTRA SUPPORT Brainstorm suitable headings with the class for each title before Sts choose which article to write.

Possible headings:
A job interview
Don't be late
Wear the right clothes
Be prepared
Ask questions
A party where you don't know anyone
Arrive early
Introduce yourself to people
Ask people about themselves
Don't eat or drink too much
A family holiday
Try not to argue with people
Spend some time on your own
Help with housework if you're in a rented flat
Take turns to choose where to go and what to eat

G uses of the gerund (verb + *-ing*)
V verbs + gerund: *like, can't stand*, etc.
P *-ing*, the letter *o*

Lesson plan

Cartoons about happiness posted on Instagram by two well-known illustrators provide the context for Sts to learn three common uses of the verb + *-ing* form (often called the gerund).

The lesson begins with the cartoons which lead Sts into Vocabulary and Grammar by focusing on common verbs which are followed by the gerund and other uses of the gerund. This is followed by a Listening and Speaking activity about the Bank of Happiness in Tallinn, Estonia, and Sts listen to an interview with the founder of the bank, Airi Kivi. In Pronunciation, Sts look at the six pronunciations of the letter *o* and the /ŋ/ sound. The lesson ends with a speaking activity, in which Sts talk about things they love / like / don't mind, etc., doing.

More materials
For teachers
Photocopiables
Grammar infinitives with *to* or verb + *-ing*? *p.191*
Communicative Questions with gerunds *p.236* (instructions *p.212*)
Vocabulary Verbs + infinitive *to* and verbs + *-ing p.266* (instructions *p.255*)
For students
Workbook 7B
Online Practice 7B

OPTIONAL LEAD-IN (BOOKS CLOSED)

Write the following words on the board:

HAPPY   SAD   DARK   WEAK

Ask Sts what part of speech these are, and elicit that they are adjectives. Then tell Sts that by adding four letters to the end of these adjectives, you make them into nouns, and see if anyone comes up with -ness. Write the nouns on the board (*happiness, sadness*, etc.), and model and drill pronunciation.

You could also teach a few more *-ness* nouns from other adjectives Sts know, e.g. *kindness, laziness, tidiness*, etc.

1 VOCABULARY & GRAMMAR verbs + gerund; uses of the gerund

Vocabulary notes

Although Sts are learning these verbs partly in a grammar context, it's important to make sure that they're clear about what they all mean, e.g. *go on* (= continue), *feel like* (want to have or do sth), etc.

a Books open. Put Sts in pairs and get them to discuss the questions. You could answer the questions yourself first.

Get some feedback from various pairs.

EXTRA SUPPORT   Do this as a whole-class activity.

b Focus on the text and Instagram posts. You may want to pre-teach some vocabulary, e.g. *a hot tub, to illustrate sth, draw – drew*, etc. or you may prefer to deal with these in context after Sts have read the text. Tell Sts to read the text once and then tick the cartoons they agree with most.

Get some feedback. You could tell Sts which ones you agree with most.

c Do this as a whole-class activity.

We use the *-ing* form after *finish*.

Elicit any other verbs Sts know which take the *-ing* form, e.g. *like, love, hate, mind*, etc.

d Here Sts learn some other common verbs which take the gerund. Tell Sts to go to **Vocabulary Bank** Verb forms on *p.158* and look at **2 Verbs + gerund (verb + *-ing*)**.

Focus on **a** and get Sts to complete the **gerund** column with the verbs from the list.

🔊 **7.6**   Now do **b**. Play the audio for Sts to listen and check.

Check answers.

🔊 **7.6**
Verbs + gerund
1 I enjoy **reading** in bed.
2 Have you finished **tidying** your room?
3 I want to go on **working** until I'm seventy.
4 I hate **being** late when I'm meeting someone.
5 I like **having** breakfast in a café.
6 I love **waking up** on a sunny morning.
7 I don't mind **doing** the ironing. It's quite relaxing.
8 She spends hours **talking** on the phone.
9 It started **raining** at five thirty in the morning.
10 Please stop **making** such a noise. I can't think.
11 I don't feel like **cooking** today. Let's go out for lunch.

Now either use the audio to drill the pronunciation of the sentences, or model and drill them yourself. Give further practice of any verbs your Sts find difficult to pronounce.

Remind Sts that *I don't mind (doing something)* = although I don't enjoy it, it isn't a problem for me. Point out the asterisk by *start* and tell Sts that it can be used with a gerund or infinitive with no difference in meaning, e.g. *It started raining* or *It started to rain*.

Now do **Activation** and tell Sts, in pairs, to cover the **gerund** column. They must try and remember the full sentences.

Tell Sts to go back to the main lesson **7B**.

 If you think Sts need more practice, you may want to give them the **Vocabulary** photocopiable activity at this point.

e Focus on the task. Either put Sts in pairs or do this as a whole-class activity.

If Sts worked in pairs, check answers.

1 without asking   **2** parking, fitting, finding, sitting, landing, reading   **3** not having to

f Tell Sts to go to **Grammar Bank 7B** on *p.138*.

Grammar notes

It is very likely that in your Sts' L1 an infinitive form will be used in places where English uses an *-ing* form.

❗ In British English it is much more common to use a gerund after *like*, *love*, and *hate* especially when you are speaking about general likes and dislikes. However, an infinitive can often be used without any real difference in meaning, and US English uses the infinitive.

Spelling rules

You may want to point out that two-syllable verbs which are stressed on the last syllable also double the final consonant, e.g. *begin – beginning*, *prefer – preferring*.

❗ *travel – travelling* is an exception: it is stressed on the first syllable, but doubles the final consonant.

Gerund or infinitive?

Sts are asked to discriminate between the gerund and infinitive in the second exercise in the **Grammar Bank**. Before doing it you could get Sts to quickly look again at the rules for both (see **Grammar Bank 7A** *p.138*).

❗ Remind Sts that *like* is usually followed by the gerund, e.g. *I like travelling*, but *would like* is followed by the infinitive, e.g. *I would like to travel around the world*.

🔊 **7.7** Focus on the example sentences and play the audio for Sts to listen and repeat. Encourage them to copy the rhythm. Then go through the rules with the class.

Now focus on the exercises for **7B** on *p.139*. Sts do the exercises individually or in pairs.

Check answers, getting Sts to read the full sentences.

a
1 swimming   **2** practising   **3** remembering   **4** Teaching
5 messaging   **6** not knowing   **7** Travelling   **8** studying
b
1 Doing   **2** to pay   **3** to park   **4** giving   **5** to get
6 raining   **7** cooking, doing   **8** getting up

Tell Sts to go back to the main lesson **7B**.

 If you think Sts need more practice, you may want to give them the **Grammar** photocopiable activity at this point.

g Tell Sts they are going to write a sentence similar to the ones in **1b**. Write HAPINESS IS… on the board and tell Sts they should write between five and ten words about their idea of happiness.

 If your Sts like drawing, you could ask them to illustrate their text.

h When Sts have finished writing, put them in small groups (of three or four). Tell Sts to read their sentences to the rest of their group. When they have finished reading all of them, they should give their opinion.

Get some feedback from various groups. If Sts have illustrated their work, you could put it up on the wall.

2 LISTENING & SPEAKING

a Focus on the task and elicit ideas from the class.

b 🔊 **7.8** Tell Sts they are going to listen to a radio interview with Airi Kivi, the woman who started the bank. They must listen and choose which description 1–3 best explains how the bank works.

Play the audio once the whole way through.

Check the answer.

 Read through the script and decide if you need to pre-teach any new lexis before Sts listen.

3 You help somebody, and then somebody else helps you.

🔊 **7.8**
(script in Student's Book on *p.123*)

P = presenter, A = Airi

P The capital city of Estonia, Tallinn, is one of the most beautiful cities on the Baltic coast. It's one of the world's 'smart cities', which means that technology plays an important role in people's lives and in business. But some people in Tallinn are using the internet for something very unusual. It's called the Bank of Happiness, but it's a very different kind of bank. Nobody pays money into the bank, and the bank doesn't lend money to anybody. Instead, the Bank of Happiness is a forum where thousands of people from Estonia, and other countries too, connect with each other, and they offer or receive services completely free of charge.
Here's how it works: you register and then you post what you're offering or what you need – it's really easy. For example, people offer to do the shopping for somebody, or walk their dog.
Other people post things like 'I need someone who can fix my car' or 'Can anybody translate an email into French for me?'
But the most important thing is that nobody pays any money. Everything is free.
The bank was started over five years ago by a thirty-nine-year-old Estonian woman called Airi Kivi. She's a psychologist and a family therapist, and her goal was to make people think and act with their hearts.

A I thought, we need something like this Bank of Happiness, where people can meet each other and help each other – do something cool. The Estonian economy was also having problems at the time. A little bit later, I thought, wow, the Bank of Happiness is perfect for this economic crisis. A lot of people are unemployed and they can use our bank.
In the Bank of Happiness people don't need to pay each other back. For example, a teenager will do the shopping for his old neighbour, and maybe the neighbour can't do anything for him in return. But then perhaps the neighbour will post a comment on the site and tell people about what the teenager did, and then another person, who sees this, will probably do something to help the teenager. The principle of the bank is that it's not money and things that make people happy. What really makes them happy is doing things for other people.

c Give Sts time to read the six multiple-choice questions and make sure they understand all the lexis.

Then play the audio again for Sts to listen and choose the correct answer. Play the audio again if necessary.

Check answers.

> **1** a **2** b **3** c **4** a **5** b **6** c

 If there's time, you could get Sts to listen again with the script on *p.123*, so they can see exactly what they understood / didn't understand. Translate / Explain any new words or phrases.

d Focus on the three questions and give Sts time to think of their answers.

Put Sts in pairs and get them to discuss the questions.

Get some feedback from various pairs.

3 PRONUNCIATION *-ing, the letter o*

> ### Pronunciation notes
>
> **-ing**
>
> *-ing* at the end of a word, as in the gerund, is always pronounced /ɪŋ/. Sts often need practice making this sound as they may not have it in their language.
>
> **the letter o**
>
> Sts often have problems with the different pronunciations of *going* and *doing*. This exercise focuses on the two most common pronunciations of the letter o, /ɒ/ (e.g. *clock*) and /əʊ/ (e.g. *phone*), and two less common ones, /ʌ/ (e.g. *mother*) and /uː/ (e.g. *boot*).
>
> Highlight that *clock* and *mother* are short sounds, *boot* is a long sound, and *phone* is a diphthong.

a 🔊 **7.9** Focus on the sound picture and elicit the word and sound (*singer* /ŋ/).

Now focus on the example words next to the sound picture, e.g. *shopping*, etc.

Play the audio once for Sts just to listen.

🔊 **7.9**
See sound and words in Student's Book on *p.57*

Then play the audio again, pausing after each word for Sts to listen and repeat. Correct pronunciation and give further practice if necessary.

b Focus on the sound pictures and elicit the six words and sounds, e.g. *phone* /əʊ/, *horse* /ɔː/, etc.

Focus on the question and play the audio again, pausing after each word for Sts to match it to a sound.

 Get Sts to do the matching exercise before they listen again.

Check answers.

> shopping 4   nothing 6   boring 2
> ironing 3   going 1   doing 5

Play the audio again for Sts to listen and repeat. Give more practice if these sounds are a problem for your Sts.

Put Sts in pairs and get them to practise saying the words.

c 🔊 **7.10** Focus on the pairs of words in 1–4 and make sure Sts know what they mean.

Tell Sts they are going to hear all the words and they should try to notice the difference between them.

Now play the audio once the whole way through for Sts just to listen.

🔊 **7.10**
See words in Student's Book on *p.57*

---

d 🔊 **7.11** Tell Sts they are going to hear one of the words in each group in **c** used in a sentence. They just have to decide if it is a or b.

Play the audio once the whole way through, pausing after each sentence. Play it again if necessary.

Check answers.

> **1** b bank   **2** a thing   **3** b sink   **4** a ping

🔊 **7.11**
1 The news about the bank really surprised me.
2 One thing I hate about supermarkets is queuing.
3 Please could you put the dirty dishes in the sink?
4 I think you have a message. I just heard your phone ping.

 Write some words on the board for each sentence to help Sts, e.g. 1 NEWS, BANK, SURPRISED; 2 HATE, SUPERMARKETS. QUEUING, etc. Then play the audio again, pausing after each sentence for Sts to listen and repeat.

 If these sounds are difficult for your Sts, it will help to show them the mouth position. You could model this yourself or use the the Sound Bank videos on the *Teacher's Resource Centre.*

4 SPEAKING

a Here Sts get some oral practice of the new vocabulary and grammar. Focus on the task. Highlight that Sts only have to choose five things they want to talk about from the ten possibilities. Give them a minute to choose their five things.

❗ Highlight that *dream of* is used for daydreaming, i.e. something we would love to do; *dream about* is used for dreaming while actually asleep, e.g. *I dreamed about you last night.*

 Sts could write down their answers to help prepare them for the speaking.

b Demonstrate the activity by choosing a few things from the list in **a** and talking about them yourself. Encourage the class to ask you for more information, e.g. *Why (not)?*.

In pairs, **A** tells **B** his / her five things and **B** asks for more information.

When you think Sts **A** have finished, get them to swap roles.

Monitor and help while Sts are talking. Correct Sts if they use an infinitive instead of an *-ing* form.

Get some feedback from the class.

 Get fast finishers to choose more topics to talk about.

Could you pass the test?

G *have to, don't have to, must, mustn't*
V adjectives + prepositions: *afraid of*, etc.
P stress on prepositions

Lesson plan

The title and main context of this lesson were inspired by an article in the British press, where an experiment was done to see how well someone could learn a foreign language in just a month. When the month was up, the person travelled to the country itself and carried out a series of tasks to see how much he had learned.

The lesson begins with Sts speaking about whether they use English outside the classroom. Then Sts read an article about British people's problems learning foreign languages, and an experiment to see how much Spanish a British student, Max, could learn in a month. Next is a grammatical focus on verbs expressing obligation: *have to / don't have to* and *must*. Then Sts listen to hear how Max got on in Spain when his course finished and do the challenges themselves. The Vocabulary and Pronunciation focus is on common verb + preposition combinations, e.g. *bad at, afraid of*, etc. as well as stress on prepositions. In Writing, Sts write a formal email to a language school asking for information.

More materials

For teachers

Photocopiables
Grammar have to, don't have to, must, mustn't p.192
Communicative In the UK p.237
(instructions p.213)

For students
Workbook 7C
Online Practice 7C

OPTIONAL LEAD-IN (BOOKS CLOSED)

Ask Sts what rules there are in their class, and elicit their ideas onto the board, writing them up in imperatives, e.g.
DO HOMEWORK EVERY DAY.
DON'T MISS CLASSES.
TURN OFF YOUR PHONE.
DON'T SPEAK IN (Sts' L1), etc.

You could leave these up on the board to be referred to later.

Then ask Sts which two they think are the most important.

1 SPEAKING

Books open. Here Sts do a short speaking activity based on their experience of using English. Quickly run through the questions before Sts start.

Put Sts in small groups and get them to discuss the questions. Encourage them to use *What about you?* after they have answered.

Get some feedback from various groups about their experiences. You could also tell them a little about your experience of language learning.

2 READING using topic sentences

a Focus on the questions and elicit some opinions from the class. Try to get a short discussion going if Sts seem to be interested in the topic.

b Tell Sts that they are going to read an article about a language learning experiment. Make sure Sts understand what *an experiment* means (= a test that you do to find out what will happen or if sth is true).

First, focus on the **Topic sentences** box and go through it with the class.

Now focus on topic sentences A–F and go through them, making sure Sts understand all the lexis, e.g. *a Brit*.

Give Sts time to read the article and complete the gaps with the topic sentences. Point out that the first (*E*) has been done for them.

Get Sts to compare with a partner, and then check answers.

EXTRA SUPPORT Before Sts read the article the first time, check whether you need to pre-teach any vocabulary.

2 D **3** F **4** B **5** C **6** A

c Go through questions 1–6 with the class.

Give Sts time to read the article again.

Get Sts to answer the questions with a partner, and then check answers.

1 Tourists sometimes try to say a few phrases in a foreign language, but stop as soon as they discover that the waiter speaks English; Many British people who live abroad never learn the language at all.
2 They think they don't need to learn a language because everyone speaks English.
3 It's too difficult.
4 By sending one of their journalists on an intensive language course.
5 Because he'd like to go to Spain and Latin America. He did a one-month intensive course.
6 He went to Madrid with a teacher to do some tests to see if he could survive.

Deal with any other new vocabulary. Model and drill the pronunciation of any tricky words.

3 GRAMMAR *have to, don't have to, must, mustn't*

a 🔊 **7.12** Focus on the tests and rules, and give Sts time to read them.

Now play the audio of Max talking about the tests. Sts listen and complete the gaps.

Check answers.

> **1** sandwich **2** follow **3** taxi **4** dictionary
> **5** speak Spanish **6** hands

🔊 **7.12**
Max
There were four tests for me to complete in Madrid. I had to order a drink and a sandwich in a bar, ask the price, and understand it. Then I had to ask for directions in the street, and follow them, then get a taxi to a famous place, and finally phone somebody and leave a message on their voicemail.
There were just three rules. You mustn't use a dictionary or phrase book app, you must only speak Spanish and you mustn't use your hands or mime or write anything down.

b Focus on the highlighted phrases in **a** and questions 1 and 2.

Give Sts a few moments to answer the questions, and then check answers.

> **1** You have to, you must   **2** you mustn't

c Do this as a whole-class activity.

> **1** I don't need to do this

d Tell Sts to go to **Grammar Bank 7C** on *p.138*.

> ### Grammar notes
> #### *must* and *have to*
> At Pre-intermediate level *have to* and *must* can be treated as synonyms as a way of expressing obligation. We tend to use *have to* more often than *must* when there is an external obligation, i.e. a law or a rule, e.g. *You have to wear a seat belt in a car in the UK.*
>
> Watch out for the typical mistake of using *to* with *must*: e.g. ~~I must to go to the bank~~.
>
> Highlight the impersonal use of *You* when we talk about rules and laws, e.g. *You have to drive on the left.*
>
> #### *mustn't* and *don't have to*
> The typical mistake here is when Sts use *don't have to* instead of *mustn't*, e.g. ~~You don't have to use your phone in class.~~ (*You mustn't use your phone…*)

Focus on the example sentences and play both audio 🔊 **7.13** and 🔊 **7.14** for Sts to listen and repeat. Encourage them to copy the rhythm. Then go through the rules with the class.

Now focus on the information box about **must and have to**, **mustn't and don't have to**, and **Impersonal you**, and go through it with the class.

Then focus on the exercises for **7C** on *p.139*. Sts do the exercises individually or in pairs.

Check answers, getting Sts to read the full sentences.

> a
> **1** Janice **has to** study very hard – she has exams soon.
> **2** You **have to** buy a ticket before you get on the bus.
> **3** **Does** your sister **have to** go to London for her job interview?
> **4** Mike **has to** wear wear a really ugly uniform at his new school.
> **5** We **have to** get up early tomorrow.
> **6** Harry **doesn't have to** work today – he has a day off.
> **7** I **have to** make a phone call.
> **8** **Do** we **have to** go to bed?
> b
> **1** mustn't
> **2** ✓
> **3** don't have to
> **4** ✓
> **5** musn't
> **6** ✓
> **7** ✓
> **8** don't have to

Tell Sts to go back to the main lesson **7C**.

EXTRA SUPPORT If you think Sts need more practice, you may want to give them the **Grammar** photocopiable activity at this point.

e Put Sts in pairs, **A** and **B**. Tell Sts to go to **Communication What are the rules?**, **A** on *p.105*, **B** on *p.110*.

Go through the instructions with Sts carefully, and make sure they know what they have to do.

Sts **A** look at photos 1–6 and complete the rules. Sts **B** do the same with photos 7–12.

EXTRA SUPPORT You could put two Sts **A** and two Sts **B** together first to complete the rules. Then put them in **A / B** pairs.

A then reads his / her rules in a different order to **B**, who looks at his / her photos and says which photo the rules apply to.

They then swap roles and do the same with photos 7–12. Finally, check the rules for photos 1–12.

> **1** You have to / must turn off your phone.
> **2** Children don't have to pay.
> **3** You have to / must wear a jacket.
> **4** You mustn't touch the door.
> **5** You have to / must be over 18 to see this film.
> **6** You mustn't take photos here.
> **7** You don't have to pay anything now.
> **8** You mustn't play football here at night.
> **9** You mustn't put your feet on the seats.
> **10** You don't have to come to class on Mondays.
> **11** You have to / must drive in one direction.
> **12** You have to / must wear sports shoes here.

Tell Sts to go back to the main lesson **7C**.

EXTRA IDEA Ask Sts what rules there are in their school and if they think, they are good rules. You could then also ask Sts to invent some new rules that they would like to see incorporated.

4 LISTENING

a 🔊 **7.15** Tell Sts to look at the tests again in **3a** and ask Sts the two questions. Get some feedback from the class.

Then play the audio of Max doing the tests in Madrid. Sts just listen to hear which test was the easiest and which was the most difficult.

EXTRA SUPPORT Read through the script and decide if you need to pre-teach any new lexis before Sts listen.

Check answers.

> The easiest test was ordering the beer and sandwich. The most difficult was getting a taxi.

🔊 **7.15**
(script in Student's Book on *p.123*)
M = Max, P = Paula, W = waiter, Pb = passer-by, T = taxi driver, L = Lola
M I arrived at Madrid airport where I met Paula. *Hola, Soy Max.*
P *Encantada. Soy Paula.*
M Paula took me to my hotel, and that evening we went to the centre of Madrid and it was time for my first test. I had to order a sandwich and a drink in a bar, then ask for the bill. I sat down at the bar and I tried to order a beer and a ham sandwich. *Por favor, una cerveza y un bocadillo de jamón.*
W *En seguida.*
M Fantastic! The waiter understood me first time. My pronunciation wasn't perfect, but I got my beer and my sandwich. I really enjoyed it. But then the more difficult bit. Asking for the bill… *¿Cuánto es?*
W *Seis noventa.*
M *¿Cómo?*
W *Seis noventa.*
M Six ninety. I understood! Paula gave me eight points for the test. I was very happy with that. Next we went out into the street. Test number two was asking for directions and – very important! – understanding them. We were in a narrow street, and I had to stop someone and ask them for the nearest chemist, *una farmacia.* I stopped a woman. At first I didn't understand anything she said!
Pb *Siga todo recto y tome la segunda por la derecha. Hay una farmacia en esa calle.*
M I asked the woman to speak more slowly.
Pb *Todo recto y tome la segunda calle por la derecha DERECHA.*
M I got it this time, I think. The second street on the right. I followed the directions and guess what. There was a chemist there! Seven points from Paula.
Test number three. I wasn't looking forward to this one. I had to get a taxi to a famous place in Madrid. Paula wrote down the name of the place on a piece of paper. It was the name of the football stadium where Real Madrid play. We stopped a taxi. *El Bernabéu, por favor.*
T *¿Qué? ¿Adónde?*
M He didn't understand me. I tried again, but he still didn't understand. I was desperate, so I said, 'Real Madrid, Stadium, football'.
T *¡Ah! El Santiago Bernabéu.*
M Finally! Paula only gave me five because I ended up using English. Still, at least I made the taxi driver understand where I wanted to go. And so to the final test. I had to leave a message in Spanish on somebody's voicemail. I had to give my name, spell it, and ask the person to call me back. Paula gave me the number – it was one of her friends called Lola – and I dialled. I was feeling a bit nervous at this point, because speaking on the phone in a foreign language is never easy.
L *Deje su mensaje después de la señal.*
M *Er. Buenas noches. Soy Max. Max. M-A-X. Er…Por favor…llámame esta noche…Oh yes…a las 8.30 er, Gracias.* Well, my grammar wasn't right, but I left the message. Half an hour later, at half past eight Lola phoned me. Success! Paula gave me eight points. That was the end of my four tests. Paula was pleased with me. My final score was seven. I was quite happy with that. So, how much can you learn in a month? Well, of course you can't learn Spanish in a month, but you can learn enough to survive if you are on holiday or on a trip. Now I want to go back to England and try and learn some more. *¡Adiós!*

b Focus on the task and quickly go through sentences 1–7 before playing the audio.

Play the audio again, pausing to give Sts time to mark them *T* (true) or *F* (false). Play all or part of the audio again if necessary. Remind Sts to correct the *F* ones.

Check answers.

> **1** F (The waiter **understood** Max.)
> **2** T
> **3** F (It was the **second** street on the right.)
> **4** F (The driver **didn't understand** the name.)
> **5** T
> **6** F (He got **seven**.)
> **7** F (You **can't** learn a language (Spanish) in a month, but you can learn enough to do some simple everyday things.)

EXTRA SUPPORT If there's time, you could get Sts to listen again with the script on *p.123*, so they can see exactly what they understood / didn't understand. Translate / Explain any new words or phrases.

c Focus on the task and give Sts time to think of their answers.

Put Sts in pairs and get them to discuss their answers to 1–4.

Get some feedback from various pairs for each test.

> **Possible answers**
> **1** (Can / Could I have) a coffee and a cheese sandwich, please? How much is that?
> **2** Excuse me, where's the nearest chemist's?
> **3** Could you take me to…, please?
> **4** Hi, it's Anna. Could you please call me back? My number is…

5 VOCABULARY & PRONUNCIATION
adjectives + prepositions; stress on prepositions

Vocabulary notes

Certain adjectives are often followed by a particular preposition, which may well be different in Sts' L1. Sts should make a note of adjective + preposition combinations when they meet them.

a Focus on the **Adjectives + prepositions** box and go through it with the class.

Then focus on questions 1–10, and get Sts to complete the gaps with a preposition from the list.

Get them to compare with a partner.

b ◆) **7.16** Play the audio for Sts to listen and check.

Check answers.

1 at **2** at **3** for **4** of **5** in **6** of **7** for **8** to **9** with **10** from

---

◆) 7.16
Languages
1 Do you think you're good at learning languages?
2 Is there anything about learning English that you're bad at?
3 Do you think listening to pop music is good for your English?
4 Are you afraid of going to places where you don't speak the language?
5 What English-speaking countries are you most interested in?
Tourism
6 Which towns or cities in your country are full of tourists in the summer?
7 What tourist attractions is your country famous for?
8 Are people in your country usually nice to tourists?
9 Do you get angry with tourists who don't to try to speak your language?
10 Are people in the capital city very different from people in the rest of the country?

Pronunciation notes

Sts are normally encouraged not to stress prepositions in sentences and questions. However, there is one situation in which prepositions are stressed, which is when they are the last word in a sentence or question, and pointing this out and getting Sts to practise it will improve their sentence rhythm.

c ◆) **7.17** Focus on the task and play the audio once the whole way through for Sts just to listen.

Then play it again pausing after the first pair of questions.

Get Sts to compare with a partner, and then repeat with the second pair of questions.

Check answers.

at is unstressed in 1 and stressed in 2.
for is unstressed in 3 and stressed in 7.

◆) 7.17
1 Do you think you're good at learning languages?
2 Is there anything about learning English that you're bad at?
3 Do you think listening to pop music is good for your English?
7 What tourist attractions is your country famous for?

Finally, ask Sts *What do you think is the rule for stress on prepositions?* to elicit that prepositions are stressed when they are the last word in a sentence or question.

d Put Sts in pairs and get them to ask and answer questions 1–10 in **a**. You could demonstrate the activity by getting Sts to ask you some of the questions first.

Get some feedback from various pairs.

6 WRITING a formal email

Tell Sts to go to **Writing A formal email** on *p.117*.

a Tell Sts to read the email and tick the questions that Marek asks the school.

Check answers.

Sts should tick

How much do the courses cost?
When do the courses start and finish?
Can I combine two kinds of classes?
Can my wife stay with me?

b Now tell Sts to look at the highlighted phrases. They are all for a formal email. Sts need to write the equivalent expressions for an informal email.

Check answers.

Formal	Informal
Dear Sir / Madam,	Dear / Hi [first name]
I am writing	I'm writing
I would like	I'd like
however	but
I look forward to hearing from you.	Looking forward to hearing from you.
Yours faithfully,	Best wishes / All the best / Love

c Get Sts to read the advertisement for a language school. They must plan a formal email to the school. They should decide how long they want to study for, what kind of course they want to do and where they want to stay. They should also ask two or three questions.

d You may like to get Sts to do the writing in class or you could set it as homework. Get them to write the email, making sure they write two paragraphs according to the model.

e Sts should check their emails for mistakes before handing them in.

Practical English At the pharmacy

Function going to a pharmacy
Vocabulary feeling ill: *a headache, a cough*, etc.

Lesson plan

In this lesson Sts get practice with describing symptoms and buying medicine. Early in the morning, Rob and Jenny go running in Central Park, and Jenny invites Rob for dinner. However, Rob isn't feeling too well, and in the afternoon he goes to a pharmacy. Later, in the evening, he has dinner at Jenny's apartment.

More materials
For teachers
Teacher's Resource Centre
Video Practical English Episode 4
Quick Test 7
File 7 Test
For students
Workbook Practical English 4
Can you remember...? 1–7
Online Practice Practical English 4
Check your progress

OPTIONAL LEAD-IN (BOOKS CLOSED)

Before starting Episode 4, elicit what Sts can remember about Episode 3, e.g. ask them *What does Rob buy? Why? What happens when he buys them? What does Rob agree to do with Jenny?*, etc.

Alternatively, you could play the last scene of Episode 3.

1 ▶ RUNNING IN CENTRAL PARK

a ◀)) **7.18** Books open. Focus on the photos and elicit what Sts think is happening. Don't tell them if they are correct or not yet.

Now focus on the question and play the video / audio once the whole way through for Sts to check their ideas.

Check answers.

Jenny is enjoying the run. Rob says he is, but he is very tired.

◀)) **7.18**
J = Jenny, R = Rob
J Are you OK?
R Me? Never better.
J It's beautiful here, isn't it? I think this is my favourite place in New York.
R Yeah, it's great.
J So how's it all going? Are you happy you came?
R To Central Park? At seven fifteen in the morning?
J To New York, Rob.
R Yeah. Of course I'm happy. It's fantastic.
J Really? You aren't just saying that.
R No, I mean it.
J You need to get in shape, Rob.
R I know. I am a bit tired of eating out all the time. It isn't good for my figure.

J It's the restaurants you go to! Why don't you come over to my place after work? I could make you something a little healthier.
R I'd really like that. Thanks.
J So, how do you feel now? Are you ready to go again?
R Oh, yes! I'm ready for anything.
J Are you sure you're OK?
R Absolutely.
J OK. We'll only go around two more times.
R Two? Excellent!

b Focus on questions 1–6 and give Sts time to read them.
Play the video / audio again the whole way through.
Get Sts to compare with a partner, and play again if necessary.
Check answers.

1 Never better.
2 It is beautiful and her favourite place in New York.
3 Yes
4 He is tired of eating out.
5 She invites him to have dinner at her place.
6 Twice / Two more times

EXTRA SUPPORT If there's time and you are using the video, you could get Sts to watch again with subtitles, so they can see exactly what they understood / didn't understand. Translate / Explain any new words or phrases.

2 ▶ VOCABULARY feeling ill

a Focus on the title and elicit / teach the meaning of *ill*.
Now focus on the question *What's the matter?* and make sure Sts understand it.
Tell Sts to match the phrases and photos.
Focus on the pronunciation of the words.
Now get Sts to compare with a partner.

b ◀)) **7.19** Play the video / audio for Sts to watch or listen and check.
Check answers.

◀)) **7.19**
What's the matter?
2 I have a headache.
4 I have a cough.
1 I have flu.
5 I have a temperature.
6 I have a bad stomach.
3 I have a cold.

Model and drill the sentences. You might want to contrast *I have a cold* (= I am ill) and *I am cold* (= I am feeling cold, but not ill).

Play the video / audio again, pausing after each phrase for Sts to repeat. Give further practice of any words your Sts find difficult to pronounce.

Tell Sts to cover the phrases and look at the photos, and practise saying the phrases with a partner.

EXTRA CHALLENGE Get Sts to give some advice.

3 ▶ GOING TO A PHARMACY

a ◀ **7.20** Focus on the title and the **British and American English** box on *p.61* and go through it with the class.

Now focus on the instructions and sentences 1–4.

Tell Sts to cover the converation in **b**.

Play the video / audio once the whole way through. Play again if necessary.

Get Sts to compare with a partner, and then check answers.

> **1** flu **2** ibuprofen **3** four hours **4** $6.99

◀ **7.20 7.21**
P = pharmacist, R = Rob
P Good morning. Can I help you?
R I'm not feeling very well. (repeat) I think I have flu. (repeat)
P What are your symptoms?
R I have a headache and a cough. (repeat)
P Do you have a temperature?
R No, I don't think so. (repeat)
P Are you allergic to any drugs?
R I'm allergic to penicillin. (repeat)
P No problem. This is ibuprofen. It'll make you feel better.
R How many do I have to take? (repeat)
P Two every four hours.
R Sorry? How often? (repeat)
P Two every four hours. If you don't feel better in forty-eight hours, you should see a doctor.
R OK, thanks. How much is that? (repeat)
P That's six dollars ninety-nine, please.
R Thank you. (repeat)
P You're welcome.

You might want to tell Sts that ibuprofen is like aspirin, it reduces pain. You could also elicit / teach that penicillin is an antibiotic.

b Now focus on the conversation in the chart. Elicit who says the **You hear** phrases (the pharmacist) and who says the **You say** phrases (the customer, here Rob). These phrases will be useful for Sts if they need to go to a pharmacy / chemist.

Give Sts a minute to read through the conversation and think what the missing words might be. Then play the video / audio again, and get Sts to complete the gaps. Play again if necessary.

Get Sts to compare with a partner, and then check answers.

> **1** temperature **2** problem **3** better **4** Two
> **5** Two **6** 48 **7** welcome

Go through the conversation line by line with Sts, helping them with any words or expressions they don't understand. Elicit / Explain the meaning of *symptoms*. You might also want to highlight the phrase *to be allergic to sth*. Model and drill *allergic* /əˈlɜːdʒɪk/. Ask a few Sts *Are you allergic to anything?*.

c ◀ **7.21** Now focus on the **You say** phrases and tell Sts they're going to hear the conversation again. They should repeat the **You say** phrases when they hear the beep. Encourage them to copy the rhythm and intonation.

Play the video / audio, pausing if necessary for Sts to repeat the phrases.

◀ **7.21**
Same as script 7.20 with repeat pauses

d Put Sts in pairs, **A** and **B**. **A** is Rob and **B** is the pharmacist. Get Sts to read the conversation aloud, and then swap roles.

e In pairs, Sts do another role-play. Go through the instructions with them. **A** (book closed) should choose another illness from **2a**. **B** (book open) starts with *Can I help you?*.

Monitor and help.

 Demonstrate the activity by getting a confident student to play the pharmacist and you pretend to feel ill.

f When they have finished, Sts should swap roles.

You could get a few pairs to perform in front of the class.

4 ▶ DINNER AT JENNY'S APARTMENT

a ◀ **7.22** Focus on the photo and ask Sts *Where are Rob and Jenny?*.

Focus on sentences 1–5 and go through them with Sts.

Then play the video / audio once the whole way through for Sts to mark the sentences *T* (true) or *F* (false). Make it clear that they don't need to correct the false sentences yet. Play again if necessary.

Get Sts to compare with a partner, and then check answers.

> **1** F **2** T **3** F **4** F **5** F

◀ **7.22**
R = Rob, J = Jenny
R That was a lovely meal. Thanks, Jenny.
J That's OK.
R It's been great being in New York. You know, your offer to work here came at a very good time for me.
J Really?
R Yeah, I was looking for something new. Something different. You see, I broke up with my girlfriend a few months before I met you.
J Oh…right…
R What about you?
J What about me?
R You know…relationships?
J Oh, I've been too busy recently to think about relationships. Getting this job at the magazine was a really big thing for me. I guess that's taken up all my time and energy.
R But that isn't very good for you. Only thinking about work, I mean.
J Why didn't you tell me you weren't feeling well this morning? We didn't have to go for a run.
R I wanted to go. It was nice.
J Well, I'm glad you're feeling better. Would you like another coffee?
R No, thanks. I think I should get back to the hotel now, I've got a really busy day tomorrow. Do you have a telephone number for a taxi?
J Yeah…but it's much easier to get a cab on the street.
R Oh, OK, then.
J I'll see you in the morning, if you're feeling OK.
R Oh, I'm sure I'll be fine! Thanks again for a great evening.
J Any time.
R Goodnight.
J Night, Rob.

b Play the video / audio again, so Sts can watch or listen again and correct the false sentences.

Get Sts to compare with a partner, and then check answers.

1 Rob broke up with his girlfriend **a few months** before he met Jenny.
3 Jenny **didn't know** that Rob wasn't feeling well in the morning.
4 Rob wants to go back to his hotel because **he wants to go to bed early, as he has a busy day the next day.**
5 Jenny **doesn't call** a taxi.

EXTRA SUPPORT If there's time and you are using the video, you could get Sts to watch again with subtitles, so they can see exactly what they understood / didn't understand. Translate / Explain any new words or phrases.

c ◗ **7.23** Focus on the **have got** box and go through it with the class.
Play the video / audio once the whole way through for Sts just to listen.

◗ **7.23**
See sentences in Student's Book on *p.61*

Now play it again, pausing after each phrase, for Sts to listen and repeat.

In *English File* Sts have been taught to use *Do you have…?, I don't have…, I have…* to talk about possession as we believe it is the easiest form for Sts to acquire and the most international. However, it is important that they are aware of, and can recognize, the *have got* form of *have*, which is especially common in spoken English among UK native speakers of English (although the *have / do you have* form is also common). We normally contract *have got*, e.g. *I've got a headache*. Point out that you cannot use *have got* when you are using *have* with another meaning, e.g. *have dinner, have a shower*. If you want to go into the grammar of *have got* in more detail with your Sts, tell them to go to *p.165*.

◗ **7.24** Go through the rules (audio ◗ **7.24**), and get Sts to do the exercises in pairs.

Answer key for the *have got* appendix
a
1 She hasn't got any brothers.
2 Have you got a big flat?
3 We haven't got a lot of work today.
4 Has your sister got a boyfriend?
5 Roger and Val have got a beautiful garden.
6 I have got a really good teacher.
7 My brother hasn't got a job at the moment.
8 They've got the same colour eyes.
9 Have we got a meeting today?
10 He hasn't got many friends at work.
b
1 I **haven't got** my umbrella today.
2 **Has** your phone **got** a good camera?
3 I**'ve got** a new iPad.
4 Sorry kids, I **haven't got** enough money to buy sweets.
5 Jane **has got** 50 pairs of shoes – can you believe it?
6 I can't call him now – I **haven't got** a signal on my phone.
7 **Have** you **got** your keys?
8 'Maria's so lucky – she**'s got** lovely curly hair.
9 **Have** you **got** any qualifications?
10 We might have problems getting there because we **haven't got** satnav in our car.

◗ **7.24**
I've got a brother and two sisters.
I haven't got any pets.
She's got a beautiful house.
He hasn't got many friends.
Have they got any children?
No they haven't.
Has the hotel got a swimming pool?
Yes, it has.

d Focus on the instructions and the example. Put Sts in pairs.
Monitor and help, making sure Sts use *have got* correctly. Get some feedback from various pairs.

EXTRA IDEA Tell Sts to add two more possessions to ask their partner about.

e Focus on the **Social English** phrases. In pairs, get Sts to see if they can remember any of the missing words.

EXTRA CHALLENGE In pairs, get Sts to complete the phrases before they listen.

f ◗ **7.25** Play the video / audio for Sts to watch or listen and complete the phrases.
Check answers. If you know your Sts' L1, you could get them to translate the phrases.

1 meal 2 good 3 glad 4 should 5 sure 6 great

◗ **7.25**
1 That was a lovely meal.
2 That isn't very good for you.
3 I'm glad you're feeling better.
4 I think I should get back to the hotel now.
5 I'm sure I'll be fine.
6 Thanks again for a great evening.

Now play the video / audio again, pausing after each phrase, for Sts to watch or listen and repeat.

g Focus on the instructions and make sure Sts understand what they have to do.
Get Sts to compare with a partner, and then check answers.

A 3 B 1 C 4 D 5 E 2 F 6

Now put Sts in pairs and get them to practise the conversations.

Finally, focus on the **CAN YOU…?** questions and ask Sts if they feel confident they can now do these things. If they feel that they need more practice, tell them to go to *Online Practice* to watch the episode again and practise the language.

G *should*
V *get*: *get angry*, *get lost*, etc.
P /ʊ/ and /uː/

Lesson plan

In this lesson Sts learn to use *should / shouldn't* for giving advice. The lesson begins with Sts reading a problem which was sent to a newspaper 'problem page' by a young woman wanting advice, and listening to the advice given. This leads into the grammar presentation, which is followed by a pronunciation focus on the /ʊ/ and /uː/ sounds. Then there is a speaking and listening activity where Sts listen to a radio phone-in programme and discuss the advice that is given to three callers. Finally, Vocabulary and Speaking focuses on different meanings of *get*, which are recycled in a questionnaire.

More materials
For teachers
Photocopiables
Grammar should / shouldn't *p.193*
Vocabulary get *p.267* (instructions *p.255*)
Communicative I need some advice *p.238*
(instructions *p.213*)
For students
Workbook 8A
Online Practice 8A

OPTIONAL LEAD-IN (BOOKS CLOSED)

Write on the board I NEED SOME ADVICE. Ask Sts what they think *advice* means, and also elicit that it is a noun, and that the verb is *advise*. Point out that the verb is /ədˈvaɪz/ and the noun is /ədˈvaɪs/. Tell Sts that *advice* is uncountable in English – it can't be used with *an* or in the plural, e.g. *My sister usually gives me good advice.* NOT ~~a good advice~~ or ~~good advices~~.

1 READING & LISTENING understanding opinions

a Books open. Focus on the question and give Sts a couple of minutes to discuss it in pairs or small groups.

Get feedback from the class. Elicit also the idea of contacting a radio programme or a magazine / online problem page. Find out from the class what they think of these more impersonal options, and ask if Sts think this is better than asking a family member or friend.

b Focus on the instructions and make sure Sts understand what *an advice column* is.

Get Sts to read the problem and then, with a partner, discuss which they think is the best advice.

Elicit some opinions. You could write the majority class opinion on the board before they listen.

EXTRA SUPPORT Before Sts read the problem and advice, check whether you need to pre-teach any vocabulary.

EXTRA SUPPORT Before Sts discuss the advice, ask a few questions to make sure they have understood the problem, e.g. *How big is the age difference? How long have they been together? Does she get on with his children?*, etc.

c 🔊 **8.1** Tell Sts they are now going to listen to Tracey reading Graham Norton's advice and they must see which piece of advice in **b** he suggests.

Play the audio once the whole way through.

Check the answer and elicit why.

EXTRA SUPPORT Read through the script and decide if you need to pre-teach any new lexis before Sts listen.

b: She should think hard about what kind of man she really wants to be with before making a decision.

🔊 **8.1**
(script in Student's Book on *p.123*)
Hi, Tracey. You know the answer to your last question, and it's 'yes'. You're making your life more difficult. But it's also true that having a long-term relationship with anyone is difficult, and in your case, you can at least see what some of the problems are. I'm sure this man loves you and will support you in all your goals in life, but it's true that he's already done all the things you want to do. It's not his fault, but it means that he'll never get as excited as you about, for example, a wedding or having another child. And everything you experience together he'll probably compare to the last time he did it. You should think carefully about what kind of partner you really want: someone who can support you and show you the way in life, or someone who will discover life with you. You shouldn't make a decision in a hurry. When you're clearer about what you want, then you can decide if you're going to stay with this man or not. Good luck!

EXTRA SUPPORT If there's time, you could get Sts to listen again with the script on *p.123*, so they can see exactly what they understood / didn't understand. Translate / Explain any new words or phrases.

2 GRAMMAR *should*

a Tell Sts to look at the three sentences and answer
questions 1–3.
Check answers.

> **1** b
> **2** No
> **3** Add *not* / *n't* for negatives; *Should* + subject + infinitive for
> questions.

b Tell Sts to go to **Grammar Bank 8A** on *p.140*.

Grammar notes

should does not usually cause problems, as it has a clearly
defined use and the form is simple. Remind Sts to use the
infinitive without *to* after *should*.

The main problem with *should* is the pronunciation,
i.e. the silent *l* (see **Pronunciation notes** in **3**).

8.2 Focus on the example sentences and play the
audio for Sts to listen and repeat. Encourage them to copy
the rhythm. Then go through the rules with the class.

Now focus on the **ought to** box and go through it with
the class.

Then focus on the exercises for **8A** on *p.141*. Sts do them
individually or in pairs.

Check answers, getting Sts to read the full sentences.

> **a**
> **1** You **shouldn't** work really long hours every day.
> **2** You **should** stop smoking.
> **3** You **should** eat more fruit and vegetables.
> **4** You **shouldn't** put so much sugar in your coffee.
> **5** You **should** start doing some exercise.
> **6** You **should** drink less alcohol.
> **7** You **should** drink more water.
> **8** You **shouldn't** go to bed so late.
> **b**
> **1** You **should wear** a scarf.
> **2** I **should study** this afternoon.
> **3** You **should book** a holiday.
> **4** You **shouldn't be** at work.
> **5** She **should relax** more.
> **6** You **shouldn't drive** so fast – this road's very dangerous.
> **7** Parents **should spend** more time with their children.
> **8** You **shouldn't buy** him an iPad – he's only seven years old.

Tell Sts to go back to the main lesson **8A**.

EXTRA SUPPORT If you think Sts need more practice, you
may want to give them the **Grammar** photocopiable
activity at this point.

c Focus on the instructions and quickly go through the
WhatsApp messages to make sure Sts understand all the
lexis, e.g. *it's driving me mad*, etc.

Give Sts time to write a short answer to each message. Tell
them to write between 10 and 20 words for each answer.

Monitor and help with vocabulary while Sts are writing.

Put Sts in small groups and get them to read their advice
for each problem. They should then choose the best piece
of advice.

Get feedback from each group by eliciting the best piece
of advice they chose for each problem.

3 PRONUNCIATION /ʊ/ and /uː/

Pronunciation notes

should (like *would* and *could*) is often mispronounced,
partly because of the silent *l*, but also because *ou* is not
normally pronounced /ʊ/.

The focus on /ʊ/ and /uː/ will give Sts further practice of
/ʊ/ and contrast it with the long /uː/. It is worth pointing
out to Sts that one of the main problems with these two
sounds is words with *oo*, which can be pronounced either
way, e.g. *good* /ɡʊd/ and *food* /fuːd/. There is no rule, so
Sts need to learn each word as it comes up.

a **8.3** Focus on the instructions and questions.
Play the audio for Sts to listen and repeat the sounds
and words.

8.3
See sounds and words in Student's Book on *p.62*

Ask the class the first question.

> /ʊ/ is short; /uː/ is long.

Now ask the second question.

> The *l* isn't pronounced in *should* and *would*.

Finally, play the audio again for Sts to listen and repeat.

b **8.4** Tell Sts to put the words in the correct row.
Remind them that this kind of exercise is easier to do if
they say the words aloud.

Play the audio for Sts to listen and check.

Check answers.

8.4
bull /ʊ/   book, could, look, pull, push
boot /uː/   cool, flew, food, lose, shoes, school

Now play the audio again for Sts to listen and repeat.

EXTRA SUPPORT If these sounds are difficult for your Sts,
it will help to show them the mouth position. You could
model this yourself or use the the Sound Bank videos on the
Teacher's Resource Centre.

c Put Sts in pairs and get them to practise saying the
sentences.

EXTRA SUPPORT Before putting Sts in pairs, read each
sentence aloud and get Sts to listen and repeat.

4 SPEAKING & LISTENING

a Tell Sts that a–c are three different pieces of advice for a problem. They should read them and then, with a partner, decide what the problem is.

Elicit some ideas, but <u>don't</u> tell Sts if they are right.

b ◗ **8.5** Focus on the task and tell Sts they are going to listen to Annabel and Peter phoning a radio programme with their problem. They must listen and make notes about the problem.

Play the audio once the whole way through. Then play it again if necessary.

Check the answer and ask a few comprehension questions to make sure Sts understood the details of the problem. Find out how many Sts guessed correctly in **a**.

EXTRA SUPPORT Read through the scripts and decide if you need to pre-teach any new lexis before Sts listen.

> Their son, Jamie, wants to go on holiday to Mexico with some friends. Annabel and Peter, his parents, don't think he should go. They think he should save his money, so he can get his own place to live.

◗ **8.5**
(script in Student's Book on *p.123*)
A = Annabel, P = Peter, E = expert
A   Hello. I'm Annabel.
P   And I'm Peter.
E   Hi there, Annabel and Peter. What's your problem?
A   We've got a son, Jamie, and he's twenty-five. He's a chef.
P   But he still lives with us because he says it's too expensive to rent a flat and he doesn't earn enough money.
A   He gives us some money every month for bills – not much, but a bit – and, you know, it's nice to have him at home, but we think he needs to be more independent.
P   Yes, absolutely.
A   But last week he told us that he's planning a two-week holiday to Mexico with his friends. I mean, it's true that he works full-time and we know he needs a break, but we really think...
P   Yes, we don't think he should go on an expensive holiday when he doesn't give us much money. We think he should save his money so that he can get his own place to live. Should we tell him that he can't go to Mexico?

c Put Sts in pairs and get them to discuss which advice in **a** they think is the best.

Elicit some feedback and ask Sts to explain why they chose their advice.

d ◗ **8.6** Now tell Sts they are going to listen to the expert's advice. They must see if the expert gives the same advice that they chose in **c** and decide whether it is good advice. They should make notes, so they can then compare it to their advice.

Play the audio once the whole way through. Then play it again if necessary.

Check the answer first, then find out what Sts think of the advice, and if they have any other suggestions.

> c – The expert's advice is to let Jamie go on holiday, but talk to him about paying rent when he gets back.

◗ **8.6**
(script in Student's Book on *p.123*)
A = Annabel, P = Peter, E = expert
E   You know, to be honest, I think you're being a bit hard on him. I mean, he's only twenty-five. It's good that he has a job, and everybody needs a holiday. My advice is that you should let him go to Mexico, but when he comes back, you should sit down with him and talk to him about starting to pay rent. That way he'll understand that he needs to start planning for the future and to start thinking about renting a flat. But I know from talking to other parents that there are a lot of young people still living at home in their twenties and thirties, and some of them don't even have jobs. So in many ways, I think you're lucky.
A   You see? That's just what I think…

e ◗ **8.7 8.8** Tell Sts they are going to hear another caller, Nick. They should follow the same steps as for Annabel and Peter, i.e. predict the problem, then listen and check and make notes, decide which advice they think is best, and then listen to the advice and see what they think of it.

> Nick's girlfriend wants to move to London to get a better job, but he has a good job and doesn't know if he should follow her or not.

◗ **8.7**
(script in Student's Book on *p.123*)
N = Nick, E = expert
N   Hi there. I'm Nick.
E   Hi, Nick. So what's your problem?
N   Well, I've been with my girlfriend for three years. We have a really great relationship although we're quite different. She's clever and popular, and I'm, er, quiet and hard-working. Anyway, now she wants to move to London because she thinks she can get a better job there, and she wants me to go to London, too – you know, London's much more exciting than Bolton, where we live now. But I have a good job in Bolton and I get a good salary. I mean, the idea of moving and having a new life is like a dream, but for me that's what it is – I mean, it's a dream; it isn't real. What should I do? Should I follow my heart and move to London with her? Or should I stay here, where I know I have a good job, but possibly lose my girlfriend?

> a – The expert's advice is for Nick and his girlfriend to sit down and discuss their future. If they want the same thing, then Nick's girlfriend should move to London and he can visit.

◗ **8.8**
(script in Student's Book on *p.123*)
E   I think you should sit down together and talk about your dreams for the future, and see if they are the same dreams. If they are, and you can see a future together, then the first thing is for her to look for a job in London. If she finds one, then maybe she can move there first, and you can go at weekends and see how you feel about life there.
N   Thanks a lot for that. I think that's really good advice.

f ◗ **8.9 8.10** Tell Sts they are going to hear a final caller, Jane. They follow the same steps as for Annabel and Peter, and Nick.

> Jane has planned a holiday with her friend Susan and is really looking forward to it. However, Susan has now invited another friend, Angie. Jane doesn't know Angie and doesn't want to go on holiday with her.

◗ **8.9**
(script in Student's Book on *p.123*)
J = Jane, E = expert
J Hello. My name's Jane.
E Hi, Jane. So, why are you calling?
J Well, a month ago, my friend Susan and I decided to go on holiday together this summer, to Turkey. So we planned everything and, er, I was really looking forward to it, as Susan's an old friend and I don't see her very often. But the other day, she told me that she was telling another friend of hers about our holiday – somebody I don't know, a woman called Angie – and Angie was really interested, and now Susan has invited her to come, too. Susan never asked me what I thought! I don't even know Angie, and I really don't want to go on holiday with someone I don't know. What should I do?

b – The expert's advice is to try to get to know Angie first. If Miriam likes her, then the holiday will be a success. If not, then she should tell her friend Susan she isn't going.

◗ **8.10**
(script in Student's Book on *pp.123–124*)
E I think your friend has been a bit insensitive, and she's put you in a difficult position. You have several different options. You could say that you aren't going if Angie goes, but then you'll put Susan in a difficult position. Or you could just cancel, and suggest having another holiday later, with just the two of you. Or you could invite someone else who you like, and then there would be four of you, which is sometimes a better number than three. But in fact, you don't know Angie, and maybe you'll like her. So I think you should try to get to know her first. If you like her, then the holiday will probably be a success. If not, then you should tell your friend you aren't going because you don't think it will work with Angie. You know, a bad holiday is worse than no holiday.

 If there's time, you could get Sts to listen again with the scripts on *pp.123–124*, so they can see exactly what they understood / didn't understand. Translate / Explain any new words or phrases.

5 VOCABULARY & SPEAKING *get*

a Focus on the instructions, the three sentences, and the meanings.

Get Sts to match them and then compare with a partner.

Check answers.

1 c **2** a **3** b

b Tell Sts to go to **Vocabulary Bank** *get* on *p.159*.

Vocabulary notes

Get is one of the most common verbs in English, mainly because it has many different meanings and there are also many phrasal verbs with *get*. It's important for Sts to be clear about the four main meanings (*become, buy / obtain, arrive,* and *receive*) and to begin learning some of the most common phrasal verbs.

When focusing on the first **become** section, highlight the difference between *be angry / divorced*, etc. and *get angry / divorced*, etc.

Highlight the different phrasal verbs for cars (*get into / out of*) and public transport, e.g. buses, planes, and trains (*get on / off*).

Focus on the *get* box and go through it with the class.

Get Sts to do **a** individually or in pairs. Many of these words / phrases may already be familiar to them.

◗ **8.11** Now do **b**. Play the audio for Sts to listen and check.

Check answers.

◗ **8.11**
7 get angry
3 get divorced
5 get fit
4 get lost
2 get married
1 get nervous
6 get ready
9 get better / get worse
8 get colder
11 get a job
12 get a newspaper
10 get a ticket
16 get into a car
15 get on a bus a bus
13 get on with somebody
14 get up
18 get home
19 get to school
17 get to work
21 get an email
20 get a present
22 get a prize

Now either use the audio to drill the pronunciation of the phrases, or model and drill them yourself. Give further practice of any words your Sts find difficult to pronounce.

Finally, do **Activation** and get Sts to cover the phrases and look at the pictures. They can test themselves or a partner.

Tell Sts to go back to the main lesson **8A**.

 If you think Sts need more practice, you may want to give them the **Vocabulary** photocopiable activity at this point.

c Focus on the questionnaire and go through the questions. Get Sts to ask you one or two of the questions.

Then get Sts to ask and answer in pairs.

Monitor and help, making sure they are using *get* correctly.

Get feedback from a few pairs.

G *if* + present, *will* + infinitive (first conditional)
V confusing verbs: *carry*, *wear*, *win*, *earn*, etc.
P homophones

Lesson plan

This lesson presents the first conditional through the humorous context of 'Murphy's Law', which states that if something bad can happen, it will happen. The lesson begins with a reading text about the origins of Murphy's Law and Sts try to match two halves of some common examples. This leads into the grammar presentation of the first conditional, which is followed by a listening activity in which Sts hear two true stories about real examples of Murphy's Law. The vocabulary and speaking focus is on verbs which are often confused, like *know / meet* and *borrow / lend*, which are practised in a questionnaire. The lesson ends with a pronunciation focus on homophones, e.g. *wear – where*, *write – right*, etc.

More materials
For teachers
Photocopiables
Grammar *if* + present, *will* + infinitive (first conditional) *p.194*
Vocabulary Confusing verbs *p.268* (instructions *p.255*)
Communicative Conditionals race *p.239* (instructions *p.213*)
For students
Workbook 8B
Online Practice 8B

OPTIONAL LEAD-IN (BOOKS CLOSED)

Write MURPHY'S LAW on the board and elicit from the class anything they know about it. Try to elicit a concrete example of one of Murphy's laws. If the class don't seem to have much idea, you could ask them *What always happens if you drop a piece of bread or toast on the floor? Which way does it fall?* (with the buttered side on the floor). You could use mime to help make this clear.

1 READING

a Books open. Focus on the question. Sts will probably try to express that the queue they were in before will move faster.

b Focus on the article and tell Sts to read the two paragraphs (up to where the examples start). Give Sts a few minutes to read and answer the questions.

Check answers.

EXTRA SUPPORT Before Sts read the article the first time, check whether you need to pre-teach any vocabulary.

Murphy was an American aerospace engineer.
His 'Law' is 'if there is something that can go wrong, it will go wrong.'

c Give Sts time to read the examples of Murphy's Law (1–8) and to match them to the correct endings A–H.

Check answers.

1 D   2 H   3 B   4 C   5 A   6 F   7 E   8 G

Deal with any other new vocabulary. Model and drill the pronunciation of any tricky words.

d In pairs, small groups, or as a whole class, Sts answer the question.

If Sts worked in pairs or small groups, get some feedback. You could tell Sts if these things happen to you.

2 GRAMMAR   *if* + present, *will* + infinitive

a In pairs, Sts cover A–H in **1c** and try to remember the laws, using the first half of the sentences in the article as prompts.

b Now tell Sts to focus on the full sentences and to decide which structures are used in both parts.

Check answers and explain that sentences with *if* are often called *conditional sentences*, and that this structure (a sentence with *if* + present, future) is often called *the first conditional*.

The verb after *if* is in the present simple and the other verb is in the future (*will* / *won't* + infinitive).

c Tell Sts to go to **Grammar Bank 8B** on *p.140*.

Grammar notes

Since first conditional sentences refer to future possibilities, some Sts may try to use the future after *if*. A typical mistake is: ~~If he'll phone, I'll tell him~~.

The present simple is also used after *when*, rather than *will*, e.g. *I'll tell him when he arrives*. You may want to point this out in this lesson.

8.12 Focus on the example sentences and play the audio for Sts to listen and repeat. Encourage them to copy the rhythm. Then go through the rules with the class.

Now focus on the exercises for **8B** on *p.141*. Sts do them individually or in pairs.

Check answers, getting Sts to read the full sentences.

a
1 D   2 G   3 E   4 F   5 A   6 B
b
1 If you **tell** me what really happened, I **won't tell** anybody else.
2 If I **don't write** it down, I **won't remember** it.
3 **Will** you **call** me if you **get** any news?
4 She**'ll help** you if you **ask** her nicely.
5 I**'ll phone** you if I **hear** from Alex.
6 You**'ll miss** your friends if you **move** to Paris.
7 If you **listen** carefully, you**'ll understand** everything.
8 Your boss **won't be** pleased if you are late for work today.
9 I'll **drive** you home if you **give** me directions.
10 If you **don't take** an umbrella, it**'ll rain**!

Tell Sts to go back to the main lesson **8B**.

d Focus on the prompts for Sts to make new 'Murphy's Laws'. Highlight that there is not one correct answer. Remind Sts of the original 'Law': *If there is something that can go wrong, it will go wrong.*

While Sts complete their laws in pairs, monitor and help with vocabulary and spelling. You may want to teach the verb *spill*.

e Put Sts in small groups or get them to stand up and move around, and get them to read their 'laws' to each other.

Get feedback and write the 'laws' on the board. Accept all logical endings.

Possible endings
1 they won't have your size
2 you won't find / see one
3 you'll spill tomato sauce / red wine on it
4 you'll get / miss an important call
5 your team / someone will score a goal

3 LISTENING understanding an anecdote

a ◗) **8.13** Focus on the instructions and make sure Sts understand what they have to do.

Play the audio once the whole way through for Sts to listen and complete the task.

Check answers.

1 recession   2 applied for   3 got cut off   4 either, or
5 in the wild   6 the whole morning

◗) **8.13**
1 It was the recession and it was very difficult to get a job.
2 I applied for lots of different jobs.
3 We got cut off because the bus went into a tunnel.
4 I was interested in either a trip to see birds or a trip to see a tiger.
5 I thought it would be really cool to see a tiger in the wild.
6 We spent the whole morning looking for the tiger.

Now put Sts in pairs and get them to discuss what they think the words and phrases they circled mean.

Check answers. Model and drill pronunciation.

1 recession = a difficult time for the economy of a country
2 applied for = sent applications and CVs to possible employers
3 got cut off = lost phone connection
4 either, or = one of two options
5 in the wild = in its natural state
6 the whole = all of

b ◗) **8.14** Tell Sts they are now going to listen to both Peter's and Sue's stories. They must decide why they are examples of Murphy's Law.

Play the audio once the whole way through. You could pause it after Peter's story to give Sts time to complete the task.

Check answers.

Peter waited four months for a job interview, but when the phone call finally came for an interview, the call got cut off.

Sue got up early for a trip to see a tiger, but didn't see one. However, other people who went on a trip to see birds saw the tiger.

◗) **8.14**
(script in Student's Book on *p.124*)
Peter wanted to get a job
I did maths at university and normally, after doing maths at university, people get a job in a bank or in IT, but when I finished it was the recession and it was very difficult to get a job. I was unemployed for quite a long time. I was looking for jobs, and I applied for lots of different jobs, but they just answered, 'Sorry, we don't want you,' and I was getting a bit depressed. This went on for about four months, and then one day, I was on a number forty-nine bus in London – I can even remember where I was sitting – and my phone rang. I said, 'Hello' and a woman said, 'Hello, you applied for a job with us a few months ago. Are you still interested?' So I said, 'Yes, absolutely. I'm very interested.' So then she said, 'We'd like you to come for an interview'...and then, at that moment, we got cut off because the bus went into a tunnel. And the phone number wasn't on my phone – it just said 'unknown number', and I couldn't remember what the name of the company was because I'd applied for so many jobs. So I thought, 'Four months of nothing, and then when they ring, I get cut off.' Luckily, they called back the next day, and in the end, I had an interview and I got the job.

Sue wanted to see a tiger
This happened when I was at a conference in Thailand. The conference hotel was amazing – it was in a beautiful national park called *Khao Yai*, north of Bangkok. We were very busy with talks and meetings most of the time, but we had one free morning, and we could choose from different trips or activities. I was interested in either a trip to see birds or a trip to see a tiger. A tiger, not tigers, because they told us that there was only one tiger in the whole park! Well, I chose the tiger trip, because I thought it would be really cool to see a tiger in the wild. But we had to leave really early in the morning because we had to travel quite a long way to the part of the park where the tiger usually was – the bird trip was nearer the hotel. So we tiger-watchers got up at five in the morning, but our guide said that we probably wouldn't see the tiger because, you know, there was only one tiger. We finally got there and we spent the whole morning looking for the tiger, but no luck. But we saw some nice birds, and it was fun, so when we got back to the conference hotel, we felt we'd had a really good morning. But then the other group got back – the ones who went to see the birds – and of course they saw lots of amazing birds, but they also saw the tiger! I suppose that day, it wasn't in its usual part of the park. And I thought, 'Isn't that typical – you go on the tiger trip and you don't see the tiger, but the people on the bird trip see the tiger!'

c Focus on the task and give Sts time to read sentences 1–6.

Play the audio, pausing at the end of Peter's story. Give Sts time to mark 1–3 *T* or *F* and then play Sue's story. Then give Sts time to do the same with 4–6 *T* or *F*. Remind them that they need to correct the *F* sentences.

Check answers.

EXTRA SUPPORT If there's time, you could get Sts to listen again with the script on *p.124*, so they can see exactly what they understood / didn't understand. Translate / Explain any new words or phrases.

d Do this as a whole-class activity. You could also tell Sts what you think, and tell any Murphy's Law stories that you can think of.

4 VOCABULARY & SPEAKING confusing verbs

a Focus on the question and elicit answers from the class.

1 looking for **2** told

b Tell Sts to go to **Vocabulary Bank Confusing verbs** on *p.160* and get Sts to do **a** individually or in pairs. Many of these words / phrases may already be familiar to them.

Vocabulary notes

Some of these verbs are often confused because in some Sts' L1, one verb may be used for both meanings. Use the notes below to help clarify where necessary. Encourage Sts to learn the verbs in a phrase, e.g. *know someone well, meet someone for the first time*, etc.

- *wear / carry*:
  You wear clothes or jewellery, i.e. have it on your body, e.g. *I wear glasses to read*.
  You carry something heavy and take it from one place to another, e.g. *He was carrying a suitcase*.

- *win / earn*:
  You win a sports match, something in a competition, the lottery, etc.
  You earn money when you work.

- *know / meet*:
  know a person = you have met and seen this person before
  meet a person = to get to know somebody for the first time, e.g. *Nice to meet you*, or to arrange to be with a person in a certain place / at a certain time, e.g. *Let's meet in the café at 6.30*.

- *hope / wait*:
  hope = what you want to happen, e.g. *I hope that it's sunny tomorrow*.
  wait = sit / stand and do nothing until something happens, e.g. *wait for the doctor*

- *watch / look at*:
  You watch something where there is movement, e.g. *We watched a cricket match in the park, We watched the children playing*.
  You look at something static, e.g. a photo, somebody's passport

- *look / look like*:
  We use *look* + adjective, e.g. *You look tired*.
  We use *look like* + a noun, e.g. *You look like Brad Pitt*.

- *miss / lose*:
  You miss a class, a bus, a plane (e.g. if you are late / ill).
  You lose a sports match or lose an object, e.g. your keys.

- *bring / take*:
  This depends on where the speaker is. The teacher (at school) says: *Don't forget to bring your book to class tomorrow*. The student (at home) says: *I must remember to take my book today*.

- *look for / find*:
  Look for is the action of trying to locate something you have lost or need, e.g. *I'm looking for a new job*.
  Find is used when you have located it, e.g. *I have found a new job*.

- *say / tell*:
  Say is used like this:
  Jack said, 'Hello.'
  Jack said hello to me yesterday.
  Susan told a lie.
  Susan told me a lie.

- *lend / borrow*:
  I lent my brother some money.
  My brother borrowed some money from me.

- *hear / listen to*:
  hear = be aware of sounds in your ears, e.g. *I heard the baby next door crying*.
  listen to = to pay attention to sb / sth that you can hear, e.g. *I listen to the news on the radio every morning*.

◖◗ **8.15** Now do **b**. Play the audio for Sts to listen and check.
Check answers.

◖◗ **8.15**
Confusing verbs
2 wear jewellery, wear clothes, carry a bag, carry a baby
8 win a match, win a medal, win a prize, earn a salary, earn money
5 know somebody well, know something, meet somebody for the first time, meet at eleven o'clock
1 hope that something good will happen, hope to do something, wait for a bus, wait for a long time
3 watch TV, watch a match, look at a photo, look at a view
11 look happy, look about twenty-five years old, look like your mother, look like a model
4 miss the bus, miss a class, lose a match, lose your glasses
9 bring your dictionary, bring something back from holiday, take an umbrella, take your children to school
6 look for your glasses, look for a job, find your glasses, find a job
10 say sorry, say hello, say something to somebody, tell a joke, tell a lie, tell somebody something
7 lend money to somebody, borrow money from somebody
12 hear a noise, hear the door bell, listen to music, listen to the radio

Now either use the audio to drill the pronunciation of the phrases, or model and drill them yourself. Give further practice of any words your Sts find difficult to pronounce.

Focus on the **hope and expect** and **bring and take** box and go through it with the class.

Finally, get Sts to do **Activation** in pairs. **A** says a verb and **B** a continuation, and then they swap roles.

Tell Sts to go back to the main lesson **8B**.

 If you think Sts need more practice, you may want to give them the **Vocabulary** photocopiable activity at this point.

c Get Sts to read questions 1–10 and circle the correct verb in each one.

Get Sts to compare with a partner, and then check answers.

> **1** look like **2** missed **3** listening to **4** earn **5** meet
> **6** tell **7** lent **8** looking for **9** wear **10** watch

Now put Sts in pairs and get them to ask and answer the questions.

Get some feedback from the class.

5 PRONUNCIATION homophones

 You could introduce the concept of homophones by dictating individual words, like *here, where, no*, etc. Then get Sts, in pairs, to compare how they've spelled them. Finally, elicit some of the words onto the board and explain that both words, e.g. *here* and *hear*, are pronounced exactly the same.

a 🔊 **8.16** Focus on the **Homophones** box and go through it with the class, stressing that the pronunciation of the words is <u>identical</u>.

Give Sts time to quickly read 1–8.

Play the audio, pausing after each **b** sentence to give Sts time to write.

Check answers by eliciting the words onto the board, getting Sts to spell them.

 Pause the audio after the first one, and elicit the answer to check Sts know what they have to do.

> **1** Where **2** no **3** meat **4** Wait **5** right **6** won **7** sea
> **8** wore

🔊 **8.16**

1 **a** What are you going to wear tonight?
  b A Where are you from?
     B I'm from Warsaw.
2 **a** I don't know what to do.
  b There's no milk in the fridge!
3 **a** Hi. Nice to meet you.
  b Do you want meat or fish?
4 **a** The maximum weight for hand luggage is ten kilos.
  b I'm coming! Wait for me!
5 **a** Please write soon.
  b Is it on the left or on the right?
6 **a** There's only one ticket left.
  b Brazil won the match five–one.
7 **a** I can't see the board!
  b I love swimming in the sea.
8 **a** Have you ever read *War and Peace*?
  b It was cold, so she wore a coat.

---

b 🔊 **8.17** Tell Sts they are going to hear four sentences and they must write them down. The first time, tell them just to listen, <u>not</u> to write.

Now play the audio again, pausing after each sentence to give Sts time to write.

Check answers, eliciting the sentences onto the board and getting Sts to spell the homophones in each sentence.

🔊 **8.17**

1 I can see the sea from here.
2 I write with my right hand.
3 He won one game.
4 I know there's no hope.

Play the audio again, pausing for Sts to listen and repeat the sentences and copy the rhythm.

Now put Sts in pairs and get them to practise saying the sentences.

8C Who is Vivienne?

G possessive pronouns
V adverbs of manner: *dreamily*, *completely*, etc.
P reading aloud

Lesson plan

The context of this lesson is a short story by the famous American writer O. Henry (1862–1910), which has a characteristic 'twist' at the end.

Sts read and listen to the first part of the story and then practise reading aloud with good sentence rhythm in Pronunciation. Examples taken from the story lead into the grammar focus on possessive pronouns. Then Sts watch or listen to both the first two parts. Parts 3 and 4 are dramatized in video listening. Finally, there is a vocabulary and writing focus on using adverbs of manner.

This lesson provides a good opportunity to remind Sts of the value of reading Graded Readers (sometimes called Easy Readers) in English. Reading Graded Readers helps to consolidate what Sts already know and to build their vocabulary. Some Graded Readers also have accompanying audio and some are available as e-books, which can be used to help to improve Sts' listening comprehension and pronunciation. You could recommend the Oxford Bookworm series level 2, which has a selection of other O. Henry stories in a book called *New Yorkers*.

More materials
For teachers
Photocopiables
Grammar possessive pronouns *p.195*
Communicative Reading questionnaire *p.240* (instructions *p.213*)
Teacher's Resource Centre
Video Girl
For students
Workbook 8C
Online Practice 8C

Get feedback from the class and use this opportunity to stress the importance of reading in English outside class. If you haven't already done so, draw Sts' attention to Graded Readers, particularly if your school has a library. If not, you could consider starting a class library by getting Sts to buy one book each and then swapping the books among all the Sts in the class. You could also have a wallchart recording the books Sts have read and a brief comment or score.

1 READING understanding a story

a Books open. Focus on the task and tell Sts to look at the all the photos in the lesson. Elicit answers from the class.

> Suggested answer: I think the story takes place in the 19th century, because of the costumes.

b 🔊 **8.18** Tell Sts they are going to read and listen to an extract from *Girl* by O. Henry. You might want to tell them that his real name was William Sydney Porter (1862–1910) and that he was a famous American author.

Play the audio once the whole way through while Sts follow **Part 1** of the story.

EXTRA SUPPORT Before Sts read the story, check whether you want to pre-teach any vocabulary.

🔊 **8.18**
See Part 1 in Student's Book on *p.66*

Then give Sts time to read **Part 1** again without the audio. In pairs, Sts answer questions 1–4 and the *Think about the story so far* question.

Check answers to 1–4 and elicit ideas for *Think about the story so far*.

> 1 He gave Hartley Vivienne's address. He offered to follow her.
> 2 He left the detective's office and went to find where Vivienne lived.
> 3 She looked about 21, her hair was red gold, and her eyes sea-blue.
> 4 Because she didn't answer his letter.

c 🔊 **8.19** Before telling Sts to read and listen to **Part 2**, go through the **Glossary** on *p.67* with them.

Then play the audio once the whole way through while Sts read **Part 2** of the story.

🔊 **8.19**
See Part 2 in Student's Book on *p.67*

Now give Sts time to read **Part 2** again without the audio. In pairs, Sts answer questions 1–5 and the *Think about the story so far* question.

Check answers to 1–4, elicit ideas for 5 and *Think about the story so far*.

❗ At this stage of the story, Sts will probably assume that Hartley is in love with Vivienne and wants her to come and live with him. They will also probably imagine that Héloise is his wife. <u>Don't</u> confirm or reject these assumptions.

> **1** She doesn't think she would enjoy living in the suburbs.
> **2** He told her she could come to the city whenever she wants.
> **3** At the Montgomerys'.
> **4** Because she has someone else.

Deal with any other new vocabulary. Model and drill the pronunciation of any tricky words.

2 PRONUNCIATION reading aloud

Pronunciation notes

Reading aloud in class is an activity which divides teachers. Some feel that it can give Sts valuable pronunciation practice, while others find it painful. We believe that in small doses, it can be helpful to improve Sts' awareness of word and sentence rhythm. However, we believe that reading aloud needs to be focused, with <u>short</u> pieces of text which all Sts can work on (with teacher correction). This can be much more effective than just getting Sts to read a text aloud around the class, with each person reading a different sentence.

a 🔊 **8.20** Focus on the task and on the last four lines of the story on *p.67* (from *"Vivienne," said Hartley masterfully* to the end). Get Sts to read the two questions, and then play the audio.

Check answers.

> **a** punctuation   **b** the adverbs, i.e. *masterfully, calmly*

🔊 **8.20**
H = Hartley, N = narrator, V = Vivienne
H   Vivienne…
N   …*said Hartley, masterfully.'*
H   You must be mine.
N   *Vivienne looked him in the eye.*
V   Do you think for one moment…
N   …*she said calmly…*
V   …that I could come to your home while Héloise is there?

Play the extract again and ask Sts to focus on the rhythm of the sentences, and how the speaker pauses.

Now give Sts a few moments to read the text aloud (quietly) to themselves. Tell them to try to get the correct rhythm, to pause momentarily when there is a comma, and to read the two lines with adverbs (*masterfully* and *calmly*) in the appropriate way.

Then choose a couple of Sts to read the text aloud to the class with good rhythm, correcting them as necessary.

b 🔊 **8.21** Play the audio, pausing after each name for Sts to listen and repeat.

🔊 **8.21**
See names in Student's Book on *p.67*

c Focus on the **Reading aloud** box and go through it with the class.

Put Sts in pairs, **A** and **B**. Then focus on the instructions. Remind Sts that they need to pay attention to the adverbs, e.g. *slowly*, etc. as they read. They also need to stress words which should be stressed and to pause momentarily when there is a comma.

Give Sts time, in pairs, to read their section of **Part 2** of the story.

EXTRA IDEA If you think your Sts would enjoy it, you could put them in groups of three, with one student playing Hartley, one Vivienne, and one being the narrator, as they heard on the audio. When they have finished, get a group to perform in front of the class.

3 GRAMMAR possessive pronouns

a Tell Sts to look at the two sentences from the story, and to complete the gaps.

Check answers. You could ask Sts what the difference between the two words is (*my* = possessive adjective and *mine* = possessive pronoun).

> **1** my   **2** mine

b Tell Sts to go to **Grammar Bank 8C** on *p.140*.

Grammar notes

Sts will probably need reminding of how possessive adjectives (*my, your, his*, etc.) are used, and in particular, how they agree with the subject of a sentence, not the object (e.g. **Jack** helps **his** *sister a lot.* NOT ~~Jack helps **her** sister a lot.~~) and how they never change (e.g. *your books* NOT ~~yours books~~).

When Sts learn possessive pronouns, e.g. *These are yours / hers / ours*, they may then tend to start adding an *s* to possessive adjectives.

🔊 **8.22** Focus on the example sentences and play the audio for Sts to listen and repeat. Encourage them to copy the rhythm. Then go through the rules with the class.

Now focus on the exercises for **8C** on *p.141*. Sts do them individually or in pairs.

Check answers, getting Sts to read the full sentences.

a
1 my   2 yours   3 ours   4 her   5 mine   6 their   7 theirs
8 your   9 hers

b
1 **Hers** is a white Peugeot
2 Maya has a new boyfriend, but I haven't met **him** yet.
3 Look. Here's a photo of Alex and Kim with **their** new baby.
4 We've finished paying for our house, so it's **ours** now.
5 Can you give Maria and Marta **theirs**?
6 Can you tell **us** how to get to the station?
7 Would you like to see **our** garden?
8 London is famous for **its** beautiful parks.

Tell Sts to go back to the main lesson **8C**.

EXTRA SUPPORT If you think Sts need more practice, you may want to give them the **Grammar** photocopiable activity at this point.

c ◑ 8.23 Focus on the instructions and the example. Tell Sts they are going to listen to seven sentences, and each time, they must change the object for a possessive pronoun.

Play the audio, pausing after each sentence for Sts to make the transformation.

◑ 8.23
1 It's my book. (*pause*) It's mine.
2 It's her scarf. (*pause*) It's hers.
3 They're our coats. (*pause*) They're ours.
4 It's his bike. (*pause*) It's his.
5 It's your phone. (*pause*) It's yours.
6 It's their house. (*pause*) It's theirs.
7 They're your sweets. (*pause*) They're yours.

Then repeat the activity, eliciting responses from individual Sts.

4 ▶ VIDEO LISTENING

a ◑ 8.18 8.19 Tell Sts to close their books and watch or listen to **Parts 1** and **2** of the story again.

Play the video / audio once the whole way through.

◑ 8.18 8.19
See Part 1 and Part 2 in Student's Book on *pp.66–67*

b ◑ 8.24 Tell Sts they are going to watch or listen to **Part 3** of the story and they must answer two questions and the *Think about the story so far* question.

Play **Part 3** of the video / audio once the whole way through. Then play it again if necessary.

Get Sts to compare with a partner, and then check answers to 1 and 2. Elicit ideas for *Think about the story so far*, but <u>don't</u> tell Sts if they are right yet.

1 He said Héloise must go.
2 She promised Hartley she would be his.

◑ 8.24
H = Hartley, N = narrator, V = Vivienne
Part 3
H Héloise will go.
H I haven't had one day without problems since I met her. You're right, Vivienne. Héloise must go before I can take you home. But she will go. I've decided…
V Then…my answer is yes. I will be yours.
H Promise me.
V I promise.
H I will come for you tomorrow.
V Tomorrow.
N *An hour and forty minutes later, Hartley stepped off the train when it stopped in the suburbs. He walked to his house, went inside and walked up the stairs.*

c ◑ 8.25 Now tell Sts they are going to watch or listen to **Part 4** of the story and they must answer questions 1–3.

Play **Part 4** of the video / audio once the whole way through. Then play it again if necessary.

Get Sts to compare with a partner, and then check answers.

1 Hartley's wife   2 The Montgomerys' cook   3 Hartley's cook

◑ 8.25
HW = Hartley's wife, H = Hartley
Part 4
HW My mother's here. But she's leaving in half an hour. She came to have dinner, but there's nothing to eat.
H I have something to tell you.
HW Oh, Mother!
HW What do you think? Vivienne is coming to be our cook! She is the cook that was with the Montgomerys. She's going to be ours! And now, dear…you must go to the kitchen and tell Héloise to leave. She's been drunk again all day.

EXTRA SUPPORT If there's time and you are using the video, you could get Sts to watch again with subtitles, so they can see exactly what they understood / didn't understand. Translate / Explain any new words or phrases.

d Do this as a whole-class activity. You could tell Sts your reaction the first time you read the story.

Vocabulary notes

Some Sts at this level still have problems distinguishing between adjectives and adverbs.

If necessary, remind them that adverbs describe actions (verbs) and elicit the basic rules for the formation of adverbs:

Adjective	Adverb	
quiet	quiet**ly**	add *-ly*
sadly	sad**ly**	
possi**ble**	possi**bly**	change *-ble* to *-bly*
comforta**ble**	comforta**bly**	
lazy	laz**ily**	y add *-ily*
angry	angr**ily**	
good	**well**	irregular
fast	**fast**	
hard	**hard**	

a Focus on the instructions and give Sts time to underline six adverbs in **Part 2**.

Get Sts to compare with a partner, and then check answers. Sts may underline the adverb well (line 39). You could also accept this as an answer.

dreamily (line 24)   slowly (line 25)   completely (line 35)
suddenly (line 43)   masterfully (line 49)   calmly (line 51)

b Focus on the instructions and get Sts to make adverbs from the adjectives in the list.

Get Sts to compare with a partner, and then check answers.

angrily lazily quietly sadly seriously slowly

c ◍ 8.26 Get Sts to read sentences 1–6 and to think what the missing adverbs from **b** might be.

Now play the audio the whole way through. Then play it again, pausing after each sentence for Sts to write an adverb to describe how the person is speaking.

Get Sts to compare with a partner, and then check answers.

1 sadly **2** angrily **3** slowly **4** quietly **5** lazily
6 seriously

◍ 8.26
1 I'm sorry, but I don't love you.
2 Give me back all my letters.
3 I think...I have an idea.
4 Don't make a noise. Everyone is asleep.
5 I don't feel like doing anything.
6 This is a very important matter.

d Focus on the task, and remind Sts that at the end of the story, Hartley's wife tells him to tell the cook (Héloise) to leave. In pairs, give Sts, e.g. five minutes to write their short scene. Tell them that they should also include at least two adverbs in their dialogues after *said*.

Get Sts to perform their dialogues in front of the class. You could get them to vote for the best ones.

EXTRA IDEA You could get pairs to read their scenes to each other and see how similar they are.

For instructions on how to use these pages, see *p.40*.

More materials
For teachers
Teacher's Resource Centre
Video Can you understand these people? 7&8
Quick Test 8
File 8 Test
For students
Online Practice Check your progress

GRAMMAR

1 a	2 c	3 b	4 c	5 b	6 a	7 a	8 c	9 c	10 b
11 a	12 b	13 b	14 c	15 b

VOCABULARY

a
1 meet   2 tell   3 miss   4 hope   5 wears

b
1 forget   2 learn   3 feel like   4 promise   5 hate   6 mind
7 enjoy   8 finish

c
1 with   2 in   3 of   4 at   5 for

d
1 lost   2 home   3 better   4 tickets   5 on   6 divorced
7 presents

PRONUNCIATION

c
1 ch**oo**se /uː/   2 l**oo**k /ʊ/   3 l**o**ve /ʌ/   4 do**ing** /ŋ/
5 **kn**ow /n/

d
1 sur**vive**   2 **hap**piness   3 a**fraid**   4 pre**tend**   5 **bor**row

CAN YOU understand this text?

a 1

b
1 c   2 a   3 f   4 e   5 b   6 d

▶ CAN YOU understand these people?

1 b	2 c	3 b	4 c	5 a

◑ 8.27

1

I = interviewer, S = Susie
I   What's your idea of happiness?
S   That's a difficult question. Um, my idea of happiness is probably relaxing with friends in my home, listening to nice music, with lovely food for everyone.

2

I = interviewer, T = Tarquin
I   What foreign languages do you speak?
T   I speak French.
I   How well do you speak it?
T   Quite well. Not fluently, but well enough to get around.

3

I = interviewer, K = Katelyn
I   If you have a problem, who do you ask for advice, friends or family?
K   When I have a problem, I usually ask close friends for advice.
I   Why?
K   My parents are a lot older than me, so their advice is really great for certain things, but most of the things I'm going through right now, my friends are pretty good.

4

I = interviewer, J = Joseph
I   What advice would you give someone who can't sleep at night?
J   If someone couldn't sleep at night, I'd usually advise them to do something like meditation, so some kind of breathing exercises which would calm them down, um, and also just to be in an environment where they feel comfortable and safe I guess, rather than in an environment that stresses them out, maybe keep their phone out of the bedroom, or something like that.

5

I = interviewer, A = Alison
I   Do you think the British are bad at learning languages?
A   I think we do tend to be rather bad at learning languages.
I   Why?
A   I think we can be a bit lazy, because everybody else speaks English.

9A Beware of the dog

G *if* + past, *would* + infinitive (second conditional)
V animals and insects: *lion, tiger, goat,* etc.
P word stress

Lesson plan

A survival quiz, where Sts have to choose what they would do in a variety of situations involving animals and insects, is the context for Sts to learn about the second conditional for hypothetical and imaginary situations.

The lesson begins with Vocabulary. Sts learn the names of common animals, and Pronunciation focuses on how to pronounce the words for animals in English which may be similar in Sts' own language. Next, Sts listen to an interview about the five most dangerous animals in the UK. This leads to Reading and Speaking, where Sts read and answer questions in a quiz and then find out if they have chosen the best option. Questions from the quiz are used to lead into Grammar, where the second conditional is analysed and practised. Finally, both the grammar and vocabulary are recycled and practised in Speaking.

More materials
For teachers
Photocopiables
Grammar *if* + past, *would* + infinitive (second conditional) *p.196*   *Vocabulary* Animal quiz *p.269* (instructions *p.256*)   *Communicative* I think you'd… *p.241* (instructions *p.213*)
For students
Workbook 9A
Online Practice 9A

OPTIONAL LEAD-IN (BOOKS CLOSED)
Give Sts, in pairs, three minutes to brainstorm words they know for animals.

Elicit answers, getting Sts to spell the words, and write them on the board. Elicit the correct pronunciation. You could also write the animals in columns, depending on whether they are wild animals, farm animals, insects, etc.

1 VOCABULARY & PRONUNCIATION
animals and insects; word stress

Vocabulary notes
Many animal words are similar in other languages, and Sts may not only have pronunciation problems, but also problems with spelling, e.g. *crocodile* in English is *cocodrilo* in Spanish.

a ◀) **9.1** Books open. This listening consists only of sound effects. Play the audio, pausing after each sound for Sts to say or write the name of the animal.
Check answers.

◀) **9.1**
(sound effects of the following)
1 chicken (or hen) 2 horse 3 monkey 4 snake 5 cat
6 dog 7 lion 8 bull

b Tell Sts to go to **Vocabulary Bank Animals** on *p.161*. Focus on the four headings and make sure Sts understand them. Model and drill the pronunciation of *insects* /ˈɪnsekts/ and *wild* /waɪld/.
Get Sts to do **a** individually or in pairs.
◀) **9.2** Now do **b**. Play the audio for Sts to listen and check.
Check answers.

◀) **9.2**

Animals

Insects	**Wild animals**	**Sea animals**
5 bee	16 bat	32 dolphin
2 butterfly	18 bear	30 jellyfish
6 fly	21 bird	33 shark
1 mosquito	14 camel	31 whale
4 spider	26 crocodile	
3 wasp	28 deer	
	17 elephant	
Farm animals	15 giraffe	
8 bull	22 kangaroo	
10 chicken	20 lion	
12 cow	19 monkey	
7 goat	23 mouse	
13 horse	25 rabbit	
11 pig	27 rat	
9 sheep	29 snake	
	24 tiger	

Either use the audio to drill the pronunciation of the words, or model and drill them yourself. Give further practice of any words your Sts find difficult to pronounce.
Go through the **bite and sting** box with the class.
Finally, do **Activation** and get Sts to cover the words and look at the photos. They can test themselves or a partner.
Tell Sts to go back to the main lesson **9A**.

EXTRA SUPPORT If you think Sts need more practice, you may want to give them the **Vocabulary** photocopiable activity at this point.

c Focus on the **Stress in words that are similar in other languages** box and go through it with the class.
Tell Sts to look at the animal words in the list and to underline the stress.

d ◀) **9.3** Play the audio for Sts to listen and check.
Check answers.

◀) **9.3**
<u>ca</u>mel <u>cro</u>codile <u>dol</u>phin <u>e</u>lephant gi<u>raffe</u> kanga<u>roo</u>
<u>li</u>on mos<u>qui</u>to

If you are teaching a monolingual class, ask them if the stress is in the same place in their L1.

e Quickly go through questions 1–7, making sure Sts understand them.

Put Sts in pairs, and get them to ask and answer the questions.

Get some feedback from the class by asking individual Sts for some of their answers.

2 LISTENING understanding facts

a Focus on the pictures and the task.

Elicit some ideas for the most dangerous animal or insect and then the least dangerous. <u>Don't</u> tell Sts if they are right.

b 🔊 **9.4** Focus on the chart in **c**, and tell Sts that as they listen and check their answers to **a**, they should write the names of the animals or insects in the headings. Tell them not to worry about the rest of the chart.

Tell Sts they are going to hear the answers in an interview, but that the answers will be given in reverse order, i.e. the least dangerous of the five will be first. Play the audio for Sts to listen and check.

Check answers.

EXTRA SUPPORT Read through the script and decide if you need to pre-teach any new lexis before Sts listen.

> **5th** a snake (the adder)   **4th** cows   **3rd** red deer   **2nd** dogs
> **1st** wasps and bees

🔊 **9.4**
(script in Student's Book on *p.124*)

P = presenter, D = David

P So David, what are the five most dangerous animals in the UK? Can you tell us in reverse order – I mean, starting with the fifth most dangerous?

D Yes, of course. At number five is a snake: the adder. The adder is the only poisonous snake in the UK. They can be about one metre long and they're quite common in some parts of the UK. They don't normally attack people, except when people step on them by accident. A bite from an adder can be very painful, and, occasionally, can kill. However, the last death from an adder bite was more than forty years ago.

P And number four?

D The fourth most dangerous animals in the UK are cows. People think cows are slow and a bit stupid, but in fact, cows kill at least one person every year. However, nearly all attacks happen when people are walking dogs in a field of cows, and they usually happen in spring or early summer, when young cows are with their mothers. So that's when you need to be careful.

P And third?

D In third place are red deer. These are large animals – they can weigh one hundred kilos. You need to be especially careful in the autumn, when the male deer can get very aggressive. They also cause frequent accidents on the road by running out in front of cars – there are about fifty thousand car accidents a year which involve deer.

P And in second place?

D Dogs. They are responsible for around two hundred thousand attacks a year in the UK, although most of them aren't serious, and very few actually cause death. Certain breeds of dog, like German shepherds, Rottweilers, and Pit Bulls, are more aggressive than others. One reason for this is that they were traditionally hunting dogs or guard dogs. Dog attacks can happen at any time, and some dogs even attack their owners.

P And in first place?

D Wasps and bees. They cause more deaths in the UK than any other type of animal or insect. About five people a year die from bee or wasp stings, and it's nearly always because they have an allergic reaction. About twenty-five per cent of the population in the UK have a bee or wasp allergy – some more serious than others. However, people are usually allergic to either bees or wasps, but not both. Bees and wasps only sting in self-defence or when they're provoked, but wasps are more aggressive than bees. So if you ever see a wasp nest in your garden, make sure you call a professional to come and destroy it.

P Definitely. Well, David, that was certainly…

c Tell Sts they are going to listen to the interview again and this time they need to complete the facts in the charts with one or two words only. Go through the items in the chart, making sure Sts understand all the lexis, e.g. *by accident*, *weigh*, etc.

Give Sts time, individually or in pairs, to try to guess what the missing words might be.

Now play the audio again. You could pause it after each animal or insect is mentioned to give Sts time to write.

Get Sts to compare with a partner, and then play the audio again if necessary.

Check answers.

> **1** one metre   **2** step on   **3** every year   **4** walking dogs
> **5** early summer   **6** 100 kilos   **7** autumn   **8** 50,000
> **9** Very few   **10** their owners   **11** five   **12** Wasps   **13** bees

EXTRA SUPPORT If there's time, you could get Sts to listen again with the script on *p.124*, so they can see exactly what they understood / didn't understand. Translate / Explain any new words or phrases.

d Do this as a whole-class activity. You could tell Sts about your own experience if you have one.

3 READING & SPEAKING

a Focus on the list of animals, and elicit the pronunciation of each one.

Now focus on the instructions and the quiz. Tell Sts, in pairs, to just complete each gap in the questions with one of the animals or insects in the list.

Check answers.

EXTRA SUPPORT Before Sts do the quiz, check whether you need to pre-teach any vocabulary, but <u>not</u> the highlighted verbs and verb phrases.

> **1** dog   **2** bee, wasp   **3** snake   **4** cows   **5** jellyfish   **6** shark

b Focus on the highlighted verbs and verb phrases. Get Sts, in pairs, to guess their meaning. Tell them to read the whole sentence, as the context will help them guess.

Check answers, either explaining in English, miming, translating into Sts' L1, or getting Sts to check in their dictionaries.

shout /ʃaʊt/ = to say something in a loud voice
keep still /kiːp stɪl/ = not move
wave /weɪv/ = to move your hand or arm from side to side in
  the air, in order to attract attention, etc.
suck /sʌk/ = to take liquid, air, etc. into your mouth with your
  lips
tie /taɪ/ = to fasten something with string, rope, etc.
rub /rʌb/ = to move your hand backwards and forwards over a
  surface while pressing firmly
float /fləʊt/ = to stay on the surface of water

Finally, go through the three alternatives for each quiz question and deal with any other new vocabulary. Model and drill the pronunciation of any tricky words.

c Give Sts a few minutes to read the questions again and choose their answers.

Get Sts to compare their choices with a partner. Encourage them to try to say why they have chosen each option.

d Put Sts into groups of three. Tell them to go to **Communication** Would you know what to do?, **A** on *p.105*, **B** on *p.110*, and **C** on *p.107*. Explain that all Sts **A** are going to read the answers to *In the city*, Sts **B** to *In the country*, and Sts **C** to *In the water*.

! If the number of Sts you have does not divide into groups of three, have one or two pairs where they read and tell each other the answers to **A** and **B**, and then simply read the answers to **C**.

Go through the instructions with them carefully. Monitor and help with vocabulary while they are reading.

When Sts have read their answers, put them back into their groups, so they can tell each other what the correct answers are and why the others are wrong.

When they have finished, they could see who in their group got the most answers correct.

Tell Sts to go back to the main lesson **9A**.

e Do the questions as a whole-class activity. If you have been in any of the situations, tell the class about it.

4 GRAMMAR *if* + past, *would* + infinitive

a Focus on the task. Get Sts, in pairs, to look at questions 1–6 in the quiz in **3**, or go through them with the whole class.

Check answers.

They are all about an imagined future situation.
The tense of the verb after *if* is the past simple. The other form is *would* + infinitive.

b Tell Sts to go to **Grammar Bank 9A** on *p.142*.

Grammar notes

Sts may find it strange to be using past tenses in the *if* half of these conditional sentences, and it needs emphasizing that they do not refer to the past, but rather to a hypothetical situation.

Sts have seen and used *would / wouldn't* + infinitive before with the verb *like*, so should not have problems with the form of *would*. You may want to tell them that this form is sometimes called the *conditional tense*.

◀)) 9.5 Focus on the example sentences and play the audio for Sts to listen and repeat. Encourage them to copy the rhythm. Then go through the rules with the class.

Now focus on the ***be* in second conditionals** box and go through it with the class.

Then focus on the exercises for **9A** on *p.143*. Sts do them individually or in pairs.

Check answers, getting Sts to read the full sentences.

a
1 E **2** D **3** C **4** F **5** G **6** B
b
1 We **would / could** get a dog if we **had** a garden.
2 If you **tried** Indian food, I'm sure you**'d like** it.
3 I **wouldn't buy** it if I **didn't like** it.
4 If we **hired** a car, we **could** drive to the mountains.
5 We**'d see** our children more often if they **lived** nearer.
6 I **wouldn't go** to that restaurant if I **were** you…
7 You**'d learn** more if you **did** more homework.
8 I**'d cycle** to work if the traffic **wasn't / weren't** so bad.
9 **Would** you **work** abroad if you **found** a well-paid job?
10 I **wouldn't be** happy if I **had** to leave.

Tell Sts to go back to the main lesson **9A**.

EXTRA SUPPORT If you think Sts need more practice, you may want to give them the **Grammar** photocopiable activity at this point.

5 SPEAKING

Go through the questions and make sure Sts understand them all.

Then focus on the **Talking about imaginary situations with *would* / *wouldn't*** box and go through it with the class.

Get some Sts to choose a question to ask you. Answer, giving as much detail as you think Sts will understand, and trying to use some of the phrases in the box.

Put Sts into groups of three, and tell them to take turns to choose a question they want to ask their partners. They should also answer that question themselves. Encourage Sts to ask for more information (*Why?*, etc.).

Monitor and help Sts, correcting any misuse of tenses in the second conditional.

Get some feedback from the class, asking if anyone found their partners' answers surprising / funny, etc.

EXTRA SUPPORT Before Sts start, you might also want to elicit some useful phrases for them to use when they are discussing the questions in their groups, e.g. *Me too.*, *I don't think that's a good idea because…*, *Really? Why (not)?*, etc.

G present perfect + *for* and *since*

V words related to fear: *afraid*, *frightened*, etc., phrases with *for* and *since*

P sentence stress

Lesson plan

In this lesson Sts study the present perfect with *for* and *since* to talk about unfinished actions or states. The context is phobias, and the lesson begins with some information about phobias from a website called *fearof.net*. Sts learn some words related to fear. In Listening and Speaking, Sts hear two women talking about the phobias they suffer from. In Grammar, examples of the present perfect are taken from the listening activity and analysed before Sts go to the Grammar Bank. Sts then look at phrases with *for* and *since*. In Pronunciation, Sts work on sentence stress in present perfect sentences to prepare them for the speaking activity – a survey in which Sts find out how long their classmates have done certain things.

More materials
For teachers
Photocopiables
Grammar present perfect + *for* and *since p.197*
Communicative Famous phobias *p.242*
(instructions *p.214*)
For students
Workbook 9B
Online Practice 9B

OPTIONAL LEAD-IN (BOOKS CLOSED)

Play *Hangman* with the word *phobia*.

When Sts have worked out the word, elicit the pronunciation (reminding Sts that *ph* is always pronounced /**f**/).

Then ask Sts *How do you feel if you have a phobia of something?* and elicit *afraid* (or *frightened / scared*).

1 READING recognizing topic links

a Books open. Do this as a whole-class activity. Check first that Sts know what all the photos represent. You could tell Sts if you are afraid of any of the things.

Then elicit any other things Sts can think of that people sometimes have phobias of, and write them on the board.

b Focus on the title of the website and, if you didn't do the **Optional lead-in**, make sure Sts understand *phobia*. You may also need to explain here that *fear* is the noun from *afraid* (though this is focused on later). Now tell Sts to read the text and complete each phobia with one of the headings in the list.

Get Sts to compare with a partner, and then check answers.

EXTRA SUPPORT Before Sts read the text, check whether you need to pre-teach any vocabulary, but <u>not</u> the highlighted words and phrases.

1 Fear of driving	**2** Fear of butterflies	**3** Fear of doctors
4 Fear of heights	**5** Fear of crowds	

c Tell Sts that five people have written about their phobias on the website. Sts need to read each comment and match it to a phobia in **b**.

Give Sts time to match comments A–E to phobias 1–5.

Get Sts to compare with a partner, and then check answers. You could ask Sts which words helped them to match the comments and fears.

A 3 **B** 1 **C** 2 **D** 5 **E** 4

d Focus on the instructions and give Sts time to match the seven highlighted words and phrases in the phobias and comments to definitions 1–6.

Get Sts to compare with a partner, and then check answers.

1 fear	**2** terrified	**3** scared, frightened	**4** dizzy	**5** panic
6 suffers from				

Deal with any other new vocabulary. Model and drill the pronunciation of any tricky words.

e Focus on the task and example.

Put Sts in pairs or small groups to discuss the three questions.

Get some feedback from the class.

2 LISTENING & SPEAKING

a ◗ **9.6** Focus on the instructions and tell Sts to copy the chart on a piece of paper, so that they have more space to write. Make sure Sts understand the meaning of *therapy* (= a way of helping people who are physically or mentally ill).

Play the audio, pausing it after the first interview to give Sts time to write.

Then play the rest of the audio. If Sts think the button phobia is unlikely, tell them it's a real interview!

b Get Sts to compare with a partner, and then play the audio again if necessary.

Check answers.

EXTRA SUPPORT Read through the script and decide if you need to pre-teach any new lexis before Sts listen.

Speaker 1 (Julia)
1 Spiders
2 Since she was 12
3 A very big spider went across the room in the flat where she lived.
4 She's better now and can sit in same room as a spider, but not for long. In the past it affected her a lot – she couldn't sit in the same room as a spider, always kept doors and windows shut.
5 Yes

Speaker 2 (Chloe)

1 Buttons
2 Since she was six or seven months old
3 Her mum tried to dress her in a cardigan with buttons.
4 She has problems buying winter coats, as there aren't many that don't have buttons. She doesn't like hugging people who are wearing clothes with buttons. Her mum had to adapt her school uniform.
5 No

◗ 9.6
(script in Student's Book on *p.124*)
I = interviewer, J = Julia, C = Chloe

Julia

I Do you have any phobias?
J Yes, I'm very, very scared of spiders.
I And how long have you had this phobia?
J I've had it since I was about twelve, so for more than thirty years.
I Did something happen to start the phobia?
J I remember – and it's when I think I started being frightened – I remember a very big spider in the flat that we lived in at the time coming out from under the television and going across the room, and me being absolutely terrified, and that's the first time I remember being scared.
I How does it affect your life?
J In the past, it was really awful. I mean, I couldn't sit in the same room as a spider, and I always had to keep all the doors and windows shut because I was frightened that spiders might come in. But I had some therapy, and I can now sit in the same room as a spider – not for long; it still has to be moved – and I can put it in a glass now and take it outside myself if I have to – if there's nobody else there. So it doesn't affect me as badly as it did before, but I still don't like them.
I What kind of therapy did you have? How long did it take?
J Probably about six weeks. I went to the therapist's office and he used a kind of hypnosis. He made me go back to that first incident with the spider and the TV, and we talked about it again and again, until it wasn't so frightening. And then in the last session, he brought in a spider in a jar, into the room, and he made me hold the jar. I couldn't put the spider on my hand, but that was a great improvement, because before I couldn't even look at a drawing of a spider in a children's book, and I certainly couldn't look at photos of spiders.
I Wow. Amazing.

Chloe

I Do you have any phobias?
C Erm, yes, I have a phobia of buttons.
I Buttons on clothes?
C Yes. I don't like touching them.
I And how long have you had the phobia?
C All my life, I think. For as long as I can remember.
I Do you know what happened to start the phobia?
C I don't know exactly, but my mum has told me that when I was very little, about six or seven months old, she tried to dress me in a cardigan, a woollen cardigan with buttons that my grandmother had made for me, and apparently I screamed and screamed until she took it off again.
I OK. And how does the phobia affect your life?
C It really affects the kind of clothes I can buy, especially in the winter, when I need a coat – there aren't many coats that don't have buttons. But it's better than it was: when I was younger, I refused to wear anything that had buttons, so for example, my mother had to adapt my school uniform so that there were no buttons.
I Have you had any therapy?
C No, no. I haven't had any therapy. It seems such a silly thing to be afraid of.
I What about if other people are wearing clothes with buttons on – is that OK?
C Well, if the buttons aren't touching me, that's fine, but I don't like hugging people that have buttons on their clothes.

Finally, ask Sts if the phobias are better now.

They both still have their phobias, but they are better.

EXTRA SUPPORT If there's time, you could get Sts to listen again with the script on *p.124*, so they can see exactly what they understood / didn't understand. Translate / Explain any new words or phrases.

c Do this as a whole-class activity, making sure Sts know the meaning of *rational* (= based on reason rather than emotions). You could also tell them what you think.

3 GRAMMAR & VOCABULARY present perfect; phrases with *for* and *since*

a Tell Sts to focus on the extract from the first interview (Julia's) and to answer the three questions.

Get Sts to compare with a partner, and then check answers.

1 When she was 12. / More than 30 years ago.   **2** Yes
3 The present perfect (*have* + past participle)

b Tell Sts to go to **Grammar Bank 9B** on *p.142*.

Grammar notes

The present perfect with *for* and *since* can be tricky for Sts as they may use a different structure in their language to express this concept, e.g. the present tense. A typical mistake is: ~~I live here since three years / since three years ago~~.

The important thing to highlight is that the present perfect with *for* and *since* is used to say how long a situation has continued from the past until now, i.e. we use it for situations which are still true, e.g. *I've been in this class for two years* (= I started two years ago and I am still in this class now).

In the following lesson, the present perfect for unfinished actions / periods of time will be contrasted with the past simple for finished actions / periods.

◗ 9.7 Focus on the example sentences and play the audio for Sts to listen and repeat. Encourage them to copy the rhythm. Then go through the rules with the class.

Now focus on the exercises for **9B** on *p.143*. Sts do the exercises individually or in pairs.

Check answers, getting Sts to read the full questions and sentences.

a 1 How long have you been afraid of flying?
2 How long has your sister had her new car?
3 How long have they lived in this town?
4 How long has your dad been a teacher?
5 How long have you known your boyfriend?
6 How long has Spain been in the EU?
7 How long have you had your cat?
8 How long has Dan been in this class?
b 1 I**'ve been afraid of flying since** I was about 15.
2 She**'s had her car for** three weeks.
3 They**'ve lived in this town for** a long time.
4 He**'s been a teacher for** more than 20 years.
5 I**'ve known my boyfriend since** May.
6 It**'s been in the EU since** 1986.
7 We**'ve had our cat for** about two years.
8 He**'s been in this class since** last month.

Tell Sts to go back to the main lesson **9B**.

c Give Sts time to complete the gaps with *for* or *since*. Get them to compare with a partner.

d 🔊 **9.8** Play the audio for Sts to listen and check. Check answers. You might want to point out to Sts the linking between *for* and *since* and the words that follow when they start with a vowel, e.g. *for ages*, *for about*, *since I*, etc.

> **since** 1990   **for** a long time   **for** about 20 years   **for** ages
> **since** I was a child   **for** six months   **since** the 4th of May
> **for** a few weeks   **since** then   **since** I got up this morning
> **since** 8.15   **for** five minutes

🔊 **9.8**
since nineteen ninety, for a long time, for about twenty years, for ages, since I was a child, for six months, since the fourth of May, for a few weeks, since then, since I got up this morning, since eight fifteen, for five minutes

---

Get Sts, in pairs, to practice saying the phrases.

4 PRONUNCIATION sentence stress

a 🔊 **9.9** Here Sts practise sentence rhythm in the present perfect to prepare for the speaking activity in **5**.
Play the audio once the whole way through.
Now play it again, pausing after each section for Sts to repeat, building up to the whole sentence or question. Encourage them to copy the rhythm.

🔊 **9.9**
See sentences in Student's Book on *p.73*

Finally, get Sts to practise in pairs.

b 🔊 **9.10** Now tell Sts they are going to hear five sentences / questions and they must write them down.
Play the audio once for Sts just to listen.
Now play it again, pausing after each line to give Sts time to write. Play the audio again if necessary.
Check answers.

🔊 **9.10**
1　How long have you worked here?
2　They've been married for twenty years.
3　She hasn't travelled by plane since two thousand and five.
4　How long has he lived in Italy?
5　We've known them for a long time.

In pairs, get Sts to practise saying the sentences.

5 SPEAKING

a Focus on the chart and instructions. Elicit the answer to the first question from the class, and tell them that all the sections have the same two tenses.

> The two verb forms are the present simple and the present perfect.

Now give Sts time to complete the questions.

b 🔊 **9.11** Play the audio for Sts to listen and check. Check answers.

> See the words in **bold** in script 9.11

🔊 **9.11**
have
Do you have a pet? What is it? How long **have you had** it?
Do you have a tablet? What kind? How long **have you had** it?
live
Do you live in a modern flat? How old is it? How long **have you lived** there?
Do you live near this school? Where exactly? How long **have you lived** there?
know
Do you know anybody from another country? Where is he or she from? How long **have you known** him or her?
be
Are you a fan of a football team? Which team? How long **have you been** a fan?
Are you a member of a club or organization? Which one? How long **have you been** a member?
Are you married? What's your partner's name? How long **have you been** married?

---

c Tell Sts they are going to move around the class, asking other Sts the questions. If someone says *Yes, I do / am* to the first question (the present simple question), then they must ask the follow-up question (including the present perfect question). They should try to find someone different for each question. Encourage Sts to ask for and give as much information as they can so that the survey becomes more of a conversation, rather than just question and answer.
When Sts have finished, get some feedback.

G present perfect or past simple? (2)
V biographies
P word stress, /ɔː/

Lesson plan

The main focus of this lesson is how to describe your or somebody else's life, and the contrast between the past simple for completed actions or situations in the past, and the present perfect for situations or actions which started in the past, but are still true now. The context is famous mothers and daughters, and famous fathers and sons.

The lesson begins with Sts learning the vocabulary for verb phrases often used in biographies. There is then a pronunciation focus on the word stress in these phrases, and on the /ɔː/ sound. This lexis is recycled in Reading, where Sts read about the lives of the actress Janet Leigh and her daughter, Jamie Lee Curtis. The contrast between the verb forms used for the mother (who is dead) and her daughter (who is still alive) is used to show Sts a fundamental difference between how the past simple and the present perfect are used in English. In Listening, Sts hear about another famous parent–child pair: David Bowie (father) and Duncan Jones (son). The lesson finishes with a speaking activity where Sts talk about the life of an older person who they know well. This leads into Writing, where Sts are asked to write a short biography about either someone they know or a famous person.

More materials
For teachers
Photocopiables
Grammar present perfect or past simple? (2) *p.198*
Communicative Like father, like son *p.243*
(instructions *p.214*)
For students
Workbook 9C
Online Practice 9C

OPTIONAL LEAD-IN (BOOKS CLOSED)

Ask Sts, in pairs, to brainstorm famous people whose parents are / were also famous.

Elicit answers, getting Sts to tell you what the people do, and write their names on the board.

Possible answers

Actors
Angelina Jolie and Jon Voight; Melanie Griffith and Tippi Hedren; Jaden Smith and Will Smith; Kiefer Sutherland and Donald Sutherland; Charlie Sheen, Emilio Estevez, and Martin Sheen, etc.

Singers
Norah Jones and Ravi Shankar; Enrique Iglesias and Julio Iglesias; Ziggy Marley and Bob Marley, Stella McCartney and Paul McCartney, etc.

1 VOCABULARY & PRONUNCIATION
biographies; word stress, /ɔː/

a Books open. Focus on the list of phrases. Elicit / Teach the meaning of *events* (= things which happen to you). Go through the list, making sure Sts understand them all. Point out that *sb* stands for *somebody*.

Now tell Sts to number the events in a logical order between *be born* and *die*.

Put Sts into pairs and get them to compare their order with a partner. Do they agree?

Finally, elicit from the class a typical order of the events.

A possible order
2 go to primary school   **3** go to secondary school   **4** leave school   **5** go to university   **6** get a job   **7** fall in love   **8** marry sb / get married   **9** have children   **10** separate   **11** divorce sb / get divorced   **12** retire

EXTRA IDEA You could get Sts to mark the expressions: *E* = everybody does it, *M* = most people do it, *S* = some people do it

b 🔊 9.12   Give Sts time to look at the highlighted words and mark the stress.

Play the audio for Sts to listen and check.

Check answers.

🔊 **9.12**
<u>marr</u>y somebody / get <u>marr</u>ied
go to <u>prim</u>ary school
have <u>chil</u>dren
go to <u>sec</u>ondary school
go to uni<u>ver</u>sity
<u>sep</u>arate
di<u>vorce</u> somebody / get di<u>vorced</u>
re<u>tire</u>

Then play the audio again for Sts to listen and repeat.

Pronunciation notes
The most common spellings of the /ɔː/ sound are *or* (when it is stressed), *al*, and *aw*.

However, words beginning *wor-* are pronounced /ɜː/, e.g. *work*, *world*, *worse*, etc., which is confusing for Sts, who often pronounce these words with the /ɔː/ sound. Learning the rule here should help them to avoid this common pronunciation error.

c 🔊 9.13   Focus on the sound picture and elicit the word and sound: *horse* and /ɔː/.

Then play the audio for Sts to listen.

🔊 **9.13**
See sound and words in Student's Book on *p.74*

Now play the audio again and get Sts to listen and repeat.

d Focus on the words in the list and tell Sts that some of them have the /ɔː/ sound. Sts should say the words and circle the ones with the /ɔː/ sound. Remind them that it is easier if they say the words aloud to themselves.

Get Sts to compare with a partner.

e ◉ **9.14** Play the audio for Sts to listen and check. Check answers.

Sts should circle:
more, small, walk, talk, ball, form, bought, four

◉ **9.14**
See words in Student's Book on *p.74*

Now ask Sts *What rule can you hear for words with* wor + *consonant?* and elicit the answer.

wor + consonant words are normally pronounced /ɜː/. You may want to point out that after other consonants, *or* is usually pronounced /ɔː/, e.g. *more*, *born*, *horse*, etc.

Now play the audio again for Sts to listen and repeat.

 If these sounds are difficult for your Sts, it will help to show them the mouth position. You could model this yourself or use the the Sound Bank videos on the *Teacher's Resource Centre.*

2 READING

a Tell Sts they are going to read a text about two actresses, Janet Leigh and Jamie Lee Curtis. Focus on the photos and ask the class if they have heard of them. You may want to explain that in the black-and-white photo, Jamie Lee Curtis (on the left) is holding a photo of her mother in the famous shower scene from the Hitchcock film *Psycho*.

Read the introduction together and then ask Sts if they have seen any of the actresses' films, and if they liked them. (Janet Leigh: *Little Women* (1949), *The Manchurian Candidate* (1962), *The Fog* (1980); Jamie Lee Curtis: *Scream Queens* (2016), *NCIS* (2012), *Freaky Friday* (2003), *A Fish Called Wanda* (1988).)

Finally, ask Sts what the title *Like mother, like daughter* means (= the daughter is doing the same as her mother did, i.e. making a career in acting).

b Focus on the task and tell Sts, in pairs, to read each paragraph and decide if it refers to Janet Leigh (*JL*) or Jamie Lee Curtis (*JLC*).

Check answers.

 Before Sts read the paragraphs the first time, check whether you need to pre-teach any vocabulary.

JL: 1, 4, 7, 9, 10
JLC: 2, 3, 5, 6, 8

Deal with any other new vocabulary. Model and drill the pronunciation of any tricky words.

c Put Sts in pairs, **A** and **B**. Sts **A** re-read the paragraphs about Janet Leigh and Sts **B** the ones about Jamie Lee Curtis.

Now, books closed, **A** tells **B** anything he / she can remember about Janet Leigh. Then Sts swap roles.

3 GRAMMAR present perfect or past simple? (2)

a Tell Sts to cover the text, and give them time to answer the questions about sentences 1–6.

Check which sentences are about Janet Leigh and which are about Jamie Lee Curtis.

1, 3, and 6 are about Janet Leigh.
2, 4, and 5 are about Jamie Lee Curtis.

Now ask Sts why the tenses in the sentences about Janet Leigh are different to the ones in the sentences about Jamie Lee Curtis.

The ones about Janet Leigh are all in the past simple because she is dead. The ones about Jamie Lee Curtis are in the present perfect because she is alive, and the actions or situations are true about her life up to now.

b Tell Sts to go to **Grammar Bank 9C** on *p.142*.

Grammar notes

The contrast between the past simple and the present perfect was first focused on in **4B** (see **Grammar Bank 4B** *p.132*).

Highlight that the present perfect is used in the examples about Jamie Lee Curtis because her career as an actress hasn't finished. She is still an actress and will probably be in more films.

The past tense is used for Janet Leigh because the sentences refer to a finished period of time. Janet Leigh won't write a book now because she is dead, so *wrote* is used. If she were still alive and writing, then *has written* would be used.

◉ **9.15** Focus on the example sentences and play the audio for Sts to listen and repeat. Encourage them to copy the rhythm. Then go through the rules with the class.

Now focus on the exercises for **9C** on *p.143*. Sts do the exercises individually or in pairs.

Check answers, getting Sts to read the full sentences.

a
1 Martin left   2 I lived   3 Anna's been   4 My sister had
5 I've worked   6 The city has changed   7 They were
8 I met, was

b
1 How long **has he lived** there?
  He **moved** there last September.
2 When **did Picasso** die?
  How long **did he live** in France?
  He **left** Spain when he was 25.
3 How long **have they been** married?
  They**'ve been** married since 1995.
  They **met** at university.
  What university **did** they **go** to?

Tell Sts to go back to the main lesson **9C**.

 If you think Sts need more practice, you may want to give them the **Grammar** photocopiable activity at this point.

4 LISTENING understanding biographical information

a Tell Sts to look at the photo of a famous father and son. Ask if they know them. If they do, then what else do they know about them? Listen to their ideas, but <u>don't</u> tell them if they are right or not.

b 🔊 **9.16** Tell Sts they are going to listen to a radio programme about the son and they need to check their answers to **a** as well as answer the question *How well did he and his father get on?*.

Play the audio once the whole way through.

Get Sts to compare with a partner, and then check answers.

EXTRA SUPPORT Read through the script and decide if you need to pre-teach any new lexis before Sts listen.

> They are Duncan Jones and his father, David Bowie.
> They had a very good relationship.

🔊 **9.16**

(script in Student's Book on *p.124*)

Good evening and welcome to *Family*, the programme where we discuss issues concerning parents and children. Last week, we talked about children following their parents into the same job, and whether children of celebrities have an easier life than other children. Today, we're going to look at a celebrity son who did something different, and has been successful without the help of his famous father. Duncan Jones may not be a name you recognize if you're not a serious cinema fan. Duncan Jones is his real name, but when he was very young, he was called Zowie Bowie. His father was the famous singer David Bowie, whose real surname was Jones. Zowie was actually Duncan's middle name.

Duncan was born in the UK in nineteen seventy-one. When he was nine, his parents divorced, and Duncan stayed with his father. He continued to visit his mother, David Bowie's first wife, Angie, until he was thirteen, but their relationship wasn't a happy one, and he hasn't seen her since then.

When he was a child, Duncan wasn't interested in music. His father tried and tried to get him to learn an instrument – the drums, the saxophone, and the piano – but Duncan just wasn't interested. He was more interested in sport, and in films. So, his father bought him a little eight-millimetre video camera, and he used it to make films with his Star Wars toys.

After he left school, Duncan went to the London Film School and studied to be a film director.

In the early years of his career, Duncan directed TV commercials, for example for the fashion label French Connection, and Heinz ketchup, and he also worked on video games.

In two thousand and six, he made his first film, called *Moon*, a science fiction drama, which was a great success. He won many awards for the film, including the prize for Best New British Director. Since then, he has made many more successful films, including *Source Code*, a science-fiction thriller starring Jake Gyllenhaal, and *Warcraft*, based on the game *World of Warcraft*.

Duncan has said that one of the reasons why he went into film directing was that he wanted to be behind the camera, not in front of it. As a child, there were often paparazzi around, which he hated. Even now, as a successful film director, he doesn't like being photographed.

Although, as he says, 'I've never needed to use my father's name,' Duncan was very close to his father all his life, and was with him when he died in January two thousand and sixteen. He said of him, 'He was a wonderful father who encouraged me to be creative, but different.'

---

c Explain the task and focus on 1–9, making sure Sts understand all the lexis, e.g. *a commercial* and *paparazzi*. Point out that the first one has been done for them. In pairs, Sts quickly try to remember what connection there might be between the information in 2–9 and Duncan Jones.

Listen to their ideas, but <u>don't</u> tell them if they are right or not.

Play the audio once and tell Sts <u>not</u> to write anything, just to listen to see whether they remembered the connections correctly.

Then play the audio again, and get Sts to make notes. Pause the audio, as necessary, to give Sts time to make notes.

Get Sts to compare with a partner, and play the audio again if necessary.

Check answers. Try to elicit as much of the information in the key as possible.

> **2** He was born in the UK in 1971.
> **3** His parents divorced when he was nine. He stayed with his father. He saw his mother, Angie, until he was 13, but hasn't seen her since then.
> **4** His father tried to get him to learn the drums, the saxophone, and the piano.
> **5** He went to the London Film School and studied to be a film director.
> **6** His father bought him an 7mm video carema, which he used to make films about his Star Wars toys.
> **7** He directed the TV commercials in the early years of his career.
> **8** He made *Moon* in 2006. It's a science-fiction drama and was very successful. He won the prize for Best New British Director.
> **9** He made *Source Code*, a science fiction thriller, and *Warcraft*, based on the game *World of Warcraft*. They have both been successful.
> **10** He wanted to be a film director because he wanted to be behind the cameras, not in front of them. He hated the paparazzi who were around when he was a child and doesn't like being photographed.

EXTRA SUPPORT If there's time, you could get Sts to listen again with the script on *pp.124–125*, so they can see exactly what they understood / didn't understand. Translate / Explain any new words or phrases.

d Do the questions as a whole-class activity and elicit opinions. You could tell Sts what you think.

5 SPEAKING & WRITING

a In this activity Sts put into practice the contrast between the past simple and the present perfect through talking about an older person – a friend or member of their family.

Focus on the activity and give Sts five minutes to think about who they are going to talk about and to prepare their answers to the questions. Stress that it should be an older person, not a younger one, because they will have had more experiences.

Focus on the question prompts. You could demonstrate the activity by getting the class to ask you about one of your grandparents, elderly relatives, or a friend.

b Sit Sts in pairs, ideally face-to-face. Set a time limit for Sts to interview each other. Encourage Sts answering to give as much information as possible, and Sts asking the questions to ask for extra information where possible.

Then Sts swap roles.

Find out if their two people had anything in common.

c Tell Sts to go to **Writing A biography** on *p.118* and to do **a**. Tell them not to worry about the gaps in the biography.

When they have finished, elicit three things about Matt Damon that they remember.

Now tell Sts to do **b** by putting the verbs in brackets in the past simple or present perfect. Point out that the first one (*was born*) has been done for them.

Check answers.

> **2** divorced **3** lived **4** became **5** appeared **6** went
> **7** wrote **8** starred **9** won **10** didn't finish **11** has become
> **12** has appeared **13** has received **14** won **15** has been

Now focus on the **Writing a biography – use of tenses** box and go through it with the class.

For **c**, get Sts to write a biography of someone who is still alive – so someone they know or a famous person. Tell them to make notes for the three paragraphs in the model.

For **d**, it is probably better to set this writing for homework to allow Sts to research the person they want to write about. They could also attach a photo of the person.

In **e**, Sts should check their biography for mistakes.

EXTRA IDEA If Sts wrote their biographies for homework, when they bring them in, get them to swap with other Sts, or put them up round the class for people to read, and then ask the class which ones they found most interesting.

Function asking how to get there
Vocabulary directions: *traffic lights*, *take the…*, etc.

Lesson plan

In this lesson Sts learn how to give and understand simple directions, both for in the street and for public transport.

In the storyline, Rob is with Holly in Brooklyn. Jenny rings to confirm their dinner date in Manhattan. She gives Rob directions on the subway to the restaurant. However, Rob arrives late. When he gets there, Jenny is leaving the restaurant, after having waited an hour, and they have an argument.

More materials
For teachers
Teacher's Resource Centre
Video Practical English Episode 5
Quick Test 9
File 9 Test
For students
Workbook Practical English 5
Can you remember...? 1–9
Online Practice Practical English 5
Check your progress

OPTIONAL LEAD-IN (BOOKS CLOSED)

Elicit from the class what happened in the previous episode. Ask some questions, e.g. *What did Rob and Jenny do in the morning? Why did Rob go to the pharmacy? What did he buy? Where did Rob go in the evening?*

Alternatively, you could play the last scene of Episode 4.

1 ▶ HOLLY AND ROB IN BROOKLYN

a 🔊 **9.17** Books open. Focus on the photos and elicit what Sts think is happening. <u>Don't</u> tell them if they are right or not yet.

Focus on sentences 1–6 and give Sts time to read them.

Now play the video / audio once the whole way through for them to mark the sentences *T* (true) or *F* (false). Make it clear that they don't need to correct the false sentences yet. Play again if necessary.

Get Sts to compare with a partner, and then check answers.

1 T   2 T   3 F   4 T   5 F   6 F

🔊 **9.17**

H = Holly, R = Rob, J = Jenny

H That was a good day's work, Rob. You did a great interview.
R You took some great photos, too. They're really nice.
H Thanks. Hey, let's have another coffee.
R I don't know. I have to get to Manhattan.
H You don't have to go right now.
R I'm not sure. I don't want to be late.
H Why do you have to go to Manhattan?
R I've got a…erm…
H A date? You have a date?

R Mm hm.
H Is it with anybody I know?
R No, it isn't. Anyway, excuse me a minute. I need to go to 'the restroom'.
H That's very American. I'll order more coffees.
R OK.
J (*on the phone*) Rob?
H Is that you, Jennifer?
J Oh, hi, Holly. Erm…is Rob there?
H Yeah, one second. Rob! Not anybody I know, huh?
R Hi, Jenny.
J Rob? Are you still in Brooklyn?
R Yeah.
J You know the reservation at the restaurant's for eight, right?
R Don't worry. I'll be there! Oh, how do I get to Greenwich Village on the subway?

b Play the video / audio again so Sts can watch or listen and correct the false sentences.

Get Sts to compare with a partner, and then check answers.

3 He has **a date** in Manhattan.
5 **Jenny** phones Rob.
6 The restaurant is booked for **eight** o'clock.

Elicit from Sts that the restaurant is in Greenwich Village, a well-known area of Manhattan, and that *Greenwich* is pronounced /ˈɡrenɪtʃ/.

Now focus on the **British and American English** box and go through it with the class.

EXTRA SUPPORT If there's time and you are using the video, you could get Sts to watch again with subtitles, so they can see exactly what they understood / didn't understand. Translate / Explain any new words or phrases.

2 ▶ VOCABULARY directions

a Tell Sts to look at the pictures and then complete phrases 1–5.

Get Sts to compare with a partner.

b 🔊 **9.18** Play the video / audio for Sts to watch or listen and check.

Check answers.

1 left   2 straight   3 next   4 traffic   5 roundabout

🔊 **9.18**
1 Turn left.
2 Go straight on.
3 Take the next turning on the right.
4 Turn right at the traffic lights.
5 Go round the roundabout and take the third exit.

Now play the video / audio again for Sts to watch or listen and repeat the phrases.

c Tell Sts to cover the phrases, look at the pictures, and say the phrases.

3 ▶ ASKING HOW TO GET THERE

a ◗ **9.19** Focus on the map of the New York subway and ask Sts *Is Rob in Manhattan or Brooklyn now?* (Brooklyn), *Is the restaurant in Brooklyn?* (No, it isn't. It's in Greenwich Village, Manhattan.)

Make sure Sts can see where Rob is on the map.

Tell Sts that they are going to hear Rob asking Jenny for directions and they need to listen to the directions and try to mark the route on the map. Play the video / audio at least twice.

Get Sts to compare with a partner, and then check that they have marked the correct route.

❗ The map in the Student's Book has been adapted and is simplified rather than strictly accurate.

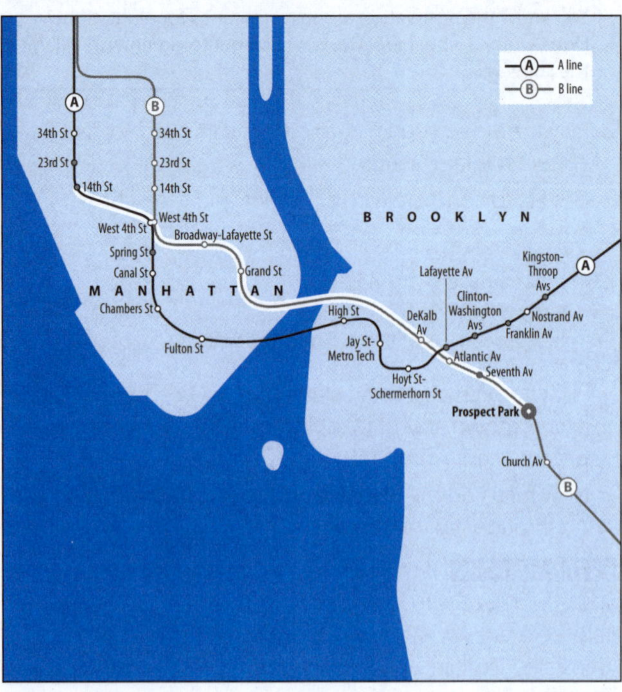

◗ **9.19 9.20**

R = Rob, J = Jenny

R How do I get to Greenwich Village on the subway? (*repeat*)
J Go to the subway station at Prospect Park. Take the B train to West Fourth Street.
R How many stops is that? (*repeat*)
J Six or seven.
R OK. And then? (*repeat*)
J From West Fourth Street, take the A train and get off at Fourteenth Street.
R Could you say that again? (*repeat*)
J OK. From Prospect Park, take the B train to West Fourth Street, and then take the A train to Fourteenth Street. That's only one stop.
R Where's the restaurant? (*repeat*)
J Come out of the subway on Eighth Avenue, go straight on for about fifty yards, and take the first left. That's Greenwich Avenue. The restaurant's on the right. It's called *The Tea Set*.
R OK, thanks. See you later. (*repeat*)
J And don't get lost!

b Now focus on the conversation in the chart. Elicit that the **You say** phrases are what Rob says and the **You hear** phrases are said by Jenny, who is giving Rob directions. These phrases will be useful for Sts if they need to ask for directions.

Give Sts a minute to read through the conversation and think what the missing words might be. Then play the video / audio again and get Sts to complete the gaps. Play again if necessary.

Get Sts to compare with a partner, and then check answers.

1 Take   **2** off   **3** stop   **4** straight   **5** first   **6** right   **7** lost

Go through the conversation line by line with Sts, helping them with any words or expressions they don't understand.

c ◗ **9.20** Now focus on the **You say** phrases and tell Sts they're going to hear the conversation again. They should repeat the **You say** phrases when they hear the beep. Encourage them to copy the rhythm and intonation.

Play the video / audio, pausing if necessary for Sts to repeat the phrases.

◗ **9.20**
Same as script 9.19 with repeat pauses

d Put Sts in pairs, **A** and **B**. **A** is Rob and **B** is Jenny. Get Sts to read the conversation aloud, and then swap roles.

e Still in their pairs, Sts role-play asking for and giving simple directions using the subway map. Go through the instructions with them. **A** starts with *Go to the subway station at…*

Monitor and help with any issues relating to directions.

EXTRA SUPPORT Demonstrate the activity by giving the class directions to somewhere on the map, and then ask them where they are.

f When they have finished, they should swap roles.

You could get a few pairs to perform in front of the class.

4 ▶ ROB IS LATE…AGAIN

a ◗ **9.21** Focus on the photos and ask Sts some questions, e.g. *What's happening? How do they look?*, etc.

Get Sts to focus on the question, or get them to close their books, and write it on the board.

Play the video / audio once the whole way through, and then check the answer.

No, it isn't.

⏺ **9.21**
R Jenny! I'm here.
J Hi.
R I'm so sorry. There was a problem on the underground.
J We call it the 'subway' here.
R Right. Anyway, the train stopped for about twenty minutes. I tried to call, but there was no signal.
J I've been here since seven forty-five.
R I know. I ran from the underground…subway station…I'm so sorry.
J You're always late. It's funny, isn't it?
R I said I'm sorry. Look, why don't we go back inside the restaurant?
J I waited for an hour for you. I don't want to stay here any more.
R Maybe we could…we could go for a walk. We could find another restaurant.
J I don't feel like a walk. It's been a long day.
R OK.
J But the night is still young. Maybe you have time to meet up with Holly again.
R Holly?
J I'm sorry. I didn't mean to say that.
R I don't care about Holly.
J Forget it, Rob. Now, if you don't mind, I'd like to go home.
R Listen to me, Jenny. Holly is just a colleague.
J I said forget it. It's OK.
R No, it isn't OK. Look, I know I'm always late. And I know the underground is the subway. But that's not the point! I'm not interested in Holly. I came to New York because of you. The only person I'm interested in is you!

b Now give Sts time to read questions 1–5.

Play the video / audio again the whole way through. Play it again if necessary.

Get Sts to compare with a partner, and then check answers.

1 He says there was a problem on the underground.
2 An hour
3 Go back in the restaurant, go for a walk, or go to a different restaurant.
4 He could meet up with Holly.
5 Jenny

EXTRA SUPPORT If there's time and you are using the video, you could get Sts to watch again with subtitles, so they can see exactly what they understood / didn't understand. Translate / Explain any new words or phrases.

c Focus on the **Social English** phrases. In pairs, get Sts to see if they can remember any of the missing words.

EXTRA CHALLENGE In pairs, get Sts to complete the phrases before they listen.

d ⏺ **9.22** Play the video / audio for Sts to watch or listen and complete the phrases.

Check answers. If you know your Sts' L1, you could get them to translate the phrases.

1 sorry   2 said   3 feel   4 long   5 mean

⏺ **9.22**
1 I'm so sorry.
2 I said I'm sorry.
3 I don't feel like a walk.
4 It's been a long day.
5 I didn't mean to say that.

Now play the video / audio again, pausing after each phrase for Sts to watch or listen and repeat.

e Focus on the instructions and make sure Sts understand what they have to do.

Get Sts to compare with a partner, and then check answers.

A 3 B 1,2 C 5 D 4

Now put Sts in pairs and get them to practise the conversations.

Finally, focus on the **CAN YOU…?** questions and ask Sts if they feel confident they can now do these things. If they feel that they need more practice, tell them to go to *Online Practice* to watch the episode again and practise the language

G expressing movement: *go over*, etc.
V sports: *team*, *player*, etc., expressing movement: *into*, *through*, etc.
P word stress

Lesson plan

In this lesson Sts learn how we express movement in English using a verb and an adverb or preposition, e.g. *walk under the bridge*, *go out of the door*, and the context is sport. At the start of the lesson, in Vocabulary and Pronunciation, Sts look at various sports, as well as verbs that go with sports. Then they practise pronouncing the names of sports in English, before doing a questionnaire about which sports they like and don't like, etc. In Vocabulary and Grammar, Sts focus on words which describe movement (*up*, *down*, *along*, *through*, etc.) and they learn how to combine these words with a verb to express movement. In Reading and Speaking, Sts read some comments posted on an American site called *The Atlantic* about women's sports. Finally, in Writing, Sts read a model essay about public running events, and then write an essay of their own about an activity they enjoy in their free time.

More materials

For teachers

Photocopiables
Grammar expressing movement *p.199*
Vocabulary Expressing movement *p.270* (instructions *p.256*)
Communicative The race *p.244* (instructions *p.214*)

For students
Workbook 10A
Online Practice 10A

OPTIONAL LEAD-IN (BOOKS CLOSED)

Write SPORTS on the board and give Sts, in pairs, two minutes to think of English words for sports. Tell them that they must try to write down at least ten. Tell them to keep their lists, as they will be using them later.

1 VOCABULARY & PRONUNCIATION sports; word stress

Vocabulary and Pronunciation notes

Some words for sports in other languages are similar to the English word, or even the same. However, they are sometimes spelled differently and the pronunciation is usually different. This means that there may often be interference from Sts' L1 when they use the English word for a particular sport.

The way the verbs *do*, *play*, and *go* are used with sports may also be different in your Sts' L1. Remind them of the difference between, e.g. *swim* and *go swimming* (see **2A**).

With sports ending in *-ing* (*cycling*, etc.), we can also use the verb, e.g. *I cycle at weekends*.

We use *do* for sport and exercise in general, e.g. *I do a lot of exercise*.

a Books open. Focus on the photos and ask Sts to name all the sports. Write their answers on the board.

1 athletics (high jump) **2** basketball **3** tennis **4** skiing
5 cycling **6** handball **7** rugby

b ◉ **10.1** Focus on the list of sports and make sure Sts know what they are.

Give Sts time to underline the stressed syllable in each one.

Play the audio once for Sts to listen and check.

See the underlining in the script below

◉ **10.1**
<u>ath</u>letics, <u>base</u>ball, <u>bas</u>ketball, <u>cyc</u>ling, <u>foot</u>ball, gym<u>nas</u>tics, <u>hand</u>ball, ka<u>ra</u>te, <u>rug</u>by, <u>ski</u>ing, <u>ten</u>nis, <u>voll</u>eyball, <u>wind</u>surfing, <u>yoga</u>

EXTRA CHALLENGE Before playing the audio, put Sts in pairs and get them to say together how they think the sports are pronounced, and to underline the stressed syllable.

c Now focus on the chart, and point out the three headings and examples.

Give Sts time to put the sports in the correct column. Check answers.

play	go	do
baseball, basketball, football, handball, rugby, tennis, volleyball	*cycling*, skiing, windsurfing	*athletics, gymnastics, karate, yoga*

Tell Sts to add two more sports to each column. If you did the **Optional lead-in**, Sts could look at their lists and see if any have not been named so far. Elicit their spelling and pronunciation, and write them on the board.

Possible answers
play: badminton, table tennis, cricket, netball, golf
go: sailing, running, jogging, swimming, ice skating
do: judo, t'ai chi, aerobics, tae kwon do

2 SPEAKING

Now focus on the sports questionnaire and go through the questions, making sure Sts understand them. Point out that *live* in the penultimate question is an adjective and is pronounced /laɪv/. Demonstrate the activity by answering some of the questions yourself.

Put Sts in pairs and get them to ask and answer the questions. Encourage them to ask for and give more information, so that this becomes a conversation, rather than just questions and answers.

Get some feedback from the class.

3 VOCABULARY & GRAMMAR expressing movement

a ◀)) **10.2** Focus on the task. Give Sts time to look at the illustration and read the passage.

Tell Sts they will hear some of the commentary before and after the passage in the Student's Book.

Play the audio once the whole way through for Sts to complete the gaps. Then play it again if necessary.

Check answers.

1 past **2** towards **3** over **4** into

◀)) **10.2**

England really need a goal now: they're losing two–one, with only five minutes left. But here comes Matthews. What can he do here? He goes past one defender, and another! The goalkeeper's coming towards him. Matthews shoots. And the ball goes over the goalkeeper, and into the goal! That is a fantastic goal! That is the Matthews magic! England: two, Germany: two!

b Tell Sts to go to **Vocabulary Bank Expressing movement** on *p.162* and get them to do **a** individually or in pairs.

Vocabulary notes

Sts may not be clear about the difference between *to* and *towards*. Highlight that *He walked to the car* = he reached the car, and *He walked towards the car* = he walked in the direction of the car.

◀)) **10.3** Now do **b**. Play the audio for Sts to listen and check.

Check answers.

◀)) **10.3**

Expressing movement

 6 under the bridge
11 along the street
10 round the lake
 8 through the tunnel
 4 into the shop
 2 across the road
 3 over the bridge
12 up the steps
 7 past the church
 9 towards the lake
 1 down the steps
 5 out of the shop

Now either use the audio to drill the pronunciation of the phrases, or model and drill them yourself. Give further practice of any words and phrases your Sts find difficult to pronounce.

Focus on the **across or through** box and go through it with the class.

Then focus on the **away and back** box and go through it with the class.

Finally, focus on **Activation**. Get Sts to cover the words in **a** and look at the pictures. From memory, they take turns to tell their partner where the woman and her dog went.

Tell Sts to go back to the main lesson **10A**.

 If you think Sts need more practice, you may want to give them the **Vocabulary** photocopiable activity at this point.

c Focus on the activity and check that Sts understand the verbs in the list and the words in bold. You could use the photos in **a** to elicit the meaning of *hoop*, *net*, etc.

Now get Sts to complete the sentences.

Check answers.

1 throw **2** kick **3** hit **4** run

d Tell Sts to go to **Grammar Bank 10A** on *p.144*.

Grammar notes

In English, movement is usually expressed by adding a preposition or adverb of movement to a verb, e.g. *walk **up** the steps*, *climb **over** the wall*. In your Sts' L1, this may be expressed in a different way, e.g. by just using a single verb.

◀)) **10.4** Focus on the example sentences and play the audio for Sts to listen and repeat. Encourage them to copy the rhythm. Then go through the rules with the class.

Now focus on the **come or go?** and **in or into? out or out of?** boxes and go through them with the class.

Then focus on the exercises for **10A** on *p.145*. Sts do the exercises individually or in pairs.

Check answers, getting Sts to read the full sentences.

a
1 to, into **2** past **3** along **4** over **5** towards
6 over, into **7** round **8** across
b
1 When I was walking under the bridge, a train went **over** it.
2 Come **in**. The door's open.
3 Go up the stairs – the office is **on** the second floor.
4 He walked **into** the café and ordered some lunch.
5 Go **out** of the building and turn left.
6 Go **away**! I don't want to talk to you.
7 I cycle **down** a big hill on my way home.

Tell Sts to go back to the main lesson **10A**.

 With a class which is very keen on sport, you could get Sts to practise more sports rules. Put Sts in groups of four: **A**, **B**, **C**, and **D**. **A** thinks of a sport he / she knows well. The others have to guess it by asking a maximum of ten *yes / no* questions, e.g. *Is it a team sport? Do you play it inside? Do you have to throw the ball?*, etc. When they have guessed, **B** thinks of a sport, etc.

 If you think Sts need more practice, you may want to give them the **Grammar** photocopiable activity at this point.

e Focus on the instructions and the example. Before Sts start, you could pre-teach some words they might need, e.g. *line, jump*, etc. Point out that the first one (*jumping over*) has been done for them.

Give Sts time to complete each sentence with the correct verb and preposition, depending on what they can see in the photos in **1**.

Get Sts to compare with a partner, and then check answers.

2 throwing…through   **3** hitting…over   **4** skiing down
5 cycling round   **6** throwing…into   **7** running towards

4 READING & SPEAKING understanding opinions

a Do this as a whole-class activity.

b Focus on the instructions and the title, and make sure Sts understand the meaning of *popular* (= liked by a lot of people).

Give Sts time to read the comments and complete the task.

Get Sts to compare with a partner, and then check answers.

! The reading text is adapted from an online forum. It is important for Sts to realize that there may be opinions expressed in this text which they strongly disagree with. The opinions expressed here do not represent the views of the authors or of Oxford University Press.

 Before Sts read the comments the first time, check whether you need to pre-teach any vocabulary, but <u>not</u> the words in **d**.

One person who obviously prefers women's sport: A (RichSmith)
One who obviously prefers men's sport: E (SimonB)

c Tell Sts to read comments A–F again and this time match them to 1–6, which represent the main idea that each person was making.

When Sts have finished, get them to compare with a partner.

Check answers.

1 F   **2** A   **3** C   **4** E   **5** B   **6** D

d Focus on the highlighted sports words. Get Sts, in pairs, to guess their meaning and how they are pronounced. Tell them to read the whole sentence, as the context will help them guess.

Check answers, either explaining in English, translating into Sts' L1, or getting Sts to check in their dictionaries. You might want to point out that *serve* and *return* can also be nouns, e.g. *Djokovic has a good serve. His return was out.*

serve /sɜːv/ = hit the ball over the net to start a point
opponent /əˈpəʊnənt/ = the person who you compete against
return /rɪˈtɜːn/ = to hit the ball back over the net
team /tiːm/ = a group of players playing together
athlete /ˈæθliːt/ = someone who competes in sport
ice skating /ˈaɪs skeɪtɪŋ/ = either dancing or racing on ice

Deal with any other new vocabulary. Model and drill the pronunciation of any tricky words.

e Give Sts time to read each comment again and tick the ones they agree with.

Now put Sts in pairs and get them to compare which comments they ticked. They should tell their partner why they agree with the comment and what they think of the other comments.

Get some feedback from various pairs, and open up the discussion to the whole class.

5 WRITING

a Do this as a whole-class activity.

b Tell Sts to go to **Writing An article** on *p.119* and to do **a**. Tell them not to worry about the gaps in the article.
When they have finished, check the answer.

2 Because she likes doing exercise with other people

Now tell Sts to do **b** by reading the article again and completing the gaps with the adjectives in the list.
Check answers.

1 faster   **2** overweight   **3** local   **4** friendly
5 young   **6** healthy

Now focus on **c**, where Sts look at the topic in each paragraph of the article. Get them to match 1–4 to the correct summary.
Check answers.

1 She gives basic information about the activity.
2 She says when and why she started doing it. She gives more details about when and where she does it now.
3 She explains why she enjoys it.
4 She recommends the activity, and explains why.

For **d**, get Sts to make notes about an activity that they enjoy doing in their free time – explain that it doesn't have to be a sport; it can be any free-time activity. Tell them they must then write an article with four paragraphs by following the model. Point out the highlighted phrases in the article. Sts should make a list of useful phrases for their activity.

For **e**, you may like to get Sts to do the writing in class, or you could set it as homework.

In **f**, Sts should check their article for mistakes. Then they should swap articles with other Sts. Find out if any Sts wrote about the same activity. Finally, find out if any Sts would like to try an activity they read about.

G word order of phrasal verbs
V phrasal verbs: *look up*, *look after*, *find out*, etc.
P linking

Lesson plan

This lesson provides an introduction to phrasal verbs and how they work. Phrasal verbs are an important feature of English, and are used very frequently by native speakers. Sts will probably have already learned some in *English File* Elementary, such as *wake up*, *get up*, *turn off*, and here they revise ones which have come up so far during the course, and learn some more common ones, including how they work grammatically.

The context is about the pros and cons of getting up early in the morning. The lesson begins with Reading and Speaking, where Sts read a text about Ella, a baker, or Peter, a DJ who has an early morning radio programme, and then tell each other what they found out. In Vocabulary, the focus is on common phrasal verbs, and in Grammar, the word order of phrasal verbs is analysed. In Listening, Sts listen to a radio programme about the advantages of getting up early. Then in Pronunciation, Sts have more practice of linking. The lesson finishes with Speaking, where the phrasal verbs Sts have learned are recycled and practised in a questionnaire.

More materials

For teachers

Photocopiables
Grammar word order of phrasal verbs *p.200*
Vocabulary Phrasal verbs *p.271* (instructions *p.256*)
Communicative Phrasal verb conversations *p.245* (instructions *p.214*)

For students
Workbook 10B
Online Practice 10B

OPTIONAL LEAD-IN (BOOKS CLOSED)

Draw a clock on the board and quickly revise telling the time.

Then say a few 'digital times' to Sts (e.g. *eight fifteen, eleven forty*, etc.) and elicit the other way of saying them (*a quarter past eight, twenty to twelve*).

Then tell Sts to continue in pairs, **A** and **B**. **A** says a digital time and **B** has to say it the other way. Then **B** says a digital time, etc. Stop the activity when you think Sts have had enough practice.

1 READING & SPEAKING

a Books open. Read the questions with the class, making sure Sts remember the meaning of all the verbs, e.g. the difference between *wake up* (= stop sleeping) and *get up* (= leave your bed).

Now put Sts in pairs and get them to interview their partner.

Get some feedback from the class. You could also tell the class about yourself.

b Focus on the photos and the captions. Elicit from Sts what time they think Ella and Peter get up, but <u>don't</u> tell them yet.

c Put Sts in pairs, **A** and **B**, and tell them to go to **Communication Early birds**, **A** on *p.105*, **B** on *p.111*. You could explain that *an early bird* is a person who gets up very early. You could also write the idiom on the board THE EARLY BIRD CATCHES THE WORM. Elicit / Explain that it means it is a good thing to get up early, and ask Sts if they have an equivalent idiom in their language.

Go through the instructions with them carefully.

Point out the **Glossary** with each text. Get Sts to read their text and answer the questions with short notes on a separate piece of paper.

Student A (about Ella)
1 She gets up at 2.35 a.m.
2 She sets the alarm on her phone, and her partner does, too.
3 She usually feels pretty terrible.
4 No, she doesn't eat or drink anything before she goes to work.
5 She walks to work.
6 She starts at 3.00 a.m. and finishes at 3.00 p.m.
7 She usually goes to bed at 8.30 p.m.
8 Yes, she would like to change her working hours, so she could sleep more.

Student B (about Peter)
1 He gets up at 4.45 a.m.
2 He has two alarms, one that repeats and a Fitbit that vibrates.
3 He feels a bit sleepy at first.
4 He has a cup of tea before going to work.
5 He drives.
6 He has to be at work at 5.30 a.m.; his show starts at 6.00 a.m. He finishes work late afternoon.
7 He usually goes to bed at 11.00 p.m.
8 No, he doesn't want to change his working hours.

Then sit Sts **A** and **B** face-to-face. **A** tells **B** about Ella's day, using his / her notes. Then **B** tells **A** about Peter's day, using his / her notes.

When they have finished, they should find similarities and differences between Ella and Peter.

Get some feedback from various pairs.

Similarities
They both get up early, live near work, set two alarms, have their clothes already chosen, have long working days, get similar amounts of sleep, and love their work. They don't go out with friends during the week.

Differences

Ella gets up two hours earlier than Peter, and goes to bed two and a half hours earlier; Ella feels terrible first thing and wants more sleep, but Peter just feels a bit sleepy first thing and gets enough sleep; Ella walks to work, Peter drives; Ella's first cup of tea is at work, Peter's is at home before going to work; Ella doesn't go out during the week at all, but Peter will go out if it is a necessary work event.

Deal with any other new vocabulary. Model and drill the pronunciation of any tricky words.

Tell Sts to go back to the main lesson **10B**.

d Get Sts to discuss the questions in pairs, or ask the questions to the whole class. You could demonstrate the activity by answering some of the questions yourself.

Get some feedback from the class.

2 VOCABULARY & GRAMMAR phrasal verbs

Vocabulary notes

Technically, a phrasal verb is a verb + particle. The particle can be a preposition or an adverb. However, at this level it is probably easier to call them *prepositions*, which many of them are, rather than confusing Sts with a new term.

Some Sts have a 'phobia' of phrasal verbs and are convinced that they are impossible to learn. It is important to make Sts realize that at the end of the day, they are just more vocabulary items. They can often use an alternative verb (e.g. *continue* instead of *go on*); however, there are some concepts which can only really be expressed with a phrasal verb (e.g. *get up*, *get on with*), and native speakers often use them, so it is important for Sts to gradually increase their knowledge.

a Focus on the **Phrasal verbs** box and go through it with the class.

Now focus on the instructions and give Sts a few minutes to work out what the highlighted verbs mean in the five sentences.

Check answers.

1 rings **2** stop sleeping **3** get out of bed **4** leave home to do something, like eat in a restaurant or meet up with friends **5** stop doing it

b Now elicit answers for questions 1–3. You might want to point out that *get on* isn't always followed by *with*, e.g. *My brother and I don't get on well*.

1 look for **2** try on **3** get on with

c Tell Sts to go to **Vocabulary Bank** **Phrasal verbs** on *p.163* and get them to do **a** individually or in pairs.

10.5 Now do **b** and play the audio for Sts to listen and check.

Check answers.

10.5
Phrasal verbs
9 The match will be over at about five thirty.
11 My alarm goes off at six o'clock every morning.
14 We set off for the airport at six thirty.
4 I want to give up chocolate.
1 Don't throw away that letter!
10 Turn down the music! It's very loud.
5 Turn up the TV! I can't hear.
7 He looked up the words in a dictionary.
2 Could you fill in this form?
13 I want to find out about hotels in Madrid.
8 It's bedtime – go and put on your pyjamas.
12 Could you take off your boots, please?
3 My sister's looking after Jimmy for me today.
6 I'm really looking forward to the holidays.

Now either use the audio to drill the pronunciation of the sentences, or model and drill them yourself. Give further practice of any words your Sts find difficult to pronounce.

Focus on the box explaining the three types of phrasal verbs and go through it with the class, making sure Sts understand the difference between them.

Now focus on **Activation**. For **a**, get Sts to cover the sentences and look at the pictures. They can test themselves or a partner. Encourage them to say phrases, e.g. *throw away a letter*, *fill in a form*, as learning phrasal verbs in context makes it easier to remember their meaning.

Now tell Sts to focus on **b**. Elicit the meaning of these phrasal verbs from Sts, or if you know your Sts' L1, translate them.

Tell Sts to go back to the main lesson **10B**.

EXTRA SUPPORT If you think Sts need more practice, you may want to give them the **Vocabulary** photocopiable activity at this point.

d Here Sts focus on the grammar of phrasal verbs. Focus on the photo and instructions.

Get Sts to compare which words they have underlined, and check answers.

1 the alarm clock **2** the alarm clock **3** it

e Focus on the instructions and check Sts know the difference between a noun and a pronoun. Get Sts to read and complete the rules.

Check answers.

1 noun **2** pronoun

f Tell Sts to go to **Grammar Bank 10B** on *p.144*.

Grammar notes

Sts will probably ask *How do we know if a phrasal verb which takes an object is type 2 or type 3?* There is no easy rule. Tell them:

1 to always put new phrasal verbs into an example sentence, and if they are type 2, to write the object in the middle, e.g. *turn (the radio) down*.

2 in a dictionary, a type 2 phrasal verb will always be given with *sth / sb* between the verb and the particle, e.g. *turn sth down*.

◄))) **10.6** Focus on the example sentences and play the audio for Sts to listen and repeat. Encourage them to copy the rhythm. Then go through the rules with the class, and remind Sts that the green phrasal verbs in the **Vocabulary Bank** are type 1; the red are type 2; and the blue are type 3.

Now focus on the exercises for **10B** on *p.145*. Sts do them individually or in pairs.

Check answers, getting Sts to read the full sentences.

> **a**
> 1 look after my little sister   2 go out this evening
> 3 ✓   4 looking for a new job   5 ✓   6 try them on
> 7 ✓   8 get on with her   9 take it back
> 10 get up in the morning
> **b**
> 1 Pick **them up**.
> 2 Put **it on**.
> 3 Look **it up**.
> 4 Please fill **them in** now.
> 5 When can you give **it back**?
> 6 Trun **it on** and see.

Tell Sts to go back to the main lesson **10B**.

 If you think Sts need more practice, you may want to give them the **Grammar** photocopiable activity at this point.

3 LISTENING understanding reasons

a ◄))) **10.7** Focus on the task and items 1–6. Point out to Sts that the first one has been done for them. Give them time to quickly read 2–6.

Play the audio once the whole way through.

Get Sts to compare with a partner, and then play the audio again if necessary.

Check answers.

 Read through the scripts and decide if you need to pre-teach any new lexis before Sts listen.

> 2 He does exercise for 30 minutes.
> 3 He goes for a walk around a local park.
> 4 He starts work at 9.00 a.m.
> 5 He studies German at 5.20 a.m. on Thursdays.
> 6 He works 70 hours a week.

b Now play the audio again for Sts to complete the sentences about Tim.

Check answers.

> …it helps him to do more during the day.

◄))) **10.7**
(script in Student's Book on *p.125*)
Tim Powell isn't a morning person. Which is surprising because on weekdays, he gets up very early. While most of us are still asleep, Powell wakes up at five forty-five, does exercise for thirty minutes in his home gym, and has a big breakfast. Then he gets ready for work and drives to the office. When he gets to the building where he works, he goes for a walk around a local park, then he goes inside to start work at nine o'clock. And on Thursdays, he gets up even earlier, at five twenty a.m., to study German.
Powell is a lawyer. He works seventy hours a week, and he says that getting up early helps him to do more during the day. He isn't the only one – many busy, successful people get up very early.

c ◄))) **10.8** Focus on the task and give Sts time to read the three sentences.

Play the audio once the whole way through.

Get Sts to compare with a partner, and then play again if necessary.

Check answers.

> 1 quiet   2 go to bed   3 do things, energy

◄))) **10.8**
(script in Student's Book on *p.125*)
Experts agree that getting up early is a big help if you have a lot of things to do. There are three main reasons for this. The first reason why it's good to get up early is that the early morning is quiet. Nobody phones you at six a.m. There aren't any important emails or messages to answer. There aren't any meetings. There aren't any people. The morning is your time.
The second reason is that if you get up early, you go to bed early. Most people don't do anything useful in the evenings. People who go to bed late spend many hours watching TV, seeing their friends, and spending time on social media. So if you want to do a lot, it's better to go to bed early, and have shorter evenings and longer mornings.
The third reason is that it's better to do things in the morning, when you have energy. Most people are tired after a day at work or college. And when you're tired, the last thing you want to do is to exercise, or to study, or to practise a musical instrument.
And if you find it impossible to get up early? Set your alarm five minutes earlier than you usually get up. And the next day set it five minutes earlier again. After three weeks, you'll have nearly two hours that you never had before!

d Tell Sts to listen and write down examples the expert gives for each reason in **c**. Sts should also listen for the advice he gives to people who have problems getting up early.

Play the audio again, pausing after each reason to give Sts time to write.

Get Sts to compare with a partner, and then play again if necessary.

Check answers.

> 1 Nobody phones you at 6.00 a.m. There aren't any important emails or messages to answer. There aren't any meetings. There aren't any people.
> 2 Most people don't do anything useful in the evenings. People who go to bed late spend many hours watching TV, seeing their friends, and spending time on social media.
> 3 Most people are tired after a day at work or university. And when you're tired, the last thing you want to do is to exercise, or to study, or to practise a musical instrument.

Now ask Sts what advice the expert gave for people who have problems getting up early.

Get up five minutes earlier every day.

Finally, ask Sts what they think of this advice.

 If there's time, you could get Sts to listen again with the scripts on *p.125*, so they can see exactly what they understood / didn't understand. Translate / Explain any new words or phrases.

e Do this as a whole-class activity. You could share your ideas with the class and also find out who gets up the earliest and who gets up the latest.

4 PRONUNCIATION linking

a ◆ **10.9** Here Sts practise deciphering connected speech, and all the examples involve phrasal verbs. Write on the board as an example GET UP and remind Sts that when a word ends with a consonant sound and the next word begins with a vowel sound, they are linked together and sound like one word, especially when people speak quickly. Draw a linking mark on the board between the *t* in *get* and the *u* in *up*.

Point out that the first one (*Please turn it off*) has been done for them. Play the audio once for Sts to hear the six sentences. Tell them just to listen, not to write.

Then play the audio again, pausing after each sentence to give Sts time to write.

Check answers, eliciting the sentences onto the board.

2 Pick it up **3** look it up **4** Put it on **5** look after it
6 Take it off

◆ **10.9**
1 I can't concentrate with the radio on. Please turn it off.
2 There's a wet towel on the floor. Pick it up.
3 If you don't know what the word means, look it up.
4 Why have you taken your coat off? Put it on!
5 This book was very expensive. Please look after it.
6 Why are you wearing your coat in here? Take it off!

 When writing the answers on the board draw the linking mark between the words to show Sts where to link words. This will help them when listening and repeating in **b**.

b Play the audio again, pausing for Sts to repeat the sentences and copy the rhythm.

Put Sts in pairs and get them to practise saying the sentences.

5 SPEAKING

a Go through the questionnaire with Sts, making sure they understand all the vocabulary.

Then give Sts some time to think about their answers.

b Put Sts in pairs, and get them to interview each other with the questionnaire. Tell them to ask alternate questions, and to return the questions to each other with *What about you?*.

Get some feedback from various pairs.

 Get Sts to choose a few questions to ask you before they interview each other.

10C International inventions

G the passive
V people from different countries
P /ʃ/, /tʃ/, and /dʒ/

Lesson plan

This lesson focuses on inventions – firstly, things that were invented by different nationalities in different centuries, and later, in the video listening, things invented by women. The lesson begins with Vocabulary and Pronunciation, where Sts look at nationality adjectives and the three sounds: /ʃ/, /tʃ/, and /dʒ/. Inventions through the ages provide the context for the introduction of the present and past passive in Grammar. Next, in Speaking, Sts ask each other quiz questions that use the passive. Finally, the lesson ends with a video listening, where Sts watch or hear a programme about six things invented by women.

More materials

For teachers

Photocopiables
Grammar the passive: *be* + past participle *p.201*
Communicative General knowledge quiz *p.246* (instructions *p.215*)

Teacher's Resource Centre
Video Invented by women

For students
Workbook 10C
Online Practice 10C

OPTIONAL LEAD-IN (BOOKS CLOSED)
Write the following phrase on the board:

THE MOST IMPORTANT INVENTION OF THE 20TH CENTURY WAS...

Give Sts, in pairs, two or three minutes to complete the sentence.

Get feedback and write Sts' ideas on the board.

Then get Sts to vote, with a show of hands, for the most useful invention.

1 VOCABULARY & PRONUNCIATION people from different countries; /ʃ/, /tʃ/, and /dʒ/

Vocabulary notes

Talking about people of different nationalities is a complicated area in English. In this lesson we just focus on people in general from different countries, rather than individuals (*an Englishman*, *a Dane*, etc.). If relevant to your Sts, you could explain that some nationalities also have a specific word for people from that country (that is different from the nationality adjective), e.g. *the Scottish – the Scots, the Turkish – the Turks, the Polish – the Poles, the Spanish – the Spaniards*, etc.

a Books open. Do this as a whole-class activity.

1 American, Belgian, Italian (all end in *an*)
2 Chinese, Swiss, French, Dutch, English, Spanish

b Focus on the **Talking about people from different countries** box and go through it with the class. You could point out to Sts that not all nationalities fit into these two categories, e.g. *Czechs*, *Greeks*, *Thais*, etc.

Focus on countries 1–8 and give Sts time to complete the gaps.

c **10.10** Play the audio for Sts to listen and check.

Check answers. Then either use the audio to drill the pronunciation of the words, or model them yourself.

10.10

1	England	English	the English
2	Brazil	Brazilian	the Brazilians
3	Russia	Russian	the Russians
4	Turkey	Turkish	the Turkish
5	Argentina	Argentinian	the Argentinians
6	Poland	Polish	the Polish
7	Japan	Japanese	the Japanese
8	Spain	Spanish	the Spanish

Pronunciation notes

The most common spelling of the /ʃ/ sound is *sh*. However, *ti* and *ci* before another vowel are also pronounced /ʃ/, as in *invention* and *musician*.

The most common spelling of the /tʃ/ sound is *ch* or *tch*.

The most common spelling of the /dʒ/ sound is *j*; *g* before *e*, *i*, or *y*; and *dge*.

d **10.11** Focus on the three sound pictures and elicit the words and sounds: *shower* /ʃ/, *chess* /tʃ/, and *jazz* /dʒ/.

Now play the audio for Sts to listen and repeat.

10.11
See sounds and words in Student's Book on *p.82*

e **10.12** Focus on the task. Remind Sts that this type of activity is easier if they say the words aloud to themselves.

Put Sts in pairs and give them time to complete the task.

Play the audio for Sts to listen and check.

Check answers.

EXTRA CHALLENGE Elicit the sounds before Sts listen to the audio.

1 b, a **2** b, b, a **3** c, b **4** c, c **5** c, a

10.12
See sentences in Student's Book on *p.82*

Now play the audio again, pausing after each sentence for Sts to listen and repeat.

Finally, put Sts in pairs and get them to practise saying the sentences.

EXTRA SUPPORT If these sounds are difficult for your Sts, it will help to show them the mouth position. You could model this yourself or use the the Sound Bank videos on the *Teacher's Resource Centre*.

2 GRAMMAR the passive

a Focus on the instructions and the photos. Make sure Sts know the meaning of *a century* (= a period of 100 years) and *to invent* (= to make or think of sth for the first time).

Put Sts in small groups and tell them to complete sentences 1–10 with the items which are shown in the photos. Tell them to look carefully at the verbs to see if the item should be in the singular or plural.

Elicit some ideas, but <u>don't</u> tell Sts if they are right.

b 🔊 **10.13** Tell Sts they are now going to hear the answers as well as some extra facts about each item. First, they just need to listen and check their answers to **a**.

Play the audio, pausing after each item to check the answer.

> 1 Guns 2 Glasses 3 The hot-air balloon 4 Stamps
> 5 The saxophone 6 Dynamite 7 The watch
> 8 The mobile phone 9 Lego 10 CDs

🔊 **10.13**

The thirteenth century

Guns were invented by the Chinese. The first guns were quite large, like small cannons. The oldest gun that still exists today was made in about twelve eighty.

Glasses were invented by the Italians in about twelve eighty-six.

Sunglasses were invented even earlier, in the twelfth century.

The eighteenth century

The hot-air balloon was invented by two French brothers, Joseph and Jacques Montgolfier. The first flight with people was in seventeen eighty-three, and the balloon flew three kilometres, over Paris.

The nineteenth century

Stamps were invented by an English teacher, Rowland Hill. The first stamp, from eighteen forty, was called the Penny Black, and it showed the head of the young Queen Victoria.

The saxophone was invented by a Belgian musician in eighteen forty-six. His name was Adolphe Sax. Saxophones were first used mainly in military bands, but are now used in all kinds of music.

Dynamite was invented by a Swedish scientist called Alfred Nobel. The Nobel Prize is named after him. Since its invention, it has been used all over the world for demolition, for making tunnels, cutting canals, and building railways.

The wrist watch was invented by the Swiss. The first one was made for a Hungarian countess by Patek Philippe in eighteen sixty-eight, a company which still makes luxury watches today.

The twentieth century

The mobile phone was invented by the Americans. It was first produced by the company Motorola. On the third of April nineteen seventy-three, Martin Cooper, a Motorola researcher and executive, made the first mobile telephone call. His phone weighed one point one kilos.

Lego was invented by a Danish businessman, Ole Kirk Christiansen. The name *Lego* comes from the Danish phrase *leg godt*, which means 'play well'. Twenty billion pieces of Lego are produced every year.

CDs were invented by a Dutch company, Philips. Sony also worked on CDs, and they were designed to play seventy-four minutes of music because that was the length of Beethoven's *Ninth Symphony* – the Sony boss's favourite piece of music.

c Tell Sts they are going to listen again and they need to write down one more piece of information about each invention.

Play the audio again, pausing after each invention to give Sts time to write.

Elicit any information Sts understood about each invention.

> See script 10.13

d Focus on the task and the example. Tell Sts to write four more true sentences using information from each column once only.

Get Sts to compare with a partner, and then check answers.

> 2 The first stamp was called the Penny Black.
> 3 Twenty billion pieces of Lego are produced every year.
> 4 The saxophone was invented by Adolphe Sax.
> 5 The Nobel Prize is named after the inventor of dynamite.

e Focus on the two sentences, a and b, and read the three questions aloud to the class. Elicit answers from the whole class, getting a majority opinion on each one and confirming if it is right or wrong.

> 1 Yes 2 b 3 a

f Tell Sts to go to **Grammar Bank 10C** on *p.144*.

Grammar notes

This lesson provides an introduction to the passive and Sts are taught present and past forms only.

The form of the passive is not difficult for Sts as it is composed of known items: the verb *be* and a past participle.

The passive is often used in English where other languages use an impersonal subject.

EXTRA CHALLENGE You may want to point out to Sts that all other forms of the passive are made simply by changing the form of *be*, e.g. *will be made, has been made*, etc.

🔊 **10.14** Focus on the example sentences and play the audio for Sts to listen and repeat. Make sure they pronounce the
-ed endings in the participles correctly, and encourage them to copy the rhythm. Then go through the rules with the class.

Now focus on the exercises for **10C** on *p.145*. Sts do the exercises individually or in pairs.

Check answers, getting Sts to read the full sentences.

> **a**
> 1 Many of the things we use every day **were invented** by women.
> 2 In the UK most children **are educated** in state schools.
> 3 DNA **was discovered** by Watson and Crick in 1953.
> 4 This morning I **was woken** up by the neighbour's dog.
> 5 Cricket **is played** in the summer in the UK.
> 6 The songs on this album **were written** last year.
> 7 Millions of toys **are made** in China every year.
> 8 Carols are songs which **are sung** at Christmas.
> 9 These birds **aren't usually seen** in northern Europe.
> 10 The London Eye **was opened** on 31 December 1999…
> **b**
> 1 St Paul's Cathedral was designed by Christopher Wren.
> 2 This olive oil is produced by a small Italian company.
> 3 Australia was discovered by the Dutch in 1606.
> 4 The *Star Wars* films weren't directed by Spielberg.
> 5 *Sunflowers* was painted by Van Gogh in 1888.
> 6 Glass wasn't invented by the Chinese.
> 7 The *Harry Potter* books were written by J.K. Rowling.
> 8 Skoda cars are made in the Czech Republic.

Tell Sts to go back to the main lesson **10C**.

3 SPEAKING

Put Sts into pairs, **A** and **B**, and tell them to go to **Communication** Passives quiz, **A** on *p.106*, **B** on *p.111*.

Give Sts time to complete their sentences and circle the correct answers.

Get Sts to sit face-to-face if possible. **A** reads his / her sentences to **B**, who listens and says if **A**'s sentences are right or wrong, and corrects the wrong answers.

Sts then swap roles.

Monitor and help as Sts do the task, making sure they are forming the passive and pronouncing the past participle correctly.

End the activity when the majority of pairs have finished.

Tell Sts to go back to the main lesson **10C**.

4 ▶ VIDEO LISTENING

a Focus on the photos and give Sts, in pairs, a couple of minutes to guess which six things were invented by women. <u>Don't</u> check answers yet.

b Play the video for Sts to check their answers.

Check answers. Make sure Sts understand what all the words mean, e.g. *disposable* = you throw it away after you have used it once. Model and drill pronunciation.

Get feedback to find out if Sts had guessed correctly.

> **The six inventions are:** the dishwasher, disposable nappies, windscreen wipers, the life raft, solar heating, and CCTV.

Invented by women

Hello, and welcome to *Science Now*. When we think of famous inventors, we usually think of men – like Alexander Graham Bell, Guglielmo Marconi, and Thomas Edison. But many of the things which make our lives easier or safer today were invented by women. And on today's show, we're going to look at six of them.

One invention that definitely improved the lives of millions of people was the disposable nappy. They were invented by a woman called Marion Donovan. Her father and uncle were inventors and, when she had young children, she invented a nappy that you could use and then throw away. Before her invention, babies wore nappies made of cotton – like these. And this meant a *lot* of washing. Although she invented the disposable nappy in the nineteen forties, it wasn't until nineteen fifty-one that an American company bought Donovan's idea. Today, millions of disposable nappies are used every day, and Donovan's invention is now more eco-friendly. You can buy biodegradable nappies!

And now another invention which has made life easier.

The dishwasher was invented by a woman called Josephine Cochrane in eighteen eighty-six. She was a rich American who gave a lot of dinner parties. But she was annoyed that her servants often broke plates and glasses when they were washing up after a party. Oops! So, Cochrane decided to invent a machine which could wash a lot of plates and glasses safely. She said, 'If nobody else is going to invent a dishwasher, then I will!' She designed the machine, and then she found a company to make it. At first, only hotels and restaurants bought Cochrane's new machine, but today, the dishwasher is used in homes all over the world.

The car was invented by a man, but it was a woman, Mary Anderson, who solved one of the biggest problems of driving. On a trip to New York in nineteen oh three, Anderson noticed that drivers had to open their windows to see where they were going when it was raining. When she returned to her home in Alabama, she invented windscreen wipers, which made driving a lot safer.

Our fourth invention made life safer for people living in flats or apartments – video entry phones. They were invented in nineteen sixty-six by Marie Van Brittan Brown, a nurse who lived in New York. Her neighbourhood was quite dangerous and Brown was often at home alone, so she decided to invent something that would make her feel safer. With the help of her husband, an electrician, she developed a camera that you could put by the front door. This camera sent a picture of the person at the door to a screen inside the flat, and there was also a microphone so you could talk to the person outside. If the person was a welcome visitor, you pushed a button to let them in. If not, you could push another button to contact a security company. This system is now common all over the world.

And now an invention that has saved a lot of lives. The modern life raft was invented by Maria Beasley in eighteen eighty and then improved in eighteen eighty-two. Before her invention, life rafts were just wooden platforms, and many people died in accidents at sea. Four of her life rafts were used on the *Titanic*, alongside the ship's normal lifeboats. When the *Titanic* sank in nineteen twelve, only seven hundred and six people survived, and nearly two hundred of them were in the life rafts designed by Beasley.

Our last invention is one of today's most important green technologies. Mária Telkes, a Hungarian-American scientist, worked at the Massachusetts Institute of Technology in the United States in the nineteen forties. She was so interested in the power of the sun, that her nickname was 'the Sun Queen'. In nineteen forty-eight, she designed the first house which was heated completely by the sun. The system worked for three years. The solar technology we use today is very different from Telkes's invention, but – like all our female inventors – she showed the world what was possible. And today solar technology has the power to change our lives and save our environment.

c Focus on the questions and give Sts time to read them.

Play the video again for Sts to watch for more detail. Pause after each invention to give Sts time to write their answers.

Get Sts to compare with a partner, then play the video again if necessary.

Check answers.

> 1 They were inventors. Nappies were made of cotton. In 1951, an American company bought her invention.
>
> 2 Her servants often broke plates and glasses when they were washing up. The first customers were hotels and restaurants.
>
> 3 She got the idea in 1903 on a trip to New York. They had to open their windows to see where they were going.
>
> 4 She was a nurse. She lived in a dangerous neighbourhood. Her husband helped her with her invention. You could push a button to contact a security company.
>
> 5 They were used on the *Titanic*. Nearly 200 survivors had used her invention.
>
> 6 She was Hungarian-American. Her nickname was 'the Sun Queen'. In 1948 she designed the first house to be heated by the sun.

d Do this as a whole-class activity.

For instructions on how to use these pages, see *p.40*.

More materials
For teachers
Teacher's Resource Centre
Video Can you understand these people? 9&10
Quick Test 10
File 10 Test
For students
Online Practice Check your progress

GRAMMAR

1 b	2 c	3 a	4 c	5 c	6 a	7 c	8 a	9 c	10 a
11 c	12 b	13 b	14 c	15 b					

VOCABULARY

a
1 goat (the others are insects)
2 lion (the others are farm animals)
3 spider (the others live in the sea)
4 retire (the others are to do with marriage)
5 cycling (the others are sports with a ball)

b
1 for   2 for   3 since   4 since   5 for

c
1 through   2 into   3 along   4 towards   5 past   6 off
7 up   8 down (off)   9 forward   10 out

d
1 Japanese   2 French   3 Swiss   4 Belgians   5 Spanish

PRONUNCIATION

c
1 giraffe /dʒ/   2 work /ɜː/   3 divorce /ɔː/   4 invention /ʃ/
5 Dutch /tʃ/

d
1 butterfly   2 retire   3 secondary   4 athletics   5 karate

CAN YOU understand this text?

b
1 Robert Bauer   2 Jon Drummond   3 Angel Matos
4 Nelson Piquet   5 Luciano Gaucci

▶ CAN YOU understand these people?

1 c	2 a	3 b	4 c	5 a

◑ 10.15

1

I = interviewer, H = Hope
I   What animal would you most like to see in the wild, for example on a safari?
H Oh, that's a really good question. Probably an elephant.
I   Why?
H I think they're amazing. They're so big, and just, they sort of live in the wilderness, and yeah.

2

I = interviewer, M = Mairi
I   Do you have a phobia?
M I'm frightened of spiders.
I   How long have you had it?
M Er, since I was about five or six I think, but I'm not sure.
I   How does it affect your life?
M Um, I normally have to check a room to see if there's a big spider in it before I go to sleep, because, one time a spider, er, joined me in my bed.

3

I = interviewer, D = Dave
I   Who's the oldest person you know well?
D My great aunt is a hundred and four, living in California.
I   What kind of life has she had?
D She has had a great life. She's still travelling at a hundred and four.

4

I = interviewer, S = Sarah
I   Do you do any sport or exercise?
S I run and I hike, and I do yoga.
I   Do you enjoy it?
S I love hiking, hiking is my favourite, and I just love being in nature and outdoors, and experiencing nature on foot.

5

I = interviewer, K = Kathy
I   Are you a morning or evening person?
K Um, I'm a morning person. Um, I feel a lot more awake in the morning than in the evening, um, so I tend to get up early, even when I'm not at, even when I'm not at work. Um, and I prefer to go to bed earlier.

 Ask the teacher

G *used to*
V school subjects: history, geography, etc.
P *used to / didn't use to*

Lesson plan

In this lesson Sts learn to use *used to* to talk about repeated past actions, and the main context is school experiences.

The lesson begins with a vocabulary focus on school subjects. Then Sts read an article in which three teachers talk about a student of theirs who became famous. Extracts from the article are used to present the grammar of *used to / didn't use to*. This is followed by a pronunciation focus on how to pronounce the new language. In Listening and Speaking, Sts listen to six people talking about whether they liked school or not, which leads into a speaking activity where Sts talk about their own experiences at primary or secondary school.

More materials
For teachers
Photocopiables
Grammar used to / didn't used to p.202
Communicative My past p.247 (instructions p.215)
For students
Workbook 11A
Online Practice 11A

OPTIONAL LEAD-IN (BOOKS CLOSED)

Write on the board:

WHAT PRIMARY / SECONDARY SCHOOL DID YOU GO TO? DID YOU LIKE IT? WHY (NOT)?

Model and drill the pronunciation of *primary* and *secondary*.

Answer the question yourself and tell Sts a bit about your school experience. If your Sts are at secondary school, they should talk about their primary school experience. Then get them to ask and answer in pairs, and get some feedback.

1 VOCABULARY school subjects

a 🔊 **11.1** Books open. Focus on the instructions. Tell Sts they are going to hear nine teachers in their classrooms. Model and drill the pronunciation of *subjects* /ˈsʌbdʒekts/.

Play the audio for Sts to listen and number the lessons they hear.

Get Sts to compare with a partner.

🔊 **11.1**
T = teacher, Sts = students, S = student
1
T OK, so now repeat after me: *du pain*.
Sts *Du pain*
T *De la salade*
Sts *De la salade*
T *Des saucisses*
Sts *Des saucisses*
2
T So last week, we looked at percentages, and today, we're going to look at fractions. Can someone give me an example of a fraction?
S Three quarters?
T Yes, exactly. And what would that be as a percentage?
S Seventy-five per cent.
3
T Can anybody tell me the dates of the First World War?
S Me sir, me sir!
T Angela?
S Nineteen thirty-nine to nineteen forty-five, sir.
T No, that's the Second World War. Try again.
4
T So we're going to start by defining a few words and phrases. I'm going to dictate the terms and I want you to write a short definition. So, for example, if I said the word *cookies*, what would you write?
S *Biscuits*?
T Very funny, Carl. Anna?
S Er, pieces of text that, er, websites put onto your computer?
T That's right. And what do internet cookies do?
S They record details of the websites you've visited and, er, how long you've spent on them.
5
T OK. Act three, scene one. OK, Jack, you can be Hamlet. This is a very important speech. Are you ready?
S Yes. *To be, or not to be, that is the question. Whether…*
6
T So I have a small piece of sodium here – about one cubic centimetre – and we're going to see what happens when we add it to water. So if you could all stand back a bit…further back… OK…Here we go…
7
T Today, we're going to look at two self-portraits from different centuries. Take a look at these.
S The one on the right looks like you, sir!
T Thank you, Jasper. Now, I want you to start by thinking about two questions. When do you think the self-portraits were painted? And how old do you think the artists were when they painted them?
8
T OK, we're going to warm up first. I want you to run round the track three times.
Sts Can't we play football?
T No, come on, three times round the track. Ready, steady, go.
9
T There are no active volcanoes in the UK, but there are quite a lot in the rest of Europe. Can anyone tell me a European country that has active volcanoes?
S France?
T Not France, no…
Sts Italy? Italy has Mount Etna.
T Yes, Italy. In fact, Etna is the highest active volcano in Europe, at over three thousand three hundred metres.

---

b 🔊 **11.2** Play the audio for Sts to listen and check. Check answers by asking the subject and which words helped Sts guess.

> **Possible answers**
> 1 foreign languages (French): *repeat after me*, all French words
> 2 maths: *percentage, fraction, three quarters, 75%*
> 3 history: *First World War, 1939 to 1945, Second World War*
> 4 IT: *cookies, website, computer, internet*
> 5 literature: *act, scene, speech, Hamlet*
> 6 science (chemistry) *sodium, add, water*
> 7 art: *self-portraits, painted, artists*
> 8 PE: *warm up, run, track, football*
> 9 geography: *active volcanoes, European countries, Mount Etna*

🔊 **11.2**

T = teacher, Sts = students, S = student

1 foreign languages
T OK, so now repeat after me: *du pain.*
Sts *Du pain*
T *De la salade*
Sts *De la salade*
T *Des saucisses*
Sts *Des saucisses*

2 maths
T So last week, we looked at percentages, and today, we're going to look at fractions. Can someone give me an example of a fraction?
S Three quarters?
T Yes, exactly. And what would that be as a percentage?
S Seventy-five per cent.

3 history
T Can anybody tell me the dates of the First World War?
S Me, sir. Me, sir!
T Angela?
S Nineteen thirty-nine to nineteen forty-five, sir.
T No, that's the Second World War. Try again.

4 IT
T So we're going to start by defining a few words and phrases. I'm going to dictate the terms and I want you to write a short definition. So, for example, if I said the word *cookies*, what would you write?
S Biscuits?
T Very funny, Carl. Anna?
S Er, pieces of text that, er, websites put onto your computer?
T That's right. And what do internet cookies do?
S They record details of the websites you've visited and, er, how long you've spent on them.

5 literature
T OK. Act three, scene one. OK, Jack, you can be Hamlet. This is a very important speech. Are you ready?
S Yes. *To be, or not to be, that is the question. Whether…*

6 science
T So I have a small piece of sodium here – about one cubic centimetre – and we're going to see what happens when we add it to water. So if you could all stand back a bit…Further back… OK…Here we go…

7 art
T Today, we're going to look at two self-portraits from different centuries. Take a look at these.
S The one on the right looks like you, sir!
T Thank you, Jasper. Now, I want you to start by thinking about two questions. When do you think the self-portraits were painted? And how old do you think the artists were when they painted them?

8 PE
T OK, we're going to warm up first. I want you to run round the track three times.
Sts Can't we play football?
T No, come on, three times round the track. Ready, steady, go.

9 geography
T There are no active volcanoes in the UK, but there are quite a lot in the rest of Europe. Can anyone tell me a European country that has active volcanoes?
S France?
T Not France, no…
Sts Italy? Italy has Mount Etna.
T Yes, Italy. In fact, Etna is the highest active volcano in Europe, at over three thousand three hundred metres.

c 🔊 **11.3** Play the audio for Sts to listen and repeat the subjects.

🔊 **11.3**
See words in **a** in Student's Book on *p.86*

Then repeat the activity, getting individual Sts to repeat. Point out that *history* /ˈhɪstri/ and *literature* /ˈlɪtrətʃə/ each have a syllable which isn't pronounced (the **o** in *history* and the **e** in *literature*).

d Focus on the task and elicit answers to the first question. Write the subjects on the board.

Now focus on the second question and the three options. Point out the speech bubble and the use of *at* after *good*, *OK*, and *bad*.

Demonstrate the activity by talking about the subjects yourself.

Put Sts in pairs and give them a few minutes to talk to each other.

Get some feedback from various pairs.

2 READING

a Focus on the task and either put Sts in pairs or do this as a whole-class activity.

If Sts worked in pairs, get some feedback.

b Focus on the title and read the introduction together. Make sure Sts understand *fame* (noun from *famous*), *academy*, and *spark* (= a special quality of energy, intelligence, or enthusiasm that makes sb very clever, amusing, etc.). Model and drill pronunciation. Point out the **Glossary**.

Give Sts time to read the article to check their answers to **a**. Check answers.

EXTRA SUPPORT Before Sts read the article the first time, check whether you need to pre-teach any vocabulary.

> **the most popular:** Alex Turner
> **the most unpopular:** Jude Law
> **the quietest:** J.K. Rowling

c Focus on the instructions and questions 1–6, making sure Sts understand all the lexis, e.g. *pupil, perform*, etc. Model and drill the pronunciation of *pupil* /ˈpjuːpl/.

Give Sts time to read the article again and answer the questions.

Check answers.

> 1 Jude Law's teacher   2 J.K. Rowling   3 Alex Turner's teacher
> 4 J.K. Rowling's teacher   5 Jude Law   6 Alex Turner

Deal with any other new vocabulary. Model and drill the pronunciation of any tricky words.

d Put Sts in pairs or small groups.

Get some feedback from various pairs or groups. You could tell the class what you think your teachers thought of you. If any of your Sts are still at school, ask them what they think their teachers think of them.

3 GRAMMAR *used to*

a Tell Sts to read the three sentences from the article and answer the questions.

Check answers.

> **1** b   **2** a

b Tell Sts to go to **Grammar Bank 11A** on *p.146*.

> **Grammar notes**
>
> *Used to* only exists in the past, and is used for past habits or states. Sts may not have an equivalent form in their language. If they do have an equivalent verb, it may also exist in the present (for present habits), which means Sts may try to say *I use to* for present habits, rather than using the present simple and an adverb of frequency (*I usually…*). A typical mistake is: ~~I use to go to the gym every Friday~~.
>
> **!** Sts might confuse *used to* + infinitive with the past of the verb *use*, e.g. *I used my dictionary when I did my English homework*.

11.4 Focus on the example sentences and play the audio for Sts to listen and repeat. Encourage them to copy the rhythm. Then go through the rules with the class.

Now focus on the **used to or usually?** box and go through it with the class.

Then focus on the exercises for **11A** on *p.147*. Sts do the exercises individually or in pairs.

Check answers, getting Sts to read the full sentences.

> **a**
> **1** He used to have long hair.
> **2** He didn't use to wear glasses.
> **3** He didn't use to have a beard.
> **4** He used to play / like / love / be interested in football.
> **5** He didn't use to wear a tie.
>
> **b**
> **1** Angie used to hate maths, but she loves it now.
> **2** Where did you use to work when you lived in Cairo?
> **3** I didn't use to like reading when I was a child.
> **4** What did you use to do in the summer holidays when you were young?
> **5** The British didn't use to cook with olive oil, but now it's very popular.
> **6** This restaurant used to be a cinema in the 1960s.
> **7** Did your sister use to eat meat, or has she always been a vegetarian?
> **8** I didn't use to be interested in athletics, but now I always watch it.
> **9** Did you use to have a motorbike when you were a student?
> **10** Telegrams used to be the quickest way to send important messages.

Tell Sts to go back to the main lesson **11A**.

EXTRA SUPPORT If you think Sts need more practice, you may want to give them the **Grammar** photocopiable activity at this point.

4 PRONUNCIATION *used to / didn't use to*

> **Pronunciation notes**
>
> As mentioned earlier, Sts might confuse *used to* + infinitive with the past of the verb *use*. As well as having a completely different meaning, the two verbs are pronounced differently (*used to* is pronounced /ˈjuːstə/ and *used* (past of *use*) is /juːzd/).
>
> The final /t/ in *used* and the /t/ in *to* are run together and make one /t/ sound. For this reason, *use to* or *used to* sound the same, and Sts sometimes write *Did you used to…?*.

a **11.5** Focus on the **Pronouncing *used to*** box and go through it with the class. Model and drill the pronunciation of *used to* /ˈjuːstə/.

Now focus on the task. Play the audio once for Sts just to listen.

Play the audio again for Sts to listen and repeat.

11.5
See sentences in Student's Book on *p.87*

Then repeat the activity, eliciting responses from individual Sts.

b **11.6** Focus on the task and the example. Tell Sts that for the first four sentences, they must make positive *used to* sentences; for the next four, negative ones; and questions for the final four.

Play the audio, pausing after each phrase to give Sts time to make the transformation.

11.6
Positive sentences
have a lot of friends (*pause*) I used to have a lot of friends.
be lazy (*pause*) I used to be lazy.
wear a uniform (*pause*) I used to wear a uniform.
play football (*pause*) I used to play football.

Negative sentences
like exams (*pause*) I didn't use to like exams.
do much homework (*pause*) I didn't use to do much homework.
be good at maths (*pause*) I didn't use to be good at maths.
enjoy PE (*pause*) I didn't use to enjoy PE.

Questions
work hard (*pause*) Did you use to work hard?
like school (*pause*) Did you use to like school?
do sport (*pause*) Did you use to do sport?
have long hair (*pause*) Did you use to have long hair?

Then repeat the activity, eliciting responses from individual Sts.

5 LISTENING & SPEAKING understanding attitude

a Focus on the instructions and make sure Sts understand what they have to do. point out that the first one (*P*) has been done for them

Get Sts to compare with a partner, and then check answers.

> **No, not really. I didn't like it at all.** N
> **I didn't hate school, but I don't think I liked it very much.** N
> **Sometimes. Yeah, most of the time.** P
> **Well, yes and no.** B
> **Yes, definitely. I really enjoyed school.** P

b 🔊 **11.7** Focus on the task and tell Sts that all the speakers are answering the same question as in **a**, *Did you like school?*.

Before playing the audio, tell Sts that one of the speakers is American. Focus on the **Education in the UK and the US** box and go through it with the class.

Play the audio, pausing after each speaker to give Sts time to match the speaker to their answer in **a**. Play again if necessary.

Check answers.

EXTRA SUPPORT Read through the script and decide if you need to pre-teach any new lexis before Sts listen.

> **Speaker 1:** I didn't hate school, but I don't think I liked it very much.
> **Speaker 2:** No, not really. I didn't like it at all.
> **Speaker 3:** Well, yes and no.
> **Speaker 4:** I didn't like it – I absolutely loved it!
> **Speaker 5:** Sometimes. Yeah, most of the time.
> **Speaker 6:** Yes definitely. I really enjoyed school.

🔊 **11.7**
(script in Student's Book on *p.125*)
I = interviewer, M = man, W = woman

1
I Did you like school?
M I didn't hate school, but I don't think I liked it very much. I used to enjoy PE; I used to enjoy sport; um, I quite liked English, but there were lots of subjects I didn't like. I didn't like maths very much, history was boring, and I found science difficult. I had a small group of friends – not many, but a close group of friends – and I used to spend time with them, talking about sport, talking about music. So it wasn't too bad, but I didn't like it very much. I've never been back to school – I've never been to a school reunion, or anything like that.

2
I Did you like school?
M No, not really. I didn't like it at all.
I Why not?
M It was a boys' school and I got bored with just being with boys all the time. And I didn't really like any of the subjects.

3
I Did you like school?
M Well, yes and no. Some things I really loved; some things I thought, 'This isn't much fun'; but I used to enjoy quite a lot of the subjects.
I Like what?
M I liked English and I liked maths.
I And what didn't you enjoy?
M I hated geography. And I hated PE. The PE teacher once caught me reading a book on the football pitch, and I was punished for that.

4
I Did you like school?
W I didn't like it – I absolutely loved it! I liked all the subjects, especially English and history. I remember one time when I was about six or seven, I got ill during the Easter holidays and I was really, really sad, and my mum thought I was sad because I was ill during the holidays, but in fact, I was terrified that I'd never get better and I'd never go back to school.

5
I Did you like school?
W Er, sometimes. Yeah, most of the time.
I What did you like about it?
W Well, I had some good friends, and I liked learning things, but there were some subjects that I didn't like very much, and I hated PE. I used to invent a lot of excuses, like saying that I was ill, because I didn't want to do it.

6
I Did you like school?
W Yes, definitely. I really enjoyed school. Elementary school was all fun and we had great teachers. I always really looked forward to getting back to school. High school was harder work and we used to have lots of exams and tests, but we had really inspiring teachers. My favourites were in math and biology. And overall, yeah, I really liked it.

Remind Sts that speakers 1–3 are men and 4–6 are women, then ask the class if the men enjoyed school more than the women, or if it was about the same.

> The women enjoyed school more than the men.

Finally, ask Sts if they think in their country girls tend to enjoy school more than boys

c Tell Sts that they are now going to hear the people again and they must make a list of the subjects they liked and disliked.

Play the audio again and then check answers. Elicit other details if possible.

> **Speaker 1:** He liked PE and English, but didn't like maths, history, and science.
>
> **Speaker 2:** He didn't really like any of the subjects.
>
> **Speaker 3:** He liked English and maths, but hated geography and PE. He enjoyed quite a lot of subjects.
>
> **Speaker 4:** She liked all the subjects, especially English and history.
>
> **Speaker 5:** She hated PE.
>
> **Speaker 6:** She really liked maths and biology.

EXTRA SUPPORT If there's time, you could get Sts to listen again with the script on *p.125*, so they can see exactly what they understood / didn't understand. Translate / Explain any new words or phrases.

d Focus on the instructions and give Sts time to think about their answers.

e Put Sts in small groups of three and get them to tell each other about their answers to **d**.

Get some feedback from various groups. You could also tell the class whether you used to like school.

Help! I can't decide!

G *might*
V word building: noun formation, e.g. *decide – decision*
P diphthongs

Lesson plan

This lesson presents the modal verb *might*, used to express possibility through the context of a person who is very indecisive. The lesson begins with Speaking, where Sts interview each other to find out whether they are indecisive. In the Grammar Bank, Sts see that *may* is an alternative to *might*. Although both forms are common, in oral practice Sts are asked simply to use *might*, in order to avoid confusion. Then in Pronunciation, Sts work on some common diphthongs. This is followed by a listening which asks whether there is too much choice in today's world. Finally, in Vocabulary and Speaking, Sts get some practice in word building (formation of nouns).

More materials
For teachers
Photocopiables
Grammar might / might not (possibility) *p.203*
Communicative I might…but I might not *p.248*
(instructions *p.215*)
For students
Workbook 11B
Online Practice 11B

OPTIONAL LEAD-IN (BOOKS CLOSED)

Write DECIDE on the board. Ask Sts what it means (= to think carefully about the different possibilities that are available and choose one of them) and which part of speech it is (verb, noun, etc.), and elicit that it's a verb. Ask where the stress is and mark it on the board (DECIDE).

Then ask *What's the noun from* decide? and elicit that it's *decision*. Teach / Elicit the phrase *make a decision*.
Then elicit / teach the adjective *decisive* and its meaning (it describes a person who can make decisions quickly), and then teach / elicit the opposite, *indecisive*.

1 GRAMMAR *might*

a Books open. Focus on the *Are you indecisive?* questionnaire and put Sts in pairs. If you didn't do the **Optional lead-in**, write INDECISIVE on the board and underline the stressed syllable. Go through the questions and make sure Sts understand the phrase *change your mind* (= make a decision and then change it). Tell them they are going to interview each other to find out who is the more indecisive of the two of them.

Give Sts time to interview each other. Monitor and encourage them to ask for / give more information, and to illustrate their answers with examples.

Get feedback from various pairs to find out which of them is more indecisive, and find out (with a show of hands) if the majority of the class is indecisive or decisive.

EXTRA IDEA You could get Sts to interview you first. Give as many examples as you can.

b 🔊 **11.8** Focus on the photo and the task, and elicit the vocabulary for all the things Sts can see in Nancy's suitcase. You could ask Sts what they think Brian might say that Nancy doesn't need to pack.

Play the audio once the whole way through.

Check answers.

1 trainers	**2** raincoat	**3** hairdryer	**4** two pairs of jeans

🔊 **11.8**

B = Brian, N = Nancy
B Have you finished packing? The taxi will be here in fifteen minutes.
N Er, nearly. I can't decide what to take.
B Well, hurry up. You don't need all that! You'll never close that suitcase. And we can only take fifteen kilos each.
N Yes, I know.
B You don't need your trainers. We're going to be on the beach most of the time!
N Yes, but I might go to the gym. There's one in the hotel.
B And why are you taking a raincoat? It's not going to rain in Greece in June.
N It might rain. It sometimes rains in the summer.
B What's that?
N It's my hairdryer.
B But the hotel will have a hairdryer.
N It might not have one. Hotels don't always have hairdryers. And I need it.
B And two pairs of jeans? We're only going to be there for a week.
N They're different styles. I'm not sure which ones I'll want to wear.
B You need to take some things out. Extra baggage costs a fortune. It's something like ten pounds per kilo.
N Yes, yes, I will. I promise.
B Well, hurry up. The traffic might be a bit slow because of the rain.
N I'll be ready in five minutes…
****
B The taxi's here.
N I've closed my case. Can you take it downstairs?
B I'm sure this is more than fifteen kilos.
N I think it'll be OK…

c Tell Sts they are going to listen again and they must write down the reasons Nancy gives for wanting to take each item mentioned in **b**.

Play the audio for Sts to listen and complete sentences 1–4.

Get Sts to compare with a partner, and then check answers.

1 I might **go to the gym**.
2 It might **rain**.
3 The hotel might not **have one**.
4 They're **different styles**.

d 🔊 **11.9** Tell the class Brian and Nancy are now at the airport. Sts must listen and answer the question *What happens?*.

Play the audio once the whole way through.

Get Sts to compare with a partner, and then play the audio again if necessary.

Check the answer.

> Nancy's suitcase is too heavy (17.5 kilos, and she can only take 15). They tell her to pay £25 extra. She tries to take some things out and put them in Brian's case.

🔊 **11.9**

BD = bag drop, B = Brian, N = Nancy

BD Can you put your case on the scales, please?
B Shall I help you?
N No, I'm fine.
BD That's seventeen and a half kilos. You can only take fifteen.
B I knew it. I told you it was too heavy.
BD You need to go to the window over there and pay for the extra two and a half kilos. That'll be twenty-five pounds.
N Twenty-five pounds? No, wait. Brian, I can put some things in your case. Yours was only ten kilos. Look, take this pair of jeans…and the hairdryer…and these books…and the raincoat…

e Do this as a whole-class activity.

> **2** a possibility

f Tell Sts to go to **Grammar Bank 11B** on *p.146*.

Grammar notes

Might and *may* are synonyms, but *might* is probably more frequent in spoken English, which is why the presentation focuses on this form. However, *may* is also commonly used, especially in writing, so it is important that this is pointed out to Sts.

At this level, *might* is taught more for recognition than production, as it is an example of 'late assimilation' language. In conversation, Sts are more likely to try to express the same idea in another way, e.g. by using *maybe*, *possibly*, or *It's possible*.

🔊 **11.10** Focus on the examples and play the audio for Sts to listen and repeat. Encourage them to copy the rhythm. Then go through the rules with the class.

Now focus on the **may / may not** box and go through it with the class.

Then focus on the exercises for **11B** on *p.147*. Sts do them individually or in pairs.

Check answers, getting Sts to read the full sentences.

> **a**
> **1** H **2** G **3** A **4** C **5** B **6** I **7** F **8** E
> **b**
> **1** She **might be** ill.
> **2** He **might be in a meeting**.
> **3** You **might not like it**.
> **4** I **might not have time**.
> **5** I **might have the pasta**.
> **6** It **might be cold** later.

Tell Sts to go back to the main lesson **11B**.

EXTRA SUPPORT If you think Sts need more practice, you may want to give them the **Grammar** photocopiable activity at this point.

g Focus on the task and the example in the speech bubbles. You could demonstrate the activity by answering a couple of the questions yourself.

Make sure Sts understand that they must give two possibilities each time and return the question with *What about you?*. Put Sts in pairs and get them to ask and answer the five questions.

Get some feedback from various pairs.

2 PRONUNCIATION diphthongs

Pronunciation notes

A diphthong is a combination of two vowel sounds which run together to produce a new sound. For example, the diphthong /ɪə/ is a combination of /ɪ/ and /ə/. There are eight diphthongs in English, which are all practised here.

a 🔊 **11.11** Look at the eight picture words and sounds, and tell Sts to listen to how they are pronounced. Or, you could elicit the ones you think Sts already know. Play the audio once for Sts to just listen.

🔊 **11.11**

1 bike /aɪ/
2 train /eɪ/
3 phone /əʊ/
4 chair /eə/
5 ear /ɪə/
6 tourist /ʊə/
7 owl /aʊ/
8 boy /ɔɪ/

Now play the audio again for Sts to listen and repeat each sound. Play again if necessary, concentrating especially on any sounds your Sts find more difficult to make.

b Tell Sts to look at all the words in each category and to find the odd word out, i.e. the one that doesn't have the same diphthong sound. Remind Sts that this kind of exercise is easier if they say the words aloud to themselves.

Get Sts to compare with a partner.

c 🔊 **11.12** Now play the audio for Sts to listen and check. Check answers.

> **1** since **2** key **3** trousers **4** fear **5** where **6** bus
> **7** throw **8** town

🔊 **11.12**

See words in Student's Book on *p.88*

Then play the audio, pausing after each line for Sts to listen and repeat.

d 🔊 **11.13** Tell Sts they are going to hear one sentence for each of the eight sounds in **b**. They must listen and repeat it.

Play the audio, pausing after each sentence for Sts to listen and repeat.

◉ 11.13
1 I might buy a white tie.
2 It may rain later.
3 We don't know where to go.
4 There's a hairdresser in the square.
5 Here's a really good idea for a souvenir.
6 The tourists are curious about Europe.
7 We're now in a small town in the south.
8 Those noisy boys are annoying me.

Then repeat the activity, eliciting responses from individual Sts.

 If these sounds are difficult for your Sts, it will help to show them the mouth position. You could model this yourself or use the the Sound Bank videos on the *Teacher's Resource Centre.*

3 LISTENING & SPEAKING identifying the main points in a talk

a Focus on the photos and the different styles of jeans, and make sure Sts know what they all are. Then put Sts in pairs or small groups to answer the questions.

Elicit some feedback from the class.

b ◉ 11.14 Focus on the task, but <u>don't</u> ask Sts their opinion as they will be giving it later. You might want to tell Sts that the speaker is American.

Play the audio once the whole way through.

Check the answer.

 Read through the script and decide if you need to pre-teach any new lexis before Sts listen.

Yes

◉ 11.14
(script in Student's Book on *p.125*)
Buying jeans isn't as easy as it used to be. Years ago, there was only one kind of jeans – probably Levi's. Nowadays, there are hundreds – different styles, different colours, different lengths, with buttons, with zips. There are so many options that you feel the perfect pair must be waiting for you somewhere…
And it isn't just jeans. In big supermarkets, we have to choose between thousands of products – my local supermarket has thirty-five different kinds of milk! When we're buying clothes or electrical gadgets, ordering a coffee in a café, looking for a hotel on a travel website, deciding which TV channel to watch, or even choosing a future partner on a dating website, we constantly have to choose from hundreds of possibilities.
People often think that being able to choose from a lot of options is a good thing. However, university researchers have discovered that too much choice is making us feel unhappy and dissatisfied. The problem is that we have so many options that we get stressed every time we have to make a decision, because we're worried about making the wrong one. Then when we choose one thing, we feel bad because we think we are missing other opportunities, and this makes us dissatisfied with what we've chosen.
Research also shows that we feel happier when we have less choice. In a study, Professor Mark Lepper at Stanford University found that people who tried six kinds of jam and then chose one felt happier with their choice than those who were offered twenty-four jams to taste.
But if all this choice is bad for us, what can we do about it? Professor Lepper suggests that we should try to relax when we have to decide what to buy. 'Don't take these choices too seriously or it will become stressful,' he says. 'If you pick a sofa from IKEA in thirty seconds, you'll feel better than if you spend hours researching sofas – because you won't know what you're missing.'

c Focus on the task and give Sts time to read the five main points and their options. Make sure Sts understand all the lexis.

Play the audio again.

Get Sts to compare with a partner, and then check answers.

 Get Sts to choose their answers before they listen again.

1 b **2** c **3** a **4** b **5** c

 If there's time, you could get Sts to listen again with the script on *p.125*, so they can see exactly what they understood / didn't understand. Translate / Explain any new words or phrases.

d Either put Sts in pairs or small groups and get them to discuss the two questions for each situation.

Get some feedback from the class.

 Do this as a whole-class activity.

4 VOCABULARY & SPEAKING word building: noun formation

Vocabulary notes
There are several ways of making nouns from verbs, but here we focus on the three most common endings: *-ion*, *-sion*, and *-ation*. More complicated for Sts is when the noun is a different word altogether – Sts learn six common examples here.

a Do this as a whole-class activity. Model and drill pronunciation of each word.

choose = verb   *choice* = noun
decide = verb   *decision* = noun

b Focus on the **Making nouns from verbs** box and go through it with the class.

Now focus on the chart, point out the two sections, and make sure Sts know all the nouns. Highlight the *-ion* ending and the spelling changes. Point out that the first one (*decide*) has been done for them, and get Sts to continue in pairs.

c ◉ 11.15 Play the audio for Sts to listen and check.
Check answers.

2 revise **3** confuse **4** invent **5** compete **6** educate
7 invite **8** pronounce **9** choose **10** advise **11** fly
12 live **13** die **14** succeed

Now get Sts to underline the stressed syllables in the verbs and nouns.

Check answers.

◀)) **11.15**

1	decide	decision
2	revise	revision
3	confuse	confusion
4	invent	invention
5	compete	competition
6	educate	education
7	invite	invitation
8	pronounce	pronunciation
9	choose	choice
10	advise	advice
11	fly	flight
12	live	life
13	die	death
14	succeed	success

2 re<u>vi</u>se, re<u>vi</u>sion   **3** con<u>fu</u>se, confusion   **4** invent, invention
5 compete, competition   **6** educate, education   **7** invite,
invitation   **8** pronounce, pronunciation   **9** choose, choice
10 advise, advice   **11** fly, flight   **12** live, life   **13** die, death
14 ucceed, success

Now you could ask Sts what the rule is for nouns which
end in *-ion*, *-sion*, and *-ation*.

With nouns ending in *-ion*, *-sion*, and *-ation*, the stressed syllable
is always the one before the ending.

Finally, play the audio one more time for Sts to listen and
repeat.

EXTRA CHALLENGE Give Sts some more verb prompts to
change into nouns, e.g. *celebrate – celebration, communicate
– communication*, etc.

d Focus on the task and give Sts time to complete questions
1–8 with nouns from **b**.

Get Sts to compare with a partner, and then check
answers.

1 decision   **2** invitation   **3** flight   **4** invention
5 competition   **6** advice   **7** life, death   **8** pronunciation

EXTRA SUPPORT Put Sts in pairs to complete the questions,
and then check as a class.

e Put Sts in pairs and get them to ask and answer the
questions in **d**. Tell them to give as much information as
possible or to ask for more information.

Get some feedback from various pairs.

G *so, neither* + auxiliaries
V similarities and differences
P /ð/ and /θ/

Lesson plan

The topic of this lesson is twins. The lesson begins with Reading and Listening about a website called *Twin Strangers*, which helps you find your lookalike anywhere in the world. The vocabulary focus is on different words / phrases used to express similarity, and the structure *So am I / Neither am I* is presented in Grammar through the true case of identical twins who were separated at birth, but reunited 40 years later. The pronunciation focus is on the two possible pronunciations of *th*, /ð/ as in *neither*, and /θ/ as in *both*. The lesson ends with a speaking activity in which Sts first complete some sentences so they are true about themselves, and then they try to find a classmate like them. At this level, Sts will find it hard to manipulate this structure with much fluency, so here they just practise using the present forms *So am / do I* and *Neither am / do I*.

More materials
For teachers
Photocopiables
Grammar so, neither + auxiliaries *p.204*
Communicative So do I! *p.249 (instructions p.215)*
For students
Workbook 11C
Online Practice 11C

OPTIONAL LEAD-IN (BOOKS CLOSED)

Draw a picture of a head on the board with as many facial features as possible, e.g. face, eyes, nose, mouth, hair, lips.

Then elicit these words from Sts and write them on the board.

1 READING & LISTENING understanding similarities and differences

a Books open. Focus on the instructions and photos. Make sure Sts know the meaning of *identical twins* and *complete strangers*.

With a show of hands, find out which photo Sts think is of identical twins. <u>Don't</u> tell them if they are right.

b Tell Sts to read about a project called Twin Strangers and check their answer to **a**. Point out the **Glossary**.

Get Sts to compare with a partner, and then check the answer.

EXTRA SUPPORT Before Sts read the article the first time, check whether you need to pre-teach any vocabulary.

Photo 2 – Thomas and Toby

c Before Sts read the article again, tell them that the Irish name *Niamh* is pronounced /ˈniːv/. Explain that *to set up a website / business*, etc. means *to start it*.

Now tell Sts to read the article again and answer the two questions.

Check answers.

It was set up by Niamh Geaney and two friends.
What was surprising was that one of the twins Niamh found is Italian.

Deal with any other new vocabulary. Model and drill the pronunciation of any tricky words.

d 🔊 **11.16** Focus on the task and make sure Sts understand the situation.

Play the audio once the whole way through for Sts to listen and answer the two questions.

Get Sts to compare with a partner, and then check answers.

EXTRA IDEA If you didn't do the **Optional lead-in**, you could do it here before Sts listen.

EXTRA SUPPORT Read through the script and decide if you need to pre-teach any new lexis before Sts listen.

Yes, Maggie found someone who looked very like her.
It was a strange feeling, but she's happy she found her 'twin'.

🔊 **11.16**
(script in Student's Book on p.125)
I went onto the *Twin Strangers* website. All you have to do is pay three dollars ninety-five, upload a photo of your face, and then describe it – your nose, mouth, and eyes. I looked in a mirror and decided that I have an oval face, blue eyes, and, unfortunately, thin lips.
Immediately, I got a lot of photos of possible matches. My first reaction was, 'They all look totally different from me.' Then something interesting began to happen. Some of the people started to look familiar, like people in my family. I found one woman who looked just like my brother. I started to wonder. Was there something there?
I called my husband to come and have a look at all these 'twins'. His first reaction was the same as mine, but then he went a bit quiet. He pointed to one woman who, at first sight, looks completely different from me, but whose picture I had stopped at several times. He said, 'She has the same mouth as you. In fact, she's a bit like you.' And he was right.
I decided to change my profile a bit. Many people tell me I look younger than I really am, so I put my age as ten years younger, and then searched again. The result was surprising. Suddenly, there seemed to be a number of women a bit like me. Especially one. I put her picture on my Facebook page and asked my friends what they thought. The first person to answer was my brother. 'Yes,' he wrote, 'she looks like you and our sister.'
It's a strange feeling. I keep looking at her picture. We're very similar, but not identical – for example, she has brown eyes, but mine are blue. But there's something there. Not just the blonde hair and the thin lips. There's something in her eyes that I recognize. It's a very strange feeling, but I'm really happy that I found her. I sent her a message through the website, but she hasn't replied yet. I'm going to keep trying. I want to know who she is.

e Tell Sts they are going to listen to Maggie again and need to answer questions 1–8.

Give Sts time to read the questions.

Now play the audio again.

Get Sts to compare with a partner, and then check answers.

1 She says 'I have an oval face, blue eyes and, unfortunately, thin lips.'
2 She thought they all looked totally different from her.
3 Her brother
4 Her husband thought one of the twins had the same mouth. Yes, she did.
5 She changed her age by making herself ten years younger.
6 He thought she looked like Maggie and their sister.
7 They both have blonde hair and thin lips.
8 No, they haven't. Maggie sent her a message, but she hasn't replied.

EXTRA SUPPORT If there's time, you could get Sts to listen again with the script on *p.125*, so they can see exactly what they understood / didn't understand. Translate / Explain any new words or phrases.

f Put Sts in pairs and get them to discuss the questions.

Get some feedback from various pairs. You could tell the class your answers, too.

2 VOCABULARY similarities and differences

a Here Sts learn some different ways of expressing similarities. Focus on the sentences about the people in **1**.

Get Sts to complete the gaps with words from the list.

b 11.17 Play the audio for Sts to listen and check.

Check answers.

1 both 2 identical 3 from 4 like 5 as 6 similar

11.17
1 Cordelia and Ciara were both on Erasmus scholarships.
2 The two girls looked identical.
3 The first photos Maggie looked at were totally different from her.
4 Maggie found one woman who looked just like her brother.
5 Her husband said, 'She has the same mouth as you.'
6 Maggie's 'twin' looks very similar to her.

EXTRA CHALLENGE You may also want to teach the rules for the position of *both*, i.e. before the main verb, but after *be* (like adverbs of frequency).

c Say the sentences about yourself. Encourage Sts to ask for more information.

Then give Sts a few moments to complete the sentences with a family word.

! For 4, they need to add other words, too. They can use the same family member more than once.

Put Sts in pairs to discuss their answers.

Get feedback by eliciting different sentences from various pairs.

3 GRAMMAR so, neither + auxiliaries

a Focus on the photo and ask Sts if the two men look similar. Elicit that they are twins.

Now focus on the instructions. Give Sts time to read the text and answer the questions.

Get Sts to compare with a partner, and then check answers.

1 They are (American) identical twins.
2 Because they were adopted by two different families when they were babies.
3 He decided to try to find his brother.
4 Six weeks

b 11.18 Either tell Sts to cover the conversation or get them to close their books. Tell Sts that the two men have a lot of things in common. They should listen to the conversation for at least three things.

Before playing the audio, you might want to tell Sts that *neither* can be pronounced /ˈnaɪðə/ or /ˈniːðə/, and that in this audio they will hear the American version /ˈniːðə/. Play the audio once the whole way through. Play again if necessary.

Elicit answers from the class onto the board. You may need to teach the word *both* here.

EXTRA CHALLENGE Tell Sts to try and hear as many things as possible that the men have in common.

Sts should mention three of these:
Both men have been married twice, they both have a son called James Allen, neither went to college, they were both terrible students, they both have a dog called Toy, they don't do any exercise, they own the same car (a Chevrolet), and they both drink Miller Lite beer.

11.18
A Hi! I'm Jim.
B So am I. Great to meet you. Sit down. Are you married, Jim?
A Yes…well, I've been married twice.
B Yeah? So have I. Do you have any children?
A I have one son.
B So do I. What's his name?
A James Allen.
B That's amazing! My son's name is James Allen, too!
A Did you go to college, Jim?
B No, I didn't.
A Neither did I. I was a terrible student.
B So was I. Hey, this is my dog, Toy.
A I don't believe it! My dog's called Toy, too!
B He wants to go outside. My wife usually takes him. I don't do any exercise at all.
A Don't worry. Neither do I. I drive everywhere.
B What car do you have?
A A Chevrolet.
B So do I!
A and B Let's have a beer, Jim.
A What beer do you drink?
B Miller Lite.
A So do I!

c Get Sts to look at the conversation. Tell them to listen again and to complete the gaps in the conversation. Play the audio once and then play it again if necessary.

Get Sts to compare with a partner, and then check answers.

1 am 2 have 3 do 4 did 5 was 6 do 7 do 8 do

Finally, ask Sts which coincidence they find the most surprising.

d Focus on the instructions and put Sts in pairs. Give them time to answer the questions.

Check answers.

1 + So am I, So have I, So was I, So do I
   - Neither did I, Neither do I
2 The auxiliary verb changes to follow the tense or form used
   by the first speaker.

e Tell Sts to go to **Grammar Bank 11C** on *p.146*.

11.19 Focus on the example sentences and play the
audio for Sts to listen and repeat. Encourage them to copy
the rhythm. Then go through the rules with the class.

Now focus on the **neither and nor** box and go through it
with the class.

Then focus on the exercises for **11C** on *p.147*. Sts do them
individually or in pairs.

Check answers, getting Sts to read the full sentences.

a
1 am 2 did 3 was 4 do 5 have 6 can 7 would
8 did 9 would 10 can
b
1 So do I. 2 Neither am I. 3 So did I. 4 Neither have I.
5 Neither do I. 6 So can I. 7 So will I. 8 So am I.

Tell Sts to go back to the main lesson **11C**.

EXTRA SUPPORT If you think Sts need more practice, you
may want to give them the **Grammar** photocopiable
activity at this point.

f **11.20** Focus on the instructions and the example. Explain
that Sts are going to hear a sentence and they have to use
So…I or *Neither…I* to say that they are the same. You might
want to stress that Sts mustn't think about themselves, but
simply answer so that they agree with the speaker.

Play the audio, pausing after the first sentence to elicit
So do I from the whole class. Continue, pausing the audio
after each sentence to elicit a response.

11.20
1 I catch the bus to work. (*pause*) So do I.
2 I like chocolate. (*pause*) So do I.
3 I'm happy. (*pause*) So am I.
4 I'm not angry. (*pause*) Neither am I.
5 I don't like football. (*pause*) Neither do I.
6 I'm going out tonight. (*pause*) So am I.
7 I have a big family. (*pause*) So do I.
8 I'm not English. (*pause*) Neither am I.
9 I live in a flat. (*pause*) So do I.

Then repeat the activity, eliciting responses from individual Sts.

EXTRA SUPPORT Write SO ______ I and NEITHER ______ I on
the board for Sts to focus on.

4 PRONUNCIATION /ð/ and /θ/

a **11.21** Focus on the two sound pictures, *mother* /ð/
and *thumb* /θ/, and play the audio once for Sts just to
listen to the sounds and words. Encourage Sts to try to
approximate the *th* sound as far as possible, and to hear
the difference between the voiced sound /ð/ and the
unvoiced sound /θ/, although they may find this quite
difficult.

11.21
See sounds and words in Student's Book on *p.91*

Then play the audio again, pausing for Sts to listen and
repeat the words and sounds.

b **11.22** Tell Sts they are going to hear four words with
the *mother* sound and then four with the *thumb* sound.
They must listen and write the words.

Play the audio for Sts to listen and write.

Check answers by eliciting the words onto the board.

11.22
mother /ð/ although, other, there, without
thumb /θ/ maths, thing, thirsty, through

Then play the audio again, pausing after each word or
group of words, and get Sts to repeat.

Put Sts in pairs and get them to practise saying the words.

EXTRA CHALLENGE Say some words for Sts to identify the
sound, /ð/ or /θ/.

EXTRA SUPPORT If these sounds are difficult for your Sts,
it will help to show them the mouth position. You could
model this yourself or use the the Sound Bank videos on the
Teacher's Resource Centre.

5 SPEAKING

a Focus on the instructions. Make sure Sts understand all
the categories in brackets, and give them a few minutes
to complete the sentences.

b Go through the instructions and focus on the speech
bubbles. Demonstrate by going to different Sts and saying
I love (whatever kind of music you like) to individual Sts
until somebody says *So do I*. If they don't like it, encourage
them to say a whole sentence, e.g. *Really? I don't like it. / I
hate it.*

Tell Sts to stand up and start saying their sentences from
a to each other to find someone who is the same. Stop
the activity when one student has a name for all his / her
sentences.

Get some feedback from the class.

Function on the phone

Lesson plan

In this final Practical English lesson Sts learn some vocabulary related to phoning, leaving messages, and responding to news.

Rob and Jenny are depressed that his stay in New York is coming to an end. Rob goes off to do his last interview. Meanwhile, Barbara is trying to get hold of him. Rob gets her message, and tries to phone her back, but has problems getting through. In the final scene, Rob and Jenny meet in Central Park. They both have news for each other. Jenny tells hers first – she has sent Barbara an email to say she is resigning as she wants to move to London. However, Rob's news is that Barbara has offered him a permanent job in New York, which he has accepted. Jenny desperately phones Barbara and tells her not to open the email, and all ends well. They have a future in New York.

The story is continued in New York in *English File Intermediate*.

More materials
For teachers
Teacher's Resource Centre
Video Practical English Episode 6
Quick Test 11
File 11 Test
For students
Workbook Practical English 6
Can you remember...? 1–11
Online Practice Practical English 6
Check your progress

OPTIONAL LEAD-IN (BOOKS CLOSED)

Elicit what happened in the last episode by asking some questions, e.g. *How did Rob get to his date with Jenny? Did they have a good meal at the restaurant?*, etc.

Alternatively, you could play the last scene of Episode 5.

1 ▶ ROB AND JENNY TALK ABOUT THE FUTURE

a ◀)) 11.23 Books open. Focus on the photo and elicit what Sts think Jenny and Rob are talking about.

Focus on sentences 1–6 and go through them with Sts.

Then play the video / audio once the whole way through for them to mark the sentences *T* (true) or *F* (false). Make it clear that they don't need to correct the *F* sentences yet. Play again if necessary.

Get Sts to compare with a partner, and then check answers.

1 F	2 F	3 T	4 F	5 T	6 F

◀)) 11.23

J = Jenny, R = Rob, B = Barbara

J I can't believe it. Your month here is nearly over. It's gone so fast.
R I know. I've had a great time, Jenny.
J Me too. It's been really special. But…
R But what?
J It won't be the same when you're in London and I'm here.
R But we'll still be in touch. You can visit me in London and I can come back here to see you.
J It still won't be the same.
R No. No, it won't.
J Maybe…I could come back to London with you?
R You can't do that, Jenny. You've just got this job.
J That's true.
R Well, we still have some time together. We're going out for dinner tonight!
J Yes, and I'm going to take you somewhere really nice.
R Look at the time. I have to go now; it's my last interview in New York. I don't want to be late.
J OK. See you later, then.
R Bye.
***
B Jenny, is Rob here?
J Oh, you just missed him, Barbara.
B I really need to talk to him. I'll try him on his cell phone… (*on the phone*) Hello, Rob? It's Barbara. Can you give me a call? There's something I'd like to talk about.

Now focus on the **British and American English** box and go through it with the class.

b Play the video / audio again so Sts can watch or listen and correct the false sentences.

Get Sts to compare with a partner, and then check answers.

1	Rob is going home **soon**.
2	He says Jenny can visit London and he can come back to New York.
4	He **doesn't think** it's a good idea.
6	Barbara wants to talk to **Rob**.

Ask Sts what they think Barbara wants to talk about, and elicit ideas, but don't tell them the answer yet.

EXTRA SUPPORT If there's time and you are using the video, you could get Sts to watch again with subtitles, so they can see exactly what they understood / didn't understand. Translate / Explain any new words or phrases.

2 ▶ ON THE PHONE

a ◀ **11.24** Focus on the photos and elicit what Sts think is happening.

Focus on the instructions and the two questions. Alternatively, you could get Sts to close their books, and write the questions on the board.

Play the video / audio once the whole way through.

Get Sts to compare with a partner, and play the video / audio again if necessary.

Check answers.

1 He wants to speak to Barbara.   **2** He has to call three times.

◀ **11.24 11.25**
M = man, R = Rob, Re = receptionist, B = Barbara
M Hello. Broadway Grill.
R Oh, sorry. I have the wrong number. *(repeat)*
***
Re *NewYork 24seven.* How can I help you?
R Hello. Can I speak to Barbara Keaton, please? *(repeat)*
Re Just a second. I'll put you through…Hello.
R Hi, is that Barbara? *(repeat)*
Re No, I'm sorry. She's not at her desk right now.
R Can I leave a message, please? *(repeat)*
Re Sure.
R Can you tell her Rob Walker called? *(repeat)* I'll call back later. *(repeat)*
Re I'll give her the message. You could try her cell phone.
R Yes, I'll do that. Thank you. *(repeat)*
***
B I'm sorry, I can't take your call at the moment. Please leave a message after the beep.
R Hello, Barbara. This is Rob, returning your call. *(repeat)*
***
Re *NewYork 24seven.* How can I help you?
R Hello. It's Rob again. *(repeat)* Can I speak to Barbara, please? *(repeat)*
Re Just a second…I'm sorry, the line's busy. Do you want to hold?
R OK, I'll hold. *(repeat)*
B Hello.
R Hi, Barbara. It's me, Rob. *(repeat)*
B Rob, hi! I tried to call you earlier.
R What did you want to talk about? *(repeat)*

b Now focus on the conversation in the chart. Ask Sts *Who says the* **You hear** *sentences in each conversation?* and elicit that first it is a man working in a restaurant, then the receptionist at *NewYork24seven*, and, finally, Barbara.

Then ask *Who says the* **You say** *sentences?* and elicit that it is Rob. Tell Sts that if they want to make a call, they will need the **You say** phrases.

Give Sts a minute to read through the conversation and think what the missing words might be. Then play the video / audio again, and get Sts to complete the gaps. Play again if necessary.

Get Sts to compare with a partner, and then check answers.

1 How   **2** put   **3** desk   **4** message   **5** call   **6** leave
7 busy

Go through the conversation line by line with Sts, helping them with any words or expressions they don't understand.

c ◀ **11.25** Now focus on the **You say** phrases. Tell Sts they're going to hear the conversation again. They should repeat the **You say** phrases when they hear the beep.

Play the video / audio, pausing if necessary for Sts to repeat the phrases. Encourage them to copy the rhythm and intonation.

◀ **11.25**
Same as script 11.24 with repeat pauses

---

d Put Sts in pairs, **A** and **B**. Tell Sts **A** to read the part of the man, the receptionist, and Barbara, and Sts **B** to read Rob. In pairs, Sts read the conversation aloud.

Then make sure **A** and **B** swap roles.

e Sts now role-play the same conversations, but this time, the person taking the part of Rob closes his / her book and does it from memory.

f Sts swap roles when they have finished.

You could get some pairs to perform in front of the class.

3 ▶ IN CENTRAL PARK AGAIN

a ◀ **11.26** Focus on the photo and ask Sts what's happening.

Get Sts to focus on the question, or get them to close their books, and write it on the board.

Play the video / audio once the whole way through and then check the answer.

It's a happy ending.

◀ **11.26**
R = Rob, J = Jenny
R Jenny!
J Rob! I have something to tell you.
R I have something to tell you, too. You go first.
J Well, I thought again about moving to London…
R But you don't need to move to London.
J What?
R Barbara called me earlier.
J What about?
R She offered me a job. Here, in New York!
J What?! Oh, that's great news.
R You don't seem very pleased.
J I am. I mean, it's great! It's just that…
R What?
J I sent Barbara an email this morning.
R And?
J I told her I was quitting and moving to London.
R Don't worry. Maybe she hasn't read your email yet.
J I'll call her.
B Hello, Barbara Keaton.
J Barbara? It's Jenny.
B Oh, hi, Jenny.
J Um, have you read your emails recently? There's one from me.
B Oh, yes. I can see it. I haven't opened it yet.
J Don't open it! Delete it! Please just delete it. I'll explain later.
B OK. It's gone. Is everything all right, Jenny?
J Yes, thanks. Never better.

b Focus on the questions and give Sts time to read them.

Play the video / audio once the whole way through.

Get Sts to compare with a partner, and then play again if necessary.

Check answers.

1 They both have news.
2 Barbara offered Rob a job in New York.
3 She sent Barbara an email. She quit her job.
4 Jenny asks Barbara to delete her email.

 If there's time and you are using the video,
you could get Sts to watch again with subtitles, so they
can see exactly what they understood / didn't understand.
Translate / Explain any new words or phrases.

c Focus on the **Social English** phrases. In pairs, get Sts to
see if they can remember any of the missing words.

 In pairs, get Sts to complete the phrases
before they listen.

d ◑ **11.27** Play the video / audio for Sts to watch or listen
and complete the phrases.

Check answers. If you know your Sts' L1, you could get
them to translate the phrases.

1 go   **2** news   **3** call   **4** later   **5** all right   **6** Never

---

◑ **11.27**
1 You go first.
2 That's great news.
3 I'll call her.
4 I'll explain later.
5 Is everything all right?
6 Never better.

Now play the video / audio again, pausing after each
phrase, for Sts to watch or listen and repeat.

e Focus on the instructions and make sure Sts understand
what they have to do.

Get Sts to compare with a partner, and then check
answers.

A 3   **B** 4   **C** 5   **D** 2   **E** 6   **F** 1

Now put Sts in pairs and get them to practise the
conversations.

Finally, focus on the **CAN YOU…?** questions and ask Sts
if they feel confident they can now do these things. If
they feel that they need more practice, tell them to go to
Online Practice to watch the episode again and practise
the language.

12A Unbelievable!

G past perfect
V time expressions
P the letter *i*

Lesson plan

In this lesson the past perfect is presented through the context of strange but true stories from around the world. The lesson begins with Reading and Vocabulary, where Sts read three stories and sequence the events in the stories in the correct order. They also study time expressions in the stories. In Grammar, a sentence from one of the stories is used to present the past perfect. In Pronunciation, Sts look at two pronunciations of the letter *i* and learn some spelling and pronunciation rules. The lesson finishes with Speaking, where Sts read two more strange but true stories, and re-tell them to each other.

More materials
For teachers
Photocopiables
Grammar past perfect *p.205*
Communicative What had happened? *p.250*
(instructions *p.216*)
For students
Workbook 12A
Online Practice 12A

OPTIONAL LEAD-IN (BOOKS CLOSED)

Revise irregular past participles by saying a verb from the **Irregular verbs** list on *p.164* and eliciting the past simple and past participle.

Then ask Sts *When do you use past participles?* and elicit in the present perfect (with *have*) and the passive (with *be*). Now tell Sts they're going to learn another form where the past participle of the verb is used.

1 READING & VOCABULARY understanding the order of events; time expressions

a Books open. Focus on the pictures and headlines, and elicit some ideas about the stories from the class. <u>Don't</u> tell them if they are right.

b Now tell Sts to read the stories and match them to the headlines. Point out the **Glossary**.

Get Sts to compare with a partner, and then check answers, making sure Sts understand the meaning of each headline.

EXTRA SUPPORT Before Sts read the stories, check whether you need to pre-teach any vocabulary, but <u>not</u> the time expressions in **d**.

Story 1 False alarm
Story 2 In the post
Story 3 Left behind

c Tell Sts to read the stories again and then put the events in each story in the correct order. Point out that the first one in *Story 1* has been done for them.

Get Sts to compare with a partner, and then check answers.

Story 1
2 The man killed the spider.
3 The police arrived at the apartment.
4 The man explained what had happened.
Story 2
1 Julie lost her cat.
2 Julie put up posters.
3 The cat jumped out of the box.
4 The vet contacted Julie.
Story 3
1 Walter went to the toilet.
2 Claudia went into the shop.
3 Walter got back into the car and drove off.
4 Walter realized what had happened.

d Tell Sts to look at the stories and find the time expressions to complete sentences 1–5.

Get Sts to compare with a partner, and then check answers.

1 immediately   2 suddenly   3 straight away   4 Meanwhile
5 eventually

e Get Sts to match the time expressions in **d** with definitions 1–4.

Check answers.

1 suddenly   2 eventually   3 meanwhile
4 immediately, straight away

Deal with any other new vocabulary, making sure especially that Sts understand *notice* and *realize* in the third story, as these are verbs often followed by the past perfect, which they are about to focus on. Model and drill the pronunciation of any tricky words.

Finally, ask Sts which of the three stories they liked best.

2 GRAMMAR past perfect

a Focus on the sentence and get Sts to number the sentences, or do it as a whole-class activity.

Check answers.

1 Walter drove 100 kilometres.
2 Walter realized his wife wasn't in the car.

b Do this as a whole-class activity and elicit answers. Some Sts may think that it is the contraction of *would*. Point out that this is impossible as *would* is followed by the infinitive, not the past participle. Explain that this form (*had* + past participle) is called the past perfect.

'd is a contraction of *had*; *driven* is a past participle.

c Give Sts time to look for two more examples of the past perfect in each story. You could tell Sts that stories 2 and 3 have a lot of examples, but they only need to underline two in each.

Get Sts to compare with a partner, and then check answers.

d Tell Sts to go to **Grammar Bank 12A** on *p.148*.

12.1 Focus on the example sentences and play the audio for Sts to listen and repeat. Encourage them to copy the rhythm. Then go through the rules with the class.

Now focus on the ***had or would?*** box and go through it with the class.

Then focus on the exercises for **12A** on *p.149*. Sts do them individually or in pairs.

Check answers, getting Sts to read the full sentences.

Tell Sts to go back to the main lesson **12A**.

EXTRA SUPPORT If you think Sts need more practice, you may want to give them the **Grammar** photocopiable activity at this point.

e Give Sts time to complete the five sentences with their own ideas. Make sure they use the past perfect.

f Put Sts in pairs and get them to compare their sentences with a partner.

Get some Sts to read their sentences to the class.

g Put Sts in pairs, **A** and **B**, and tell them to go to **Communication What had happened?, A** on *p.106*, **B** on *p.112*.

Demonstrate the activity by writing in large letters on a piece of paper the following sentence:

I WASN'T VERY HAPPY BECAUSE MY BOYFRIEND HAD EATEN ALL THE BISCUITS.

Don't show the piece of paper to the Sts yet. Then write on the board:

I WASN'T VERY HAPPY BECAUSE MY BOYFRIEND _____________ ALL THE BISCUITS. +

Tell Sts that what's missing is a positive form of a verb in the past perfect. Tell them that they must guess the exact sentence that you have written on the piece of paper. Elicit ideas. If they are wrong, say *Try again*, until someone says the correct answer. Then show them your piece of paper with the sentence on it.

Tell Sts to look at instruction **a**. Give them a few minutes to think of how to complete their sentences in a logical way, and remind them not to write anything yet. Explain that their partner has the same sentences already completed and the idea is to try and complete the sentences in the same way. Emphasize, too, that they must use a verb in the past perfect. Monitor and help while they are doing this.

Now tell Sts to look at instruction **b**. **A** must read out his / her first sentence and **B** tells him / her if he / she has completed the sentence correctly. If not, **A** has to guess again. When the guess is correct, **A** writes the answer in the gap.

When **A** finishes, **B** reads his / her sentences to **A**, etc.

Tell Sts to go back to the main lesson **12A**.

3 PRONUNCIATION the letter *i*

a Focus on the box **The letter *i*** and go through it with the class.

Now focus on the activity and elicit the two sounds and words, *bike* /aɪ/ and *fish* /ɪ/.

Give Sts two minutes to put the words in the correct row.

Get Sts to compare with a partner.

b **12.2** Play the audio for Sts to listen and check.

Check answers.

fish /ɪ/ driven, kill, miracle, notice, signal
bike /aɪ/ alive, arrive, outside, spider, surprise, survive, while, wife

Now ask Sts which two words in the /ɪ/ row don't follow the rules.

driven and *notice* are exceptions

Play the audio again for Sts to listen and repeat.

Then play the audio again, eliciting responses from individual Sts.

Finally, put Sts in pairs and get them to practise saying the words.

EXTRA SUPPORT If these sounds are difficult for your Sts, it will help to show them the mouth position. You could model this yourself or use the the Sound Bank videos on the *Teacher's Resource Centre*.

4 SPEAKING

a Focus on the instructions and the pictures. Make sure Sts know *shark*, *waves*, and *a luggage belt*.

Then either put Sts in pairs to discuss what they think the stories are about, or do it as a whole-class activity.

If Sts worked in pairs, elicit some ideas from the class. <u>Don't</u> tell Sts if they are right.

b Put Sts in pairs, **A** and **B**, and tell them to go to **Communication Two more stories**, **A** on *p.107*, **B** on *p.112*.

Go through the instructions with them carefully.

Give Sts time to read their stories and answer the questions. Monitor and check their answers while they do this, to make sure they are answering the questions correctly.

Student A
1 The swimming pool was in Sydney, close to the sea; it was outdoors.
2 The pool assistant shouted, 'Get out…' because there was a shark in the pool.
3 A large wave had carried the shark into the pool.
4 No one was hurt. The shark was put back into the sea.

Student B
1 The airport was in Stockholm, in Sweden.
2 The airport workers were surprised because they saw an old lady on the luggage belt.
3 She had got on the luggage belt with her suitcase because she was confused.
4 She only travelled a few metres.

When they are ready, sit **A** and **B** face-to-face. **A** tells his / her story to **B**. Then **B** tells **A** his / her story.

Tell Sts to go back to the main lesson **12A**.

c Ask the questions to the class and elicit opinions and any stories they may have heard.

G reported speech
V *say* or *tell*?
P double consonants

Lesson plan

This lesson provides a clear introduction to reported (or indirect) speech. Sts simply learn to deal with reported statements – reported questions are taught in *English File* Intermediate. The context for the lesson is the topic of gossiping. The lesson begins with Listening, where Sts listen to a conversation between two elderly women who are gossiping about a conversation one of them overheard between a young couple, Jack and Emma, who live next door. However, Sts find out later that she had completely misunderstood what she heard, as often happens! The grammar section presents reported speech by contrasting what Emma actually said with how the woman reported it to her friend. After practising the grammar, in Vocabulary, Sts focus on how *say* and *tell* are used, and in Speaking, they practise reporting what other Sts have said. Pronunciation focuses on how double consonants are pronounced, and the effect they have on the preceding vowel sound. The lesson finishes with a traditional story about the harmful effect of gossip, and Sts talk about the subject.

More materials
For teachers
Photocopiables
Grammar reported (or indirect) speech *p.206*
Communicative The celebrity interview *p.251*
(instructions *p.216*)
For students
Workbook 12B
Online Practice 12B

OPTIONAL LEAD-IN (BOOKS CLOSED)

Write the word GOSSIP on the board. Elicit the meaning and tell Sts that it's a noun and a verb.

Ask Sts *Who do people often gossip about? How do you feel when people gossip about you?* Elicit ideas and opinions. You could also tell them what you think.

1 LISTENING

a Focus on the question and picture, and elicit some ideas from the class.

b ◀) **12.3** Focus on the instructions.

Now play the audio once the whole way through. Play it again if necessary.

Get Sts to compare with a partner, and then check answers.

EXTRA SUPPORT Read through the scripts and decide if you need to pre-teach any new lexis before Sts listen.

Jack and Emma are Rosemary's neighbours. They have broken up.

◀) **12.3**
(script in Student's Book on *p.125*)
I = Iris, R = Rosemary
I Hello, Rosemary. How are you this morning?
R Hello, Iris. I'm fine, thanks, but you'll never guess what's happened. Jack and Emma have broken up!
I No! Jack and Emma from number thirty-six? That can't be true. I saw them last week and they looked really happy.
R No, it's definitely true. I heard them shouting. They were having a terrible argument.
I No! When?
R Last night. After he came home from work.
I What did they say?
R Well, I wasn't really listening…
I Of course not.
R But I couldn't help hearing. She was talking so loudly, and of course, the walls are very thin…
I So what did they say?
R Well, she said that she was going to stay with her mum! She told him that she wouldn't come back.
I Ooh, how awful. What about the children?
R She said she'd taken them to her sister's. I suppose she'll take them with her in the end. And anyway, then five minutes later I saw her leaving the house with a suitcase!
I No! Why do you think she's leaving him? Is he seeing another woman?
R I don't know. Ooh, here's my bus.
I I must go and tell Mrs Jones at number fourteen. She's always thought there was something…something strange about him.

c Now tell Sts they will hear the conversation again and they must answer questions 1–4. Give them a few minutes to read all the options.

Now play the audio the whole way through. Play it again if necessary.

Get Sts to compare with a partner, and then check answers.

1 a	2 c	3 b	4 c

d ◀) **12.4** Now tell Sts they are going to listen to what Jack and Emma really said when Rosemary overheard them. They must listen for any differences between what Rosemary told Iris and what Jack and Emma really said.

Play the audio once the whole way through. Play it again if necessary.

Get Sts to compare with a partner, and then check answers.

No, she wasn't. She either misunderstood a lot of what she heard, or only heard part of the conversation. In fact, Emma isn't leaving Jack; she's going to look after her mother, who has had an accident.

🔊 **12.4**
(script in Student's Book on *p.125*)
J = Jack, E = Emma
J   Hi, Emma. I'm back. Where are you?
E   I'm upstairs in the bedroom. I'm packing.
J   Why? Where are you going?
E   I'm going to stay with my mum.
J   Your mum? Why?
E   She's had an accident. She fell over in the street yesterday, and she's broken her leg.
J   How awful! Poor thing. Shall I go and make you a cup of tea?
E   That'd be lovely. Thanks, darling.
J   How long do you think you'll have to stay?
E   I won't come back until the weekend, I don't think.
J   Sorry, until when?
E   Until the weekend. I'll have to make sure she's OK. I've taken the children to my sister's for the night, and she'll take them to school tomorrow morning. Can you pick them up after school?
J   Of course I can, darling. Now don't worry about anything. We'll be absolutely fine. Drink your tea, and I'll go and get your suitcase.
E   Thanks, darling. The taxi'll be here in five minutes.

EXTRA CHALLENGE   Ask Sts some comprehension questions, e.g. *Why was Emma packing?* (to go and stay at her mother's), *Why was she going to her mother's?* (because her mother had broken her leg), etc.

EXTRA SUPPORT   If there's time, you could get Sts to listen again with the scripts on *p.125*, so they can see exactly what they understood / didn't understand. Translate / Explain any new words or phrases.

e   Put Sts in pairs and get them to discuss the questions.
Get some feedback from various pairs.

2 GRAMMAR & VOCABULARY reported speech; *say* or *tell*?

a   Focus on the instructions and the extracts. Give Sts time, in pairs, to underline the words that are different.
Check answers.

She said that <u>she</u> <u>was</u> going to stay with <u>her</u> mum.
She told him that <u>she</u> <u>wouldn't</u> come back.
She said <u>she'd</u> taken them to <u>her</u> sister's.

b   Tell Sts to go to **Grammar Bank 12B** on *p.148*.

Grammar notes

This is an introduction to reported (or indirect) speech. The reporting of sentences with *say* and *tell* is covered here, but not reported questions, e.g. *He asked me if I lived near here.*

When people report a past tense statement, they sometimes do not make the change to the past perfect, e.g.

Direct speech: *'I saw Jack at the party.'*

Reported speech: *Jane told me she saw / had seen Jack at the party.*

However, this may confuse Sts, who prefer to be given one rule, so you may not want to highlight it at this level.

Sts tend to confuse the verbs *say* and *tell*, and may try to use *say* with a person. A typical mistake is: ~~He said me that he was tired.~~

🔊 **12.5**   Focus on the example sentences and play the audio for Sts to listen and repeat. Encourage them to copy the rhythm. Then go through the rules with the class.

Now focus on the **say or tell?** box and go through it with the class.

Then focus on the exercises for **12B** on *p.149*. Sts do the exercises individually or in pairs.

Check answers, getting Sts to read the full sentences.

a
1   Ana said that she **was hungry**.
2   He said he **would call the doctor**.
3   Paul told us that he **had bought a new phone**.
4   She said that she **lived in the city centre**.
5   They said that they **couldn't do it**.
6   Julie said that she **had seen a great film at the cinema**.
7   Ben told her he **didn't like dogs**.
b
1   'I'm studying German.'
2   'My car has broken down.'
3   'I'll send you an email.'
4   'We're in a hurry.'
5   'I haven't finished my essay yet.'
6   'I won't arrive on time.'
7   'I've just arrived in London.'

Tell Sts to go back to the main lesson **12B**.

EXTRA SUPPORT   If you think Sts need more practice, you may want to give them the **Grammar** photocopiable activity at this point.

c 🔊 **12.6**   Focus on the instructions and examples. Tell Sts that they must begin the sentences with *He said that* or *She said that*, depending on whether they hear a male voice or a female voice. Do the first two as a class.

Play the audio, pausing after the direct speech sentence for the class to make the transformation into reported speech.

🔊 **12.6**
1   I'm in a hurry. (*pause*) She said that she was in a hurry.
2   I'll write. (*pause*) He said that he would write.
3   I didn't see it. (*pause*) She said that she hadn't seen it.
4   I'm hungry. (*pause*) He said that he was hungry.
5   I'll be late. (*pause*) She said that she would be late.
6   I've finished. (*pause*) He said that he had finished.
7   I'm coming. (*pause*) She said that she was coming.
8   I'll do it again. (*pause*) He said that he would do it again.
9   I had a great time. (*pause*) She said that she had had a great time.
10   I'm tired. (*pause*) He said that he was tired.

Then repeat the activity, eliciting responses from individual Sts.

d   Focus on the task and give Sts time to complete the sentences.

Get them to compare with a partner, and then check answers.

1 said   **2** told   **3** said   **4** told   **5** said   **6** tell   **7** say   **8** tell, say

3 SPEAKING

a Focus on the task. Give Sts a minute or so to think about their answers. Remind them that the information must be true, except for one answer which they must invent.

b Put Sts into pairs and give them time to interview each other. Remind Sts that the person listening must take some notes.

Make sure Sts swap roles.

c Get Sts to change partners, and explain that they must now tell their new partner what their first partner told them. To do this, they must change the information into reported speech.

Give Sts time to report their conversations to their new partners and to decide together which answer their previous partners invented.

EXTRA IDEA To help Sts to get the idea of the activity, begin by whispering a piece of real or invented gossip to one student. Then get the class to ask the student *What did he / she say?* Now encourage the student to report what you said, using reported speech.

d Then Sts should go back to their original partners and find out which answer they invented.

Get feedback by asking individual Sts to report one exchange.

4 PRONUNCIATION double consonants

Pronunciation notes

Here Sts learn two clear rules about double consonants.

Firstly, vowel sounds are normally short before a double consonant. This is the reason why we double the final consonant before adding *-er* in comparatives, and *-ed* in past tenses – that is, to maintain the short vowel sound.

Secondly, double consonants (e.g. *ss*, *rr*, etc.) are usually pronounced exactly the same as a single consonant, unlike in many other languages, where they are different.

a Tell Sts to look at the five vowel sound pictures and to match each one to a group of words 1–5.

b 🔊 **12.7** Play the audio for Sts to listen and check. Check answers.

1 /ɒ/ clock 2 /ʌ/ up 3 /ɪ/ fish 4 /æ/ cat 5 /e/ egg

🔊 **12.7**

4 cat /æ/ happy, married, accident, rabbit, baggage
2 up /ʌ/ hurry, rubbish, funny, summer, butterfly
3 fish /ɪ/ written, miss, bitten, different, middle
5 egg /e/ letter, leggings, message, umbrella, tennis
1 clock /ɒ/ gossip, offer, opposite, bottle, borrow

Play the audio again, pausing after each group of words for Sts to listen and repeat.

Put Sts in pairs and get them to practise saying the words.

c Focus on the **Double consonants** box and go through it with the class.

Tell Sts, in pairs, to try to pronounce the words in the list. Then they should look them up and find out how to pronounce them and what they mean.

Check answers.

kettle /ˈketl/ = a kitchen appliance used for boiling water
nanny /ˈnæni/ = a person who takes care of young children in the children's own home
pillow /ˈpɪləʊ/ = a piece of cloth filled with soft material, e.g. feathers, used to rest your head on in bed
pottery /ˈpɒtəri/ = pots, dishes, etc. made with clay that is baked in an oven
supper /ˈsʌpə/ = the last meal of the day, either a main meal or a snack before you go to bed, sometimes used as an alternative to *dinner*

Still in pairs, Sts practise saying the words.

5 READING & SPEAKING recognizing text type

a This is a traditional story which exists in slightly different versions in many countries. Focus on the title and make sure Sts know what it means. Use the illustrations to teach the word *feather*.

Now tell Sts to read the text and answer the two questions.

Get Sts to compare with a partner, and then check answers.

EXTRA SUPPORT Before Sts read the story the first time, check whether you need to pre-teach any vocabulary.

It's b (a traditional story) because it starts with 'Once upon a time…', the characters have no names, and the time and place aren't specific.

b Focus on the task and make sure Sts know the meaning of the noun *moral* (= a practical lesson that a story teaches you).

Tell Sts to read the story again. Then ask Sts what they think the moral of the story is. Elicit ideas, but <u>don't</u> tell Sts if they are right.

Now tell Sts to go to **Communication Blowing in the wind** on *p.107*. Give Sts time to read the ending of the story.

Finally, ask Sts what the message of the story is.

The message is that gossip can't be controlled. It can travel a long way and do a lot of damage – so think before you speak.

Deal with any other new vocabulary. Model and drill the pronunciation of any tricky words.

Tell Sts to go back to the main lesson **12B**.

c Focus on the instructions and questions 1–7, making sure Sts understand all the lexis, e.g. *celebrity*, *spread*, etc.

Put Sts in pairs to discuss the questions.

Get some feedback from various pairs.

The *English File* quiz

G questions without auxiliaries
V revision of question words
P question words

Lesson plan

In this final lesson Sts learn to use questions without auxiliaries (*Who painted this picture?*, etc.) and contrast them with questions with auxiliaries (*When did he paint it?*).

The lesson begins with some revision of question words in Pronunciation and Vocabulary. The grammar is presented through a quiz which tests Sts' memory on information that has come up in the book. If your Sts have only used the second half of *English File* Pre-intermediate (i.e. Multipack B), they should just do the second half of the quiz, i.e. questions 8–15. Then in Speaking, Sts practise making questions with or without auxiliaries, and then ask and answer them with a partner. Finally, the lesson finishes with a video listening of a pub quiz, and Sts join in to answer the questions in teams.

More materials
For teachers
Photocopiables
Grammar questions with and without auxiliaries *p.207*
Communicative Hollywood quiz *p.252*
(instructions *p.216*)
Teacher's Resource Centre
Video Pub quiz
For students
Workbook 12C
Online Practice 12C

OPTIONAL LEAD-IN (BOOKS CLOSED)

Ask eight different Sts these questions and tell them to answer them. Tell the rest of the class to listen carefully and note down just the answers to the questions.

- *How did you get to class today?*
- *What's your favourite TV programme?*
- *When do you usually get up?*
- *Where would you like to go for your next holiday?*
- *Which do you prefer, coffee or tea?*
- *Who do you live with?*
- *Whose bag is that? (pointing to another student's bag)*
- *Why are you learning English?*

Then tell Sts that you asked eight questions with eight different question words. Tell them, in pairs, to look at the eight answers and try to write down the eight question words you used.

Then get Sts to open their books and check in **1a**.

1 PRONUNCIATION & VOCABULARY
revision of question words

a Books open. Now focus on the activity and elicit the two sounds and words, *witch* /w/ and *house* /h/.

Give Sts two minutes to put the words in the correct row. Get Sts to compare with a partner.

b 🔊 **12.8** Play the audio for Sts to listen and check. Check answers.

🔊 **12.8**
witch /w/ what, when, where, which, why
house /h/ how, who, whose

Play the audio again, pausing after each group of words for Sts to listen and repeat.

EXTRA CHALLENGE Elicit any other words beginning with *wh* that Sts know, e.g. *whale, whole, wheel, while*, and ask Sts how they are pronounced.

c Give Sts time to complete the questions with the question words from **a**.

Get Sts to compare with a partner, and then check answers.

1 How	**2** Who	**3** What	**4** How	**5** whose	**6** How
7 where	**8** When / What	**9** Which	**10** Why		

d Put Sts in pairs and get them to ask and answer the questions in **c**.

Get some feedback from various pairs.

2 GRAMMAR questions without auxiliaries

a Focus on the instructions and tell Sts that the questions in the quiz are based on lessons (Files 1–11) in the Student's Book.

Put Sts in pairs and set a time limit for them to answer as many questions as possible from memory. Tell Sts to use the pictures to help them. (See **Lesson plan** above if you are using Multipack B.)

b When the time limit is up, ask Sts how many questions they could answer from memory.

Now tell them that they must find the answers to the questions they couldn't answer by looking back at lessons in Files 1–11. Tell them not to look for the answers they have already given.

Check answers. Find out which pair(s) got the most answers correct.

EXTRA CHALLENGE You could do **2a** as a competition and when the time limit is up, find out which pair(s) got the most answers correct.

1 Vermeer **2** In his jacket pocket **3** An owl **4** A guided tour when you have a stopover at an airport **5** Because she didn't do the housework. **6** Helsinki **7** Murphy's Law **8** O. Henry **9** Wasps and bees **10** A fear of butterflies **11** Janet Leigh **12** Duncan Jones **13** Adolphe Sax **14** Snape **15** His twin brother

c Now tell Sts to only focus on the quiz and to answer questions 1–4.

Get Sts to compare with a partner, and then check answers.

> **1** Who
> **2** Stuart
> **3** In question 1, *painted* is the past simple form with no auxiliary. In question 2, we use the auxiliary *did* + the infinitive *find*.
> **4** Questions 6, 8, 11, 12, and 13 are similar.

Highlight that when the question word (usually *who* or *which*) is the subject of the sentence, QuASI (**Qu**estion word, **A**uxiliary verb, **S**ubject, **I**nfinitive) does not apply because the question word and the subject are the same.

d Tell Sts to go to **Grammar Bank 12C** on *p.148*.

Grammar notes

Sts will already have met questions without auxiliaries, e.g. *Who knows the answer?*, etc., but until now, this type of question has not been focused on.

Highlight that:

- the vast majority of questions in the past and present follow the **QuASI** rule.
- the only question words which can be the subject of a question, and may not need an auxiliary verb, are:
  Who…?, e.g. *Who wrote the song?*
  Which…?, e.g. *Which singer sang My Way?*
  What…?, e.g. *What happened?*
  How many / much…?, e.g. *How many students came?*
- questions beginning with *When, Why, Where, How long*, etc. always need an auxiliary.

◀)) **12.9** Focus on the example sentences and play the audio for Sts to listen and repeat. Encourage them to copy the rhythm. Then go through the rules with the class.

Now focus on the exercises for **12C** on *p.149*. Sts do the exercises individually or in pairs.

Check answers, getting Sts to read the full sentences.

> **a**
> **1** happened **2** does this word mean **3** came **4** goes
> **5** won **6** did the teacher say **7** made
> **b**
> **1** When **did Barack Obama become** president of the USA? (in 2008)
> **2** Which US state **starts** with the letter *H*? (Hawaii)
> **3** Which books **did George R.R. Martin write?** (*A Song of Ice and Fire, A Game of Thrones*, etc.)
> **4** Who **won** the football World Cup in Russia in 2018? (TBC)
> **5** Which sport **uses** the lightest ball? (ping-pong / table tennis)
> **6** Where **did the 2016 Olympics take place**? (Rio)
> **7** Which company **did Steve Jobs start**? (Apple Inc.)

Tell Sts to go back to the main lesson **12C**.

3 SPEAKING

Put Sts into pairs, **A** and **B**, and get them to sit face-to-face if possible. Tell them to go to **Communication General knowledge quiz**, **A** on *p.107*, **B** on *p.112*.

Focus on the instructions and make sure Sts are clear what they have to do. Remind Sts that the correct answer is the one in red. Highlight that all the questions in the quiz are questions <u>without</u> auxiliaries.

Give Sts time to complete their questions. Monitor and make sure Sts are forming the questions correctly.

> **Student A**
> **1** lost **2** starred **3** wrote **4** won **5** said **6** broke
> **7** cut **8** discovered
>
> **Student B**
> **1** became **2** played **3** became **4** painted **5** wrote
> **6** used **7** refused **8** invented

Now tell Sts **A** to ask their questions first. Highlight that they should give the three alternatives each time.

Then Sts swap roles.

Get feedback to see who got the most answers correct.

Tell Sts to go back to the main lesson **12C**.

4 ▶ VIDEO LISTENING

a Do this as a whole-class activity. Tell Sts if you have ever been on a quiz team and whether you enjoyed it.

b Focus on the task and put Sts in teams of three or four.

Now play the video for Sts to watch or listen and answer the questions in their teams.

Check answers.

> **Round 1 Sports**
> **1** Manchester United
> **2** ten
> **3** three
> **4** basketball
> **5** Roger Federer
> **Round 2 Music**
> **1** Chris Martin
> **2** Andrea Bocelli
> **3** four
> **4** Stockholm
> **5** Ludwig
> **Round 3 Geography**
> **1** Venice
> **2** The Amazon
> **3** Istanbul
> **4** Dublin
> **5** Venezuela

Pub quiz

Good evening, everyone! Welcome to this week's quiz. I hope you've got a drink and you're feeling confident. Here are a few rules as always.

You'll hear each question twice. Write your answers on your answer sheets, and remember: you mustn't use your phone to Google any of the answers! We might even get a fair result that way, who knows?! And lastly: please remember to write your team name on your answer sheets.

Right, everyone, round one – sports!

Question 1: Which English football team plays at Old Trafford?

[repeat]

2 How many events are there in the decathlon?

[repeat]

3 How many times did Usain Bolt win the Olympic 100 metres race?

[repeat]

4 Which is the biggest, a football, a volleyball, or a basketball?

[repeat]

5 Who won the men's singles at Wimbledon seven times between 2003 and 2012?

[repeat]

OK – next round…music.

Question 1: What's the name of the lead singer in the band Coldplay?

[repeat]

2 Which Italian opera singer became blind at the age of 12 after a football accident?

[repeat]

3 How many strings does a violin have?

[repeat]

4 In which country did the pop group Abba form in 1972?

[repeat]

5 What was Beethoven's first name?

[repeat]

And the final round is Geography.

Question 1: In which European city could you visit the Doge's Palace and St Mark's Square?

[repeat]

2 Which rainforest produces over 20% of the world's oxygen?

[repeat]

3 Which is the only city in the world that is in two separate continents?

[repeat]

4 What is the capital of the Republic of Ireland?

[repeat]

5 Angel Falls is the world's highest waterfall. Which country is it in?

[repeat]

OK, time for the answers. Swap your answer sheets please.

Here are the answers for Round 1: Sport

Which English football team plays at Old Trafford? Manchester United.

2 How many events are there in a decathlon? Ten.

3 How many times did Usain Bolt win the Olympic 100 metres race? Three.

4 Which is the biggest, a football, a volleyball, or a basketball? A basketball.

5 Who won the men's singles at Wimbledon seven times between 2003 and 2012? Roger Federer.

Music

Question 1: What's the name of the lead singer in the band Coldplay? Chris Martin.

2 Which Italian opera singer became blind at the age of 12 after a football accident? Andrea Bocelli.

3 How many strings does a violin have? Four.

4 In which country did the pop group Abba form in 1972? Sweden.

5 What was Beethoven's first name? Ludwig.

And finally…Geography.

Question 1: In which European city could you visit the Doge's Palace and St Mark's Square? Venice.

2 Which rainforest produces over 20% of the world's oxygen? The Amazon.

3 Which is the only city in the world that is in two separate continents? Istanbul.

4 What is the capital of the Republic of Ireland? Dublin.

5 Angel Falls is the world's highest waterfall. Which country is it in? Venezuela.

OK, add up the scores and bring the answer sheets to me…

OK, and the winners are…

EXTRA SUPPORT If there's time, you could get Sts to watch again with subtitles, so they can see exactly what they understood / didn't understand. Translate / Explain any new words or phrases.

For instructions on how to use these pages, see *p.40*.

More materials
For teachers
Teacher's Resource Centre
Video Can you understand these people? 11&12
Quick Test 12
File 12 Test
Progress Test Files 7–12
End-of-course Test
For students
Online Practice Check your progress

GRAMMAR

1 b 2 c 3 a 4 c 5 a 6 c 7 c 8 b 9 a 10 c
11 a 12 c 13 a 14 c 15 c

VOCABULARY

a
1 invention 2 decision 3 choice 4 invitation 5 death
b
1 literature 2 maths 3 geography 4 science (biology)
5 history
c
1 identical 2 as 3 similar 4 like 5 both
d
1 suddenly 2 Meanwhile 3 immediately 4 eventually
5 straight away
e
1 Tell 2 say 3 say 4 say 5 tell

PRONUNCIATION

c
1 ma**th**s /θ/ 2 **s**ure /ʊə/ 3 nei**th**er /ð/ 4 **f**ear /ɪə/
5 w**r**itten /r/
d
1 inde**ci**sive 2 i**d**entical 3 i**mme**diately 4 nei**gh**bour
5 a**cc**ident

CAN YOU understand this text?

a
They both happened in / near an airport.
b
1 T 2 F 3 T 4 F 5 F 6 T 7 T 8 F

▶ CAN YOU understand these people?

1 c 2 b 3 a 4 b 5 c

🔊 12.10
1
I = interviewer, M = Mark
I Did you like school?
M I loved school actually. Um, I think I preferred senior school more than junior school, but yeah, um, lots of friends, lots of, sort of sporting activities and things, so yeah, I loved it.
I What were your best and worst subjects?
M My best subject was probably mathematics. Um, loved mathematics and found I was, sort of, very capable at it, so it was quite easy. Um, I think it's one of those things that's natural. But, um, worst subject, maybe Latin. Never very good at languages even though I use them every day now, but never very, I like languages now but I hated them at school.

2
I = interviewer, C = Caroline
I Did you have a favourite or least favourite teacher at school?
C Um, let me think about that. Yes, I, um, liked the French teacher. She was probably my favourite, favourite teacher because, um, she was French and she taught us to speak with a very good French accent.
I Did she inspire you?
C She did, and I'm still learning French and go, I live in Australia, um, and I go to France every year and I go to French language schools.

3
I = interviewer, J = John
I Do you have a problem making decisions? What about?
J It depends what sort of decision it is. If it's a sort of instant decision, I make pretty good instant decisions, but the longer you think about them, then I probably decide, or try to decipher, which is the best decision. So, instant decisions is a better way for me.

4
I = interviewer, A = Alison
I Do you know any twins? Are they identical?
A Yes, I'm a twin myself. I have a twin brother. And my sister has got twin boys. They're aged 16 and they're not identical. They don't look very similar and they don't have similar personalities either.

5
I = interviewer, K = Kathy
I Who do you think gossips more, men or women? Why?
K I think stereotypic-, stereotypically people say women gossip more, um, but I actually think men gossip quite a lot as well. I think, I think men gossip more in a factual way, whereas women gossip more, maybe, in more of a personal, emotional way, so maybe in kind of a nastier way than what men do, I would say. But I would say that they probably gossip the same, or in a similar way.

Photocopiable activities

Overview

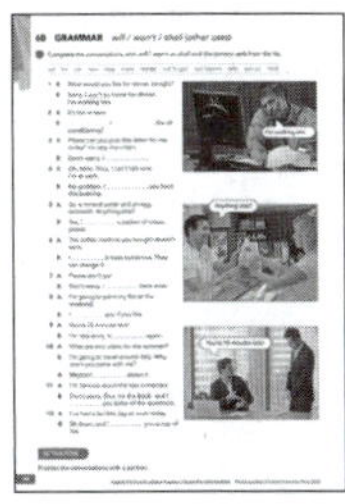  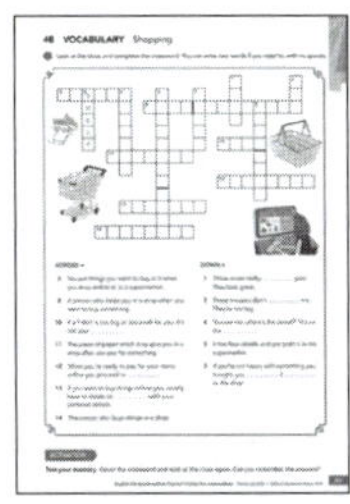

- There is a **Grammar activity** for each main (A, B, and C) lesson of the Student's Book.
- There is a **Communicative activity** for each main (A, B, and C) lesson of the Student's Book.
- There is a **Vocabulary activity** for each section of the Vocabulary Bank in the Student's Book.

All the photocopiable material is also available on the **Teacher's Resource Centre** (TRC). It is also available on the **Classroom Presentation Tool** (CPT), allowing you to display the worksheets on an interactive whiteboard or projector. This will make it easier to set up and demonstrate the activities, and show answers.

Using extra activities in mixed ability classes

Some teachers have classes with a very wide range of levels, and where some Sts finish Student's Book activities much more quickly than others. You could give these fast finishers a photocopiable activity (Grammar, Vocabulary, or Communicative) while you help the slower Sts. Alternatively, some teachers might want to give faster Sts extra oral practice with a communicative activity while slower Sts consolidate their knowledge with an extra grammar activity.

Tips for using Grammar activities

- The grammar activities are designed to give Sts extra practice in the main grammar points from each lesson. How you use these activities depends on the needs of your Sts and the time available. They can be used in the lesson if you think all of your class would benefit from the extra practice or you could set them as homework for some or all of your Sts.
- Before using the worksheets in class, check for any vocabulary that may be either new or difficult for your Sts.
- All of the activities start with a writing stage. If you use the activities in class, get Sts to work individually or in pairs. Allow Sts to compare before checking answers.
- If Sts are having trouble with any of the activities, make sure they refer to the relevant Grammar Bank in the Student's Book.
- All of the activities have an **Activation** section. Some of them have a task that gets Sts to cover the sentences and test their memory. If you are using the activities in class, Sts can work in pairs and test their partner. If you set them for homework, encourage Sts to use this stage to test themselves. Alternatively, you could set the main activity for homework and then get Sts to do the **Activation** at the start of the next class.

- Make sure that Sts keep their worksheets and that they review any difficult areas regularly. Encourage them to go back to activities and cover and test themselves.

Tips for using Communicative activities

- Before using the worksheets in class, check for any vocabulary that may be either new or difficult for your Sts.
- We have suggested the ideal number of copies for each activity. However, you can often manage with fewer, e.g. one worksheet per pair instead of one per student.
- When Sts are working in pairs, if possible get them to sit face-to-face. This will encourage them to really talk to each other and also means they can't see each other's worksheet.
- If your class doesn't divide into pairs or groups, take part yourself, get two Sts to share one role, or get one student to monitor, help, and correct.
- If some Sts finish early, they can swap roles and do the activity again, or you could get them to write some of the sentences from the activity.

Tips for using Vocabulary activities

- These worksheets are intended to recycle and consolidate Sts' understanding of the vocabulary in the Student's Book Vocabulary Banks. As such, we suggest not using them directly after doing these exercises. Instead, get Sts to do them in a subsequent lesson.
- If Sts are having trouble with any of the activities, make sure they refer to the relevant Vocabulary Bank page.
- You could ask Sts to check their answers by referring to the relevant Student's Book Vocabulary Bank.
- All the activities are suitable for use in class. However, you may wish to set some of the tasks for homework.
- Most of the Vocabulary worksheets have an **Activation** task and this can be treated in a similar way to the Grammar ones.
- Make sure that Sts keep their and that they review any difficult areas regularly. Encourage them to go back to activities and cover and test themselves.

Customisable worksheets

There are customisable versions of some of the Grammar, Communicative, and Vocabulary activities on the **Teacher's Resource Centre**. These allow you to adapt the material to make it more applicable and/or relevant to your Sts. For instance, you could:

- change some of the names to the names of Sts in your class.
- change place names to ones that are more relevant and/or familiar to your Sts.
- change items of grammar or vocabulary to focus on the needs and interests of your Sts and/or adapt the level of challenge.
- reduce the number of items if you are short of time.

Grammar activity answers

1A word order in questions

a **2** What year were you born?
3 How are you today?
4 How many brothers and sisters do you have?
5 Do you live with your family?
6 What do your parents do?
7 Why are you learning English?
8 When did you start learning English?
9 Can anyone in your family speak English?
10 What kind of films do you like?
11 How often do you go out for dinner?
12 Are you reading a book at the moment?
13 Where did you go for your last holiday?
14 Did you do any sport yesterday?
15 Where were you at ten o'clock last night?

1B present simple

2 do you see, visit
3 Does it snow; rains
4 does Sam's new girlfriend look like; has
5 do you go; don't like
6 Is; doesn't eat
7 does your Italian class finish; finishes
8 looks; doesn't talk
9 's your English teacher like; 's
10 Do you always do; forget
11 don't get on; Do they make
12 does the supermarket open; don't know

1C present simple or present continuous?

1 2 want **3** don't understand **4** play
5 love **6** 'm selling **7** want
2 8 Do you need **9** 'm just looking **10** Are…looking
11 'm thinking **12** have **13** wear
3 14 're reading **15** don't believe **16** hate **17** need **18** 's
studying **19** 's walking **20** isn't walking **21** 's flying

2A past simple: regular and irregular verbs

1 2 did…stay **3** stayed **4** booked **5** arrived **6** didn't
like **7** left **8** rented **9** were **10** started **11** didn't
finish **12** loved
2 13 was **14** wasn't **15** didn't sleep **16** watched
17 Did…like **18** was **19** had **20** met **21** didn't want
22 Did…take **23** took
3 24 Did…have **25** was **26** stayed **27** thought
28 didn't go **29** did…do **30** Did…go **31** visited
32 argued **33** bought **34** didn't buy

2B past continuous

a **2** was travelling; met
3 found; were cleaning
4 were waiting; saw
5 started; were cycling
6 ran; was driving
b **2** woke up
3 was
4 was shining
5 felt
6 didn't need
7 decided
8 were working
9 was visiting
10 went

11 arrived
12 was
13 were sunbathing
14 were playing
15 were swimming
16 was enjoying
17 put
18 began
19 shouted
20 couldn't
21 saw
22 didn't attack
23 swam
24 didn't stay
25 went

2C time sequencers and connectors

a **2** d; because **3** e; although **4** a; so **5** i; but **6** h;
because
7 j; so **8** f; but **9** b; although **10** c; but
b **2** when **3** although / but **4** because **5** but
6 One evening **7** so **8** Although **9** suddenly **10** so
11 two minutes later **12** so **13** because **14** The next day
15 but

3A *be going to* (plans and predictions)

a **2** Are…going to do
3 'm not going to do
4 're going to visit
5 are…going to go
6 're going to get
7 's going to work
8 Is…going to have
b **2** 're going to crash
3 's going to make
4 's going to cry
5 aren't going to win
6 is going to eat
7 's going to be late
8 's going to break

3B present continuous (future arrangements)

3 Who's he taking to the hospital on Tuesday? He's taking
his mum.
4 When is he working? He's working on Monday morning and
Wednesday afternoon.
5 Is he having dinner with Frank on Monday? Yes, he is.
6 What's he doing on Sunday morning? He's meeting Ellie at
the station.
7 What's he doing on Friday night? He's going to Frank's party.
8 When is he going to the dentist? He's going on Friday
morning.
9 What's he doing on Saturday morning? He's going
shopping / buying Ellie's present.
10 When is he playing tennis? He's playing tennis on Tuesday
afternoon.
11 Who's he seeing on Saturday afternoon? He's seeing George.
12 When is he helping his dad? He's helping his dad on
Thursday afternoon.
13 Is he going to the theatre on Wednesday? Yes, he is.
14 Is he meeting George at the museum? No, he isn't.
15 What's he doing on Sunday afternoon? He's driving to Wales
with Ellie.

3C defining relative clauses

a **2** who cuts **3** where…borrow **4** where…sleep
  5 which…keeps **6** which changes **7** who designs
  8 where…see **9** where…look at **10** which help
  11 where…buy **12** which has **13** which opens
  14 who flies **15** who visits
b 1, 2, 5, 6, 7, 10, 12, 13, 14, 15

4A present perfect + *yet*, *just*, *already*

a **2** He's just been on holiday.
  3 They've just arrived.
  4 She's just washed her hair.
  5 He's just bought a ring.
  6 We've just had lunch.
b **3** He hasn't done the ironing yet.
  4 He hasn't taken out the rubbish yet.
  5 He's already done the shopping.
  6 He's already done the washing.
  7 He hasn't cleaned the windows yet.
  8 He hasn't tidied his desk yet.
  9 He's already laid the table.
  10 He hasn't made his bed yet.

4B present perfect or past simple? (1)

a **2** I've never flown in a helicopter.
  3 Has she ever been late for work?
  4 Luke hasn't answered my messages.
  5 She's met a lot of famous people.
  6 We've never been to South America.
  7 She's won a lot of prizes for her novels.
  8 Have you ever lost a credit card?
  9 I've never worked in a shop or a restaurant.
  10 Have you ever sold something on eBay?
b **2** have
  3 went
  4 've…wanted
  5 Did…enjoy
  6 had
  7 were
  8 loved
  9 Have…heard
  10 have
  11 Have…ever seen
  12 saw
  13 Was

4C *something, anything, nothing,* etc.

  2 anywhere; somewhere
  3 anything; nowhere
  4 nobody
  5 something
  6 anywhere
  7 Somebody; anybody
  8 anything; nothing; anything
  9 somewhere
  10 Somebody; anything; anybody

5A comparative adjectives and adverbs, *as…as*

a **2** Belgium is hotter than France.
  3 Surfing is more exciting than fishing.
  4 Sophie plays tennis better than Emily.
  5 Sydney is further / farther from London than Delhi.
  6 Jason gets up earlier than his wife.
  7 Claire works harder than Sally.
  8 The traffic is worse at 8.30 than at 9.30.
  9 Harry writes more quickly than Paul.
  10 Life in the city is more stressful than life in the country.

b **2** France isn't as hot as Belgium.
  3 Fishing isn't as exciting as surfing.
  4 Emily doesn't play tennis as well as Sophie.
  5 Delhi isn't as far from London as Sydney is.
  6 Jason's wife doesn't get up as early as him.
  7 Sally doesn't work as hard as Claire.
  8 The traffic at 9.30 isn't as bad as at 8.30.
  9 Paul doesn't write as quickly as Harry.
  10 Life in the country isn't as stressful as life in the city.

5B superlatives (+ *ever* + present perfect)

a **2** the cheapest
  3 the most boring
  4 the meanest
  5 the most impatient
  6 the quietest
  7 the emptiest
  8 the laziest
  9 the furthest / farthest
  10 the easiest
  11 the least stressed
  12 the healthiest
b **2** What's the most difficult language you've ever learnt?
  3 What's the best restaurant you've ever eaten at?
  4 What's the most expensive thing you've ever bought?
  5 What's the hardest thing you've ever learnt to do?
  6 What's the longest journey you've ever made?
  7 What's the most interesting historic building you've
     ever visited?
  8 What's the most beautiful place you've ever been to?
  9 What's the most exciting film you've ever seen?
  10 What's the furthest / farthest you've ever run?
  11 What's the coldest place you've ever been to?
  12 What's the most important exam you've ever taken?

5C quantifiers, *too*, *(not) enough*

  2 a lot of **3** too **4** enough money **5** much
  6 too **7** a little **8** a few **9** much **10** patient enough
  11 Too much **12** many **13** too much **14** enough time
  15 too many **16** a few **17** well enough **18** very little
  19 a little **20** too many

6A *will / won't* (predictions)

  2 h; won't understand **3** g; won't be **4** i; won't have
  5 a; won't get **6** e; 'll feel **7** k; 'll lose **8** l; 'll get
  9 d; 'll wear **10** f; 'll be **11** c; 'll pass **12** j; 'll love

6B *will / won't / shall* (other uses)

  2 Shall…turn on **3** won't forget **4** 'll call **5** 'll have
  6 'll take **7** 'll be **8** 'll help **9** won't happen **10** 'll think
  11 'll ask **12** 'll make

6C review of verb forms: present, past, and future

  2 doesn't work; 'll call
  3 haven't made
  4 'm going to sell
  5 did…get; got
  6 'll help
  7 was driving
  8 don't drink
  9 Have…spoken
  10 came; weren't; was having
  11 won't hurt
  12 'm not working
  13 've…offered
  14 are…doing; Do…want
  15 did…take; was walking

7A uses of the infinitive with *to*
2 to pass   3 not to tell   4 to build   5 to use   6 to print
7 to turn off   8 to go   9 to be   10 to swim
11 not to worry   12 to learn   13 to lock   14 to see
15 to get   16 to rain   17 to make   18 to say
19 to ask   20 not to remember

7B infinitive with *to* or verb + *-ing*?
3 to come
4 not talking
5 to see
6 to earn
7 relaxing; not doing
8 to give
9 to learn
10 winning
11 not to hit
12 drinking; talking
13 to go
14 stopping
15 going
16 to be
17 to go
18 Eating
19 not to understand
20 remembering

7C *have to, don't have to, must, mustn't*
2 don't have to pay   3 must wear   4 mustn't touch
5 mustn't put   6 mustn't take   7 have to be   8 mustn't play
9 don't have to pay   10 don't have to come   11 must drive
12 must wear

8A *should / shouldn't*
2 should ask   3 should tell   4 should get   5 shouldn't sit
6 should get up   7 shouldn't think   8 shouldn't go
9 should learn   10 should go

8B *if + present, will / won't + infinitive*
(first conditional)
1 3 get   4 'll catch   5 catch   6 won't do   7 don't do
8 won't get
2 9 lend   10 'll buy   11 have   12 'll start   13 have
14 'll lend   15 lend   16 'll be able to buy
3 17 can't   18 won't go   19 don't go   20 won't meet
21 don't meet   22 'll never get   23 don't get   24 won't have
4 25 talk   26 'll miss   27 miss   28 'll be   29 'm   30 will be
31 is   32 'll lose

8C possessive pronouns
a 2 her
3 your; my
4 ours
5 My; Our
6 yours; mine
b 2 you; My; it; It; it; me
3 She; her; her
4 They; their; them
5 your; mine; hers
6 Our; we

9A *if + past, would + infinitive (second conditional)*
a 2 would you say; asked; 'd say
3 wouldn't have; went
4 knew; 'd tell
5 'd cycle; lived
6 'd buy; had; 'd have; didn't go
7 won; would you spend; 'd buy
8 'd sleep; didn't cry
b 3 studied
4 'll lend
5 weren't / wasn't
6 don't see
7 won't say
8 don't hurry up
9 wouldn't go
10 would…do

9B present perfect + *for* and *since*
a 2 has…worked; 's worked; for
3 have…been married; 've been married since
4 has…been; 's been; since
5 have…known; 've known; for
6 have…lived; 've lived; since
7 have…had; 've had; since
8 have…played; 've played; since

9C present perfect or past simple? (2)
a 1 've loved; was; started
2 Has…finished; finished; hasn't decided
3 've lived; lived; did…leave; retired; wanted
4 saw; told; Have…lived; 've never been; 's visited
5 Have…heard; 've separated; thought
6 's been; met; got; were

10A expressing movement
2 down   3 under   4 (a)round   5 towards   6 along
7 through   8 up   9 into   10 across   11 out of / through
12 down

10B word order of phrasal verbs
a 2 putting on   3 writing down   4 picking up   5 going away
6 throwing away   7 looking for   8 getting up   9 taking off
10 getting on
b 2 turn it up   3 looking after them   4 call her back   5 ✓
6 pick them up   7 look for them   8 pay me back

10C the passive: *be + past participle*
a 2 was designed   3 are spoken   4 were built   5 are shown
6 was discovered   7 weren't used   8 were written
9 was invented   10 is played   11 was painted   12 is visited

11A *used to / didn't use to*

a 3 She used to play
4 She used to wear
5 She didn't use to have
6 She didn't use to have
7 She didn't use to wear
8 She didn't use to play
9 He used to watch
10 He didn't use to do
11 He didn't use to wear
12 He used to have
13 He used to be
14 He used to wear
15 He didn't use to eat
16 He used to have

11B *might / might not* (possibility)

a 2 might be
3 might like
4 might not go
5 might meet
6 might buy
7 might not have
8 might phone
9 might go
10 might not tell
11 might be

11C *so, neither* + auxiliaries

a 3 Neither can I
4 Neither am I
5 So have I
6 Neither did I
7 So was I
8 Neither do I
9 So am I
10 So do I
11 Neither do I
12 So did I
13 So was I
14 Neither have I
15 So do I
16 Neither will I
17 So am I
18 So would I
19 So will I
20 So do I

12A past perfect

2 was; hadn't taken
3 didn't work; hadn't turned it on
4 couldn't take; had forgotten
5 'd never flown; were
6 arrived; hadn't brought
7 wasn't; 'd just had
8 had to; 'd lost
9 ran; hadn't paid
10 arrived, had put out
11 could; 'd learnt
12 was; 'd been

12B reported (or indirect) speech

a 2 he didn't like the music
3 he'd tidied his room
4 it would be expensive
5 she wasn't going to the party
6 he'd lost the match
7 he loved her
8 she'd found his keys
b 2 'It won't hurt.'
3 'It's my mother's car.'
4 'I've finished my homework.'
5 'I can't swim.'
6 'I'll always love you.'
7 'We want to check out.'
8 'I'm lost.'

12C questions with and without auxiliaries

2 Francis Ford Coppola
3 Who painted *The Scream*? Edvard Munch
4 Where do manga comics come from? Japan
5 Which country produces more coffee? Brazil
6 Which country has a blue and yellow flag? Sweden
7 When did the Second World War end? 1945
8 Which country won the most gold medals at the 2016 Olympics? USA
9 Which character did Ian Fleming create? James Bond
10 How many countries belonged to the original European Economic Community in 1957? 6
11 Which company did Kevin Systrom and Mike Krieger start? Instagram
12 Where do people speak Yorùbá? West Africa
13 Which film won the Oscar for best film in 2017? *Moonlight*
14 Which fruit contains more sugar? Orange

1A GRAMMAR word order in questions

a Put the words in order to make the questions.

1 name / your / 's / what   _What's your name_? Luca.

2 year / what / you / born / were

____? 1983.

3 how / you / are / today

____? Fine, thank you.

4 have / and / do / brothers / you / sisters / how / many

____? Two brothers and one sister.

5 with / your / do / family / you / live

____? No, I live alone.

6 your / what / do / parents / do

____? My mum's an engineer and my dad's a teacher.

7 English / why / are / learning / you

____? Because I need it for my job.

8 learning / English / did / when / start / you

____? When I was 12 years old.

9 speak / your / anyone / in / English / can / family

____? Yes, my brother speaks English really well.

10 do / of / what / kind / like / films / you

____? I love action films.

11 do / out / go / how / dinner / you / often / for

____? Once or twice a month.

12 a / the / book / reading / are / at / moment / you

____? Yes, I'm reading some short stories in English.

13 your / go / holiday / did / last / where / you / for

____? I went to Thailand.

14 do / did / you / any / yesterday / sport

____? Yes, I went swimming.

15 last / you / were / where / night / ten o'clock / at

____? I was at my friend's house.

b Cover the questions and look at the answers. Can you remember the questions?

Work with a partner. Ask and answer the questions.

English File fourth edition Teacher's Guide Pre-intermediate   Photocopiable © Oxford University Press 2019

1B GRAMMAR present simple

● Complete the conversations with the present simple form of the verbs in brackets.

1　A　Your dog *is* a bit overweight. (be)
　　B　Yes, he *eats* too much food! (eat)

2　A　How often _________________ your grandparents? (you / see)
　　B　I usually _________________ them twice a year. (visit)

3　A　_________________ here in winter? (it / snow)
　　B　No, but it _________________ a lot. (rain)

4　A　What _________________________________? (Sam's new girlfriend / look like)
　　B　She _________________ long blonde hair and big dark brown eyes. (have)

5　A　How often _________________ to the gym? (you / go)
　　B　Hardly ever! I _________________ doing exercise. (not like)

6　A　_________________ your husband a vegetarian? (be)
　　B　No, but he _________________ much meat. (not eat)

7　A　What time _________________? (your Italian class / finish)
　　B　It _________________ at seven o'clock. (finish)

8　A　Your daughter_________________ very shy. (look)
　　B　Yes, she _________________ much. (not talk)

9　A　What _________________? (your English teacher / be like)
　　B　She _________________ really kind and funny. (be)

10　A　_________________ your English homework? (you / always do)
　　B　No, I sometimes _________________! (forget)

11　A　We _________________ very well with our neighbours. (not get on)
　　B　Why not? _________________ a lot of noise? (they / make)

12　A　What time _________________? (the supermarket / open)
　　B　I _________________. Look online. (not know)

ACTIVATION

Write three sentences about what you do at the weekend, and three sentences about
what a person in your family does. Use adverbs or expressions of frequency.

1C GRAMMAR present simple or present continuous?

Complete the conversations with the present simple or present continuous form of the verbs in brackets.

1

A Why [1]**_are_** you _taking_ (take) a photo of your guitar?

B I [2]___________ (want) to sell it on eBay.

A Why? I [3]___________ (not understand). You [4]___________ (play) your guitar every day! You [5]___________ (love) it!

B I [6]___________ (sell) my old one because I [7]___________ (want) to buy a new one.

A Oh, OK.

2

A Hi. [8]___________ you ___________ (need) any help?

B No, thanks. I [9]___________ (just look).

A [10]___________ you ___________ (look) for anything in particular?

B Yes, I [11]___________ (think) of getting a jacket.

A This is one of our best-sellers. It's real leather. I [12]___________ (have) it, and I [13]___________ (wear) it all the time.

B Yes, it's lovely. Where can I try it on?

3

A You [14]___________ (read) a book about modern art! I [15]___________ (not believe) it! You [16]___________ (hate) modern art!

B I know. But now I [17]___________ (need) to learn about it.

A Why?

B Because my girlfriend [18]___________ (study) it at college this year, and she loves it.

A What's that picture on the left? Can I see it?

B It's a woman, and I think she [19]___________ (walk) in a garden…I don't really know.

A Let me see…No, she [20]___________ (not walk). She [21]___________ (fly).

B Oh, yes!

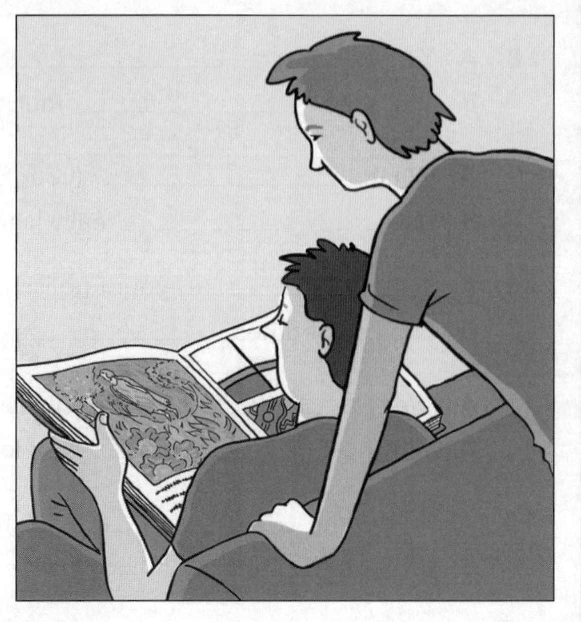

ACTIVATION

Practise the conversations with a partner.

English File fourth edition Teacher's Guide Pre-intermediate   Photocopiable © Oxford University Press 2019

2A GRAMMAR past simple: regular and irregular verbs

● Complete the conversations with the past simple form of the verbs in brackets.

1 A Is this your first time in the UK, Anna?
   B No, I [1]*had* (have) a holiday in Scotland last year.
   A Really? I love Scotland! Where [2]__________ you __________ (stay)?
   B We [3]__________ (stay) in Edinburgh. We [4]__________ (book) a hotel online, but unfortunately when we [5]__________ (arrive) we [6]__________ (not like) it. So we [7]__________ (leave) that hotel and [8]__________ (rent) an apartment. It was great! What about you? When [9]__________ (be) you in Scotland?
   A Oh, a long time ago. I [10]__________ (start) a university course there. I [11]__________ (not finish) the course, but I [12]__________ (love) Scotland!

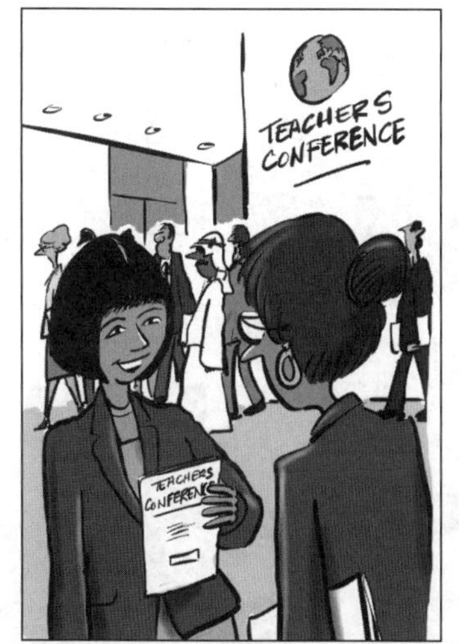

2 A Hi, Oliver. Welcome home! How [13]__________ (be) your flight?
   B Hi, Mum. It [14]__________ (not be) bad. I [15]__________ (not sleep) much, but I [16]__________ (watch) some good films.
   A And [17]__________ you __________ (like) New Zealand?
   B Yes! It [18]__________ (be) fantastic. I [19]__________ (have) a great time. It's a really beautiful country and I [20]__________ (meet) some amazing people. I [21]__________ (not want) to come home!
   A [22]__________ you __________ (take) many photos?
   B Yes, I [23]__________ (take) a lot. I can show you when we get home.

3 A Ruth! You're back! [24]__________ you __________ (have) a good holiday?
   B No. It [25]__________ (be) awful.
   A Why? What happened?
   B We [26]__________ (stay) in a horrible apartment, and Tom [27]__________ (think) the city was dangerous at night, so we [28]__________ (not go) out much in the evening.
   A What [29]__________ you __________ (do) during the day? [30]__________ you __________ (go) sightseeing?
   B Yes, we [31]__________ (visit) all the famous places. But we [32]__________ (argue) a lot. Tom [33]__________ (buy) very expensive souvenirs for all his family! I [34]__________ (not buy) anything.

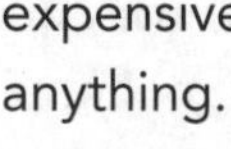

ACTIVATION

Test your memory. Cover the conversations and look at the pictures. Try to remember what happened to Anna, Oliver, and Ruth and Tom.

2B GRAMMAR past continuous

a Look at the pictures and complete the sentences with the past simple and past continuous form of the verbs in brackets.

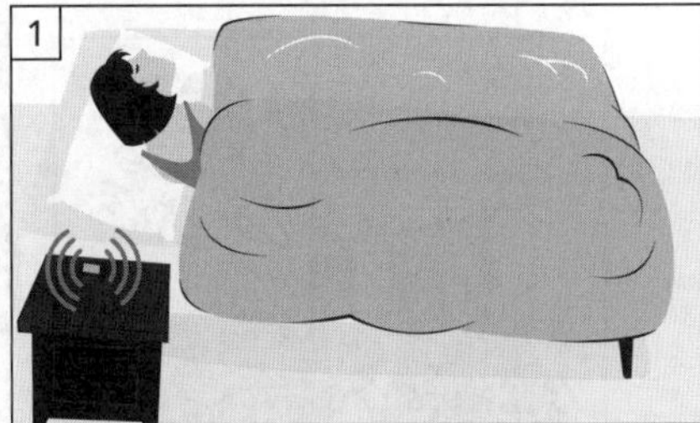  

1 I _was sleeping_ when you _sent_ me the message. (sleep, send)

2 Susan ______________ around Italy when she ______________ her boyfriend. (travel, meet)

3 We ______________ some old photos when we ______________ the house. (find, clean)

4 They ______________ for the bus when they ______________ the accident. (wait, see)

5 It ______________ to rain when they ______________ to school. (start, cycle)

6 A dog ______________ into the road when I ______________ home. (run, drive)

b Complete the story with the past simple or past continuous form of the verbs in brackets.

Last summer, I [1]_was living_ (live) in Hawaii. One Saturday morning, I [2]______________ (wake up) early, and it [3]______________ (be) a beautiful day. The sun [4]______________ (shine), and I [5]______________ (feel) really happy. I [6]______________ (not need) to go to work that day, so I [7]______________ (decide) to go surfing. Most of my friends [8]______________ (work) and my girlfriend [9]______________ (visit) her parents, so I [10]______________ (go) to the beach alone. When I [11]______________ (arrive), the beach [12]______________ (be) already crowded. A lot of people [13]______________ (sunbathe), children [14]______________ (play) games and people [15]______________ (swim) in the sea. Everyone [16]______________ (enjoy) the lovely summer day. I [17]______________ (put) my things down on the beach, and then I [18]______________ (begin) walking to the sea with my surfboard. Suddenly, a man [19]______________ (shout), 'Shark! Shark! Get out of the water!' At first, I [20]______________ (not can) see anything, but then I [21]______________ (see) a big shark. Luckily, it [22]______________ (not attack) anyone and [23]______________ (swim) away quickly. I [24]______________ (not stay) at the beach after that, and I [25]______________ (go) home without going surfing!

Test your memory. Cover the sentences in **a** and look at the pictures. Try to remember the sentences.

a Match the sentence halves and (circle) the correct word: *so, but, because,* or *although*.

1	The weather was awful,	*g*	a	**so** / **but** I invited her to dinner.
2	I didn't give him my phone number		b	**because** / **although** it had a happy ending.
3	Paul came to work		c	**but** / **so** we couldn't find the house.
4	It was her birthday,		d	**because** / **although** I didn't want him to call me.
5	Jake is an intelligent student,		e	**although** / **because** he was ill.
6	I ran to the shop		f	**so** / **but** we had a wonderful evening.
7	They didn't want to dance,		g	**but** / (**so**) we didn't go out.
8	We didn't go anywhere special,		h	**although** / **because** I was in a hurry.
9	It was a sad story		i	**because** / **but** he's very lazy.
10	We drove along the street very slowly,		j	**so** / **because** they left the club early.

b Complete the story with the time sequencers and connectors from the list.

although (x2)   because (x3)   but (x2)   the next day   one evening   so (x3)   suddenly   two minutes later   when

Don't always listen to the satnav...

Oscar Peters never wanted a satnav [1] *because* he didn't like technology. And [2]______________ his brother gave him one as a birthday present, it directed him into a difficult situation.

'My brother Jez loves gadgets and technology. Last year, he gave me a satnav for my birthday, [3]______________ he knew I didn't really want one. Jez uses his satnav all the time [4]______________ he likes listening to instructions, [5]______________ I prefer using a map.

[6]______________, a friend of a friend phoned. She needed my help, [7]______________ I agreed to drive to her house. [8]______________ I had a map in the car, I decided to use the satnav to find her village. It was dark, and I wanted to get there as quickly as possible.

Everything was going fine. I was nearly there, but then [9]______________ I saw there was a small river on the left. I could see that there was a road which went through the water to the other side of the river. The satnav said 'Turn left!', [10]______________ I followed the instruction and turned left into the water. The satnav said 'Go straight on!', but [11]______________ my car was completely stuck in the mud. I had my phone with me, [12]______________ I phoned my friend and she came to the river to help. I felt terrible [13]______________ she got very cold and wet in the water.

[14]______________ a tractor pulled my car out of the river, [15]______________ it was completely ruined by the water. I can't believe I made such a stupid – and expensive – mistake!'

ACTIVATION

Complete the sentences with your own ideas.

Although Jack was very good looking,…
The party was really boring, so…
I enjoyed the film, but…

We decided to eat out because…
Louisa met her husband when…
I was watching TV when suddenly…

3A GRAMMAR *be going to* (plans and predictions)

a Complete the conversations with the correct form of *be going to* and a verb from the list.

do   have   ~~get~~   get   go   not do   visit   work

1 **A** What are you doing?

 B I ¹*'m going to get* a trolley. I can't carry all these bags.

2 **A** ² ___________ you ___________ your homework this evening?

 B No, I'm not. I'm really tired. In fact, I ³ ___________ anything – just sleep!

3 **A** So, do you like it here in Oxford?

 B Yes, we love it! But we're only here for a short time. We ⁴ ___________ lots of different places.

 A Where ⁵ ___________ you ___________ next?

 B Liverpool. We ⁶ ___________ the train there.

4 **A** How's your daughter?

 B She's fine, thanks.

 A Does she have any plans for the summer?

 B Yes. She ⁷ ___________ in a bookshop for six weeks.

 A ⁸ ___________ she ___________ a holiday?

 B No, I don't think she is.

b What's going to happen? Write a sentence with *be going to* and a verb from the list for pictures 1–8.

be late   break   crash   cry   eat   make   ~~miss~~   not win

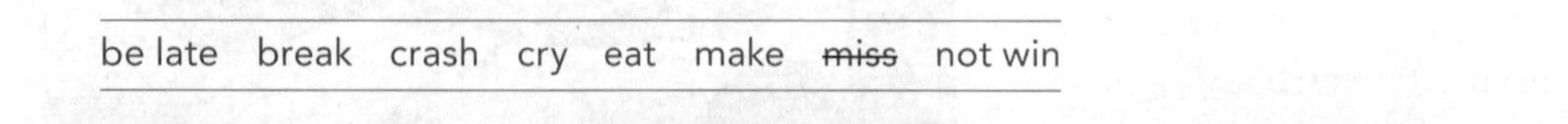

1 He *'s going to miss* the bus.
2 They ___________ .
3 He ___________ a cake.
4 She ___________ .
5 They ___________ the race.
6 The dog ___________ the sausages.
7 He ___________ for work.
8 She ___________ the window.

Test your memory. Practise the conversations in **a** with a partner. Then cover sentences 1–8 in **b**. Look at the pictures and remember the sentences.

3B GRAMMAR present continuous (future arrangements)

Look at Luke's diary. Write the questions and the answers. Use the present continuous.

MONDAY	TUESDAY	WEDNESDAY	THURSDAY
Work 9.00–12.00 a.m. Dinner with Frank 8.00 p.m.	10.00 a.m. Take Mum to the hospital 3.00 p.m. Tennis	Work 4.00–6.00 p.m. 7.30 p.m. Theatre with Yaz and Omar	10.00 a.m. Meet Sam to study Help Dad with the garden

FRIDAY	SATURDAY	SUNDAY
Dentist 11.30 a.m. Party at Frank's! 8.00 p.m.	9.00 a.m. Go shopping — buy Ellie's present 4.00 p.m. George — Café Tivoli	10.30 a.m. Meet Ellie at station! 5.00 p.m. Drive to Wales — with Ellie

1 he / meet Sam on Monday?
   'Is he meeting Sam on Monday?' 'No, he isn't.'

2 When / he / go to the station?
   'When is he going to the station?' 'He's going to the station on Sunday.'

3 Who / he / take to the hospital on Tuesday?
   ____

4 When / he / work?
   ____

5 he / have dinner with Frank on Monday?
   ____

6 What / he / do on Sunday morning?
   ____

7 What / he / do on Friday night?
   ____

8 When / he / go to the dentist?
   ____

9 What / he / do on Saturday morning?
   ____

10 When / he / play tennis?
   ____

11 Who / he / see on Saturday afternoon?
   ____

12 When / he / help his dad?
   ____

13 he / go to the theatre on Wednesday?
   ____

14 he / meet George at the museum?
   ____

15 What / he / do on Sunday afternoon?
   ____

ACTIVATION

Write down one arrangement that you have each day next week.
Tell a partner. Use the present continuous.

a Complete the definitions with *who*, *which*, or *where* and the correct form of a verb from the list.

borrow ~~build~~ buy change cut design fly have help keep look at open see sleep visit

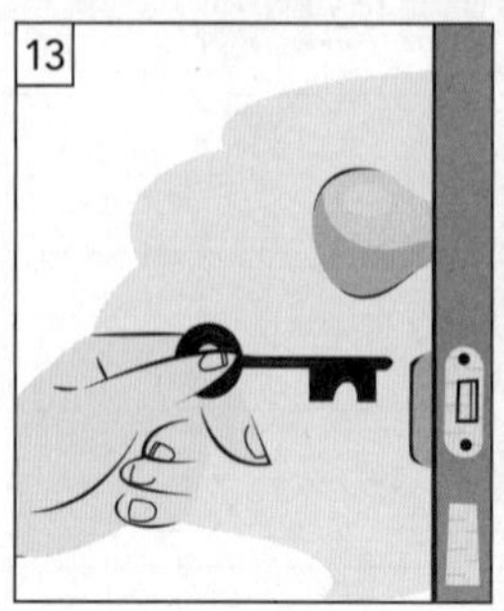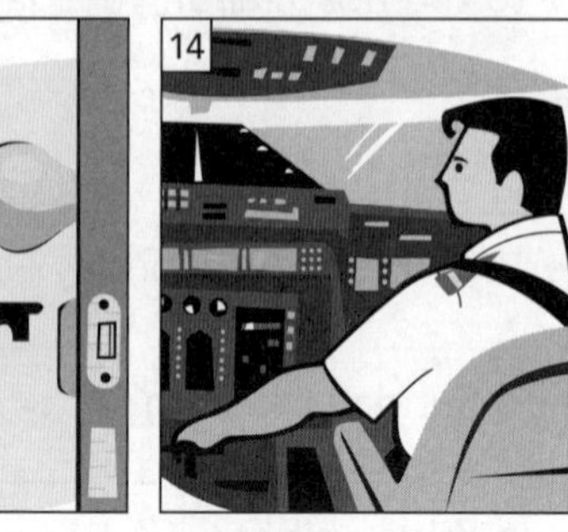

1 **A builder** is a person _who_ _builds_ houses. ☐
2 **A hairdresser** is somebody ___________ ___________ your hair. ☐
3 **A library** is a place ___________ you can read or ___________ books. ☐
4 **A campsite** is a place ___________ people ___________ in tents. ☐
5 **A fridge** is something ___________ ___________ food cold. ☐
6 **A remote control** is something ___________ ___________ TV channels. ☐
7 **An architect** is someone ___________ ___________ buildings. ☐
8 **A cinema** is a place ___________ you can ___________ a film. ☐
9 **An art gallery** is a place ___________ you ___________ paintings. ☐
10 **Glasses** are things ___________ ___________ you to see well. ☐
11 **A bookshop** is a place ___________ you ___________ books. ☐
12 **A giraffe** is an animal ___________ ___________ a very long neck. ☐
13 **A key** is something ___________ ___________ a door. ☐
14 **A pilot** is a person ___________ ___________ planes. ☐
15 **A tourist** is a person ___________ ___________ another town or country. ☐

b Look again at the relative pronouns in sentences 1–15 in **a**. Tick (✓) the sentences in which the relative pronouns can be replaced with *that*.

ACTIVATION

Test your memory. Cover the definitions and look at the pictures. Can you remember the definitions?

a Write sentences for the pictures. Use present perfect + *just*.

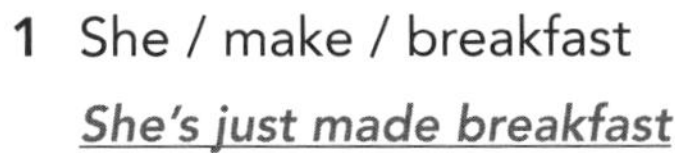
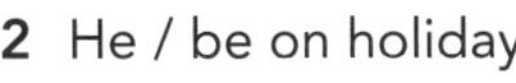

1 She / make / breakfast
She's just made breakfast.

2 He / be on holiday
_________________________________.

3 They / arrive
_________________________________.

4 She / wash her hair
_________________________________.

5 He / buy a ring
_________________________________.

6 **A** Would you like a cake?
   B No, thanks. We / have lunch
_________________________________.

b Write sentences for the picture. Use present perfect + *yet* or *already*.

1 do / the washing-up
He hasn't done the washing-up yet.

2 clean / the floor
He's already cleaned the floor.

3 do / the ironing
____

4 take out / the rubbish
____

5 do / the shopping
____

6 do / the washing
____

7 clean / the windows
____

8 tidy / his desk
____

9 lay / the table
____

10 make / his bed
____

ACTIVATION

Work with a partner. Look at the picture in **b** and ask and answer questions.

Has he done the washing-up yet? *No, he hasn't.*

a Write sentences in the present perfect.

1   you / ever eat / octopus
    Have you ever eaten octopus?

2   I / never fly / in a helicopter
    ____.

3   she / ever be / late for work
    ____?

4   Luke / not answer / my messages
    ____.

5   she / meet / a lot of famous people
    ____.

6   we / never be / to South America
    ____.

7   she / win / a lot of prizes for her novels
    ____.

8   you / ever lose / a credit card
    ____?

9   I / never work / in a shop or a restaurant
    ____.

10   you / ever sell / something on eBay
    ____?

b Complete the conversations with the present perfect or past simple form of the verbs in brackets.

1   

A   ¹*Have* you *ever been* (ever / be) to the USA?
B   Yes, I ²__________. I ³__________ (go) to New York last summer.
A   I ⁴__________ always __________ (want) to go to New York! ⁵__________ you __________ (enjoy) it?
B   Yes, I ⁶__________ (have) a great time.
A   What ⁷__________ (be) your favourite places?
B   I really ⁸__________ (love) Central Park and Fifth Avenue.

2   

A   ⁹__________ you __________ (hear) this band?
B   Of course I ¹⁰__________! They're my favourite band.
A   Really? ¹¹__________ you __________ (ever / see) them in concert?
B   Yes, I ¹²__________ (see) them at Wembley last month.
A   Lucky you! ¹³__________ (be) it a good concert?
B   It was amazing! They were fantastic.

ACTIVATION

Practise the conversations in **b** with a partner. Then ask each other questions beginning *Have you ever been to…(place)?* and *Have you ever heard…(a song or a musician)?* and have short conversations.

4C GRAMMAR *something, anything, nothing, etc.*

Complete the conversations with the words from the list. Write in the column on the right.

anybody (x2)   anything (x4)   anywhere (x2)   nobody (x2)   nothing
nowhere   somebody (x3)   something   somewhere (x2)

1   A   Why are you looking out of the window?
    B   I think there's ▮▮▮ in the house opposite.   *somebody*
    A   But ▮▮▮ has lived there for years!   *nobody*
    B   I know! That's why I'm looking.

2   A   Are you going ▮▮▮ this summer?   _______
    B   We haven't decided yet. But my wife wants to go ▮▮▮ nice and hot.   _______

3   A   I'm so bored. There isn't ▮▮▮ to do in this town!   _______
    B   That's not true. There are lots of things to do.
    A   But there's ▮▮▮ for young people to go.   _______

4   A   I phoned your office at 2.00 today, but ▮▮▮ answered.   _______
    B   Sorry, there was a problem with the phone lines.

5   A   I'm hungry. I need ▮▮▮ to eat.   _______
    B   Well, there's food in the fridge.

6   A   Where did you go last night?
    B   I didn't go ▮▮▮. I was too tired. I stayed in.   _______

7   A   ▮▮▮ told me that their new album is very good.   _______
    B   Really? I don't know ▮▮▮ who likes it.   _______

8   A   Did you buy ▮▮▮ this afternoon?   _______
    B   No, ▮▮▮. I didn't see ▮▮▮ that I liked.   _______   _______

9   A   Where are my car keys?
    B   I think they're ▮▮▮ in the kitchen.   _______

10 A   ▮▮▮ told Eva about the party. Was it you?   _______
    B   Me? No, I haven't said ▮▮▮ to ▮▮▮.   _______   _______

Test your memory. Work with a partner. Cover the column on the right.
Read the conversations aloud with the missing words.

5A GRAMMAR comparative adjectives and adverbs, *as…as*

a Write sentences about the pictures using comparative adjectives and adverbs.

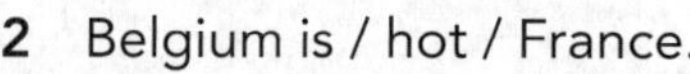

1 French / easy to learn / Russian

French is easier to learn than Russian.

2 Belgium is / hot / France.

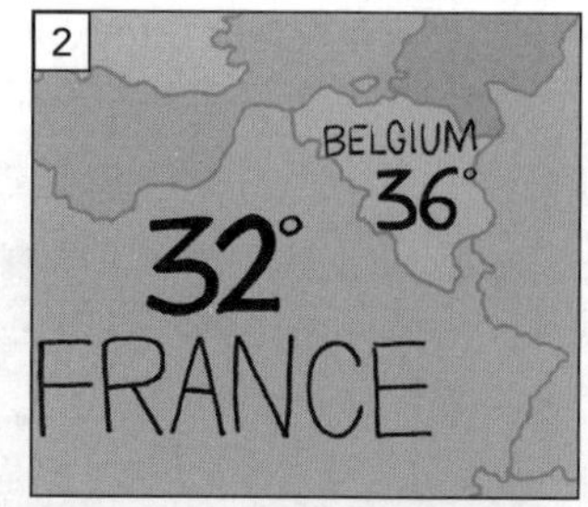

3 Surfing is / exciting / fishing

4 Sophie plays tennis / well / Emily

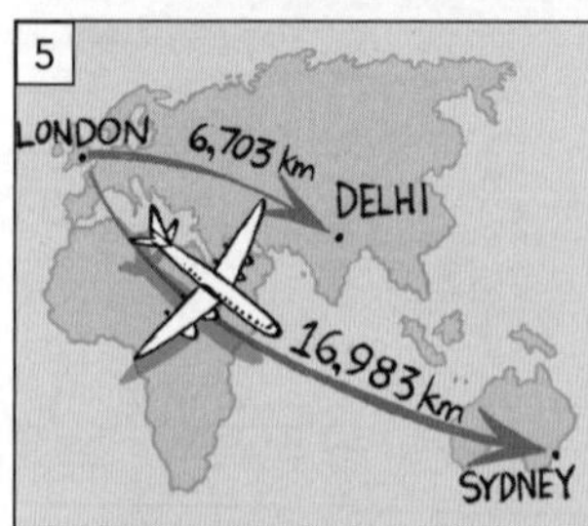

5 Sydney is / far from London / Delhi

6 Jason gets up / early / his wife

7 Claire works / hard / Sally

8 The traffic is / bad at 8.30 / at 9.30

9 Harry writes / quickly / Paul

10 Life in the city is / stressful / life in the country

b Rewrite the sentences from **a** using *not as…as*.

1 Russian *isn't as easy as French*.
2 France ___________________________________ .
3 Fishing ___________________________________ .
4 Emily ___________________________________ .
5 Delhi ___________________________________ .

6 Jason's wife ___________________________________ .
7 Sally ___________________________________ .
8 The traffic at 9.30 ___________________________________ .
9 Paul ___________________________________ .
10 Life in the country ___________________________________ .

ACTIVATION

Test your memory. Cover the sentences and look at the pictures. For each picture,
say a sentence with a comparative adjective or adverb from **a** and *not as…as* from **b**.

English File fourth edition Teacher's Guide Pre-intermediate   Photocopiable © Oxford University Press 2019

5B GRAMMAR superlatives (+ *ever* + present perfect)

a Write the opposite superlatives.

1 the most unfriendly *the friendliest*
2 the most expensive _______________
3 the most exciting _______________
4 the most generous _______________
5 the most patient _______________
6 the loudest _______________

7 the most crowded _______________
8 the most hard working _______________
9 the nearest _______________
10 the most difficult _______________
11 the most stressed _______________
12 the most unhealthy _______________

b Write the questions using the superlative form of the adjective + *ever* + present perfect.

1 Who / generous person you / meet
Who's the most generous person you've ever met?

2 What / difficult language you / learn
_______________?

3 What / good restaurant you / eat at
_______________?

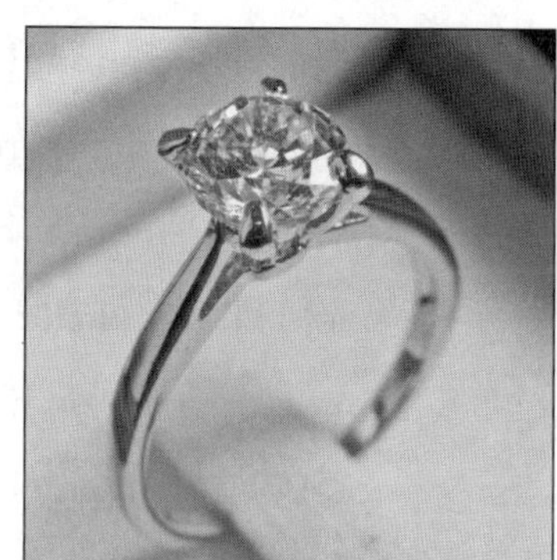

4 What / expensive thing you / buy
_______________?

5 What / hard thing you / learn to do
_______________?

6 What / long journey you / make
_______________?

7 What / interesting historic building you / visit
_______________?

8 What / beautiful place you / be to
_______________?

9 What / exciting film you / see
_______________?

10 What / far you / run
_______________?

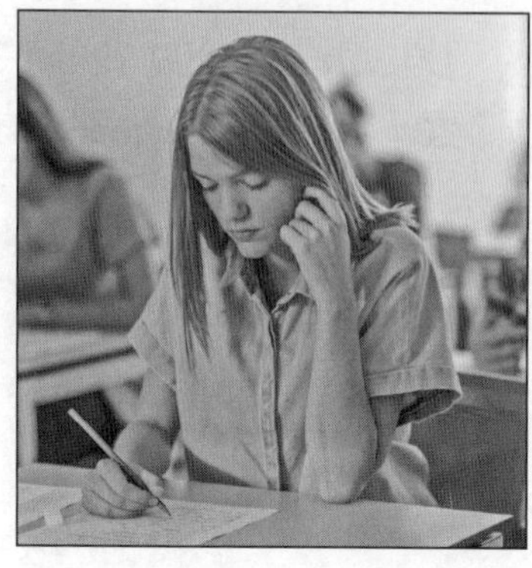

11 What / cold place you / be to
_______________?

12 What / important exam you / take
_______________?

ACTIVATION

Work with a partner. Ask and answer the questions in **b**.

5C GRAMMAR quantifiers, *too, (not) enough*

● Choose the correct word or phrase for each sentence. Circle the correct form.

1 Jackie spends **too many** / **too much** money on shoes.

2 A good diet can prevent **lot of** / **a lot of** illnesses.

3 'How was the job interview?' 'It was OK. I wasn't **too** / **enough** nervous.'

4 I think I have **enough money** / **money enough** to pay for this.

5 How **much** / **many** fruit do you eat?

6 Can you help me? This case is **too** / **too much** heavy.

7 Could I have **a little** / **a few** milk, please?

8 I'm going away on holiday for **a few** / **a little** days next week.

9 You don't do **many** / **much** exercise. Why don't you come jogging with me?

10 I can't teach children. I'm not **patient enough** / **enough patient**.

11 **Too much** / **Too many** chocolate isn't good for you.

12 How **many** / **much** hours do you work a day?

13 I spend **too much** / **too many** time at the computer.

14 I couldn't finish the report because I didn't have **time enough** / **enough time**.

15 I have **too many** / **too much** clothes. I can never decide what to wear.

16 We're going to buy **a little** / **a few** things for our new flat today.

17 Are you **enough well** / **well enough** to go to work today?

18 I'm going to have **very little** / **very few** free time this weekend.

19 My husband does **a few** / **a little** housework every day.

20 We buy **too many** / **too much** vegetables. We never eat them all!

Look at the sentences and say if they are true for you. Compare with a partner.

I watch too much TV.
I don't drink enough water.
I don't do enough exercise.
I'm not organized enough.

I spend too much time on social media.
I have too many clothes.
I drink too much caffeine.
I don't eat enough fruit and vegetables.

Yes, I watch too much TV. *How many hours a day?*

Maybe an hour. What about you? *I don't watch much TV.*

6A GRAMMAR *will / won't* (predictions)

Read sentences 1–12 and match them to predictions a–l. Complete the predictions with *will / won't*. Use the verbs in brackets.

1	'The meeting starts at 2.30.'	b
2	'John is going to see a film in French tonight.'	
3	'There's a new drinks machine in the office.'	
4	'The teacher isn't going to be here today.'	
5	'My brother's going to sell his car.'	
6	'I've started going swimming every day.'	
7	'Esther's going to buy another phone.'	
8	'My daughter has a degree in IT.'	
9	'My new coat was really expensive!'	
10	'I don't believe it. I've broken my brother's laptop.'	
11	'I'm taking my driving test tomorrow.'	
12	'We're going to Brazil next month.'	

a 'He ______________ much money for it. It's very old.' (not get)

b 'Yes, and I'm sure it*'ll be* really boring!' (be)

c 'Don't worry. You ______________ easily.' (pass)

d 'Yes, but you ______________ it a lot.' (wear)

e 'That's good. You ______________ much healthier.' (feel)

f 'Oh no. He ______________ really angry.' (be)

g 'The coffee ______________ very good.' (not be)

h 'He ______________ anything!' (not understand)

i 'Great! We ______________ the exam!' (not have)

j 'Lucky you! You ______________ the people and the scenery.' (love)

k 'She ______________ it, just like the other two.' (lose)

l 'She ______________ a good job, I'm sure.' (get)

ACTIVATION

Work with a partner. **A** read sentences 1–12. **B** read the predictions. Then swap roles.

6B GRAMMAR *will / won't / shall* (other uses)

● Complete the conversations with *will / won't* or *shall* and the correct verb from the list.

ask   be   call   have   help   make   ~~not be~~   not forget   not happen   take   turn on   think

1 A What would you like for dinner tonight?

  B Sorry, I _won't be_ home for dinner. I'm working late.

2 A It's hot in here.

  B ______________ I ______________ the air conditioning?

3 A Please can you post this letter for me today? It's very important.

  B Don't worry, I ______________.

4 A Oh, hello, Nina. I can't talk now. I'm at work.

  B No problem. I ______________ you back this evening.

5 A So, a mineral water and an egg sandwich. Anything else?

  B Yes, I ______________ a packet of crisps, please.

6 A The coffee machine you bought doesn't work.

  B I ______________ it back tomorrow. They can change it.

7 A Please don't go!

  B Don't worry. I ______________ back soon.

8 A I'm going to paint my flat at the weekend.

  B I ______________ you if you like.

9 A You're 15 minutes late!

  B I'm very sorry. It ______________ again.

10 A What are your plans for the summer?

  B I'm going to travel around Italy. Why don't you come with me?

  A Maybe! I ______________ about it.

11 A I'm nervous about the test tomorrow.

  B Don't worry. Give me the book, and I ______________ you some of the questions.

12 A I've had a terrible day at work today.

  B Sit down, and I ______________ you a cup of tea.

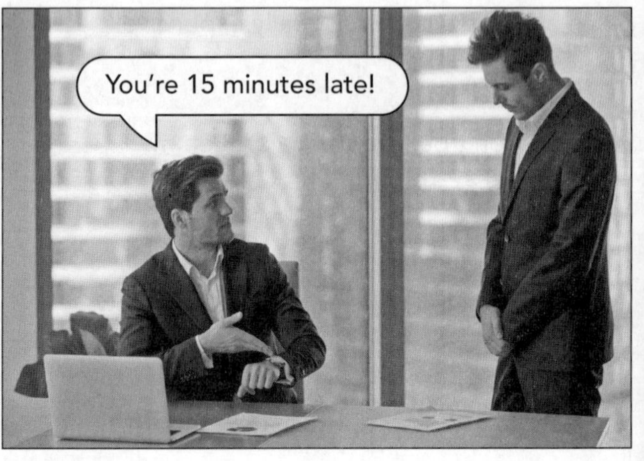

ACTIVATION

Practise the conversations with a partner.

English File fourth edition Teacher's Guide Pre-intermediate   Photocopiable © Oxford University Press 2019

Complete the conversations with the correct form of the verbs in brackets: present simple, present continuous, past simple, past continuous, present perfect, *be going to* + infinitive, *will / won't* + infinitive.

1 A <u>Does</u> your sister sometimes <u>get</u> (get) angry with you?
  B Only if I take her clothes without asking.

2 A Can I speak to Anna, please?
  B Sorry, she _______________ (not work) on Wednesdays.
  A OK, thanks. I _______________ (call) back tomorrow then.

3 A I _______________ (not make) anything for dinner yet.
  B That's OK. I'm not very hungry.

4 A Have you decided what to do with your car?
  B Yes. I _______________ (sell) it next month.

5 A How __________ you __________ (get) home last night?
  B I __________ (get) a taxi.

6 A Oh dear, I'm not very good at filling in forms.
  B Don't worry. I _______________ (help) you.

7 A Did you hear about the election result?
  B Yes, I heard it on the news when I _______________ (drive) home.

8 A Soft drinks aren't very good for you, you know.
  B Well, I _______________ (not drink) very many – just one or two cans a day.

9 A __________ you ever __________ (speak) to your mother about the problem?
  B Yes, I have. But that was a long time ago.

10 A I _______________ (come) to see you last night, but you _______________ (not be) at home.
  B No, I _______________ (have) dinner at my parents' house.

11 A I'm a bit nervous about the injection, Doctor.
  B Don't worry. It _______________ (not hurt).

12 A Hi, can you talk now?
  B Sure, I _______________ (not work) at the moment.

13 A You look happy!
  B I am. They __________ just __________ (offer) me the job in Paris.

14 A What _______________ you _______________ (do) tomorrow evening?
  B Nothing. Why?
  A __________ you __________ (want) to see a film?

15 A Wow! This is a great photo. Where __________ you __________ (take) it?
  B When I _______________ (walk) in the Himalayas.

20

16–20 Excellent. You can use the past, present, and future very well.

11–15 Quite good, but check the rules in the Grammar Bank (Student's Book p.136) and look at the exercise again.

1–10 This is difficult for you. Read the rules in the Grammar Bank (Student's Book p.136). Then ask your teacher for another photocopy and do the exercise again at home.

7A **GRAMMAR** uses of the infinitive with *to*

● Complete the sentences with *to* + a verb from the list. Write in the **INFINITIVE WITH *TO*** column.

ask be build get go learn ~~leave~~ lock make not tell pass
print not remember rain say see swim turn off use not worry

		INFINITIVE WITH *TO*
1	I was ready ▮ when my phone rang.	*to leave*
2	It isn't difficult ▮ the first year exam.	__________
3	Promise ▮ anyone about this. It's a secret.	__________
4	They're planning ▮ a supermarket there.	__________
5	Can you show me how ▮ the new photocopier?	__________
6	You need ▮ your boarding pass before you go to the airport.	__________
7	Don't forget ▮ the computer when you leave.	__________
8	Does Fabio know where ▮ when he arrives?	__________
9	She won't pretend ▮ happy if she isn't.	__________
10	Is it safe ▮ in this river?	__________
11	Try ▮ about your driving test. I'm sure you'll pass.	__________
12	What's the best way ▮ a new language?	__________
13	Did you remember ▮ the front door when you left?	__________
14	It was really nice ▮ you again after all this time.	__________
15	I can't decide what ▮ my girlfriend for her birthday.	__________
16	It started ▮, so we came home early from the beach.	__________
17	It's really important ▮ a good impression on your first day in a new job.	__________
18	He phoned her ▮ that he was sorry.	__________
19	I have a problem, but I don't know who ▮ for advice.	__________
20	It's quite normal ▮ your dreams.	__________

ACTIVATION

Test your memory. Cover the **INFINITIVE WITH *TO*** column. Read the sentences aloud with the missing infinitives.

7B GRAMMAR   infinitive with *to* or verb + *-ing*?

Complete the sentences with the *-ing* form or infinitive with *to* of the verbs in brackets.

1   I can't promise *to be* (be) on time.

2   *Swimming* (swim) is better exercise than running.

3   Would you like ______________ (come) to a concert on Saturday?

4   Do you mind ______________ (not talk) so loudly?

5   It was very interesting ______________ (see) my old school friends again.

6   Duncan works at weekends ______________ (earn) more money.

7   On Sundays, Emma likes ______________ and ______________ (relax, not do) anything.

8   We were unhappy with the service, so the restaurant offered ______________ (give) us a free dinner.

9   Is it difficult ______________ (learn) Japanese?

10   James is very competitive. He thinks ______________ (win) is the most important thing.

11   She tried ______________ (not hit) the man, but she was driving too fast.

12   We spent all evening ______________ coffee and ______________ (drink, talk).

13   Excuse me, I need ______________ (go) to the bathroom.

14   They drove without ______________ (stop) for six hours.

15   We're thinking of ______________ (go) to Mexico for our holidays next year.

16   I'm very happy ______________ (be) here again.

17   We've decided ______________ (go) camping this summer because it's cheaper.

18   ______________ (eat) just before you go to bed can make it difficult to sleep.

19   The man pretended ______________ (not understand) the policeman.

20   Are you good at ______________ (remember) people's names?   ☐ 20

16–20   Excellent. You can use the infinitive with *to* and the *-ing* form very well.

11–15   Quite good, but check the rules in the Grammar Bank (Student's Book p.138) and look at the exercise again.

1–10   This is difficult for you. Read the rules in the Grammar Bank (Student's Book p.138). Then ask your teacher for another photocopy and do the exercise again at home.

Complete the sentences with *have to*, *don't have to*, *must*, or *mustn't* + a verb from the list.

be   come   drive   pay (x2)   play   put   take   touch   ~~turn off~~   wear (x2)

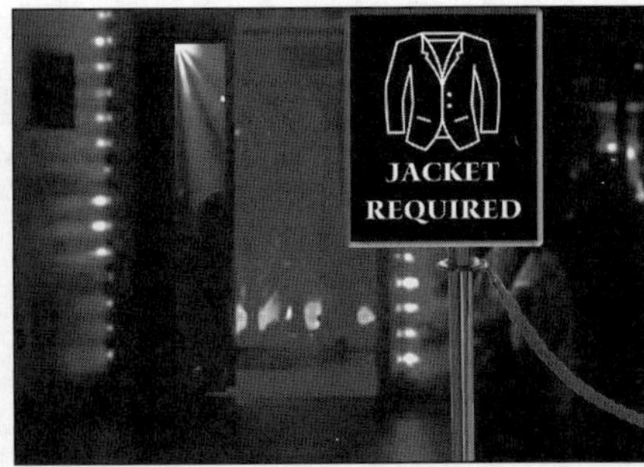

1 You *must turn off* your phone.

2 Children _______________________ _______________________.

3 You _______________________ a jacket.

4 You _______________________ the door.

5 You _______________________ your feet on the seats.

6 You _______________________ photos.

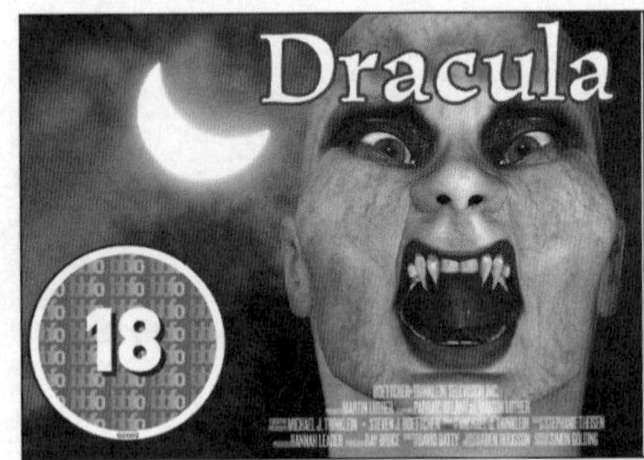

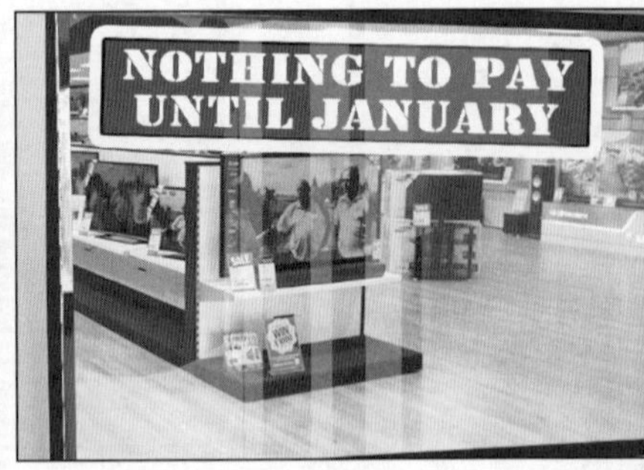

7 You _______________________ over 18 to see this film.

8 You _______________________ football here.

9 You _______________________ anything now.

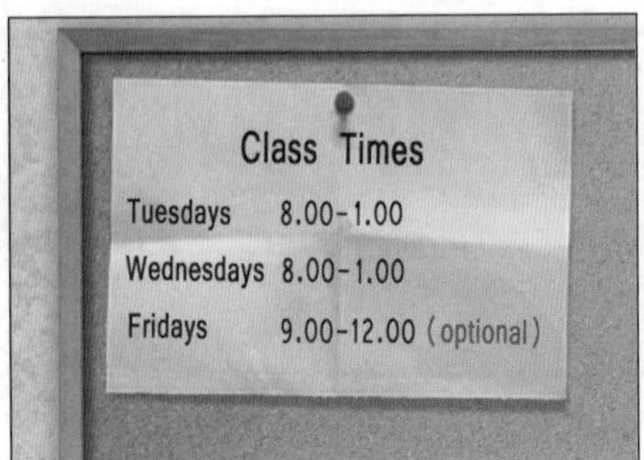

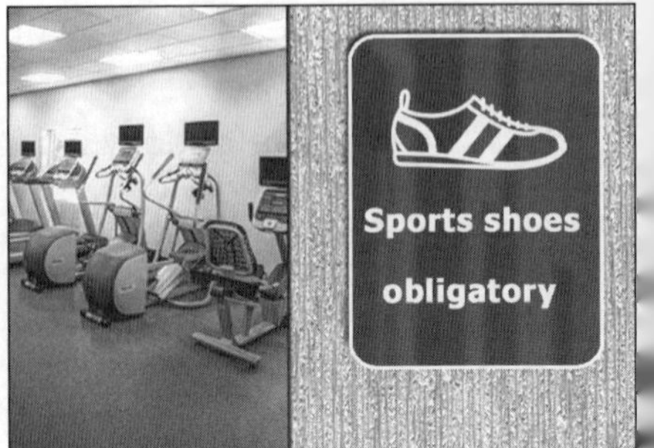

10 You_______________________ to class on Fridays.

11 You _______________________ in one direction.

12 You_______________________ sports shoes here.

ACTIVATION

Test your memory. Cover the sentences. Look at the signs and remember the sentences.

● Look at pictures 1–10. Complete the conversations with *should / shouldn't* + a verb from the list.

ask   get   get up   go (x2)   learn   sit   tell   think   ~~use~~

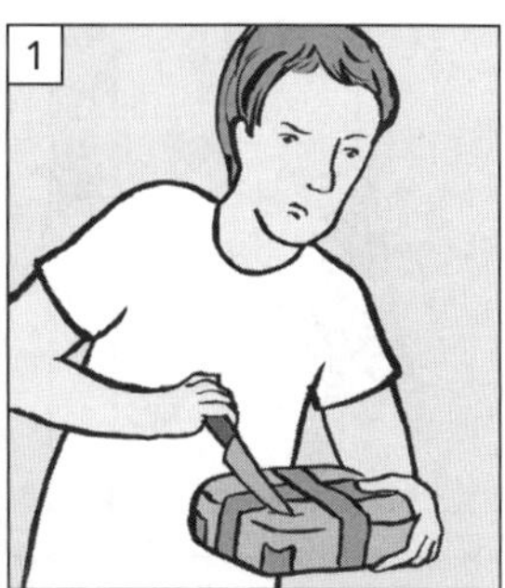

1 **A** What are you doing?

  B I'm trying to open this packet.

  A You <u>shouldn't use</u> a knife! You'll cut yourself!

2 **A** I can't do this exercise. It's too difficult.

  B You ___________________ the teacher for some help.

3 **A** I'm really annoyed with Paula.

  B Why?

  A Because she's always on the computer. She never talks to me!

  B You ___________________ her how you feel. Maybe she doesn't know.

4 **A** Angela's leaving work at the end of the month. She's going to have a baby.

  B We ___________________ her a present.

5 **A** You ___________________ so near the television.

  B Why not?

  A It isn't good for your eyes.

6 **A** I miss the bus for college nearly every day.

  B You ___________________ earlier.

7 **A** Good luck for the match!

  B Thanks, but I'm sure I'm going to lose.

  A You ___________________ like that! Be positive! Say to yourself, 'I'm going to win! I'm going to win!'

8 **A** Come on. Get up. It's 9.30.

  B But I'm tired.

  A You ___________________ to bed so late.

9 **A** Can you make me an omelette, please?

  B Make it yourself!

  A I don't know how to.

  B You ___________________ how to cook then!

10 **A** I'd love to travel round the world.

  B Do you have enough money for the trip?

  A Well, yes.

  B Then I think you ___________________!

ACTIVATION

Test your memory. Cover the conversations. Look at the pictures and remember the advice.

8B GRAMMAR *if* + present, *will / won't* + infinitive (first conditional)

● Complete the stories with the correct form of the verbs in brackets.

1 If you ¹*don't take* an umbrella, you ²*'ll get* wet. (not take, get)

If you ³_____________ wet, you ⁴_____________ a cold. (get, catch)

If you ⁵_____________ a cold, you ⁶_____________ well in your exam tomorrow. (catch, not do)

If you ⁷_____________ well in your exam, you ⁸_____________ a place at university. (not do, not get)

2 If you ⁹_____________ me £3,000, I ¹⁰_____________ a good computer. (lend, buy)

If I ¹¹_____________ a good computer, I ¹²_____________ my own business. (have, start)

If I ¹³_____________ my own business, I ¹⁴_____________ you some money. (have, lend)

If I ¹⁵_____________ you some money, you ¹⁶_____________ a new car. (lend, can buy)

3 If I ¹⁷_____________ borrow your dress, I ¹⁸_____________ to the party. (not can, not go)

If I ¹⁹_____________ to the party, I ²⁰_____________ anyone. (not go, not meet)

If I ²¹_____________ anyone, I ²²_____________ married. (not meet, never get)

If I ²³_____________ married, you ²⁴_____________ any grandchildren. (not get, not have)

4 If I ²⁵_____________ to you now, I ²⁶_____________ the train. (talk, miss)

If I ²⁷_____________ the train, I ²⁸_____________ late for work. (miss, be)

If I ²⁹_____________ late for work, my boss ³⁰_____________ angry with me. (be, be)

If my boss ³¹_____________ angry with me, I ³²_____________ my job. (be, lose)

ACTIVATION

Test your memory. Cover the sentences and look at the pictures. Try to remember the situations.

1 *If you don't take an umbrella,...*
2 *If you lend me £3,000,...*
3 *If I can't borrow your dress,...*
4 *If I talk to you now,...*

English File fourth edition Teacher's Guide Pre-intermediate   Photocopiable © Oxford University Press 2019

8C GRAMMAR possessive pronouns

a (Circle) the correct word in the conversations.

1 A Is that the neighbours' cat?
   B No, **their** / **theirs** is brown, not black.

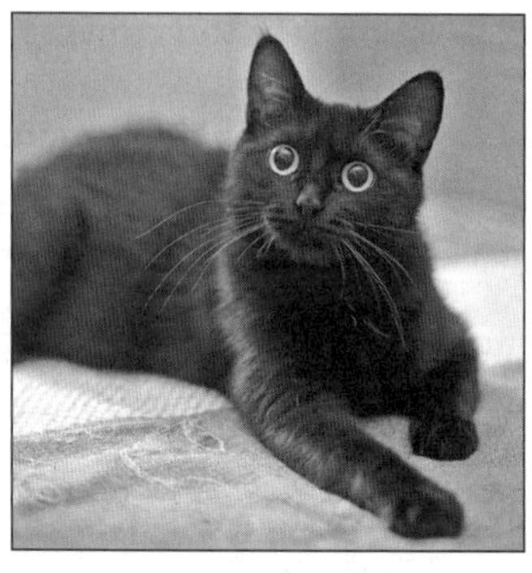

2 A Where does your girlfriend live?
   B She lives in the city centre with **her** / **hers** parents.

3 A Can you move **your** / **yours** car, please?
   B That's not **my** / **mine** car.

4 A Is that Bill's camera?
   B No, it's **our** / **ours** . Why?

5 A **My** / **Mine** son's just got a new job in London.
   B Oh, really? **Our** / **Ours** daughter's working there at the moment.

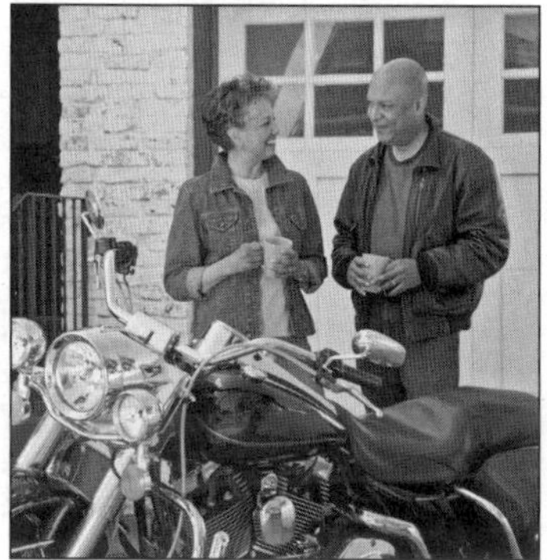

6 A I love this motorbike! Is it **your** / **yours**?
   B No, it's not **my** / **mine**, unfortunately.

b Complete the sentences with the correct subject or object pronouns
(*I*, *me*, etc.) and possessive adjectives or pronouns (*my*, *mine*, etc.).

1 If Andrew doesn't leave soon, *he*'ll miss the train. I think you should
   tell *him* to hurry.

2 A What are ___________ looking for, Mum?
   B ___________ purse. I can't find ___________ anywhere.
   A ___________'s on the table in the dining room.
   B Oh, great! Can you get ___________ for ___________?

3 Do you know where Sally is? ___________ isn't at ___________ desk,
   and one of the administrators is looking for ___________.

4 My brothers are very lazy. ___________ spend most of ___________
   free time sleeping or watching TV. My dad's always angry
   with ___________.

5 A Is that ___________ umbrella, Lucy?
   B No, it isn't ___________. Ask Claire. I think it's ___________.

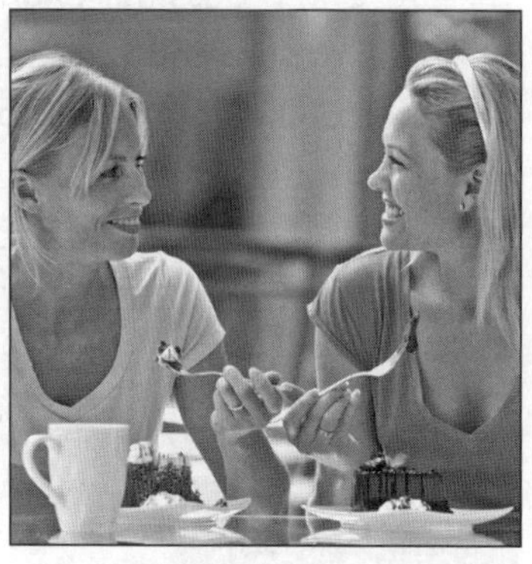

6 My sister and I work in the same office. ___________ hours are the
   same, so ___________ often have lunch together.

ACTIVATION

Write four sentences that are true for you using *I*, *me*, *my*, and *mine*.

9A GRAMMAR *if* + past, *would / wouldn't* + infinitive (second conditional)

a Complete the conversations with the second conditional forms of the verbs in brackets.

1 A Look at Hannah. She's so lazy.

   B I know. If the boss _came_ in now, he _wouldn't be_ very happy. (come, not be).

2 A What ____________ if Adam ____________ you out on a date? (you say, ask)

   B I think I ____________ 'yes'! (say)

3 A Ouch! My tooth hurts.

   B You ____________ so many problems with your teeth if you ____________ to the dentist more often. (not have, go)

4 A Is the answer to number 5 A or B?

   B If I ____________ the answer, I ____________ you. But I don't! (know, tell)

5 A Why don't you cycle to work?

   B I ____________ if I ____________ nearer the office, but I live too far away. (cycle, live)

6 A Wow! Those shoes are great. I ____________ them if I ____________ more money. (buy, have)

   B Well, you ____________ more money if you ____________ shopping so often. (have, not go)

7 A If you ____________ the lottery, how ____________ the money? (win, you spend)

   B I ____________ a big house in the country. (buy)

8 A I'm so tired!

   B We ____________ much better if the neighbours' baby ____________ all night. (sleep, not cry)

b First or second conditional? Complete the sentences with the correct form of the verbs in brackets.

1 What will we do tomorrow if it _rains_ (rain)?

2 If I had a lot of money, I_'d buy_ (buy) a horse.

3 She'd pass her exams if she ____________ (study) harder.

4 I'm sure she ____________ (lend) you the money if you ask her nicely.

5 I'd like your dog more if he ____________ (not be) so noisy!

6 If I ____________ (not see) you this evening, I'll see you on Friday.

7 I ____________ (not say) anything to James if you don't want me to.

8 If you ____________ (not hurry up), we'll miss the train.

9 If I were you, I ____________ (not go) to the UK in the winter.

10 What ____________ you ____________ (do) if you found a snake in your bed?

ACTIVATION

Complete the sentences with your own ideas.

If I could live in another country, I...

If the weather is good this weekend, I...

If I were the President, I...

If I get bored this evening, I...

English File fourth edition Teacher's Guide Pre-intermediate Photocopiable © Oxford University Press 2019

9B GRAMMAR present perfect + *for* and *since*

a Complete the conversations with the present perfect form of the verb + *for* or *since* if necessary.

have

1 **A** How long *have* you *had* your cat?

 B I *'ve had* him *for* two months now.

work

2 **A** How long _________ your daughter _________ in New York?

 B She _________ there _________ four years.

be married

3 **A** How long _________ you _________?

 B I _________ _________ 1981.

be

4 **A** How long _________ your mum _________ a journalist?

 B She _________ a journalist _________ she left university.

know

5 **A** How long _________ they _________ each other?

 B They _________ each other _________ 50 years.

live

6 **A** How long _________ you _________ here?

 B We _________ here _________ 2006.

have

7 **A** How long _________ you _________ this phobia?

 B I _________ it _________ about 2010.

play

8 **A** How long _________ you _________ for this team?

 B I _________ for them _________ I was 17.

b **Test your memory.** Cover the conversations and look at the pictures. Can you remember the conversations?

ACTIVATION

Write four sentences about yourself, two with the present perfect + *for*, and two with the present perfect + *since*.

9C GRAMMAR present perfect or past simple? (2)

a Complete the conversations with the present perfect or the past simple form of the verbs in brackets.

1
A How long have you _played_ (play) the violin?
B Since I _was_ (be) four. I ___________ (love) music all my life.
A Was it a difficult instrument to learn?
B It ___________ (be) very hard when I ___________ (start).

2
A ___________ your brother ___________ (finish) university?
B Yes, he ___________ (finish) three weeks ago.
A What's he going to do now?
B He ___________ (not decide) yet.

3
A Where do your parents live?
B In Brighton. They ___________ (live) there since last year. Before that they ___________ (live) in Birmingham.
A Why ___________ they ___________ (leave) Birmingham?
B Because my dad ___________ (retire), and they ___________ (want) to live near the sea.

4
A I ___________ (see) Oliver yesterday. He ___________ (tell) me about your plans to move to Australia.
B Yes, I'm very excited...and a bit nervous too.
A ___________ you ever ___________ (live) abroad before?
B No, never. I ___________ (never be) very interested in travelling.
A How about your wife?
B Oh, Lily loves travelling! She ___________ (visit) lots of different countries.

5
A ___________ you ___________ (hear) about Andy and Francesca?
B No. What?
A They ___________ (separate).
B Really? That's a pity. I ___________ (think) they were very happy together.

6
A Is your brother married?
B Yes, he ___________ (be) married for ages – about ten years. He ___________ (meet) his wife Sarah when they were both at secondary school. They ___________ (get) married when they ___________ (be) only 18.

b Practise the conversations with a partner.

ACTIVATION

Complete the sentences with information about real people (either people you know or famous people).

1 ___________ and ___________ were married for about ___________ years.
2 ___________ and ___________ have been married since ___________.
3 ___________ lived in ___________ for about ___________ years.
4 ___________ have / has lived in ___________ for about ___________ years.

10A   GRAMMAR   expressing movement

Look at the pictures. Complete the sentences with a preposition of movement.

1   A police helicopter flew _over_ the houses.
2   The robber fell ___________ the stairs.
3   A bird flew ___________ the bridge.
4   They danced ___________ the fire.
5   The policeman walked ___________ the car.
6   The cat ran ___________ the wall.
7   The road goes ___________ the village.

8   The boy is climbing ___________ the tree.
9   He jumped ___________ the swimming pool.
10 The dog swam ___________ the river.
11 The rock star threw a TV ___________ the window.
12 The skiers are skiing ___________ the mountain.

Test your memory. Cover the sentences and look at the pictures. Say the sentences.

10B GRAMMAR word order of phrasal verbs

a What are the people doing? Complete each sentence with a phrasal verb. Use one word from each list.

get (x2) go look pick put take throw ~~turn~~ write	away (x2) down for off on (x2) up (x2)

1 She's _turning on_ the TV.

2 He's ________________ his shoes.

3 They're ________________ the questions.

4 He's ________________ her books.

5 She's ________________ for the weekend.

6 He's ________________ the newspaper.

7 She's ________________ her phone.

8 He's ________________ early.

9 She's ________________ her coat.

10 They're ________________ well.

b Circle the right answer. Tick (✓) if both are correct.

1 Can I **try on this jacket** / **try this jacket on**, please? ✓
2 I can't hear the music. Can you **turn it up** / **turn up it**?
3 They're my sister's children. I'm **looking after them** / **looking them after**.
4 Jane called when you were out. Can you **call her back** / **call back her**?
5 **Turn off your mobiles** / **Turn your mobiles off** before the exam begins.
6 Your clothes are all over the floor. Please **pick up them** / **pick them up**.
7 I can't find my car keys. Can you help me **look for them** / **look them for**?
8 If I lend you the money, when will you **pay me back** / **pay back me**?

ACTIVATION

Test your memory. Cover the sentences in **a**. Look at the pictures and say what's happening.

a Look at the pictures. Complete the sentences with the present or past passive form of the verbs in brackets.

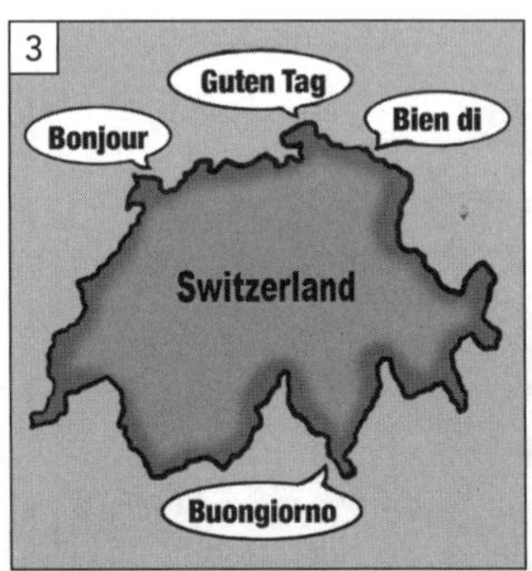

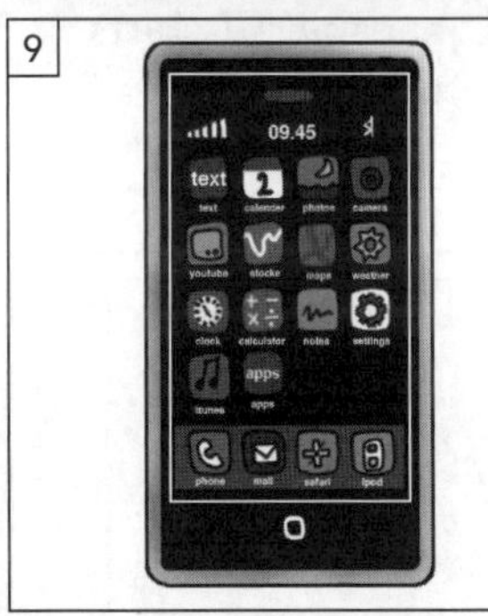

1 The film *Jurassic Park* *is based* on the book by Michael Crichton. (base)
2 The symbol of the Olympic Games _____________ in 1912. (design)
3 Four national languages _____________ in Switzerland. (speak)
4 The pyramids _____________ nearly 5,000 years ago. (build)
5 About 350 films _____________ at the Berlin Film Festival every year. (show)
6 P4 is a very small new moon which _____________ in 2011. (discover)
7 Seat belts _____________ in planes until the 1930s. (not use)
8 The Hunger Games books _____________ by Suzanne Collins. (write)
9 The first smartphone _____________ in 1992 by IBM. (invent)
10 *Pétanque* _____________ a lot all over France. (play)
11 *The Last Supper* _____________ by Leonardo da Vinci. (paint)
12 The Eiffel Tower _____________ by about seven million people a year. (visit)

b Cover the sentences and look at the pictures. Can you remember the sentences?

ACTIVATION

1 Write two past passive sentences about inventions or discoveries made by someone from your country.

2 Write two present passive sentences about things that are produced, grown, or made somewhere in your country.

11A GRAMMAR *used to / didn't use to*

Look at how Alice and Johnny have changed. For each person, write eight sentences using *used to / didn't use to* about what they were like in the past.

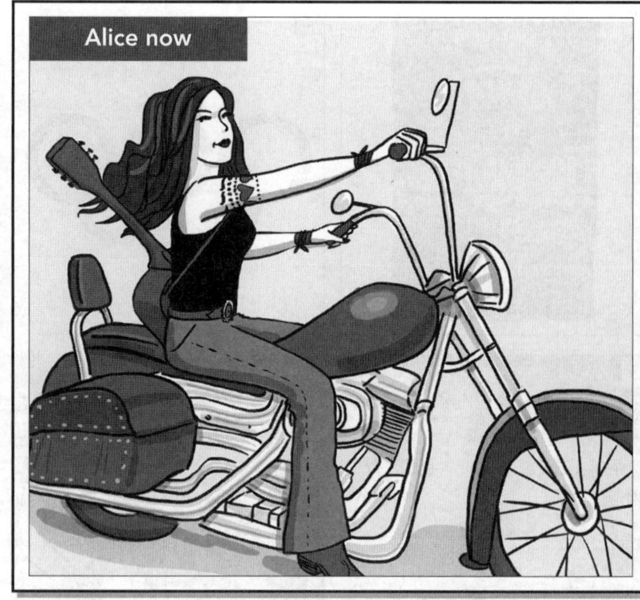

1 She *used to wear* dresses.
2 She *didn't use to ride* a motorbike.
3 ___________________ the violin.
4 ___________________ glasses.

5 ___________________ a tattoo on her arm.
6 ___________________ very long hair.
7 ___________________ jeans and T-shirts.
8 ___________________ the guitar.

9   ___________________ TV all day.
10 ___________________ any sport or exercise.
11 ___________________ a suit and tie.
12 ___________________ a beard and
    a moustache.

13 ___________________ a bit overweight.
14 ___________________ jeans.
15 ___________________ healthy food.
16 ___________________ long hair.

1 Look at the pictures. Make sentences with *used to* and *didn't use to* about Alice and Johnny.

2 Write two sentences with *used to* and two sentences with *didn't use to* about yourself.

English File fourth edition Teacher's Guide Pre-intermediate   Photocopiable © Oxford University Press 2019

11B GRAMMAR *might / might not* (possibility)

a Complete the conversations with *might / might not* and a verb from the list.

be (x2) buy ~~fall~~ go (x2) have like meet phone tell

1 **A** Look, Mummy, I can ride a bicycle without using my hands!

  B Oh, be careful! You *might fall*!

2 **A** Are you going to go to the party?

  B I'm not sure. My ex-husband ___________________ there, and I really don't want to see him.

3 **A** What's this? It looks very strange.

  B It's a special dish from my country. Try it, you ___________________ it.

4 **A** I ___________________ to class tomorrow. I think I'll have to work late.

  B OK. I'll text you and tell you if there's any homework.

5 **A** Are you going to be at home this evening?

  B I'm not sure. I ___________________ some friends for a drink.

6 **A** I think I ___________________ buy this T-shirt.

  B Don't be silly. It's much too small for you.

7 **A** Where are you going for your holiday?

  B I don't know. I'm really busy at work, so I ___________________ a holiday this year.

8 **A** Are you going to send Adam an email?

  B No, I think I ___________________ him. It's quicker.

9 **A** How are you going to get there?

  B I ___________________ by train...but maybe it's better to drive...I don't know...

  A Come on – you need to make a decision!

10 **A** Are you going to tell Anna about seeing Mike with that woman in the pub?

  B I ___________________ her. I'm not sure.

11 **A** I ___________________ late for class tomorrow. I'm seeing the doctor at 8.30.

  B OK. Thanks for telling me.

b Practise the conversations in **a** with a partner.

ACTIVATION

Write two things you might do next weekend, and two things you might not have time to do tomorrow.

11C GRAMMAR *so, neither* + auxiliaries

a Complete the conversations with *so* + auxiliary + *I* or *neither* + auxiliary + *I*.

1 A I don't like that new building much.
   B *Neither do I*. It looks like a spaceship.

2 A I passed the exam!
   B *So did I*! I got 92%.

3 A I can't swim, I'm afraid.
   B ___________________. Perhaps we should have lessons.

4 A I'm not very hungry.
   B ___________________. I'll just have a sandwich.

5 A I've finished university.
   B ___________________. I'm looking for a job now!

6 A I didn't like the film.
   B ___________________. It was too slow.

7 A I was born in 1989.
   B Really? ___________________.

8 A I don't have any brothers or sisters.
   B ___________________. But I have a lot of cousins.

9 A I'm going to stay at home this evening.
   B ___________________. I'm quite tired.

10 A I have to go to work on Saturday.
    B ___________________. I hate working at the weekend.

11 A I don't get on with Lydia very well.
    B ___________________. We don't really have much in common.

12 A I got married in 2005.
    B ___________________. But I got divorced a year later!

13 A I was working in London last year.
    B ___________________. What a coincidence!

14 A I haven't been to South America.
    B ___________________, but I'd love to go.

15 A I want to go to the beach today.
    B ___________________. It's a beautiful day.

16 A I won't go to that restaurant again.
    B ___________________. The food was awful.

17 A I'm going to stop using Facebook.
    B ___________________. I spend too much time on it.

18 A I'd like to go to New Zealand.
    B ___________________. They say it's beautiful.

19 A I'll do my homework on the bus.
    B ___________________. It's very easy.

20 A I have a twin sister.
    B ___________________. That's amazing!

b Practise the conversations in **a** with a partner.

ACTIVATION

Write a two-line conversation with *so* + auxiliary + *I*, and another with *neither* + auxiliary + *I*.

12A GRAMMAR past perfect

Look at the pictures. Complete the sentences with the past simple
and past perfect form of the verbs in brackets.

1   When they *got* (get) to the station the train *had already left* (already leave).

2   Kate ________________ (be) very cold because she ________________ (not take) her coat.

3   The printer ________________ (not work) because he ________________ (not turn it on).

4   I ________________ (not can) take a photo of the crocodile because I ________________ (forget)
    to charge the battery.

5   They ________________ (never fly) before and they ________________ (be) very nervous.

6   When he ________________ (arrive) at the pool he realized he ________________ (not bring) his
    swimsuit.

7   She ________________ (not be) hungry because she ________________ (just have) dinner.

8   She ________________ (have to) pay again because she ________________ (lose) her ticket.

9   The waitress ________________ (run) after him because he ________________ (not pay) the bill.

10 The fire engine ________________ (arrive) after the men ________________ (put out) the fire.

11 They ________________ (can) speak French because they ________________ (learn) it at school.

12 She ________________ (be) tired because she ________________ (be) in the queue all night.

ACTIVATION

Continue these sentences with the past perfect.

I didn't recognize him because…
My father was really angry because…
When I got to work / school today I realized that…

We couldn't get a table at the restaurant because…
I didn't want anything for dinner because…
I didn't want to go to the cinema because…

12B GRAMMAR reported (or indirect) speech

a Look at the pictures. Change the direct speech to reported speech.

1 She said that *she couldn't see anything*.
2 He told her that ___________________.
3 He told his father that ___________________.
4 The man said that ___________________.

5 She said that ___________________.
6 He told his wife that ___________________.
7 He told her that ___________________.
8 She said that ___________________.

b Look at the pictures. Change the reported speech to direct speech.

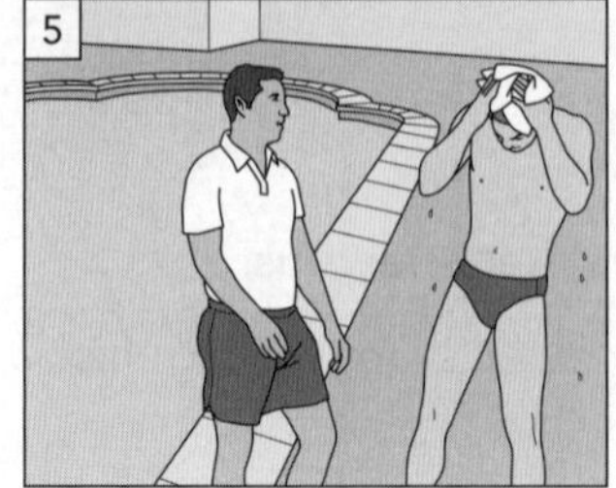

1 She said that she wasn't very hungry.
   'I'm not very hungry.'
2 The nurse told the man that it wouldn't hurt.
   ____
3 He told the police that it was his mother's car.
   ____
4 She said that she had finished her homework.
   ____

5 He told the instructor that he couldn't swim.
   ____
6 He told her that he would always love her.
   ____
7 They said that they wanted to check out.
   ____
8 He told the woman that he was lost.
   ____

ACTIVATION

Test your memory. Cover the sentences and look at the pictures in **a** and **b**.
Use reported speech to say what each speaker said.

She said that she couldn't say anything.

12C GRAMMAR questions with and without auxiliaries

Make questions using the present simple or past simple. Then circle the correct answer.

1 Where / polar bears / live

   Where do polar bears live?　　　　　　　　　　the North Pole / the South Pole

2 Who / direct / the film *The Godfather*

   Who directed the film The Godfather?　　　　Martin Scorsese / Francis Ford Coppola

3 Who / paint / *The Scream*

   _______________________________________? Gustav Klimt / Edvard Munch

4 Where / manga comics / come from

   _______________________________________? Japan / China

5 Which country / produce / more coffee

   _______________________________________? Brazil / Colombia

6 Which country / have / a blue and yellow flag

   _______________________________________? Greece / Sweden

7 When / the Second World War / end

   _______________________________________? 1945 / 1955

8 Which country / win / the most gold medals at the 2016 Olympics

   _______________________________________? China / USA

9 Which character / Ian Fleming / create

   _______________________________________? James Bond / Sherlock Holmes

10 How many countries / belong to / the original European Economic Community in 1957

   _______________________________________? 6 / 12

11 Which company / Kevin Systrom and Mike Krieger / start

   _______________________________________? Instagram / Facebook

12 Where / people / speak / Yorùbá

   _______________________________________? West Africa / East Africa

13 Which film / win / the Oscar for best film in 2017

   _______________________________________? *La La Land* / *Moonlight*

14 Which fruit / contain / more sugar

   _______________________________________? a pineapple / an orange

ACTIVATION

Test your memory. Cover the questions and look at the answers. Can you remember the questions?

1A Student profile

A pairwork activity

Sts interview each other and complete a profile of their partner. The profile revises question forms and provides the teacher with useful information about Sts. Copy one sheet per student.

> **LANGUAGE**
>
> *What's your name? What do you do? Where were you born?*, etc.

- Give out the sheets. Focus on the question beginnings in **a**. Give Sts, in pairs, a few minutes to decide what each question should be.

EXTRA SUPPORT Remind Sts about the present continuous and its question form. Tell Sts that they need it for question 8.

- Check answers. Model and drill the questions for Sts to copy the rhythm.

1	What's your first name?	8	Why are you learning English?
2	What's your surname?	9	What languages do you speak?
3	Where are you from?	10	What do you like doing in your free time?
4	Where do you live?		
5	What's your email address?	11	Which social networking sites do you use? / Which social networking sites do you like?
6	What do you do?		
7	Where were you born?		

- Now focus on **b**. Demonstrate the activity by getting Sts to ask you the first two questions. Encourage them to ask you to spell your name and surname. Put Sts in pairs to interview each other and tell them to write the information in the profile. You could tell Sts that they can invent their address and email address if they want to.
- You could collect in the forms for your own reference.

EXTRA CHALLENGE Get Sts to interview each other. They could cover the questions and ask them from memory.

1B Ask me some questions…

A group board game

Sts practise making questions using the present simple tense. Make one copy for every three or four Sts. You will also need one dice per group, and one counter per student.

> **LANGUAGE**
>
> *What does your mother look like?*
> *What do you do to relax?*, etc.

- Put Sts in groups of three or four. Give each group a copy of the board game, a dice, and some counters. Demonstrate the activity by writing on the board WHAT TIME / YOU GET UP? WHERE / YOUR MOTHER WORK? Elicit the completed questions and write *do* and *does* in the missing space. Ask a few Sts the questions.

- In their groups, Sts take turns to roll the dice and move the counter. They then ask the questions to the student on their right.
- Encourage Sts to ask for and give as much information as possible.
- When Sts have finished, get some feedback from various groups.

EXTRA IDEA If you want to make it longer, Sts can play with coins (heads = move 1 square, tails = move 2).

1C What are they doing?

A class guessing activity

Sts draw on the board and the others have to guess. Copy and cut up one sheet per 18 Sts.

> **LANGUAGE**
>
> Prepositions of place, clothes
> *He's wearing a big hat.*

- Draw a man walking in the park. Ask: *What is the man doing?* Elicit the answer and only accept *A man is walking in the park.* Give each student one card.
- Call Sts to the board and let them draw what they have on their cards. Give other Sts a minute or two to guess. Sts guess the sentence until someone gets it exactly right. Remind Sts that they must get the sentence exactly right.

NON-CUT ALTERNATIVE Cut it in half and Sts play in pairs, taking turns to draw and guess.

2A Truth or lie?

A group guessing activity

Sts create two stories, one real and one false, while practising the past simple. Copy and cut up one sheet per group of four or five Sts.

> **LANGUAGE**
>
> Past simple

- Write on the board: A TIME WHEN I WAS LATE TO WORK AND A TIME WHEN I ARGUED WITH MY BROTHER. Tell them a short story about those two times and tell them one is true and one isn't. Let Sts decide which one they think is true and give them the correct answer. Tell them they are going to tell two stories in their groups.
- Put Sts in groups of four or five. Give each group a set of cards and tell Sts to take two cards each. Give Sts time to look at their cards and think of two stories.
- Sts tell each other the stories and try to guess which ones are true and which ones are false.
- Get some feedback from various groups.

2B Who did it?

A group mingle activity

Sts try to find out who is guilty by asking and answering questions using the past continuous. Copy and cut up one sheet per 12 Sts.

> **LANGUAGE**
>
> Past continuous
> *At four o'clock, I was having a bath.*

- Read the paragraph from the top of the sheet. Elicit the relevant information from Sts and write on the board. Tell Sts that they are all characters in this mystery and they have to find out who stole Sophie Hatcher's money. Elicit from Sts the questions they should ask: *What's your name? What do you do? Why are you in the hotel?*. Now tell them the police are interested in two times: four o'clock and 4.30. Elicit the question: *What were you doing at...?*. Leave the questions on the board for Sts to refer to. Tell them they all have to tell the truth, except for the thief.

- Now give out the cards. **Tell Sts they mustn't show their cards to other Sts!** You could choose a stronger student to play Alex Cameron (the thief). If you have fewer than 12 Sts, make sure one of them is Alex Cameron (the thief). If you have more than 12 Sts, make two big groups and have them work separately – make sure one student in each group is the thief. Give Sts a couple of minutes to look at their cards and think about their answers to the questions on the board. This also gives the thief time to invent one lie.

- Give Sts a fixed amount of time, e.g. ten minutes, to move around asking questions. Encourage them to write down the information they find out.

- When the time runs out, give Sts a couple of minutes to decide, using their information, who stole Sophie's money.

- Find out who Sts think is the thief. Reveal who stole the money. If any Sts guessed correctly, they win!

2C Sentence race

A group activity

Sts race to complete sentences. Copy and cut one sheet per four or five Sts.

> **LANGUAGE**
>
> Connectors: *so, because, but, although*

- Put Sts in groups of four or five. Give each group one strip, face down. Put the other strips on your desk in separate piles for each group.

- Tell Sts they have to finish the sentence as quickly as they can in a logical and correct way and then bring it to you. If it is correct, they will get another one. If it isn't, they will have to correct it.

- Say *Go!* and tell Sts to turn over their strip and start writing.

- Check sentences when Sts bring them to you. If the sentence is correct, give them another one. If it isn't, let them take it back and try to correct it. When the time limit is up (or when one group has completed 20 sentences), stop the activity. The group with the most correct sentences is the winner.

NON-CUT ALTERNATIVE Put Sts in pairs and give them a sheet face down. Tell Sts they have to finish the sentences as quickly as they can in a logical and correct way. Say *Go!* and tell Sts to turn over their sheet and start writing. Set a time limit and monitor while Sts are writing. When the time limit is up or a pair has finished, stop the activity and check answers. The pair with the most correct sentences is the winner.

3A A day in...

A pairwork/group activity

Sts choose a city and plan a day using the information given. Copy one sheet per pair.

> **LANGUAGE**
>
> *be going to*
> *We're going to have breakfast at New York Bagels.*

- Put Sts in pairs. Tell them they're going to plan a day in Paris or New York. Give each pair a sheet.

- Explain that first they should decide together whether they want to go to New York or Paris. Then, they can choose any activities from the list, or any of the shopping options, but they have to pay attention to the time they take (in brackets) and the times they have on the schedule. Give them a set time, e.g. ten minutes, to plan their day. Monitor to make sure they're doing the activity correctly.

- Now put two pairs of Sts together. Sts have to explain their plan for the day to the other group using *be going to* and, where appropriate, explain why they have decided to do each of the things in their plan. Put an example on the board: WE'RE GOING TO VISIT THE MUSEUM OF MODERN ART BECAUSE IT'S ONE OF THE BEST ART MUSEUMS IN THE WORLD. Elicit further questions from Sts, e.g. *Where are you going to go after that? What are you going to do there?*. Encourage them to ask extra questions.

- Now ask Sts to talk about the plan they heard in pairs and decide if they would like to go on that trip or not, and why. Get feedback.

EXTRA IDEA Cut the sheet in half, so half the groups will do Paris and the other half New York. Get some Sts to explain their plan to the class.

3B Come fly with me!

A pairwork information gap activity

Sts complete questions and ask each other for some missing information. Copy one sheet per pair and cut into **A** and **B**.

> **LANGUAGE**
>
> Present continuous for future arrangements
> *Who are you flying with? How much are you taking?*
> Travel vocabulary

- Put Sts in pairs, **A** and **B**, and give out the sheets. Sit Sts face to face if possible. Explain that they have one completed boarding card and another boarding card with missing information.
- Give Sts time to read both boarding cards and deal with any vocabulary problems.
- Focus on the questions in **a**. Tell Sts to look at the boarding card with the missing information and point out that the first question has been done for them. They have to complete questions 2–7 individually using the present continuous to find out the missing information from their partner.
- Check all the questions before starting the activity. Write them on the board if necessary.

2	Where are you flying from?	6	What time are you
3	Where are you flying to?		arriving?
4	When are you leaving?	7	Where are you sitting?
5	What time are you leaving?		

- Now focus on **b**. **A** asks **B** his / her questions and completes his / her boarding card with the missing information. Then Sts swap roles.

EXTRA IDEA Fast finishers could look at the boarding cards, cover the questions and ask the questions from memory.

3C Can you explain the word?

A group card game

Sts practise giving definitions using relative pronouns. Copy and cut up one set of cards per group of four Sts.

> **LANGUAGE**
>
> *It's a thing which... / a person who... It's a kind of... It's like... You do it when...*

- If necessary, revise language for giving definitions before you start. Put Sts in groups of four. Give each group a set of cards face down or in an envelope.
- Demonstrate the activity. Pick up a card and describe the word/phrase until Sts guess it. Insist they say the exact word/phrase on the card with the correct pronunciation before showing them the card.
- Sts play the game, taking turns to take a card and define the word. Tell Sts they must <u>not</u> use the word on the card. The first student in the group who says the word or phrase correctly gets the card. The winner is the student with the most cards.

NON-CUT ALTERNATIVE Copy one sheet per pair and cut in half. Put Sts in pairs and give them one half each. **A** begins by defining one of the words on his / her sheet. If **B** can say the word, then it's **B**'s turn to give a definition.

4A Find the response

A pairwork activity

Sts match sentences to appropriate responses. Copy one sheet per student.

> **LANGUAGE**
>
> Present perfect
> *yet, just, already*
> *I've just spoken to her. I haven't met her yet. They've already gone home.*

- Give out the sheets and focus on **a**. Point out that the first one (1h) has been done for them. Now get Sts to match 1–14 to responses a–n.
- Check answers.

2e	3a	4m	5k	6n	7b	8l	9c	10j	11i	12g	13f	14d

- Now focus on **b**. Elicit or teach the meaning of *fold*, and tell Sts that they should fold their sheets vertically.
- Put Sts in pairs **A** and **B**. Ask them to look only at the sentences and not to look at the responses. Read out the first one and see who can remember what the response was, e.g. *Have you done your English homework?* (Yes, I've just finished it.)
- Sts continue in pairs. Sts **A** read out the sentences first and Sts **B** have to remember what the responses were (without looking at the sheet).
- They then swap roles. Monitor and check pronunciation.

4B Have you ever...?

A group activity

Sts practise making questions from prompts and describe events, contrasting the present perfect and the past simple. Copy and cut up one sheet per group of three or four Sts.

> **LANGUAGE**
>
> *Have you ever* + past participle...?
> Past and present tense follow-up questions
> Past tense **+** and **−** forms
> *Have you ever been to London? Yes, I have. No, I haven't. When did you go there?*

- Copy the exchange in the **Language** box on the board and elicit that this is a typical exchange which begins in the present perfect, and then goes on to the past simple to ask for details.
- Put Sts in groups of three or four and give each group an envelope with a copy of the strips. Sts take it in turns to take a strip out of the envelope and ask the other Sts in their group the question.
- Demonstrate the activity first by getting a student to ask you the question they've drawn out of the envelope. Answer the question and elicit a follow-up question.
- Encourage the Sts to ask follow-up questions.
- Get some feedback from various groups.

NON-CUT ALTERNATIVE Make one copy per pair and cut in half horizontally. Give Sts half each and get them to ask and answer the questions.

4C The same or different?

A pairwork activity

Sts compare information about their lifestyle and practise using *something, anything, nothing,* etc. They agree with or contradict a series of statements and explain why. Copy one sheet per student.

> **LANGUAGE**
> *something, nothing, anything, somebody / someone, anyone,* etc.
> *I don't usually watch anything on TV in the evenings.*

- Put Sts in pairs and give out the sheets. Focus on **a**. Demonstrate the activity by completing the first sentence, *I always have something to eat...,* and writing it on the board.
- Ask Sts to complete the sentences individually or in pairs. Give Sts enough time to complete their sheets.
- Check answers and write them on the board if necessary.

> 1 something   2 anywhere   3 something   4 anything
> 5 anything   6 nobody / no one   7 somewhere   8 anything
> 9 something   10 nothing   11 nobody / no one
> 12 anywhere   13 anyone / anybody   14 somewhere
> 15 nowhere   16 anything   17 somebody / someone
> 18 somewhere

- Now focus on **b**. Demonstrate the activity by telling the class about the first statement, e.g. *Sentence 1 isn't true for me because I never eat anything.* Encourage the class to ask for more information, e.g. *What do you drink? When do you have something to eat?.*
- Sts talk about each statement and say if it's true or not true for them and why not.
- Stop the activity when most pairs seem to have finished and get some feedback.

5A Which do you prefer? Why?

A pairwork / group speaking activity

Sts say which of two things or activities they prefer and why. Personalize the activity by writing local things to compare on the last two cards. Copy and cut up one sheet per group of four or five Sts.

> **LANGUAGE**
> Comparative forms
> *I prefer swimming in a pool because it's cleaner.*

- Put Sts in groups of four or five and give out a set of cards face down.
- Demonstrate the activity by asking a student to pick a card and ask you. Sts take turns to pick a card and ask the other Sts: *Which do you prefer, ...or...? Why?*
- Monitor while Sts are talking, correcting any mistakes with comparative forms. When Sts have finished, get feedback from a few pairs or groups.

NON-CUT ALTERNATIVE Give out one uncut sheet to each pair or group. Get them to discuss the topics on each card saying which they prefer and why.

5B Superlative questions

A pairwork quiz

Sts practise forming superlatives to complete questions to ask their partner. Copy one sheet per pair and cut into **A** and **B**.

> **LANGUAGE**
> Superlatives: *the biggest, the heaviest,* etc.

- Put Sts in pairs, **A** and **B**, and give out the sheets.
- Focus on **a** and tell Sts to complete the questions using the superlative form of the adjective in brackets. Explain that sometimes the question asks about the superlative in the world / history and sometimes it's the superlative from the three options *(Which of these...)*. Point out that the answer is in bold.

> **A**
> 1 the richest   2 the most populated   3 the most dangerous
> 4 the largest   5 the most recent   6 the most popular
> **B**
> 1 the noisiest   2 the smallest   3 the most popular
> 4 the largest   5 the youngest   6 the longest

- Sts **A** asks Sts **B** their questions, giving the three options. When **A** has finished, they swap roles. The student with the most correct answers wins.

5C How much / How many...?

A group activity

Sts read out and answer questions using *How much / How many*. Copy and cut up one sheet per group of three or four.

> **LANGUAGE**
> Quantifiers: *how much / how many, too much / (not) enough*

- Write on the board: HOW ____ CLASSES DO YOU TEACH A WEEK? Elicit the missing word (*many*) and ask Sts to guess. Write down, as they say them (*a lot, quite a lot, not many, too many, not enough, a few*). Give them the answer and write possible answers on the board for Sts to use as reference.
- Put Sts in groups of three or four and give each group a set of cards. Each student takes a turn taking a card, asking the question (using *much* or *many*) to the student to their left. Then they ask the follow-up questions for more information. Sts take cards and ask questions until the cards or the time run out.

6A Positive or negative?

A pairwork activity

Sts practise making positive predictions. Copy one sheet per pair or per student.

> **LANGUAGE**
> *will / won't* (predictions)
> *It'll be great! It won't work.*

- Give out one sheet per pair or per student. Go through sentences 1–12 in **You say** and **The optimist says**.

- Tell Sts to imagine that they are all optimists. Focus on sentence 1 and elicit a prediction, e.g. *Don't worry. I'm sure you'll find it.*
- Sts continue in pairs, writing positive predictions. Monitor and help.
- When Sts have finished, get them to mingle (alone or in pairs) and read sentences from **You say** to another student/pair and listen to their answers.
- Get feedback. You could get Sts to tell you which answer they liked best or get them to volunteer their own answers.

EXTRA IDEA Repeat the activity, but ask Sts to be pessimists this time. Give them some alternative starts *That's not good, That sounds awful/boring, Oh no!*, etc. Give them enough time to write the responses. Monitor and help. You could get Sts to decide which sentences (optimistic or pessimistic) they would use.

6B Guess my sentence

A pairwork activity

Sts practise *will / shall* sentences by trying to guess the missing part of the sentence. Copy one sheet per pair and cut into **A** and **B**.

> **LANGUAGE**
> *will / shall* + verb
> *I think I'll buy them.*
> *Shall I call you on your mobile?*

- Demonstrate the activity. On a piece of paper, write the sentence, *I'm very tired. I think I'll sit down for half an hour.* Then write on the board the sentence: I'M VERY TIRED. I THINK I _______________ FOR HALF AN HOUR.
- Tell the class they have to guess the missing phrase, which is a verb or a verb phrase with *'ll*. Elicit a possibility, making sure Sts say the whole sentence. If their guess is not the same as you have on your piece of paper, say *Try again* until someone says your sentence. Then show them your piece of paper and say *That's right.*
- Put Sts in pairs, **A** and **B**, and give out the sheets. Sit **A** and **B** face to face if possible.
- Focus on the sheets and explain that half of their sentences have gaps, and their partner has the complete sentences.
- Give Sts a minute or so to read their sentences and <u>think</u> of possible completions, but <u>not</u> to write them in the gaps.
- Sts take turns to guess the missing parts of the sentences. Stress that Sts should say the whole sentence each time, not just the missing words. Their partner should help and prompt if necessary. When a student correctly guesses the exact sentence he / she writes in the missing words.

6C Talk about it

A group board game

Sts revise past, present, and future forms. Make one copy of the board game for groups of three or four Sts. You also need one dice per group and one counter per student.

> **LANGUAGE**
> Sentence formation in past and present forms

- Put Sts in small groups of three or four. Give each group a copy of the board game and a dice.

❗ If you don't have a dice, give each group a coin. Sts toss the coin for their go and move 1 for heads and 2 for tails.

- Explain the rules of the game. Sts throw a dice and move the corresponding number of circles on the board. When they land on a circle, they must talk for 30 seconds about the topic. Then each of the other Sts in the group must ask them a question about the topic.
- Sts play the game in their groups. The game finishes when someone reaches the *Finish* square.

7A I'm going to tell you about…

A pairwork discussion activity

Sts choose six topics to discuss with a partner. Copy one sheet per student.

> **LANGUAGE**
> Verbs + *to*

- Put Sts in pairs and give out the sheets.
- Focus on the instructions. Tell Sts to choose six topics they want to talk about with a partner. Tell them to think about what they want to say. Set a time limit.
- Tell Sts to discuss the topics, taking turns to choose the topic. Encourage Sts to ask for and give as much information as possible.
- Monitor and help where necessary, particularly with the verb forms.
- When Sts have finished, get feedback on some of the topics.

7B Questions with gerunds

A pairwork question and answer activity

Sts complete the questions and then ask a partner. Copy one sheet per pair and cut into **A** and **B**.

> **LANGUAGE**
> Verb + *-ing*
> *Do you enjoy reading in bed? Are you good at cooking?*

- Put Sts in pairs, **A** and **B**, and give out the sheets.
- Focus on **a**. Give Sts time to complete their questions with verbs from the list in the gerund. Then check answers.

> **A**
> **1** getting up **2** flying **3** waiting **4** going **5** reading
> **6** cooking **7** doing **8** doing
>
> **B**
> **1** walking **2** doing **3** going **4** going **5** playing **6** eating
> **7** getting **8** being

- Elicit that the answer to the question *Do you mind…?* is either *No, I don't mind* or *Yes, I hate it.*
- Focus on **b**. Sts take turns asking their questions and asking for more information.

7C In the UK

A pairwork speaking activity

Sts decide if sentences about laws in the UK are true or false, and then talk about the situation in their own country. Copy one sheet per student.

- Put Sts in pairs and give out the sheets.
- Focus on **a** and give Sts a few minutes to read all the sentences and make sure they understand them. Set a time limit, e.g. ten minutes, for pairs to discuss each sentence and decide if it is true or not true.
- Now focus on **b** and elicit ideas. Find out if any pair identified all the false sentences.

1 F **2** F (The age limit is 18.) **3** T **4** F **5** F (Nobody has to do military service.) **6** F (You can ride a 50cc motorbike at 16.) **7** T **8** F **9** T **10** F **11** F (You have to be 18.) **12** T **13** F **14** F **15** F **16** T **17** F **18** T

- Finally, focus on **c**. Tell Sts to go through each law and say if the laws are the same or different in their country, and which ones they'd like to have in their country.
- Get some feedback from various pairs.

8A I need some advice

A group speaking activity

Sts practise giving advice to each other. Copy and cut up one sheet per group of four or five Sts.

- Put Sts in groups of four or five. Give each group a set of cards, face down.
- Sts take turns reading the situations. Each student in the group has to give a different piece of advice. The person who the reader thinks gave the best advice keeps the card. Demonstrate by picking up a card and reading the problem. Let Sts give you advice, get as many to talk as possible. Then choose one of the options and say *I'll do that*.
- Sts continue until the cards are finished. The student with the most cards is the winner.

NON-CUT ALTERNATIVE Copy one sheet per pair and cut it in half. Put Sts in pairs and give them half each. They alternate reading their problems and giving advice.

8B Conditionals race

A pairwork activity

Sts complete first conditional sentences as fast as they can and then compare them with a different pair. Copy one sheet per pair.

- Write on the board: IF I GIVE YOU AN EXERCISE,... and elicit different answers (e.g. *we'll do it / we won't know how to do it / we won't have a break*).
- Put Sts in pairs and give them a copy of the sheet. Sts then try to complete the sentences in **a** as fast as they can. Declare the first pair to finish the winners (but make sure you give an extra minute or so for all the pairs to finish).
- Now focus on **b** and put two pairs together. Get them to compare their sentences and choose the ones they like best. Get some feedback.
- Finally, in **c**, get the pairs to cover the second part of the conditional and try to remember their sentences.

EXTRA IDEA Make this into a group activity by cutting up the sentences and giving each group one sentence at a time. When they complete a sentence they have to bring it to you and, if it's correct, get another sentence. The first group to complete all the sentences are the winners.

8C Reading questionnaire

A pairwork activity

Sts answer questions about their reading habits. Copy one sheet per pair.

- Put Sts in pairs. Give out the sheets and focus on the pictures. Ask *What / Who can you see?*.
- Give Sts a time limit to read the questions. Help with any vocabulary problems.
- Get one student to ask you the main question, *Do you like reading books?* Answer *Yes, I do* or *No, I don't*. Then get Sts to ask you the first question (depending on what you said). Answer the question giving as much information as possible and encourage Sts to ask follow-up questions.
- Sts **A** ask the main question and then ask all the questions in the **Yes** or **No** column to Sts **B** with follow-up questions, if possible. They then swap roles.
- Get feedback from the class.

9A I think you'd...

A pairwork activity

Sts practise second conditional sentences by trying to complete sentences about their partner. Copy one sheet per pair and cut into **A** and **B**.

- Demonstrate the activity by writing on the board: IF SOMEBODY OFFERED YOU A DRINK NOW, I THINK YOU'D ORDER A ___________.
- Elicit that you need to complete the sentence with a noun. Then tell Sts to guess which drink you'd order. Elicit answers and then tell the class which drink you really would order.

- Put Sts in pairs, **A** and **B**, face to face if possible, and give out the sheets. Focus on **a** and tell Sts to complete the sentences, trying to guess how their partner would complete each one. They must <u>not</u> look at what their partner writes. Monitor and check that they are using the right words.
- Now focus on **b** and tell Sts to take turns to read their completed sentences to their partner, who tells them if they have guessed correctly or not. Encourage them to react by contradicting what their partner has said, and then giving the real answer if the guess is wrong, e.g. *No, I wouldn't. I don't like cats! But I love dogs.*
- Get feedback from various pairs and find out who in the pair had more correct guesses.

EXTRA CHALLENGE If you want to give more practice, get Sts to repeat the activity, but swapping roles **A** and **B**.

9B Famous phobias

A pairwork speaking activity

Sts practise using the present perfect simple + *for* or *since* by reading about famous people and their phobias. Copy one sheet per pair and cut into **A** and **B**.

LANGUAGE
Present perfect simple + *for* or *since*

- Put Sts in pairs, **A** and **B**, and give out the sheets. Tell Sts <u>not</u> to look at each other's sheets.
- Set a time limit for Sts to read about the famous people and their phobias. Monitor and help with any comprehension or pronunciation problems.
- Now get **A** to tell **B** about his / her three people. Encourage Sts to improvise and only look at their sheet if absolutely necessary. Then **A** and **B** decide together which two phobias are true.
- Sts then swap roles.
- Get feedback to find out which ones they think are true.

They are all true.

9C Like father, like son

A pairwork information gap activity

Sts question each other to discover missing biographical information about a famous father and son using the present perfect simple and past simple. Copy one sheet per pair and cut into **A** and **B**.

LANGUAGE
Past simple and present perfect

- Put Sts in pairs, **A** and **B**, and give out the sheets. Tell them <u>not</u> to look at each other's sheets. Explain that they have one complete biography and one with missing information.
- Give Sts time to read both biographies. Monitor and deal with any vocabulary problems.
- Focus on the questions in **b**. Tell Sts **A** and **B** to read the first biography they have again and to complete questions 1–7. Set a time limit. Monitor and check that Sts are writing the correct questions.

- Now focus on **c** and get Sts to ask and answer their questions to complete their biographies.

Bob Dylan
1 When was he born?   **2** Where did he go to in 1961?
3 What was his real surname?   **4** How did Joan Baez help him become famous?   **5** How many albums has he recorded?
6 What kind of books has he written?   **7** What prize did he win / receive in 2016?

Jakob Dylan
1 What does he do?   **2** When was he born?   **3** How many brothers and sisters does he have?   **4** How many albums have The Wallflowers released?   **5** Which David Bowie song have they recorded?   **6** Who has Jakob Dylan composed music for?
7 How long has he been married?

10A The race

A pairwork activity

Sts practise giving instructions using prepositions of movement. Copy one sheet per pair and cut into **A** and **B**.

LANGUAGE
Prepositions of movement: *into, over, through, past*, etc.

- Put Sts into pairs, **A** and **B**, and give out the sheets. If possible, put Sts face to face.
- Focus on the instructions in **a**. Tell Sts that they have a map with a route on it. Their routes are different. They have to describe it to each other and draw it on their second map.
- Give Sts time to plan how to describe the route.
- Sts take it in turns to describe their route to their partner, who draws it in the blank map. Monitor and help.
- When they have finished, get Sts to compare routes to see if they drew them correctly.

EXTRA IDEA Get Sts to use pencil when they draw. They can then erase the route on the blank map and draw their own routes.

10B Phrasal verb conversations

A pairwork activity

Sts practise using phrasal verbs by choosing the correct response to a situation. Copy one sheet per pair and cut into **A** and **B**.

LANGUAGE
Phrasal verbs: *fill in, take off, take back*, etc.

- Put Sts in pairs, **A** and **B**. Tell them to look at sentences 1–8 and especially the phrasal verb sentences. Give them a minute or two.
- Sts **A** start by reading the first sentence. Sts **B** choose an answer from the speech bubbles. They both decide if they think it's right or wrong. Student **A** reads all his / her sentences and then they swap roles. Monitor to make sure Sts are doing the activity correctly.

> **A reads, B responds**
> 1 OK, I'll pick it up.   2 Sorry, I'll give it back tomorrow.   3 Sorry. I'll turn it down.   4 Look it up in the dictionary!   5 Sorry, I threw it away.   6 The film will be over in ten minutes, I promise!   7 Don't worry. I'll look after him.   8 Why don't you take it back?
>
> **B reads, A responds**
> 1 I think you should give it up.   2 Don't worry, I'll take them off.   3 Yes, I get on very well with her.   4 We've run out.   5 Yes, I'm really looking forward to it.   6 I'll help you look for it.   7 OK, I'll put them away.   8 Sorry, I'll fill it in now.

- Now focus on **c**. Sts **A** read their sentences again and this time Sts **B** respond without looking at their sheet. Then they swap roles.

10C General knowledge quiz

A pairwork general knowledge quiz

Sts practise using the present simple passive and past simple passive by asking and answering questions. Copy one sheet per pair and cut into **A** and **B**.

> **LANGUAGE**
>
> Questions in the present simple passive and past simple passive
>
> *Which month is named after a Roman emperor?*
>
> *In which city was the Titanic built?*

- Put Sts in pairs, **A** and **B**. Get them to sit face to face and make sure that they can't see each other's questions.
- Set a time limit, e.g. five minutes, for Sts to read their questions. Monitor and help if necessary.
- Sts **A** start. Highlight that they should give the three alternatives each time and note down which answers **B** gets right. (The correct answers are in **bold** on the sheet.) Sts then swap roles.
- Get feedback to see who got the most correct answers.

11A My past

A pairwork speaking activity

Sts complete some boxes and then use the information to talk about past habits using *used to* and *didn't use to*. Copy one sheet per student.

> **LANGUAGE**
>
> *I used to listen to Justin Bieber, but I don't now.*
> *I didn't use to like cabbage, but now I love it.*

- Put Sts in pairs and give out the sheets. Sit them so they can't see each other's sheets. Focus on **a**. Go through phrases 1–14 and make sure Sts know what they have to do. Demonstrate by giving some personal examples for 1–3. Make it clear that Sts only have to do this with words or phrases, e.g. *spiders, a Barbie doll, Justin Bieber*, and not complete sentences.
- Give Sts time to write something in as many boxes as they can (sometimes they may not be able to think of anything). Monitor and help.
- Focus on **b**. Sts use what they have written in the boxes to tell their partner about their past habits using *I used to / I didn't use to*. Again, demonstrate the activity yourself and

give more information, e.g. *I used to have a cat. He was black, and his name was Max.* If necessary, remind Sts of the pronunciation of *used to / didn't use to*.

- Sts work together, talking about their past habits.
- Get some feedback from various pairs.

11B I might…but I might not

A board game activity

Sts practise using *might* and *might not* by completing sentences. Copy one sheet per group of three or four Sts. You will also need one counter per student and a dice per group.

> **LANGUAGE**
>
> *He might lose his job. We might not find it.*

- Write the first sentence on the board: THE WEATHER IS REALLY NICE TODAY. WE... and ask Sts to complete it using *might*. Choose an answer and write it on the board. Now ask Sts to complete the sentence using *might not*. Choose an answer and write it on the board.
- Put Sts in groups of three or four. Give out the sheets and tell Sts to take turns to roll the dice and then create two sentences for each prompt, one with *might* and one with *might not*. If they can't make two sentences, they go back to their previous square. Monitor and help.

> **Possible answers**
> 1 might go to the beach. / might not need a jacket.
> 2 might forget it. / might not remember it.
> 3 might stay at home more. / might not go out very much.
> 4 might be angry with me. / might not have her phone.
> 5 might get hungry. / might not find a restaurant.
> 6 might go to Spain. / might not go abroad.
> 7 might win. / might not lose.
> 8 might see the new Star Wars film. / might not go.
> 9 might wear the black dress. / might not wear the pink dress.
> 10 might stay in bed. / might not go to work tomorrow.
> 11 might order a takeaway. / might not have dinner.
> 12 might record it. / might not watch it today.
> 13 might throw it away. / might not tell her I don't like it.
> 14 might go to the park. / might not go out.
> 15 might take it back. / might not read it.

- Sts play until one of them finishes or time runs out.

11C So do I!

A class mingle activity

Sts practise agreeing using *So do I / Neither do I* and disagreeing. Copy and cut up one sheet per group of six Sts.

> **LANGUAGE**
>
> *So can I. / Neither have I.*

- Give each student a card. Ask them to fill in the gaps with things that are true for them.
- Write I LIKE... and complete the sentence with an animal. Get Sts to agree or disagree with you. Elicit *So do I. / I don't*. Now write I DIDN'T GO OUT YESTERDAY. Elicit *Neither did I. / I did*.
- Get Sts to stand up and mingle, reading their sentences to each other and agreeing or disagreeing. Monitor and help.
- Get feedback about things Sts agreed / disagreed with.

NON-CUT ALTERNATIVE   Cut the sheet in half and put Sts in pairs. Give each student half a sheet and ask them to complete the sentences. They can then read the sentences to their partner and agree / disagree with their choices.

12A What had happened?
A group activity

Sts practise using the past perfect by giving reasons for situations they read on cards. Copy and cut up one sheet for groups of four or five Sts.

LANGUAGE

Past perfect
We couldn't use our car because someone had stolen it.

- Write on the board I WENT TO SEE MY BROTHER YESTERDAY. HE WAS SAD BECAUSE… and try to elicit answers using the past perfect (e.g. *his football team had lost / his dog had died*). Now put Sts in groups of four or five and give them a set of cards, face down.
- Sts take turns taking a card, reading the situation and completing the sentence. Remind Sts that they must use the past perfect. The rest of the group decide if the sentence is correct and think of alternatives. Monitor and help.
- Sts repeat the activity until they run out of cards. Sts then decide in their groups who was the best at inventing reasons.

Possible answers
1 I left the house in a hurry, and when I got to the airport, I suddenly remembered that I had forgotten my passport.
2 I was angry with my husband because he hadn't taken out the rubbish.
3 When I looked at my phone, I realized that Sarah had called me ten times.
4 I couldn't read the menu because I had left my glasses at home.
5 I didn't do well in my exam because I hadn't studied very hard.
6 I couldn't use my credit card because I had forgotten my pin.
7 The burglars got into our house while we were on holiday because we had left the door open.
8 The police got to the bank very quickly, but the robbers had already left.
9 My dad was very happy when he arrived because his team had won the match.
10 I went back to the shop to buy you that shirt you liked, but it had gone.
11 When we got to Joe and Hannah's house we were very surprised because they hadn't got up yet.
12 We decided not to go to the London Eye that day because we had heard it wasn't very good.
13 I was incredibly tired that day because I had watched TV until really late.
14 The moment I pressed 'send' I realized that I had sent the text message to the wrong person.
15 When I saw Mary at the school reunion, I didn't recognize her because she had lost weight.

12B The celebrity interview
A pairwork speaking activity

Sts practise using reported speech by interviewing their partner and then telling another student about the interview. Copy one sheet per pair and cut into **A** and **B**.

LANGUAGE

Reported statements
Jay-Z said that his best work had been his album, 4:44.

- Put Sts in pairs, **A** and **B**, and give out the sheets. Focus on the instructions and tell Sts to choose a famous person. They will then give an interview as that famous person.
- Give Sts some time to read the questions and imagine the answers their famous person would give.
- Sts **B** start by asking Sts **A** the questions and writing down the answers. Then they swap roles.
- Make Sts swap partners. They now talk about their interview using the answers their first partner gave and putting them in reported speech. Monitor and help.
- You could get confident Sts to report their interview to the class.

EXTRA IDEA   Ask Sts to write an article about their partner's celebrity using the information they have and reported speech.

12C Hollywood quiz
A pairwork information gap activity

Sts practise forming past simple and subject and object quiz questions to ask their partner. Copy one sheet per pair and cut into **A** and **B**.

LANGUAGE

Past simple and subject and object questions
Which actor appeared in most of Hitchcock's films?

- Put Sts in pairs, **A** and **B**, and give out the sheets. Give Sts time to complete the questions.
- Check answers, but don't write them on the board.

Student A
1 lived / lives   2 did / does an actor say   3 did Walt Disney win
4 appeared / appears   5 did / does Marty McFly go   6 did / does Tony fall   7 played / plays   8 does Batman have

Student B
1 did Peter Jackson film   2 appeared / appears   3 does an Oscar weigh   4 played / plays   5 won   6 played / plays   7 did / does Arnold Schwarzenegger say   8 directed

- Sts **A** start by asking Sts **B** the questions, without giving the three options (the option in bold is the correct answer). If **B** can answer correctly, he / she gets two points. If **B** can't answer, **A** gives him / her the three options. If **B** gets the correct answer, he / she gets one point.
- **A** asks all of his / her questions first. Sts then swap roles.
- Find out who scored the most points in the class.

1A **COMMUNICATIVE** Student profile

a Complete the questions you need to ask to fill in the form.

1 What ____?

2 What ____?

3 Where ____?

4 Where ____?

5 What ____?

6 What ____?

7 Where ____?

8 Why ____?

9 What languages ____?

10 What ____ in your free time?

11 Which social ____?

b Interview a partner and complete the form. Ask him / her to spell names and places if necessary.

STUDENT PROFILE

1 First name

2 Surname

3 Nationality

4 Address

5 Email address

6 Occupation

7 Place of birth

8 Reason for learning English

9 Languages

10 Interests

11 Social networking sites

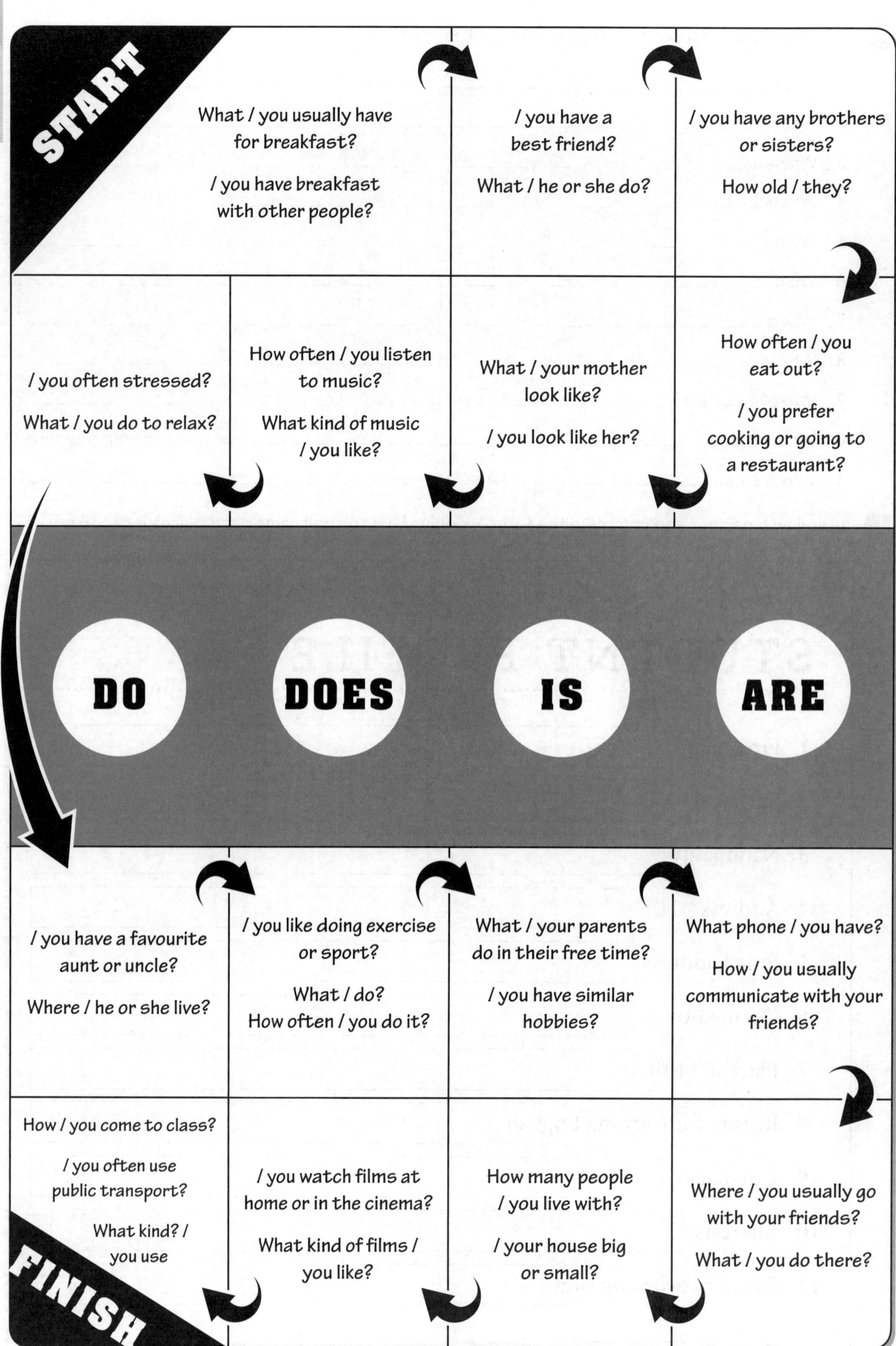

English File fourth edition Teacher's Guide Pre-intermediate   Photocopiable © Oxford University Press 2019

A man is reading the newspaper.	**A baby is crying.**
A woman is wearing a long dress.	**An old woman is carrying a bag.**
A girl is looking at a painting.	**A boy is standing next to a girl.**
A man is sitting behind a desk.	**A man is eating an apple.**
A man is buying a tie.	**A girl is cleaning her shoes.**
A dog is drinking under a table.	**A cat is sleeping on a sofa.**
A man is wearing socks and sandals.	**A woman is dancing in the kitchen.**
A baby is sitting in the garden.	**A woman is opening a window.**
A man is wearing a big hat.	**A boy is waiting for a bus.**

2A COMMUNICATIVE   Truth or lie?

A time when I lost my phone...

- When?
- How did you lose it?
- Did you find it?

A time when I sent an email or text message to the wrong person...

- Who did you send it to?
- Who did you want to send it to?
- What happened?
- When was this?

A time when I bought something and then decided that I didn't like it...

- When?
- What was it?
- Where did you buy it?
- What did you do with it?

A time when I found something in the street...

- What did you find?
- When?
- Where?
- What did you do with it?

A time when I broke something really valuable...

- How old were you?
- What did you break?
- What happened?

A time when I won a prize / competition...

- What did you win?
- How did you win it?
- What did you do with what you won?

A time when I forgot an important date...

- When?
- What date did you forget?
- What happened?

A time when I lent something to a friend and he / she didn't give it back...

- When?
- What was it?
- Who did you lend it to?
- What happened in the end?

A time when I found a large insect in my house...

- What was it?
- How did you feel?
- What did you do?

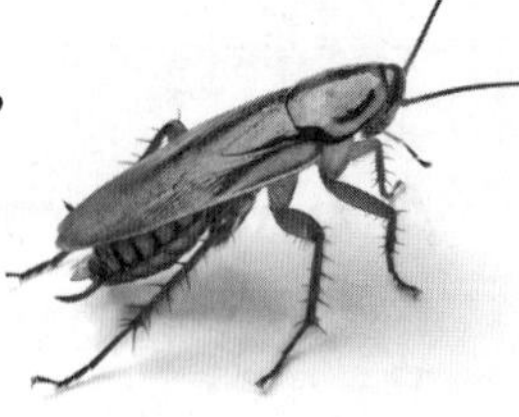

A time when I ate something really horrible...

- When?
- Where?
- What did you eat?
- Why did you eat it?

2B COMMUNICATIVE Who did it?

You're all staying at the Empire City Hotel. Sophie Hatcher, a famous model, is staying there too. At 3.55 p.m., Sophie left her room. She didn't close the door. She came back at 4.45 p.m. and her purse with all her money and credit cards wasn't there! She called the manager of the hotel and he has put everyone who is staying in the hotel in this meeting room. One of you stole Sophie Hatcher's money! Help the police find out who it was.

John Snow

You're a photographer. You're married to Cath Snow and you're on holiday together, but you aren't very happy.

4.00 p.m. – (argue) with your wife in your hotel room.

4.30 p.m. – (call) your mother on your mobile in the hotel lobby.

Cath Snow

You're a teacher. You're married to John Snow and you're on holiday together, but you aren't very happy.

4.00 p.m. – (argue) with your husband in your hotel room.

4.30 p.m. – (cry) in the hotel bar. Ella Chandler, a friend of Sophie's, was there too.

Eric Pyke

You're an architect. You are Sophie Hatcher's boyfriend. You're on holiday with her and her friend Ella Chandler.

4.00 p.m. – (listen) to music in your hotel room.

4.30 p.m. – (talk) to Jane Smith, a woman you met in the hotel, on the terrace.

Jane Smith

You're a flight attendant. You're staying in the hotel for work.

4.00 p.m. – (play) games on your phone in your room.

4.30 p.m. – (talk) to Eric Pyke, Sophie's boyfriend, on the terrace.

Mary Rivers

You're a singer.

You're in the hotel to write some songs.

4.00 p.m. – (play) the piano in the dining room.

4.30 p.m. – (drink) coffee in the dining room with Edward Strong, a journalist.

Emily Davies

You're a police officer. You're on holiday with your friend Lydia Brown.

4.00 p.m. – (do) exercise in the gym with Lydia Brown.

4.30 p.m. – (watch) a film in your room.

Ella Chandler

You're an artist. You are Sophie Hatcher's best friend. You're on holiday with her and her boyfriend, Eric Pyke.

4.00 p.m. – (do) yoga in your room.

4.30 p.m. – (dance) in the hotel bar. Cath Snow, a teacher, was there.

Edward Strong

You're a journalist. You're in the hotel because you want to write an article about Sophie and her life.

4.00 p.m. – (write) some notes in your room.

4.30 p.m. – (drink) coffee in the dining room with Mary Rivers, a singer.

David Hill

You're a security guard. You're on holiday in the hotel.

4.00 p.m. – (give) Peter Stone, a lawyer, advice about security cameras in the hotel lobby.

4.30 p.m. – (talk) with the receptionist in the hotel lobby.

Lydia Brown

You're an engineer. You're on holiday with your friend Emily Davies.

4.00 p.m. – (do) exercise in the gym with Emily Davies.

4.30 p.m. – (swim) in the pool with Alex Cameron, a man you met in the hotel.

Peter Stone

You're a lawyer. You're on holiday at the hotel.

4.00 p.m. – (ask) David Hill, a security guard, for advice about security cameras in the hotel lobby.

4.30 p.m. – (write) an email in your room.

Alex Cameron

You're a car salesman. You're on holiday and staying at the hotel. You sold Sophie Hatcher a car but she hasn't paid you. You stole her purse!

4.00 p.m. – (steal) Sophie Hatcher's purse from her room.

4.30 p.m. – (swim) in the pool with Lydia Brown, a woman you met in the hotel.

1	I'm a vegetarian, **so**…
2	I'm really happy today **because**…
3	My friend invited me to dinner, **but**…
4	**Although** my job isn't very well paid,…
5	Nora felt really ill, **so**…
6	My brother doesn't go to his English class very often, **so**…
7	**Although** her written English is excellent,…
8	Maria didn't buy the jeans **because**…
9	Paul has a lot of money, **but**…
10	It was really sunny yesterday, **so**…
11	Jack is a bit overweight **because**…
12	**Although** Katie is very attractive,…
13	It's a great restaurant **although**…
14	The match was really boring, **so**…
15	We enjoyed our holiday **although**…
16	They live together, **but**…
17	I can't go to the party tonight **because**…
18	It isn't a great film, **but**…
19	I live with my parents **because**…
20	I didn't like David when I first met him, **but**…

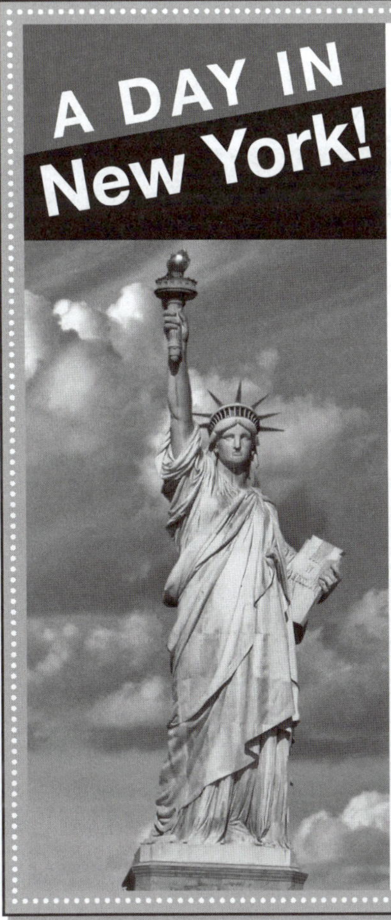

Schedule for tomorrow:

Breakfast

10 a.m.

11.30 a.m.

Lunch

3.30 p.m.

6 p.m.

Dinner

Sightseeing:

Statue of Liberty (1h 30), Museum of Modern Art (1h), Central Park (1h), Museum of Natural History (1h), NYC bus tour (1h 30), New York Library (30 mins), Empire State Building (30 mins), Bronx Zoo (1h), see a musical (*The Lion King*) (2h 30), Yankee Baseball Stadium (1h), Chinatown (1h)

Shopping:

- SoHo (small independent shops, some souvenirs)
- Fifth Avenue (famous luxury shops, lots of souvenirs)

Places to eat:

- Delmonico's (American food, burgers)
- Lombardi's Pizza (Italian food)
- Red Farm (Chinese food)
- New York Bagels (sandwiches, breakfast and lunch)
- Café Blossom (has vegetarian food)

Schedule for tomorrow:

Breakfast

10 a.m.

11.30 a.m.

Lunch

3.30 p.m.

6 p.m.

Dinner

Sightseeing:

Louvre Museum (1h 30), Boat trip on River Seine (1h), Arc de Triomphe (30 mins), Notre-Dame cathedral (1h), Eiffel Tower (1h 30), Orsay Museum of Art (1h), Paris bus tour (1h), Latin Quarter (1h), Luxembourg Gardens (30 mins), Versailles Palace (2h 30), Picasso Museum (1h)

Shopping:

- Rue Saint Honoré (luxury shops)
- Marché Aux Puces (outdoors, lots of small shops)
- The Marais (shopping streets, souvenirs, international shops)
- Galleries Lafayette (big department store)

Places to eat:

- Taste Eat (Vietnamese food)
- Midi 12 (French food)
- Pizza Julia (Italian food)
- Breton (crêpes, breakfast and lunch)
- My Kitchen (café, has vegetarian food)

3B COMMUNICATIVE   Come fly with me!

Student A

FLIGHT INFORMATION A   FLIGHT INFORMATION B

a Look at the missing information on boarding card **B**. Write the questions you need to ask **B** to complete boarding card **B**.

1 Who *are you flying* with? (fly)
2 Where _____________ from? (fly)
3 Where _____________ to? (fly)
4 When _____________? (leave)
5 What time _____________? (leave)
6 What time _____________? (arrive)
7 Where _____________? (sit)

b Ask **B** the questions and complete boarding card **B**.

c Now **B** will ask you for the information on boarding card **A**. Answer his / her questions.

Student B

FLIGHT INFORMATION A   FLIGHT INFORMATION B

a Look at the missing information on boarding card **A**. Write the questions you need to ask **A** to complete boarding card **A**.

1 Who *are you flying* with? (fly)
2 Where _____________ from? (fly)
3 Where _____________ to? (fly)
4 When _____________? (leave)
5 What time _____________? (leave)
6 What time _____________? (arrive)
7 Where _____________? (sit)

b **A** will ask you for the information on boarding card **B**. Answer his / her questions.

c Now ask **A** the questions and complete boarding card **A**.

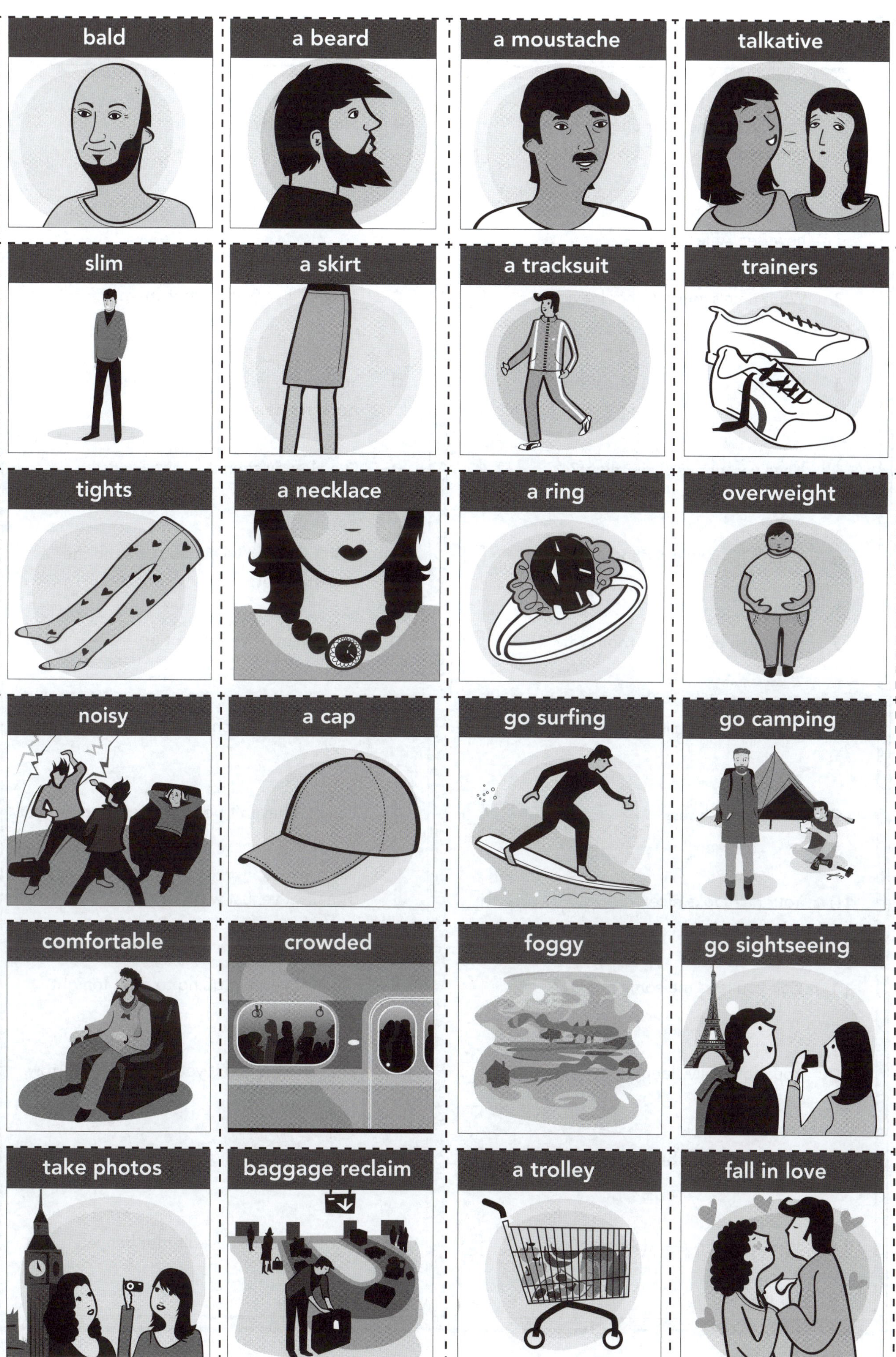

bald
a beard
a moustache
talkative
slim
a skirt
a tracksuit
trainers
tights
a necklace
a ring
overweight
noisy
a cap
go surfing
go camping
comfortable
crowded
foggy
go sightseeing
take photos
baggage reclaim
a trolley
fall in love

a Match the sentences with the responses and then check your answers with your teacher.

1 Have you done your English homework?	`h`	**a** She's already left.
2 Do you want to come and see the new Ben Affleck film?	☐	**b** No, not yet. I'm going to tidy it later.
3 What time's your mother leaving?	☐	**c** Thanks. I've just bought them.
4 Would you like a cup of coffee?	☐	**d** You're too late. They've already gone home.
5 Have you booked your flight?	☐	**e** I've already seen it.
6 What's his new girlfriend like?	☐	**f** Don't worry! I've already been to the supermarket.
7 Have you tidied your room yet?	☐	**g** Yes, I know. I've just got up.
8 What's your English course like?	☐	**h̶** Yes, I've just finished it.
9 I love your shoes!	☐	**i** I can't. I haven't been to the cashpoint yet.
10 Your hair looks nice.	☐	**j** Thanks. I've just washed it.
11 Can you lend me some money?	☐	**k** No, not yet. I'm going to do it tonight.
12 You look really sleepy.	☐	**l** I haven't started it yet. It starts tomorrow.
13 Don't forget to buy some milk!	☐	**m** No, thanks. I've just had one.
14 Where are Pete and Andrew?	☐	**n** I don't know. I haven't met her yet.

FOLD

b Fold the paper in half. **A** say sentences 1–14. **B** can you remember the responses? Then swap roles.

4B COMMUNICATIVE   Have you ever...?

1	/ ever speak English to somebody outside class? Who / speak to? What about?
2	/ ever break your arm or your leg? How / break it?
3	/ ever do an extreme sport? Which one / do?
4	/ ever be to an English speaking country? Which country / go to? / speak English there?
5	/ ever live abroad? Where / live? Why / live there?
6	/ ever do volunteer work? What / do? How long / do it for?
7	/ ever sing or play an instrument in public? What / do? How / feel?
8	/ ever run a marathon or a half marathon? When / run it? / finish it?
9	/ ever post a selfie online? Where / post it? Where / take the photo?
10	/ ever complain in a hotel or restaurant? Why / complain?
11	/ ever sleep outside all night? Where / sleep? / sleep well?
12	/ ever speak in public? What / speak about? How / feel?

4C COMMUNICATIVE   The same or different?

a Complete the sentences with *something, anywhere, nobody,* etc.

1 I always have _______________ to eat before I go to work / school.

2 I never have problems sleeping on buses or planes. I can sleep _______________.

3 I usually watch _______________ on TV in the evening.

4 When I watch films in English, I don't usually understand _______________.

5 I don't usually do _______________ interesting at weekends.

6 In my family, _______________ speaks any English except me!

7 I went _______________ really exciting last weekend.

8 I never read _______________ in English except my coursebook.

9 There's _______________ I really want to buy at the moment, but I don't have any money.

10 I love doing _______________ on Sunday mornings, just staying in bed late.

11 I hate smoking, and luckily _______________ in my family smokes.

12 I don't want to go _______________ this weekend. I just want to stay at home.

13 I don't know _______________ in this class very well.

14 There's _______________ I really want to go on holiday.

15 In my town, there's _______________ for young people to go at night. It's really boring here.

16 I never say _______________ in English in class. I'm worried about making mistakes.

17 I met _______________ very interesting last weekend.

18 I always go _______________ quiet when I want to study.

b Talk to a partner. Tell him / her if the sentences are true or not true for you, and why.

   English File fourth edition Teacher's Guide Pre-intermediate   Photocopiable © Oxford University Press 2019

swimming in the sea **OR** swimming in a pool	a holiday with your family **OR** a holiday with friends
watching a film in your language **OR** watching a film with subtitles	watching a film at the cinema **OR** watching a film at home
texting **OR** messaging	watching sport **OR** doing sport
doing English homework **OR** doing housework	reading a traditional book **OR** reading a book on screen
eating in a restaurant **OR** eating at home	buying things in a shop **OR** buying things online
going on holiday in your country **OR** going on holiday abroad	listening to music with headphones **OR** listening to music without headphones
going clothes shopping alone **OR** going clothes shopping with another person	
studying during the day **OR** studying at night	

5B COMMUNICATIVE Superlative questions

a Complete the questions with the superlative form of the adjective in brackets.

1 Which of these people is _________? (rich)
   a Michael Bloomberg, founder of Bloomberg   **b Amancio Ortega, the founder of Zara**
   c Mark Zuckerberg, the founder of Facebook
   Amancio Ortega has a fortune of over 80 billion dollars.

2 Which of these is _________ city? (populated)
   a Tokyo in Japan   b New Delhi in India   c Mexico City in Mexico
   Over 37 million people live in Tokyo's metropolitan area.

3 Where is _________ road in the world? (dangerous)
   a Russia   b Australia   **c Bolivia**
   Thousands of people have died on the Camino de la Muerte (Death Road) in Bolivia.

4 Which is _________ lake in the world? (large)
   a Lake Superior in North America   b Lake Baikal in Russia   c Lake Victoria in Africa
   Lake Superior has an area of 82,100 square km.

5 Which of these inventions is _________? (recent)
   a glasses   b the microscope   **c the telescope**
   The telescope was invented by Galileo Galilei in 1609.

6 Which of these cities is _________ with tourists? (popular)
   a Istanbul in Turkey   b New York in the USA   **c Bangkok in Thailand**
   More than 20 million people visit Bangkok every year.

b Ask **B** your questions, reading the three options. Tell **B** if he / she is right or wrong (the correct answer is in **bold**) and give the extra information. Then try to answer **B**'s questions.

- -

a Complete the questions with the superlative form of the adjective given.

1 Which is _________ city in the world? (noisy)
   a Madrid in Spain   b Cairo in Egypt   **c Mumbai in India**
   The noise in Mumbai is often over 100 decibels. That's as loud as a plane flying near you.

2 Which of these is _________ planet? (small)
   a Mercury   b Venus   c Mars
   Mercury has a radius of 2440 km.

3 Which of these videogames is _________? (popular)
   a Super Mario Bros   b Minecraft   **c Tetris**
   Tetris has sold 495 million copies.

4 Which is _________ museum in the world? (large)
   a The National Gallery in London   b The National Museum of China   **c The Louvre in Paris**
   The Louvre has an area of 72,735 square metres.

5 Who is _________ person to win a Nobel Prize? (young)
   a Guglielmo Marconi for inventing the telegraph   **b Malala Yousafzai for fighting for
   women's right to education**   c Marie Curie for discovering radioactivity
   Malala Yousafzai won the Nobel Peace Prize when she was 17 years old.

6 Which was _________ film to win an Oscar for Best Film? (long)
   a *Lord of the Rings: Return of the King*   **b *Gone with the Wind***   c *Titanic*
   Gone with the Wind lasts 3 hours and 58 minutes.

b Try to answer **A**'s questions. Then ask **A** your questions, reading the three options. Tell **A** if he / she is right or wrong (the correct answer is in **bold**) and give the extra information.

How ___________ people are there in your (workplace / class)?

- Do you think it's a good number?
- Is it a big place or is it small?
- Do you enjoy working / studying there?
- How many of your colleagues / classmates do you know well?

How ___________ time do you spend in front of a computer every day?

- Is it for work or for pleasure?
- What kind of things do you normally do on your computer?
- Do you enjoy doing them?
- Do you think you're good with computers? Why (not)?

How ___________ different drinks do you have a day?

- What's your favourite drink?
- How often do you have it?
- When you go out with your friends, what do you normally drink?
- What do you normally drink for breakfast?

How ___________ fast food do you eat?

- What's your favourite fast food restaurant?
- What things do you normally order?
- How long do you have to wait for it?
- How much money do you normally spend when you eat there?

How ___________ times a week do you see your friends?

- How many friends do you normally meet with?
- Where do you normally go?
- What do you normally do?

How ___________ luggage do you usually take on holiday?

- Is it usually enough or too much?
- Do you often forget to take something?
- Do you buy a lot of things when you are on holiday?
- What kind of things do you buy?

How ___________ music do you listen to in a day?

- What do you normally use to listen to music (your phone / the radio, etc.)?
- What is your favourite song at the moment?
- How often do you listen to it?
- Do you have a favourite band?

How ___________ does the cinema cost in your town / city?

- Do you think it's expensive?
- How often do you go to the cinema?
- What was the last film you saw at the cinema?
- Did you enjoy it? Why (not)?

How ___________ hours a week do you spend doing housework?

- What housework do you usually do?
- Do you live alone or with other people?
- How much of the housework do they do?
- What housework do you hate doing?

How ___________ time do you have for yourself every day?

- Do you think it's enough?
- What do you like doing when you have free time?
- Do you think you're going to have more or less free time in the future? Why?

How ___________ times do you use social media in a day?

- Do you like social media? Why (not)?
- What social media sites / apps do you use?
- What do you use them for?
- Do you have a lot of friends or followers?

How ___________ do you travel during the year?

- Would you like to travel more?
- What places would you like to visit? Why?
- How do you prefer to travel?
- Do you ever travel for your work / studies?

a Complete **THE OPTIMIST SAYS** column with positive predictions.

YOU SAY	THE OPTIMIST SAYS 🙂
1 I lost my wallet in the street yesterday.	Don't worry. _______________
2 I've just broken up with my partner.	Cheer up! I'm sure _______________
3 We just bought a dog – a Labrador!	Congratulations! _______________
4 I have a really difficult exam tomorrow.	Good luck! I'm sure _______________
5 We're going to see the new Star Wars film!	Fantastic! _______________
6 I'm going to start going to the gym next week!	That's great! _______________
7 I have a date tonight. I'm really nervous!	Don't worry. I'm sure _______________
8 I'm going to study in the UK next year.	That's really good. _______________
9 My team are playing an important match today.	That's fantastic! _______________
10 I'm going to Mary's party tonight.	Great! I'm sure _______________
11 I've just lost my job.	Cheer up! _______________
12 My plane leaves in ten minutes. I can't find my passport!	Don't worry. _______________

b Talk to other students. Read a **YOU SAY** sentence and listen to their **THE OPTIMIST SAYS** prediction.

Student A

1 I like these shoes. I think I _____________ them.

2 **I'll pick you up at eight o'clock. Shall I call you before I leave home?**

3 Please don't worry, Mum. I _____________ you when I get to Paris.

4 **Your suitcase looks really heavy. Shall I carry it?**

5 I _____________ you the money for Maria's present tomorrow.

6 **I'll help you with your English homework. I can see you're having problems.**

7 It's really hot in here. _____________ I _____________ the air conditioning?

8 **There's somebody at the door. I'll go and see who it is.**

9 I _____________ for lunch today. You paid last time.

10 **Don't worry! I'll remember to phone the bank tomorrow. I have a good memory.**

11 The phone's ringing. _____________ I _____________ it?

12 **Have you forgotten your book? Don't worry. I'll lend you mine.**

13 I need to go now. I _____________ you tomorrow.

14 **You do the cooking and I'll do the washing-up.**

- -

Student B

1 **I like these shoes. I think I'll buy them.**

2 I'll pick you up at eight o'clock. _____________ I _____________ you before I leave home?

3 **Please don't worry, Mum. I'll text you when I get to Paris.**

4 Your suitcase looks really heavy. _____________ I _____________ it?

5 **I'll give you the money for Maria's present tomorrow.**

6 I _____________ you with your English homework. I can see you're having problems.

7 **It's really hot in here. Shall I turn on the air conditioning?**

8 There's somebody at the door. I _____________ and see who it is.

9 **I'll pay for lunch today. You paid last time.**

10 Don't worry! I _____________ to phone the bank tomorrow. I have a good memory.

11 **The phone's ringing. Shall I answer it?**

12 Have you forgotten your book? Don't worry. I _____________ you mine.

13 **I need to go now. I'll see you tomorrow.**

14 You do the cooking and I _____________ the washing-up.

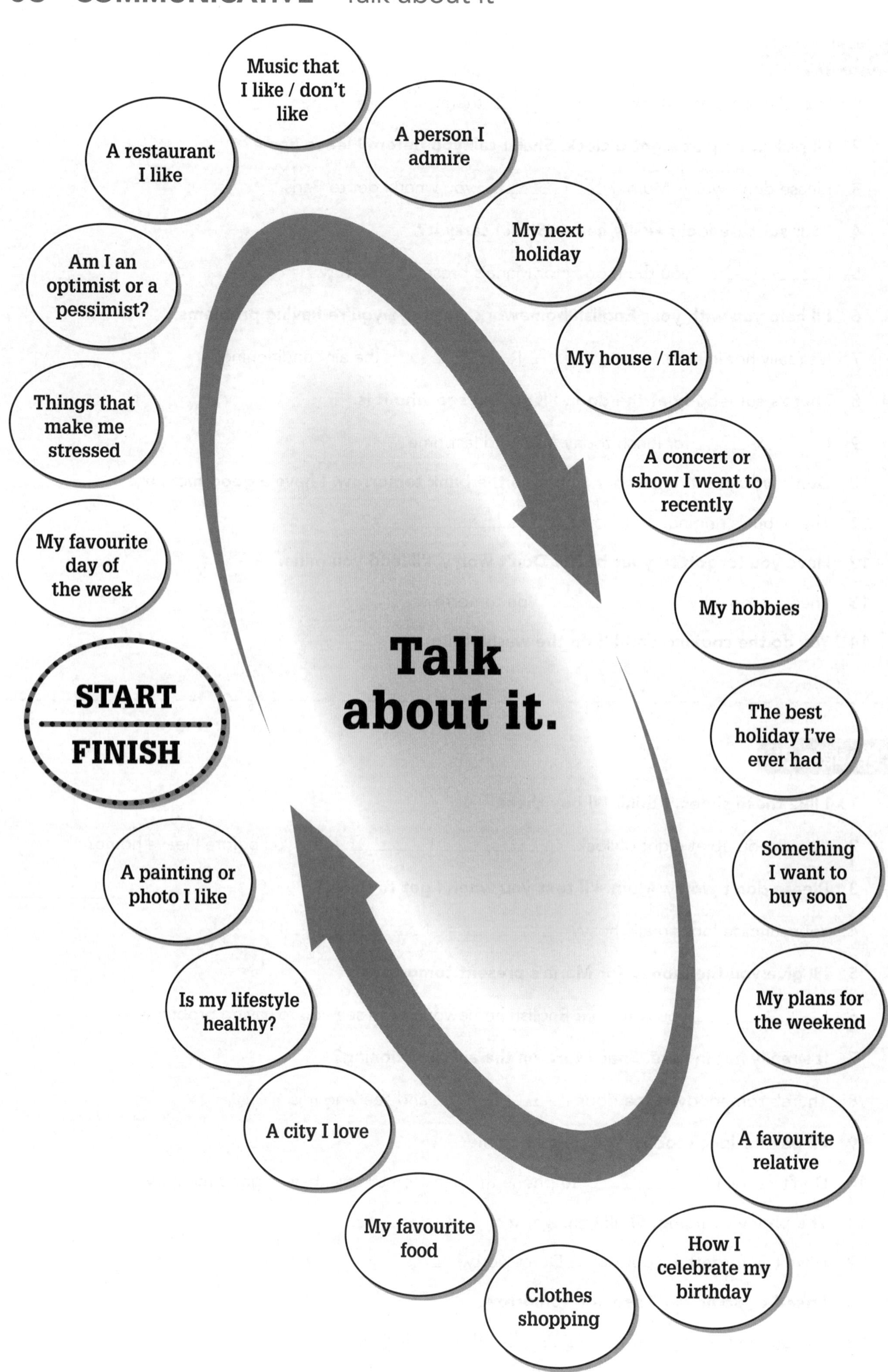
Music that I like / don't like
A restaurant I like
A person I admire
My next holiday
Am I an optimist or a pessimist?
My house / flat
Things that make me stressed
A concert or show I went to recently
My favourite day of the week
My hobbies
START
FINISH
The best holiday I've ever had
Something I want to buy soon
A painting or photo I like
Talk about it.
Is my lifestyle healthy?
My plans for the weekend
A city I love
A favourite relative
My favourite food
How I celebrate my birthday
Clothes shopping

Choose six topics and think about what you're going to say. Talk to a partner. Give and ask for more information.

what I think is the best way **to learn** a language	something I learned **to do** as a child but can't do now
something I think is important **to teach** young children	something I often forget **to do**
why tourists choose **to come** to my country	something I need **to buy** soon
the things I do **to relax** after a hard day	something I've decided **to do** in the future
a sport or activity I tried **to learn** but couldn't	something I find difficult **to do** in English
something I wanted **to be** when I was younger	what I want **to do** tonight
somebody I would like **to meet**	what I think is the best way **to make** new friends
something I thought of buying but decided **not to**	things that are important **to do** if you go for a job interview
the things I think are important **to do** for a healthy life	a film that's good **to watch** when I'm feeling sad

Student A

a Complete the questions with the *-ing* form of the verbs from the list.

cook   do (x2)   fly   get up   go   read   wait

1 Do you like ________________ early?

2 Are you afraid of ________________?

3 Do you mind ________________ for people who are late?

4 Did you hate ________________ to school when you were younger?

5 Do you enjoy ________________ in bed?

6 Are you good at ________________?

7 Have you started ________________ a new activity recently?

8 Do you think ________________ exercise is boring?

b Ask **B** your questions. Ask for more information.

Student B

a Complete the questions with the *-ing* form of the verbs from the list.

be   do   eat   get   go (x2)   play   walk

1 Do you spend much time ________________ in the country?

2 Have you stopped ________________ an activity recently?

3 Do you enjoy ________________ to the cinema alone?

4 Do you feel like ________________ out tonight?

5 Do you think ________________ computer games teaches you anything?

6 Did you like ________________ fruit and vegetables when you were a child?

7 Are you thinking of ________________ a new haircut soon?

8 Do you dream of ________________ famous?

b Ask **A** your questions. Ask for more information.

a Work in pairs. Read the sentences about the UK and decide if they are true or false.

		True	False
1	You mustn't cycle in bus lanes.	☐	☐
2	You have to be 21 to buy alcohol.	☐	☐
3	You don't have to pay to use motorways.	☐	☐
4	All dogs and cats must have a microchip with the name and address of their owner.	☐	☐
5	Everybody has to do six months military service.	☐	☐
6	You have to be 18 to ride a 50cc motorbike.	☐	☐
7	You don't have to have an ID card.	☐	☐
8	All shops must close on Sundays.	☐	☐
9	You mustn't leave a child under 12 alone at home.	☐	☐
10	You mustn't play loud music in your house after 9.00 p.m.	☐	☐
11	You have to be 17 years old to vote in a general election.	☐	☐
12	You don't have to vote in a general election.	☐	☐
13	You have to be over 16 to have a Facebook or Twitter account.	☐	☐
14	If you have a dog, you must have a special licence.	☐	☐
15	TV programmes before 9.00 p.m. mustn't include bad language.	☐	☐
16	You don't have to study a foreign language at secondary school.	☐	☐
17	You don't have to wear seat belts in the back of the car.	☐	☐
18	Parents don't have to send their children to school. They can educate them at home.	☐	☐

b Check your answers with your teacher.

c Work with a partner. Are the laws the same or different in your country? }
Which of these rules would you like to have in your country?

I have a job interview in English next week. I really want the job.

How should I prepare for it?

I want to be fitter, but I don't really like going to the gym.

What should I do?

Some friends are coming to dinner and I don't have time to cook.

What should I do?

Another company has offered me a job. The salary is lower than my present job, but the work is much more interesting.

What should I do?

I had an argument with my best friend yesterday. It was my fault. Now she's not talking to me.

What should I do?

I don't like my brother's new girlfriend, but he is very happy with her.

What should I say to him?

I want to buy a present for my grandmother. She's 90 and she likes reading, travelling and classical music.

What should I buy?

I want to learn another foreign language so I can get a good job.

Which one should I learn?

I'd like to learn to play a musical instrument.

Which one should I choose?

My family wants to get a pet. We have a small house and we're all very busy.

What kind of pet should we get?

I have two tickets for a concert. My dad and my sister really like the band and want to come with me.

Who should I take to the concert?

I'm really bad with money. I always spend more than I have, especially when I go out.

What should I do?

My friend wants to be a singer, but I don't think he sings very well.

What should I say to him?

My partner's mother doesn't like me very much.

What should I do?

I can't sleep at night.

What should I do?

I want to go on holiday to a really beautiful place this summer. I love the beach.

Where should I go?

I want to become a vegetarian, but my family really loves meat.

What should I do?

My cousin is coming to visit me. He's allergic to cats and I have a cat.

What should I do?

a Complete the conditional sentences.

1	We're playing really well, it's 3–1.	If we win, _______________
2	The film starts at 6.30.	If we don't leave now, _______________
3	There are a lot of things I want to buy!	If I don't have enough money, _______________
4	We don't have any sandwiches for the trip.	If we're hungry later, _______________
5	We really need a holiday.	If we can get a cheap flight, _______________
6	It's getting really late.	If we don't go to the supermarket now, _______________
7	It's going to be really cold tomorrow.	If it snows, _______________
8	I can't see my car keys anywhere.	If I don't find them, _______________
9	That exam was really hard.	If I don't pass it, _______________
10	You look tired.	If you don't want to go out this evening, _______________
11	My girlfriend is working late today.	If she doesn't finish work before 9.00, _______________
12	We're at the station, waiting for Dave.	If he doesn't come soon, _______________
13	I've bought a lot of food for the party.	If we don't eat it all, _______________
14	The teacher has just told us the date of the exam.	If you don't write it down, _______________
15	I know you don't like Anne, but I don't think she's coming to the party.	If she comes, _______________

FOLD

b Compare your answers with another pair. Who do you think wrote more interesting sentences?

c Fold the paper and look at the first part of the sentences. Try to remember what you wrote.

Do you like reading books?

YES

1. Do you have a favourite place or time of day to read? Why do you like it?
2. What kind of books do you like reading?
3. Do you have a favourite author? How many of his / her books have you read?
4. Do you prefer to read traditional books or e-books? Why?
5. What was the last book you bought? Where did you buy it?
6. Are you a fast reader or a slow reader?
7. Do you sometimes read more than one book at a time?
8. Is there a book everyone liked but you hated? Which one?
9. Have you ever started reading a book but not finished it? Why not?
10. Whose advice on books do you always listen to?
11. How do you choose books to read / buy?
12. Do you ever read books more than once?

NO

1. Do you read any magazines or newspapers? Which ones?
2. Do you read online? What do you read?
3. How do you find out about the news?
4. Did your parents read to you when you were a child? What kind of books did they read?
5. Did you read comics when you were a child? Which ones?
6. Is there anybody in your family who likes reading? Who?
7. Have you ever written a blog? Do you like reading blogs? Why?
8. Do you think women like reading more than men? Why?
9. If somebody gives you a book as a present, what do you do?
10. Did you have a favourite book when you were a child?
11. Do you think that people today read more or less than 20 years ago? Why?
12. Do you follow many people on social media? Do you like reading what they post?

9A COMMUNICATIVE   I think you'd...

Student A

a Complete the sentences about **B**.

1 If you could be anywhere in the world right now, I think you'd choose to be in ______________.

2 If you bought a new car today, I think you'd buy a ______________.

3 If you didn't study English, I think you'd like to study ______________.

4 If we had lunch together, I think we'd go to ______________.

5 If you could go to a concert tonight, I think you'd go and see ______________.

6 If you could go to an English-speaking country, I think you'd go to ______________.

7 If you could choose your ideal job, I think you'd like to be a / an ______________.

8 If you did a new sport / hobby, I think you'd like to ______________.

9 If you bought a new flat or house, I think you'd buy one in ______________.

10 If you got a new pet, I think you'd get a ______________.

b Read your sentences to **B**. Were you right?

c Listen to **B**'s sentences about you. Tell him / her if they are right or wrong, and why.

Student B

a Complete the sentences about **A**.

1 If you had a big problem, I think you'd speak to ______________.

2 If you could be an animal, I think you'd like to be a / an ______________.

3 If you went to a karaoke bar, I think you'd sing ______________.

4 If you had enough money, I think you'd buy a ______________.

5 If somebody wanted to buy you a present, I think you'd love a / some ______________.

6 If you could change one thing in your house or flat, I think you'd ______________.

7 If you could learn to play a musical instrument well, I think you'd choose ______________.

8 If someone invited you to a very expensive restaurant, I think you'd order ______________.

9 If you could appear on a TV programme, I think you'd appear on ______________.

10 If you could meet a famous person, I think you'd like to meet ______________.

b Listen to **A**'s sentences about you. Tell him / her if they are right or wrong, and why.

c Read your sentences to **A**. Were you right?

Student A

Scarlett Johansson This famous American actress has katsaridaphobia, which means she's afraid of cockroaches. She's had the phobia since she was a child, but it got worse when she lived in New York at the beginning of her career. Once, she woke up with a cockroach on her face and another one in her shoe! Since then, she's absolutely hated them. She's also quite afraid of birds, which was a bit of a problem for her while filming *We Bought A Zoo*.

True or false?

Orlando Bloom Have you seen Pirates of the Caribbean? If you have, then you'll probably remember this actor who appears in the film. But this 'brave' actor has a serious phobia which is swinophobia. This means that he is afraid of pigs. He has been afraid of them since he was a teenager. Although this phobia isn't very common, it's had a direct effect on his career. A director asked him to be in the film *Animal Farm* but Orlando said no because it meant that he had to work with a pig.

True or false?

Oprah Winfrey This American talk show host and producer is one of the most influential women in the world. However, she suffers from chiclephobia, which means she has a fear of chewing gum. Apparently, she has banned people from chewing gum at her production studio. She has had the phobia since she was a child. It started when she saw her grandmother putting her chewing gum in the kitchen cupboards.

True or false?

Student B

Justin Timberlake This singer and actor is from the USA. He has to travel a lot because of his job, and sometimes the arachnophobia he suffers from is a problem for him. He's been afraid of spiders for a long time. He thinks his phobia started at the age of seven or eight when he found a spider in his bed. Last year, he was staying in a hotel and saw a spider in the bathroom. He couldn't kill it, so he asked the receptionist to come and kill it for him!

True or false?

Rihanna This famous singer and actress comes from the island of Barbados. So perhaps it's strange that she has ichthyophobia – she is afraid of fish and other sea animals. She's had this phobia for a long time. Once, she was on a beach in Barbados and she went in the water. She could see lots of small fish swimming around her feet. She was so afraid that a man had to take her out of the water. Since then, she's been really afraid of them.

True or false?

Robert De Niro This Hollywood mega-star is probably one of the greatest actors of all time. However, many of us have something in common with him. He has dentophobia, which means he's afraid of the dentist. He has suffered from it since he made the film *Cape Fear*. Before filming, he paid a dentist $5,000 to make his teeth look bad enough for the role of Max Cady in the film. Then, after filming, he paid a dentist $20,000 to repair his teeth. That's dedication to his job!
True or false?

9C COMMUNICATIVE Like father, like son

Student A

a Read the biographies.

Bob Dylan is a singer and songwriter who was born in Minnesota in ¹________________. In 1961, he left university, and he went to ²________________. His real surname was ³________________, but he changed it to Dylan in 1962 after the famous Welsh poet Dylan Thomas. He became very famous in the 60s with songs like *The Times They are a-Changin'* and *Blowing in the Wind*, which inspired people to protest against war and injustice. The folk singer Joan Baez helped him become famous because ⁴________________________________. In 1965, he married Sara Lownds and they had five children, but they divorced in 1977. He has recorded ⁵________________ albums, and he still writes music and plays in concerts. He's also an artist; he has produced seven books of ⁶________________. In 2016, he received the ⁷________________.

Jakob Dylan is a singer and songwriter. He was born in New York in 1969. His father is the famous musician Bob Dylan. He has two brothers and two sisters. When he was in high school, Jakob played the guitar in several bands. In 1988, he moved to New York to study Art, but he started writing songs instead. He formed a band, The Wallflowers, and they have released six albums and won two Grammy awards. They also recorded a version of David Bowie's song *Heroes* for the soundtrack of the film *Godzilla*. Jakob has composed some music for TV shows and other musicians. He has also recorded two solo albums. He's been married to his wife Paige since 1992, and they have four children.

b Complete the questions you need to ask **B** to find out the missing information about Bob Dylan.

1 When ________________ born?
2 Where ________________ to in 1961?
3 ________________ his real surname?
4 How ________________ him become famous?
5 How many albums ________________?
6 What kind of books ________________?
7 What prize ________________ in 2016?

c Ask **B** the questions and complete Bob Dylan's biography. Answer **B**'s questions about Jakob Dylan. What do the father and son have in common?

Student B

a Read the biographies.

Bob Dylan is a singer and songwriter who was born in Minnesota in 1941. In 1961, he left university and he went to New York. His real surname was Zimmerman, but he changed it to Dylan in 1962 after the famous Welsh poet Dylan Thomas. He became very famous in the 60s with songs like *The Times They are a-Changin'* and *Blowing in the Wind*, which inspired people to protest against the government. The folk singer Joan Baez helped him become famous because she sang his songs and made them popular. In 1965, he married Sara Lownds and they had five children, but they divorced in 1977. He has recorded more than 35 albums, and he still writes music and plays in concerts. He's also an artist; he has produced seven books of paintings and drawings. In 2016, he received the Nobel Prize in Literature.

Jakob Dylan is a ¹________________. He was born in New York in ²________________. His father is the famous musician Bob Dylan. He has ³________________ brothers and ________________ sisters. When he was in high school, Jakob played the guitar in several bands. In 1988, he moved to New York to study Art, but he started writing songs instead. He formed a band, The Wallflowers, and they have released ⁴________________ albums and won two Grammy awards. They also recorded a version of David Bowie's song ⁵________________ for the soundtrack of the film *Godzilla*. Jakob has composed some music for ⁶________________. He has also recorded two solo albums. He's been married to his wife Paige since ⁷________________ and they have four children together.

b Complete the questions you need to ask **A** to find out the missing information about Jakob Dylan.

1 What ________________ do?
2 When ________________ born?
3 How many brothers and sisters ________________?
4 How many albums ________________?
5 Which David Bowie song ________________?
6 Who ________________ music for?
7 How long ________________ married?

c Answer **A**'s questions about Bob Dylan. Ask **A** the questions and complete Jakob Dylan's biography. What do the father and son have in common?

Student A

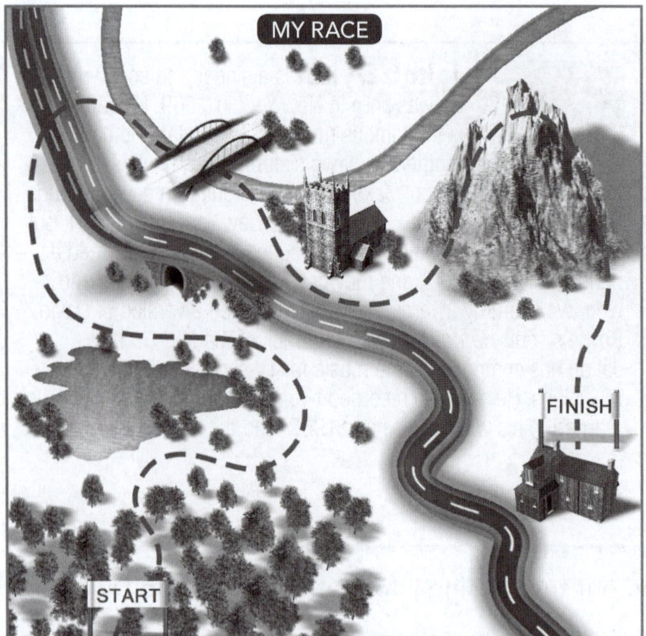

a You are going to run an extreme race! You can climb, run, or swim. Describe the route on the MY RACE map to **B**.

b Listen to **B** describe a route and draw it on your second map.

c Compare your maps with **B**'s. Did you draw the route correctly? Did **B**?

Student B

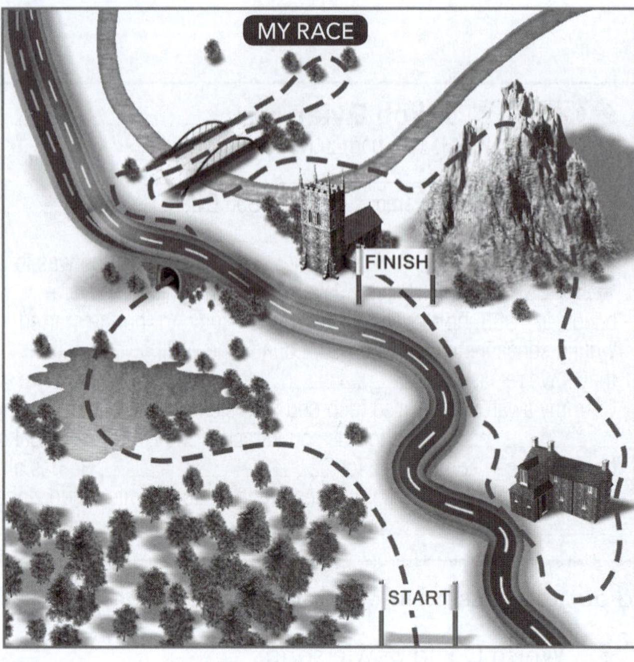

a Listen to **A** describe a route and draw it on your second map.

b You are going to run an extreme race! You can climb, run, or swim. Describe the route on the **MY RACE** map to **A**.

c Compare your maps with **A**'s. Did you draw the route correctly? Did **A**?

10B COMMUNICATIVE Phrasal verb conversations

Student A

a Read these sentences to **B** and listen to his / her answers. Do they go together?

1 You've left your towel on the floor again.
2 I really need the book that you borrowed from me.
3 The music is too loud!
4 I don't know what this word means.
5 Where is that letter from the bank?
6 Are you watching a film? I want to watch the news!
7 I don't want to leave my dog alone this weekend.
8 This T-shirt that I bought doesn't fit.

b Listen to **B**'s situations and answer them using one of the phrasal verb sentences below.

We've run out.   *Yes, I'm really looking forward to it.*

Yes, I get on very well with her.   *Don't worry, I'll take them off.*

I think you should give it up.   *I'll help you look for it.*

Sorry, I'll fill it in now.   *OK, I'll put them away.*

c Now repeat the activity, but try to remember (not read) the phrasal verb sentences. Can you both remember your answers?

Student B

a Listen to **A**'s situations and answer them using one of the phrasal verb sentences below.

The film will be over in ten minutes, I promise!   *Sorry, I threw it away.*

Why don't you take it back?   *OK, I'll pick it up.*

Sorry, I'll turn it down.   *Don't worry, I'll look after him.*

Sorry, I'll give it back tomorrow.   *Look it up in the dictionary!*

b Now read these sentences to **A** and listen to his / her answers. Do they go together?

1 I think I drink too much coffee.
2 Don't come in here in those dirty boots!
3 Do you like your boss?
4 I can't find any eggs in the fridge.
5 Are you excited about going to Rome?
6 I can't find my phone!
7 You've left all your clothes on the bed!
8 You forgot to complete this form.

c Now repeat the activity, but try to remember (not read) the phrasal verb sentences. Can you both remember your answers?

Student A

1   Which month is named after a Roman emperor?
   a **August**   b July   c January
2   What sport is played at Flushing Meadows, USA?
   a basketball   b baseball   c **tennis**
3   Where are polar bears found?
   a the South Pole   b **Alaska**   c Antarctica
4   What is the Greek goddess of victory called?
   a Adidas   b Reebok   c **Nike**
5   On a computer keyboard, which letter is found between Z and C?
   a V   b P   c **X**
6   What was the first song sung in space?
   a **Happy Birthday to You**   b *Space Oddity*   c *We Are the Champions*
7   In which European city is the Nobel Peace Prize given?
   a Stockholm   b Paris   c **Oslo**
8   What is *tofu* made of?
   a goat's milk   b **soya milk**   c cow's milk
9   What drink was created by The Coca-Cola Company in Germany during World War II?
   a Coca-Cola   b Dr Pepper   c **Fanta**
10   In which country was golf first played?
   a England   b **Scotland**   c the USA

- -

Student B

1   In which city was the *Titanic* built?
   a **Belfast**   b New York   c Portsmouth
2   Who was the ball point pen invented by?
   a Jacques Bic   b **László Biró**   c Frank Parker
3   On which day is Thanksgiving celebrated in the USA?
   a **the fourth Thursday in November**   b the second Thursday in July
   c the first Thursday in December
4   Which toy was invented in Denmark in 1949?
   a the Barbie doll   b the Rubik's Cube   c **Lego**
5   Which style of music was created by Antônio Carlos Jobim and João Gilberto in Brazil?
   a salsa   b **bossa nova**   c samba
6   In which film was the word 'supercalifragilisticexpialidocious' used?
   a *Mary Poppins*   b *Harry Potter and the Goblet of Fire*   c *E.T.*
7   Who was the ceiling of the Sistine Chapel painted by?
   a Tintoretto   b da Vinci   c **Michelangelo**
8   The Canary Islands are named after which animal?
   a a canary   b a cat   c a dog
9   How many squares are there on a chess board?
   a 144   b 96   c **64**
10   Which is the most visited tourist attraction in the world?
   a the Taj Mahal   b **the Eiffel Tower**   c the Empire State Building

a   How have you changed? Write a name or phrase in as many boxes as you can.

1   Something you used to be afraid of

2   A favourite toy you used to have

3   A singer or band you used to listen to

4   A kind of food or drink you didn't use to like

5   Something you used to collect

6   A game you used to play a lot

7   A pet you used to have

8   A place where you used to go to on holiday with your family

9   A friend you used to have at school

10   A subject you used to be very bad at

11   A TV programme you used to love

12   A teacher at school you didn't use to like

13   A house / flat you used to live in

14   An instrument you used to play

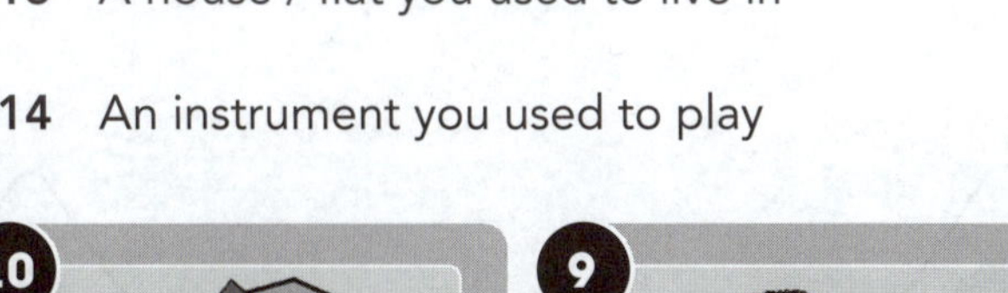

b   Compare your boxes with a partner's. Ask for and give more information about how and why you've changed.

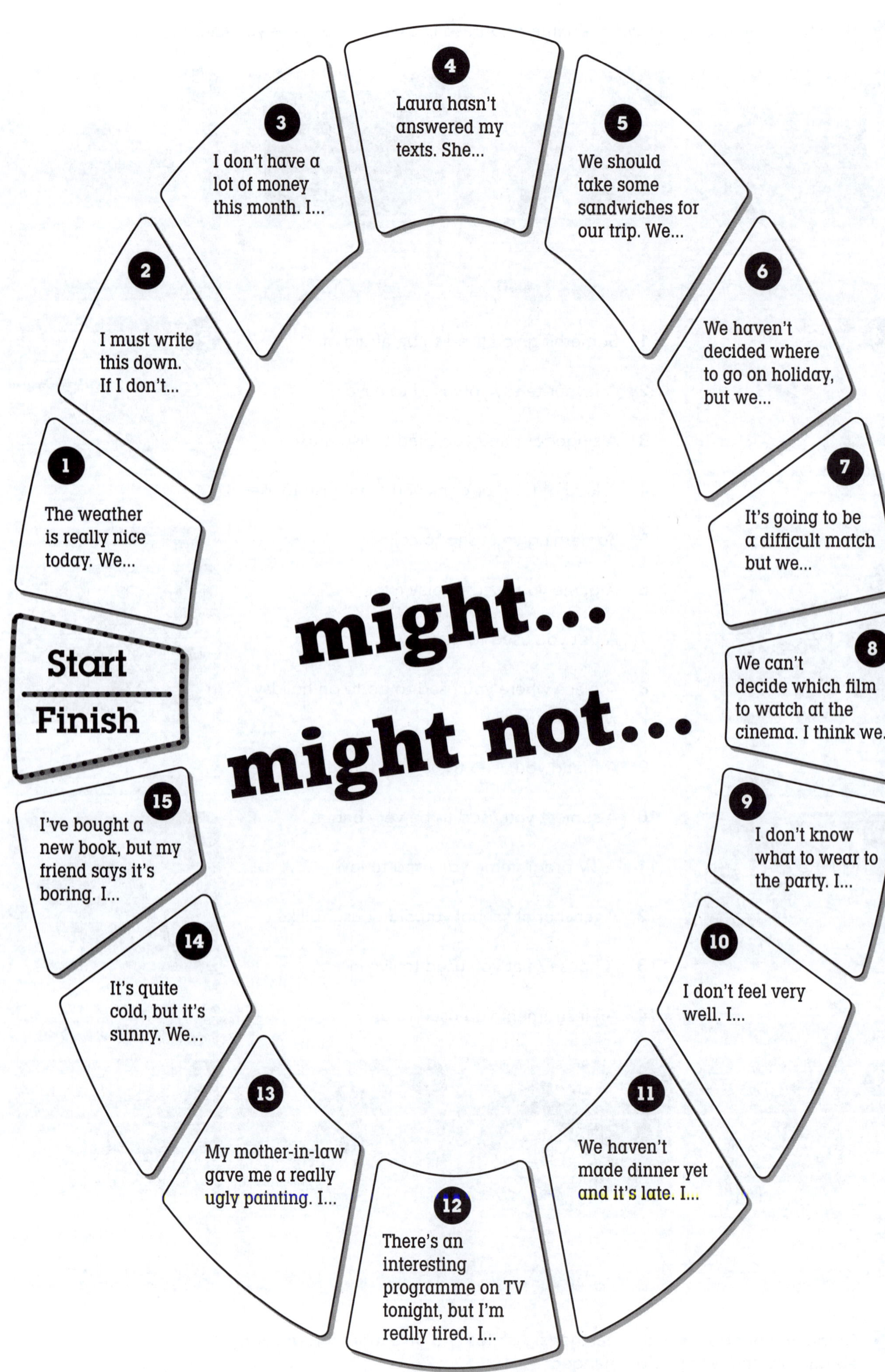
might...
might not...

Start
Finish

1 The weather is really nice today. We...

2 I must write this down. If I don't...

3 I don't have a lot of money this month. I...

4 Laura hasn't answered my texts. She...

5 We should take some sandwiches for our trip. We...

6 We haven't decided where to go on holiday, but we...

7 It's going to be a difficult match but we...

8 We can't decide which film to watch at the cinema. I think we...

9 I don't know what to wear to the party. I...

10 I don't feel very well. I...

11 We haven't made dinner yet and it's late. I...

12 There's an interesting programme on TV tonight, but I'm really tired. I...

13 My mother-in-law gave me a really ugly painting. I...

14 It's quite cold, but it's sunny. We...

15 I've bought a new book, but my friend says it's boring. I...

11C COMMUNICATIVE So do I!

Who else?

I love _____________________. (a kind of food or drink) _____________

I wouldn't like to _____________________. (an activity) _____________

I can't _____________________ very well. (a skill) _____________

Who else?

I'm a big fan of _____________________. (an actor / actress) _____________

I often watch _____________________. (a TV programme) _____________

I haven't been to _____________________. (a city or country) _____________

Who else?

I'm really good at _____________________. (an activity) _____________

I didn't go out last _____________________. (a day of the week) _____________

I've always wanted to try _____________________. (an activity) _____________

Who else?

I can't play _____________________. (a musical instrument) _____________

I like reading _____________________. (a kind of book / magazine) _____________

I'd like to go to _____________________. (a country) _____________

Who else?

I haven't seen _____________________. (a famous film) _____________

I can _____________________ very fast. (an action) _____________

I'm not interested in _____________________. (a sport) _____________

Who else?

I went to _____________________ last weekend. (a place) _____________

I don't like travelling by _____________________. (a kind of transport) _____________

I'm going to have _____________________ for dinner today. (a kind of food) _____________

1	I left the house in a hurry, and when I got to the airport, I suddenly remembered that…
2	I was angry with my husband / wife because…
3	When I looked at my phone, I realized that…
4	I couldn't read the menu because…
5	I didn't do well in my exam because…
6	I couldn't use my credit card because…
7	The burglars got into our house while we were on holiday because we…
8	The police got to the bank very quickly, but…
9	My dad was very happy when he arrived because his team…
10	I went back to the shop to buy you that shirt you liked, but…
11	When we got to Joe and Hannah's house, we were very surprised because they…
12	We decided not to go to the London Eye that day because…
13	I was incredibly tired that day because I…
14	The moment I pressed 'send' I realized that…
15	When I saw Mary at the school reunion, I didn't recognize her because she…

12B COMMUNICATIVE The celebrity interview

a Imagine that you are a famous person (e.g. an actor, musician, etc.). You are going to be interviewed on TV. Look at the questions. Try to imagine how the famous person you chose would answer.

1 Where are you living at the moment?
2 What countries have you been to?
3 What's the most interesting thing you've ever done?
4 What's the most expensive thing you've ever bought?
5 What do you like doing in your free time?
6 What are you going to do next?
7 What do you like best about your career?
8 What are you preparing for at the moment?
9 What's your ambition?
10 What do you do to relax?

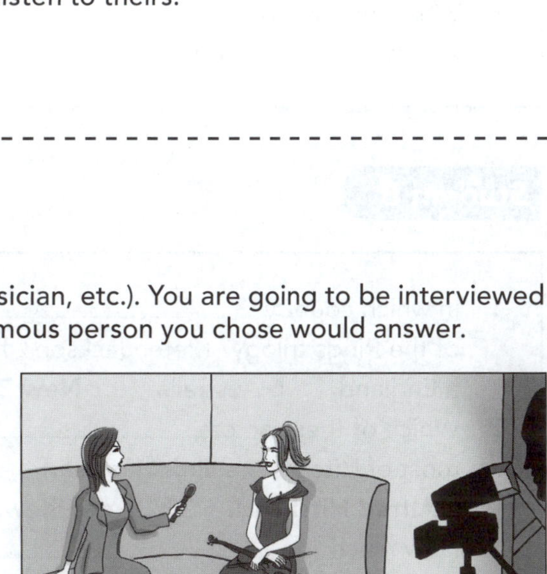

b Tell **B** who you are. Now answer **B**'s questions.

I'm Katy Perry. *Hi, Katy! Thank you for agreeing to this interview.*

c Ask **B** your questions and write down his / her answers.

d Now change partners. Tell them about **B**'s answers and listen to theirs.

Katy Perry said that what she liked best about her career was travelling around the world.

- -

a Imagine that you are a famous person (e.g. an actor, musician, etc.). You are going to be interviewed on TV. Look at the questions. Try to imagine how the famous person you chose would answer.

1 Where are you living at the moment?
2 What countries have you been to?
3 What's the most interesting thing you've ever done?
4 What's the most expensive thing you've ever bought?
5 What do you like doing in your free time?
6 What are you going to do next?
7 What do you like best about your career?
8 What are you preparing for at the moment?
9 What's your ambition?
10 What do you do to relax?

b Ask **A** your questions and write down his / her answers.

I'm Ryan Gosling. *Hi, Ryan! Thank you for agreeing to this interview.*

c Tell **A** who you are. Now answer **A**'s questions.

d Now change partners. Tell them about **A**'s answers and listen to theirs.

Ryan Gosling said that what he liked best about his career was travelling around the world.

Student A

1 Which fictional family ________________________ at
  4 Privet Drive? (live)
  a The Dursleys   **b** The Griffins   **c** The Simpsons
2 In which film series ________________________ 'May the
  force be with you'? (an actor / say)
  a Star Trek   **b** Back to the Future   **c Star Wars**
3 How many Oscars ________________________ in his
  life? (Walt Disney / win)
  a 2   **b** 12   **c 22**
4 Who ________________________ in all the Marvel superhero films? (appear)
  a Robert Downey Jr   **b Stan Lee**   **c** Chris Evans
5 What year ________________________ to in *Back to the Future*? (Marty McFly / go)
  a 1955   **b** 1975   **c** 1985
6 In which film ________________________ in love with Maria? (Tony / fall)
  a *West Side Story*   **b** *PS: I Love You*   **c** *Love Actually*
7 Who ________________________ Indiana Jones' father in *Indiana Jones and the
  Last Crusade*? (play)
  a Michael Caine   **b** Michael Douglas   **c Sean Connery**
8 What superpower ________________________? (Batman / have)
  a immortality   **b none**   **c** invisibility

- -

Student B

1 In which country ________________________ The Lord
  of the Rings trilogy? (Peter Jackson / film)
  a England   **b** Australia   **c New Zealand**
2 Which of these actors ________________________ in
  most of Hitchcock's films? (appear)
  a Alfred Hitchcock   **b** James Stewart   **c** Cary Grant
3 How much ________________________?
  (an Oscar / weigh)
  a 2.5 kilos   **b 4 kilos**   **c** 7 kilos
4 Which actor ________________________ James Bond in more films? (play)
  a Sean Connery   **b Roger Moore**   **c** Pierce Brosnan
5 Which series of films ________________________ more Oscars? (win)
  a The Lord of the Rings   **b** Star Wars   **c** The Godfather
6 Which actress ________________________ the part of Belle in the Disney film *Beauty and
  the Beast*? (play)
  a Scarlett Johansson   **b** Natalie Portman   **c Emma Watson**
7 In which film ________________________ 'Hasta la vista, baby'? (Arnold Schwarzenegger / say)
  a *Terminator 2*   **b** *The Terminator*   **c** *Terminator 3*
8 Who ________________________ *Alien*? (direct)
  a Ridley Scott   **b** Steven Spielberg   **c** JJ Abrams

Vocabulary activity instructions

1B Describing people

A pairwork vocabulary race

Sts look at photos and definitions and complete the missing words. Copy one sheet per pair or one sheet per student.

LANGUAGE
Appearance and personality adjectives

- Put Sts in pairs and give out the sheets. Tell Sts to read the definitions, look at the photos and write as many words as they can within a time limit. The lines indicate how many letters are in each word. Set the time limit.
- The first pair to complete all the words correctly is the winner. Check answers.

1 moustache **2** funny **3** slim **4** bald **5** mean
6 medium-height **7** blonde **8** beard **9** clever
10 hard-working **11** overweight **12** curly **13** dark
14 quiet **15** nice

- Now focus on **Activation** and get Sts to cover the words on the right and say the words.

1C Things you wear

A pairwork brainstorm activity

Sts think of one, two, or three words connected to clothes. Copy one sheet per pair or one sheet per student.

LANGUAGE
Clothes

- Put Sts in pairs and give out the sheets. Don't go through all the questions, but demonstrate the activity, eliciting the answer to the first question (*gloves*).
- Set a time limit, and tell Sts to start. Give more time if you can see that Sts need it.
- When the time limit is up, check answers and find out which pair has the most correct answers.

1 gloves **2** jumper **3** hat, cap **4** sandals, boots, shoes, socks
5 trousers, jeans **6** scarf, tie **7** leggings, tights **8** necklace,
bracelet, ring **9** T-shirt, shorts, trainers, tracksuit **10** hat,
jacket, sweater

- Now focus on **Activation** and point out the example. Give Sts time to write five sentences about what they are wearing. Make sure they include colours.
- Finally, put Sts in pairs and get them to read their sentences to each other.

2A Holidays

A gapfill activity

Sts complete three texts connected to holidays. Copy one sheet per student.

LANGUAGE
Holiday verbs and phrases

- Give out the sheets. Tell Sts to complete the texts with an appropriate word or verb in the correct form. Point out that the first letter(s) is given to help them.
- Set a time limit for Sts to complete the task.
- Get Sts to compare with a partner and then check answers.

Story 1 **1** away **2** go **3** stay **4** book **5** camping
Story 2 **1** skiing **2** hired **3** rent **4** had
Story 3 **1** sightseeing **2** swimming **3** sunbathe
  4 spend **5** take

- Now focus on **Activation** and give Sts time to write about their last holiday.
- Finally, put Sts in pairs and get them to read their texts to each other. You could get some Sts to read their text in front of the class.

2B Prepositions *at, in, on*

A preposition gapfill activity

Sts complete sentences which have missing prepositions. Copy one sheet per student.

LANGUAGE
Prepositions of time and place

- Give out the sheets. Tell Sts to write the correct preposition in the **PREPOSITION** column. They should complete as many sentences as they can. Set a time limit.
- Check answers.

1 in **2** in **3** at **4** at **5** on **6** in **7** in **8** on **9** at **10** in **11** at
12 in **13** on **14** at **15** at **16** on **17** at **18** in **19** at **20** in

- Now focus on **Activation** and tell Sts to cover the **PREPOSITION** column and say the sentences.

3B What's the preposition?

An error correction activity

Sts correct preposition mistakes. Copy one sheet per student.

LANGUAGE
Prepositions

- Put Sts in pairs and give out the sheets. Point out that the first two have been done for them.
- Sts continue in pairs. Check answers.

> 3 ✓
> 4 ✓
> 5 ✗ Can you ask the teacher **for**...?
> 6 ✗ When I arrive **at**...
> 7 ✓
> 8 ✓
> 9 ✗ He worries **about**...
> 10 ✗ Does this coat belong **to**...?
> 11 ✓
> 12 ✗ How often do you speak **to**...?
> 13 ✗ Maria's invited me **to**...
> 14 ✗ She's fallen in love **with**...
> 15 ✗ He depends **on**...

- Now focus on **Activation** and make sure Sts understand all the lexis, e.g. *arguments*. Give Sts time to complete the five sentences.
- Put Sts in pairs and get them to read their sentences to each other. Find out if any pairs completed a sentence in the same way.

4A Housework, *make* or *do*?

A gapfill revision activity

Sts complete sentences with the correct form of the verb. Copy one sheet per student.

LANGUAGE
Housework phrases, *make* or *do*

- Put Sts in pairs and give out the sheets. Make sure Sts know they have to use the right form of the verb. Elicit the answer to 1 (*make*).
- Tell Sts to complete as many sentences as they can.
- Check answers.

> 1 make 2 puts 3 doing 4 does 5 made 6 do 7 lay 8 do
> 9 made 10 doing 11 make 12 making 13 tidy 14 put /
> take 15 did 16 pick 17 make 18 do 19 do 20 made

- Now focus on **Activation** and give Sts time to write their sentences.
- Finally, put Sts in pairs and get them to read their sentences to each other.
- Find out if any Sts do or don't do the same housework jobs.

4B Shopping

A crossword puzzle activity

Sts read clues and complete the crossword. Copy one sheet per student or one sheet per pair.

LANGUAGE
Shopping and online shopping

- Explain to Sts that they are going to complete a crossword. Make sure Sts understand *across* and *down*.
- Either give each student a sheet or put Sts in pairs and give each pair a sheet. Tell Sts to write the words in the crossword. Point out that the first one (*shelf*) has been done for them.
- Give Sts time to complete the crossword.
- Check answers.

> **ACROSS** 3 basket 8 shop assistant 10 size 11 receipt
> 12 checkout 13 account 14 customer
> **DOWN** 1 suit 2 fit 5 trolley 6 changing room 7 sales
> 9 take...back

- Now focus on **Activation** and get Sts to cover the crossword and read the clues. Can they remember the answers? You could put Sts in pairs. **A** reads a clue from the sheet and **B** (not looking at the sheet) guesses the word. Make sure they swap roles.

5B Describing a town or city

A gapfill activity

Sts read the blog posts and complete the missing words. Copy one sheet per student or one sheet per pair.

LANGUAGE
Adjectives and nouns connected to towns and cities

- Either give each student a sheet or put Sts in pairs and give each pair a sheet. Tell Sts to complete the blog posts with the correct words. The first letter is given and the lines indicate how many letters are in each word. Set a time limit.
- Check answers.

> **Valencia:** 1 coast 2 medium-sized 3 crowded 4 noisy
> 5 historic 6 town hall 7 Cathedral
> **Shanghai:** 8 south 9 modern 10 Temple 11 Museum
> 12 exciting 13 market 14 harbour
> **St Petersburg:** 15 Palace 16 lake 17 department store
> 18 centre 19 Bridge

- Now focus on **Activation** and put Sts in pairs to discuss the questions.
- With a show of hands, find out which city Sts would most like to visit. Ask a few Sts to say why.

6A Opposite verbs

A memory activity

Sts read the sentences and write the opposite of the verb in bold. Copy one sheet per student or one sheet per pair.

> **LANGUAGE**
> High frequency verbs and their opposites

- Either give each student a sheet or put Sts in pairs and give each pair a sheet. Elicit the answer to 1 (*lent...to*). Point out that the verb must be in the correct form.
- Give Sts time to complete the task.
- Check answers.

> **1** lent...to **2** failed **3** lose **4** pull **5** forgets **6** got / received... from **7** arrive **8** finishes **9** teach **10** sell **11** Turn on **12** lost **13** fixing **14** miss **15** drop...off **16** upload

- Now focus on **Activation** and put Sts in pairs to test each other. **A** reads a sentence or just says a verb from the sheet to **B**, who (not looking at the sheet) says the opposite verb. Make sure they swap roles.

7B Verbs + infinitive *to* and verbs + *-ing*

A sentence completion activity

Sts complete the sentences in conversations with the correct form of the verb. Copy one sheet per student.

> **LANGUAGE**
> Verbs + infinitive with *to* and verbs + *-ing*: *like, want*, etc.

- Give out the sheets. Tell Sts to complete the conversations with the verbs from the list. Point out that these verbs are either followed by an infinitive or a gerund. Point out that the first one (*started*) has been done for them.
- Give Sts time to complete the task.
- Get Sts to compare with a partner, and then check answers.

> **2** stop **3** want **4** like **5** try **6** mind **7** Remember **8** forget **9** promise **10** spend **11** feel like **12** need **13** hoping **14** offer **15** go on **16** wants

- Now focus on **Activation** and get Sts to practise the conversations in pairs.

8A *get*

A sentence completion activity

Sts complete sentences with the correct form of *get* and a word from the list. Copy one sheet per student or one sheet per pair.

> **LANGUAGE**
> *get* + its different collocations, e.g. *get divorced, get colder, get a job, get up, get home, get a text message*

- Give out the sheets. In pairs or individually, Sts choose the correct word from the list and the correct form of *get* to complete the sentences.
- If Sts did the activity individually, get them to compare answers.
- Check answers.

> **1** get fit **2** got divorced **3** get...present **4** get home **5** getting up **6** get tickets **7** get lost **8** get married **9** get on **10** get...nervous **11** Get better **12** get...newspaper **13** gets colder **14** get to **15** getting worse **16** get...job **17** got...message **18** gets...angry

- Now focus on **Activation** and get Sts to discuss the questions in pairs.
- Get some feedback from various pairs.

8B Confusing verbs

A vocabulary discrimination activity

Sts circle the correct verb. Copy one sheet per student or one sheet per pair.

> **LANGUAGE**
> Verbs with similar meanings

- Either give each student a sheet or put Sts in pairs and give each pair a sheet. Give Sts time to circle the verbs.
- If Sts did the activity individually, get them to compare answers.
- Check answers.

> **1** won **2** wearing **3** met **4** watching **5** bring **6** looks like **7** found **8** telling **9** take **10** lend **11** hope **12** missed **13** known **14** looking at **15** earn **16** look **17** looking for **18** carrying **19** said **20** waiting **21** borrow **22** lose **23** hear **24** expect

- Now focus on **Activation** and give Sts time to write their six sentences.
- Put Sts in pairs and get them to read their sentences to each other.
- Get some feedback from various pairs.

9A Animal quiz
A pairwork vocabulary quiz

Sts read a series of definitions and write the words. Copy one sheet per student or one sheet per pair.

> **LANGUAGE**
> Animals

- Put Sts in pairs and give out the sheets. Tell Sts that they have to write as many words as they can. Set a time limit.
- Check answers.

> **1** kangaroo **2** bee **3** dolphin **4** camel **5** rabbit **6** jellyfish **7** giraffe **8** cows / goats **9** sheep **10** mosquito **11** mouse **12** crocodile **13** elephant **14** snake **15** horse **16** lion **17** tiger **18** pig **19** bull **20** bat

- Now focus on **Activation** and get them to cover the **ANIMAL** column and read the definitions. They can test themselves or a partner.

10A Expressing movement
A pairwork vocabulary race

Sts race to think of 1, 2, or 3 answers to questions containing a preposition of movement. Copy one sheet per student or one sheet per pair.

> **LANGUAGE**
> Expressing movement

- Put Sts in pairs and give out the sheets. Tell Sts to read the questions and write down the answers. Set a time limit, but give Sts more time if you see they need it.
- Check answers.

> **Possible answers**
> 1 river, swimming pool
> 2 stairs, hill, mountain
> 3 a road, a room
> 4 tennis, badminton, volleyball
> 5 a lipstick, keys, phone
> 6 a (white) rabbit
> 7 cinema, theatre
> 8 bus, train
> 9 marathon
> 10 tree, umbrella
> 11 The London Eye, St Paul's Cathedral
> 12 waiter, driver
> 13 Formula 1, athletics
> 14 monkey, cat, bear
> 15 chess

- Now focus on **Activation** and put Sts in pairs. **A** asks a question about something on the sheet to **B**, who (not looking at the sheet) answers. Elicit an example. Make sure they swap roles.

10B Phrasal verbs
A vocabulary discrimination activity

Sts circle the correct phrasal verb. Copy one sheet per student or one sheet per pair.

> **LANGUAGE**
> Phrasal verbs

- Either give each student a sheet or put Sts in pairs and give each pair a sheet. Point out that the first one (*look after*) has been done for them. Set a time limit for Sts to circle the phrasal verbs.
- If they did the activity individually, get them to compare answers with a partner.
- Check answers.

> **2** set off **3** throw it away **4** turn the music down **5** give it up **6** fill in **7** try it on **8** run out of **9** look after **10** looking forward to **11** turn up **12** find out **13** go off **14** go on **15** put on **16** send it back **17** drop you off **18** write down **19** looking for **20** looked it up

- Now focus on **Activation** and give Sts time to think of their answers.
- Put Sts in pairs and get them to tell each other their answers.
- Get some feedback from various pairs.

1B VOCABULARY Describing people

● Work with a partner. Look at the pictures and the definitions. Write the words.

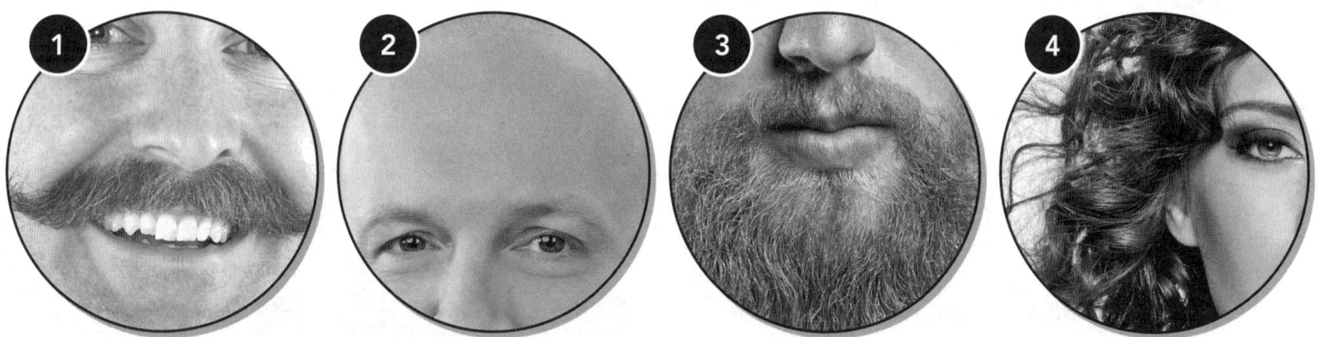

1	picture 1	_ _ _ _ _ _ _ _
2	**a person who can make other people laugh**	_ _ _ _ _
3	another way of saying **thin**	_ _ _ _
4	picture 2	_ _ _ _
5	an adjective to describe **someone who doesn't like spending money**	_ _ _ _
6	**not tall, not short**	_ _ _ _ _ _ - _ _ _ _ _ _ _
7	another word for **fair**	_ _ _ _ _ _
8	picture 3	_ _ _ _ _
9	a synonym of **intelligent**	_ _ _ _ _ _
10	the opposite of **lazy**	_ _ _ _ - _ _ _ _ _ _ _
11	**heavier** than is healthy	_ _ _ _ _ _ _ _ _ _
12	picture 4	_ _ _ _ _ (hair)
13	the opposite of **light** brown hair	_ _ _ _
14	**somebody who doesn't talk a lot**	_ _ _ _ _
15	**a person who's friendly and kind**	_ _ _ _

Test your memory. Cover the words on the right and look at the pictures and the definitions.
How many words can you remember?

Can you think of...?

1 `one` thing you wear on your hands in winter

____

2 `one` synonym for sweater

____

3 `two` things you can wear on your head

____

____

4 `two` things you wear on your feet

____

____

5 `two` things which men or women wear on their legs

____

____

6 `two` accessories you can wear around your neck

____

____

7 `two` things which women wear on their legs under a skirt or dress

____

____

8 `three` pieces of jewellery

____

____

9 `three` things you wear to do sport

____

____

____

10 `three` things you can wear if you're cold

____

____

____

ACTIVATION

Write down five things you are wearing with their colours.

I'm wearing a blue shirt.

2A VOCABULARY Holidays

● Complete the texts with one word in each gap.

1 I love going ¹a_______________ for the weekend with my friends. We usually ²g_______________ by car to a town or village and ³st_______________ in a hotel. We don't have much money, so we always ⁴b_______________ our hotel months before, as sometimes it's cheaper that way. We never go ⁵c_______________ because we want to be comfortable, and we don't like sleeping in tents.

2 

Last winter, my best friend and I decided to go ¹sk_______________ in the Alps. I didn't have any skis, so I ²h_______________ some when I got there. We decided to ³r_______________ a small apartment near the ski slopes, and we ⁴h_______________ a very good time. We'll definitely go back there next year.

3 If you like the beach and big cities, go to Barcelona! In the mornings, you can go ¹s_______________ and see all the museums and monuments. In the afternoons, you can go ²sw_______________ in the sea or simply ³s_______________ on the beach. You don't have to ⁴sp_______________ a lot of money as everything is very cheap. Make sure you ⁵t_______________ a lot of photos!

ACTIVATION

Write a short text describing your last holiday.

2B VOCABULARY Prepositions *at*, *in*, *on*

● Complete each sentence with the correct preposition. Write in the **PREPOSITION** column.

PREPOSITION

1 The children are playing ▭ the park. ____________________

2 I love sunbathing ▭ the garden. ____________________

3 He's studying physics ▭ university. ____________________

4 Let's meet ▭ the bus stop. ____________________

5 Look! That's a Picasso ▭ the wall. ____________________

6 The course starts ▭ May. ____________________

7 My grandfather died ▭ 2012. ____________________

8 I was born ▭ 25th October. ____________________

9 We have lunch ▭ work. ____________________

10 Do you go skiing ▭ winter? ____________________

11 Will you be ▭ home tonight? ____________________

12 Do you have a big meal ▭ the evening? ____________________

13 My English classes are ▭ Tuesdays and Thursdays. ____________________

14 My son usually does his homework ▭ night. ____________________

15 The flight leaves ▭ 7.00 a.m. ____________________

16 They got married ▭ Valentine's Day. How romantic! ____________________

17 We usually go away ▭ Christmas. ____________________

18 I think you left your bag ▭ the kitchen. ____________________

19 I'm always very busy ▭ the weekend. ____________________

20 I live ▭ the centre of London. ____________________

Test your memory. Cover the **PREPOSITION** column and say the sentences.
Can you remember the prepositions?

3B VOCABULARY What's the preposition?

Are the prepositions in **bold** right (✓) or wrong (✗)? Correct the wrong ones.

1 What time did your plane arrive **in** Madrid? ✓

                                 for

2 It's your birthday. I'll pay **to** dinner tonight. ✗

3 Sally waited 30 minutes **for** the bus. ☐

4 I completely agree **with** you. ☐

5 Can you ask the teacher **to** a photocopy? ☐

6 When I arrived **to** the museum, it was closed. ☐

7 Do you spend a lot of money **on** clothes? ☐

8 She writes **to** him every day. ☐

9 He worries **with** not passing the exam. ☐

10 Does this coat belong **with** you? ☐

11 I can't think **about** anybody except Pete at the moment! ☐

12 How often do you speak **at** your sister on Skype? ☐

13 Maria's invited me **for** a concert, but I don't want to go. ☐

14 She's fallen in love **to** her sister's boyfriend! ☐

15 Sometimes I walk to work, but it depends **on** the weather. ☐

ACTIVATION

Complete the sentences with a preposition and your own ideas.

Before going on holiday, I often worry…*about finishing all of my work.*
When we have family arguments, I usually agree…
We were really happy when we arrived…
If I don't like the food in a restaurant, I usually speak…
How I usually spend my holiday depends…

4A VOCABULARY   Housework, *make* or *do*?

● Complete the sentences with the correct form of a verb (e.g. *put, do, make*).

1 Shhh, don't __________ a noise. The baby's asleep.

2 She's very untidy. She never __________ away her clothes.

3 I don't like __________ the ironing.

4 My mother __________ the washing on Mondays.

5 When I was little, I always __________ my bed before I went to school.

6 Can you __________ the shopping for me, please?

7 Please __________ the table! We're eating in five minutes.

8 How often do you __________ exercise?

9 My children have __________ a lot of friends at their new school.

10 I broke a glass while I was __________ the washing-up.

11 Can I use your phone? I need to __________ a call.

12 Do you like __________ plans for the future?

13 Please __________ your room. There are books and clothes all over the floor.

14 It's my job to __________ out the rubbish at night.

15 When was the last time you __________ an exam?

16 You've left your towel on the floor. Please __________ it up.

17 I don't have time to __________ lunch. Let's eat out.

18 Did you __________ anything exciting at the weekend?

19 Please can you __________ exercise 1 on page 46?

20 I __________ the mistake of telling her my secret.

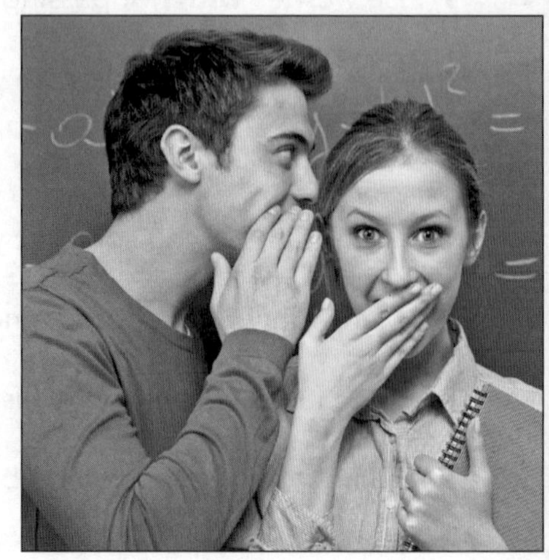

ACTIVATION

Write six sentences about:

- one housework task you do at home
- two housework tasks you never do
- three things you often make

Look at the clues and complete the crossword. You can write two words if you need to, with no spaces.

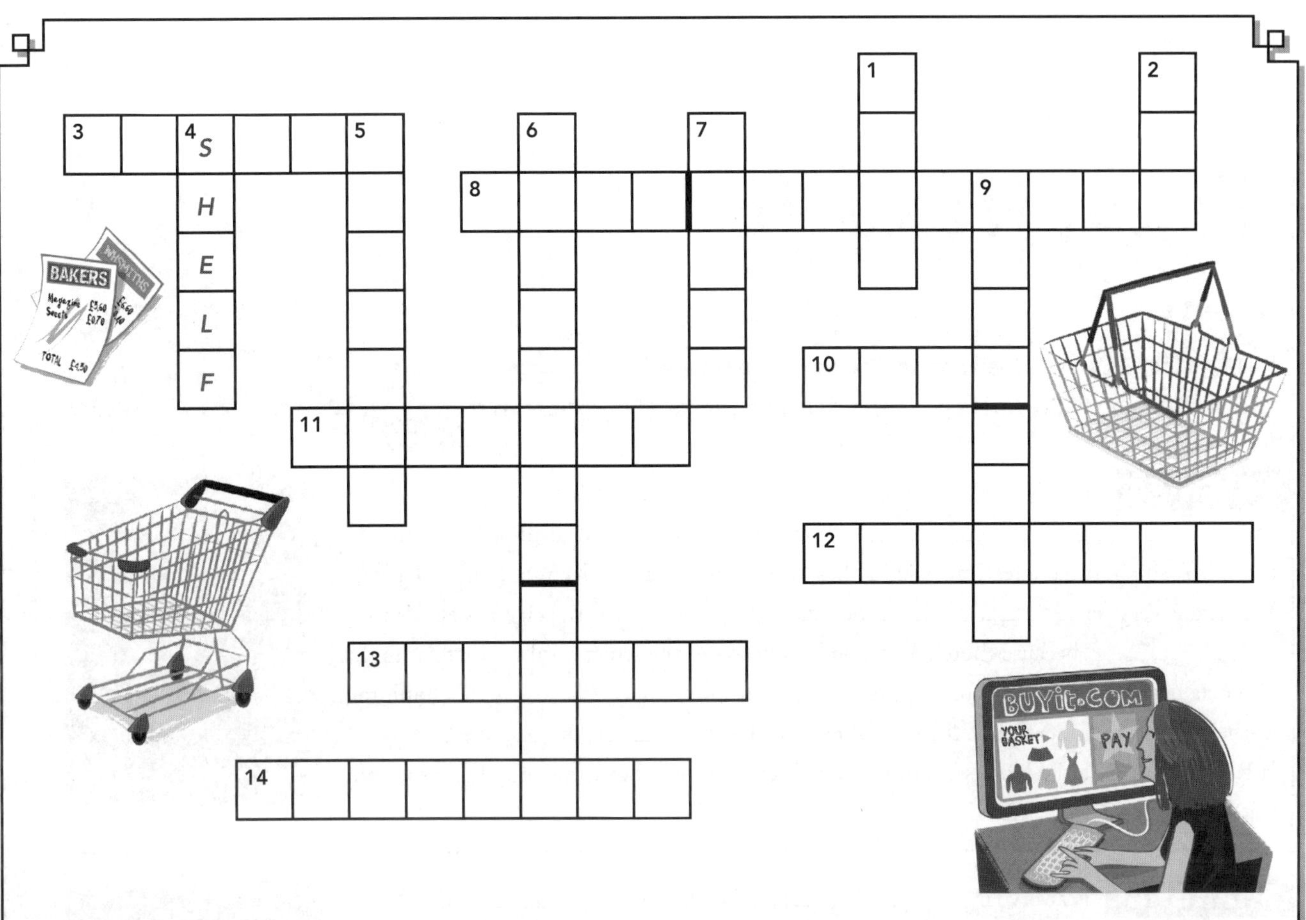

ACROSS →

3 You put things you want to buy in it when you shop online or in a supermarket.

8 A person who helps you in a shop when you want to buy something.

10 If a T-shirt is too big or too small for you, it's not your __________.

11 The piece of paper which they give you in a shop after you pay for something.

12 When you're ready to pay for your items online you proceed to __________.

13 If you want to buy things online, you usually have to create an __________ with your personal details.

14 The person who buys things in a shop.

DOWN ↓

1 Those shoes really __________ you! They look great.

2 These trousers don't __________ me. They're too big.

4 'Excuse me, where's the cereal?' 'It's on the __________.'

5 It has four wheels and you push it in the supermarket. .

6 You go into the __________ __________ to try things on.

7 When shops reduce the price of items.

9 If you're not happy with something you bought, you __________ it __________ to the shop.

5B VOCABULARY Describing a town or city

Complete the blog posts with the missing words. The first letters are given.

Travelling Jo

About me

Hi! My name's Jo. I love travelling and discovering new places! I created my blog to share all my adventures with you. I hope you enjoy reading about all the cities I visit! xxx

VALENCIA is a city on the east ¹c＿＿＿＿ of Spain. It's a ²m＿＿＿＿＿-＿＿＿＿ city. It isn't as big as Madrid or Barcelona, but it isn't small. It has a festival called Fallas, which takes place in March. During Fallas, Valencia is very ³cr＿＿＿＿＿ because lots of people visit the city. It's also very ⁴n＿＿＿＿ because there's music and fireworks in the street until very late at night. Valencia has many new buildings, but it has some ⁵h＿＿＿＿＿＿ buildings in the city centre, for example, the post office and the ⁶t＿＿＿ h＿＿＿. It has some really old religious buildings, too! There are some beautiful churches, especially the ⁷C＿＿＿＿＿＿＿.

SHANGHAI is a very large city in China. It's 1,200 km ¹s＿＿＿＿ of Beijing on the Yangtze river. Shanghai's a really ²m＿＿＿＿＿ city with lots of very tall buildings. It has many beautiful things to see, for example, the City God ³T＿＿＿＿＿ and the Yu Yuan Gardens. There is also the China Art ⁴M＿＿＿＿＿, which is the largest in Asia. Shanghai is an ⁵e＿＿＿＿＿＿ city – there are so many things happening and so much to see… and eat! Go to an outdoor ⁶m＿＿＿＿＿ and try some of the delicious street food, like noodles, rice balls, and pancakes. For the best views in the city, take a walk around the beautiful ⁷h＿＿＿＿＿ and enjoy looking at the boats and the lovely tall buildings!

ST PETERSBURG is one of the largest cities in Russia. Apart from the world-famous Hermitage Museum, it has many interesting things to see. If you want to visit an amazing building, go to see Gatchina ¹P＿＿＿＿＿, which was a summer residence for the Russian tsars. It's full of interesting art, and you can then walk around Gatchina Park and enjoy the ²l＿＿＿ and its beautiful clear water. When you get back to St Petersburg, you can go shopping, for souvenirs in Svetlanovsky ³d＿＿＿＿＿＿＿＿ st＿＿＿. If you want more shopping, you can visit the Galleria shopping ⁴c＿＿＿＿＿, which also has a cinema and a lot of different restaurants. To complete a fabulous day, go for a walk to the mysterious Egyptian ⁵Br＿＿＿＿ over the Fontanka river and take photos of the amazing Egyptian statues on it!

ACTIVATION

Work with a partner. Which of the three cities would you like to visit most? Why?

In each sentence, change the verb in **bold** to the opposite verb in the same form.
Write in the **OPPOSITE** column.

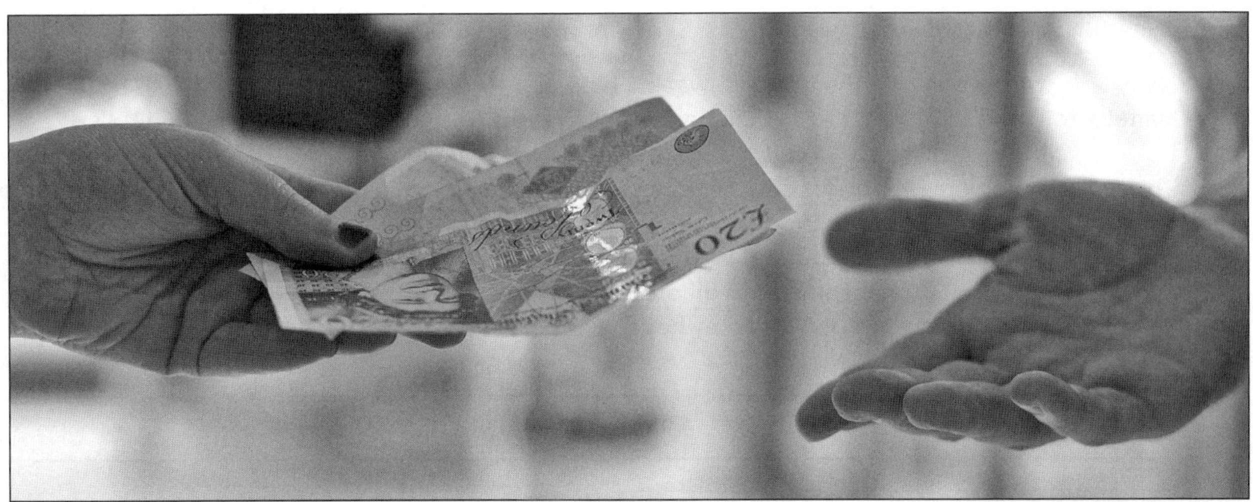

		OPPOSITE
1	Have you ever **borrowed** money **from** a friend?	_____________
2	I **passed** my final exams last week.	_____________
3	Do you think Liverpool are going to **win** the match?	_____________
4	You need to **push** the door to open it.	_____________
5	Emma always **remembers** people's names.	_____________
6	I **sent** an email **to** my sister yesterday.	_____________
7	What time does the plane **leave**?	_____________
8	The concert **starts** at 9.00 p.m.	_____________
9	This summer I'm going to **learn** French in Paris.	_____________
10	eBay's a good website if you want to **buy** something.	_____________
11	**Turn off** your computer!	_____________
12	I **found** my car keys in the garden.	_____________
13	Maria's very good at **breaking** things.	_____________
14	Do you think I'll **catch** the five o'clock train if I leave now?	_____________
15	I'll **pick** Tom **up** at the airport at six o'clock.	_____________
16	This video is taking ages to **download**.	_____________

ACTIVATION

Test your memory. Cover the sentences and look at the **OPPOSITE** column.
How many verbs can you remember from the sentences?

7B VOCABULARY Verbs + infinitive *to* and verbs + *-ing*

● Complete the conversations using the correct form of the verbs in the list.

1

like mind ~~start~~ stop try want

Amy   I ¹*started* going to the gym last week. I hate it!
Janet   You have to ² ___________ being negative! Do you
³ ___________ me to go with you?
Amy   The problem is I don't ⁴ ___________ doing exercise
there. It's really boring!
Janet   I agree that gyms are boring! Why don't we
⁵ ___________ to do something different together?
There's a swimming pool near my house…
Amy   Oh, that's a good idea! I don't ⁶ ___________ swimming.

2

feel like forget promise remember spend

Mother   OK, I'm leaving. ⁷ ___________ to load the
dishwasher, please.
Boy   Yes, Mum.
Mother   And don't ⁸ ___________ to call me if
anything happens. And you ⁹ ___________
to take out the rubbish, don't you?
Girl   Yes, Mum!
Mother   And you won't ¹⁰ ___________ all evening
playing video games, right?
Boy   No, Mum.
Mother   You know, maybe I don't ¹¹ ___________
going to this party…
Boy / Girl   MUM!

3

go on hope need offer want

Harry   I really ¹² ___________ to make some money this
summer. I'm ¹³ ___________ to go on a trip around
Europe before I go to university next year.
Sam   Wow. What kind of job are you thinking of?
Harry   Well, I thought I could ¹⁴ ___________ to walk dogs
for people. And I sometimes help a friend with his
bar in the evenings. I can probably ¹⁵ ___________
doing that for the summer. But I need another
small job…
Sam   I have an idea! My dad really ¹⁶ ___________ to
learn Italian. He loves the language, and they
often go there on holiday. You can speak Italian,
right? You could teach him for a couple of hours
every day.
Harry   That's a great idea!

ACTIVATION

Work with a partner. Practise the conversations.

English File fourth edition Teacher's Guide Pre-intermediate   Photocopiable © Oxford University Press 2019

8A VOCABULARY *get*

Complete the sentences with the correct form of *get* and a word from the list.

angry better colder divorced fit home job lost married
message nervous newspaper on present tickets to up worse

1 What's the best way to _______________? Yoga or aerobics?

2 They were married for 20 years, but they _______________ last year.

3 It's Diana's birthday next week. Shall we _______________ her a _______________?

4 How long does it take you to _______________ after work?

5 I don't like _______________ early on Sunday mornings.

6 You need to _______________ for the concert soon. They say it's going to sell out quickly.

7 We've been to your house before, so we won't _______________.

8 In the UK, you can _______________ in a church or in a registry office.

9 Do you _______________ well with your parents?

10 Most people _______________ really _______________ before doing an exam.

11 _______________ soon! And don't come back to work till you feel 100%.

12 I didn't _______________ a _______________ yesterday, so I read the news online.

13 It _______________ after 6 p.m. Temperatures go down to –10°C.

14 What time do you usually _______________ school?

15 I think the unemployment situation in my country is _______________ and not better.

16 How did the interview go? Did you _______________ the _______________?

17 I _______________ a _______________ from Pete to say he's going to be late.

18 Lucy _______________ very _______________ when people park in her parking space.

Work with a partner. Can you think of a time when…?

- you got angry with a friend
- you got a present you didn't like
- you got to school / work really late
- you got lost

8B VOCABULARY Confusing verbs

● (Circle) the correct verb to complete each sentence.

1 Have you ever **won** / **earned** a prize or cup for something?

2 I love those shoes you're **wearing** / **carrying**.

3 Mark and Charlotte **met** / **knew** at a party last year.

4 Can you help me or are you **watching** / **looking at** the news on TV?

5 Did you **bring** / **take** me anything back from New York?

6 She **looks** / **looks like** her mother. They have the same eyes.

7 Alba's **looked for** / **found** a new job. She starts next week.

8 I'm not very good at **saying** / **telling** jokes.

9 It's going to rain later, so I'll **bring** / **take** an umbrella with me.

10 Would you **lend** / **borrow** a lot of money to a good friend?

11 I **hope** / **wait** the weather is good tomorrow.

12 We got to the airport late, so we **missed** / **lost** the plane.

13 I've **known** / **met** my best friend for ten years.

14 Do you like **watching** / **looking at** photos of yourself?

15 How much money do you **win** / **earn** a month?

16 You **look** / **look like** really sad. What's wrong?

17 Can you help me? I'm **looking for** / **finding** my keys.

18 She's **wearing** / **carrying** a really heavy bag.

19 Nicky **said** / **told** that she was sorry for what happened.

20 Do you mind **hoping** / **waiting** for a few minutes? I'm not ready yet.

21 We had to **lend** / **borrow** money from the bank to buy our new car.

22 I always **miss** / **lose** my glasses.

23 Did you **listen to** / **hear** that noise? I think it was a car crash.

24 Paul is always late. I **expect** / **hope** he'll be late again today.

ACTIVATION

Write six true sentences about you using the verbs in the list.

____

borrow   earn   hope   lend   wait   win

English File fourth edition Teacher's Guide Pre-intermediate   Photocopiable © Oxford University Press 2019

9A VOCABULARY Animal quiz

● Read the definitions and write the animals in the **ANIMAL** column.

ANIMAL

1   This animal lives in Australia and carries its baby in a pocket. _______________

2   It's an insect which makes honey. It's yellow and black. _______________

3   This animal lives in the sea and is very clever. _______________

4   It's an animal which can live for two weeks with no water. _______________

5   The cartoon character Bugs Bunny is one of these. _______________

6   They're soft round sea animals. If one touches you, it really hurts! _______________

7   This animal has a very long neck and lives in Africa. _______________

8   These animals give milk which people drink. _______________

9   This animal has a very warm, white coat. _______________

10   It's a very small insect which bites people at night. _______________

11   The plural of this animal is *mice*. _______________

12   This animal lives in rivers. It's green or grey and has a lot of teeth. _______________

13   It's a very big, grey animal from Africa or India. _______________

14   This animal is a long, thin reptile, and many people are scared of it. _______________

15   People rode this animal before they had cars. _______________

16   This animal is 'the king of the jungle'. _______________

17   It's a very big, orange and black cat. _______________

18   This animal lives on a farm and has a curly tail. _______________

19   People say this animal will attack you if you're wearing something red. _______________

20   This animal comes out at night. It can fly, but it isn't a bird. _______________

ACTIVATION

Test your memory. Cover the **ANIMAL** column and look at the definitions 1–20.
Can you remember the animals?

Work with a partner. Read the questions and write the words.

Can you think of...?

1 `two` things you can **swim across**
___________________   ___________________

2 `two` things you can **go up**
___________________   ___________________

3 `two` places you can **walk across**
___________________   ___________________

4 `three` sports where you **hit** something **over** a net
___________________   ___________________   ___________________

5 `three` objects you sometimes **put into** your pocket
___________________   ___________________   ___________________

6 `something` a magician **takes out of** a hat
____

7 `two` places you can't **go into** without a ticket
___________________   ___________________

8 `two` forms of transport you can **get on** or **get off**
___________________   ___________________

9 `one` Olympic sport where you **run around** a city
____

10 `two` things you can **stand under** if it's raining
___________________   ___________________

11 `two` things you might see if you **fly over** London
___________________   ___________________

12 `two` jobs where people **take** things **from** one place **to** another
___________________   ___________________

13 `two` sports where you **go round and round** a track
___________________   ___________________

14 `two` animals which can **climb up** trees
___________________   ___________________

15 `one` game where you **move** pieces **across** a board
____

ACTIVATION

Test your partner.

(*Can you remember...?*

10B VOCABULARY Phrasal verbs

● Circle the correct phrasal verb to complete each sentence.

1 Can you look after our cat? We're **going away** / **going out**.

2 We have to **be over** / **set off** at 6.00 if we want to get to the cinema in time.

3 I really can't cook. I tried to make a cake last week, but we had to **throw it away** / **give it up**.

4 Could you **turn the music down** / **turn the music up**? I'm trying to sleep!

5 I think I drink too much coffee. I should **give it up** / **look it up**.

6 To get a passport you have to **write down** / **fill in** two forms.

7 A That's a really nice shirt.
  B They have it in your size. Why don't you **turn it on** / **try it on**?

8 Could you go to the supermarket? We've **run out of** / **put on** eggs and oil.

9 I had to **look for** / **look after** my mother last week because she was ill.

10 A When's your birthday?
   B Next Saturday! I'm really **looking forward to** / **looking round** it because I'm having a big party.

11 I can't hear what they're saying on the news! Could you **turn up** / **turn off** the volume?

12 Can you send me a link to that travel blog? I want to **find out** / **set off** things to do in Valencia.

13 The alarm will **go off** / **be over** at 7.00 tomorrow morning because I need to be at work by 8.00. Sorry!

14 I don't like this book very much, but Martin says I should **go on** / **get off** reading it because it gets better.

15 It's snowing! Are you going outside? You should **put on** / **take off** a warm jacket.

16 I bought this skirt online, but I don't like it. I think I'm going to **give it back** / **send it back**.

17 Do you want to go home now? I'm leaving and I could **drop you off** / **take you out** on the way.

18 I need to **write down** / **look up** his phone number or I'll forget it!

19 Nicola is **looking for** / **looking up** a new flat. She doesn't like where she's living now.

20 I didn't know how to pronounce 'quiet' until I **looked it up** / **turned it up** in the dictionary.

ACTIVATION

Work with a partner. Can you think of two things you can...?
- turn up or down
- run out of
- look after
- put on or take off